READER'S DIGEST

LOCAL HISTORY DETECTIVE

READER'S DIGEST

LOCAL HISTORY DETECTIVE

Published by the Reader's Digest Association Ltd
London • New York • Sydney • Montreal

Contents

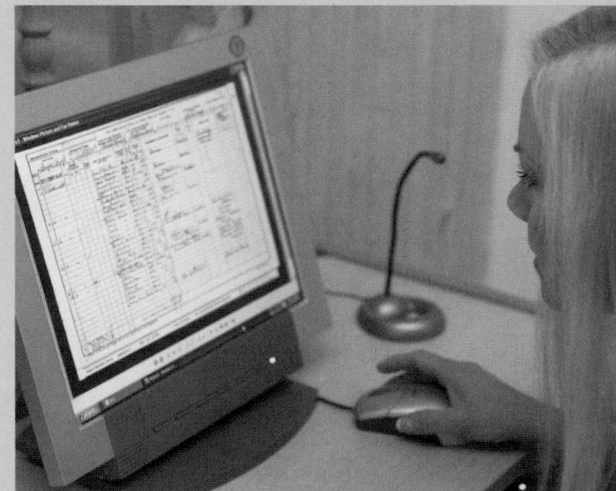

TOWNEND
CYCLES
BEST
VALUE
IN THE
WORLD.
NEND BROS
LIMITED
VENTRY.
1896.

Introduction

Every day of our lives is affected by where we live – in a house or flat, village or town, against a backdrop of fields, hills or coastline, or simply bricks and mortar as far as the eye can see. The people, places and events that entwine to make the story of our homes, our communities and our landscapes have built up layer upon layer of history over the centuries. The *Reader's Digest Local History Detective* helps you to unpeel the layers, with the reward of discovering all the engrossing tales about the place that you call home.

Maybe you long to find out when your home was built, and why, and who lived there before you, or how the land it stands on was once used. Perhaps you are curious about the origin of some of the street names in your town; or what was made at a former factory before it was turned it into an arts centre; or who made the old stone-cobbled lanes that run over the moors. Whatever intrigues you, this book is packed with the expert knowledge that will guide you towards the information you seek.

Incredible stories on your doorstep

The three main sections of the book, 'Explore Your Landscape', 'Explore Your Community' and 'Explore Your Home', show you how to understand the clues to history that can be found in Britain's rural and urban landscapes. How we live today in our villages, towns and cities and what surrounds us is the product of changes and patterns that span the centuries. The many stories and remarkable facts found here build into an understanding of why Britain is like it is. But, above all, the *Reader's Digest Local History Detective* is a practical tool. It encourages you to get out and about in your streets and landscape and interpret what you see, and equips you with the information you need – records, websites, publications, places to visit – to become your own local history detective. You will be amazed at how much there is to learn about where you live.

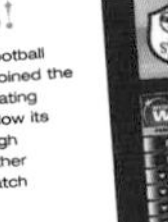

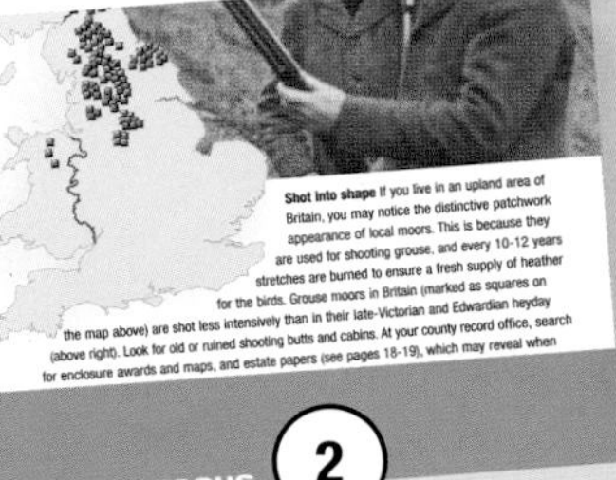

Making the most of the book

The *Reader's Digest Local History Detective* is easy to dip into so you can quickly find the information you need. Each spread covers a new topic or moves the story on, providing you with a comprehensive picture of how Britain has evolved and all the necessary tools to uncover the tales behind your own area.

1 The three main sections – on landscape, community and the home – show you how to interpret your surroundings and carry out your own research, whether at home or in archives.
2 'In Focus' features appear regularly throughout the book, offering an in-depth look at key topics.
3 Special feature boxes highlight interesting examples and case histories.
4 'Find out more' boxes list carefully researched sources – museums, organisations, books and websites – that will help you take your research further. When 'see DIRECTORY' appears in the text after a source of information, you will find contact details in the 'Directory of sources' on pages 162-169.
5 Maps appear regularly to show how historical and natural developments affected the regions of Britain, and even individual towns or cities.

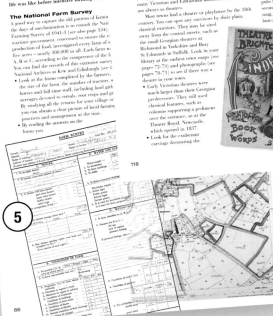

GETTING STARTED

How do you start uncovering the story of where you live? What are the best lines of enquiry to follow, and places to turn to for finding out what you want to know? This section will help you to set out your goals, draw up a step-by-step plan of action, find the best sources of information, and gather together and present your discoveries.

The first steps

Start by asking some questions, and try to decide whether your main interest is in your community, your home and the buildings around it or your local landscape.

Why am I interested? You may just be curious about the history of where you live. Perhaps you would like to know more about an area you have just moved to. Or you may have decided to trace your family's involvement in the shaping of your community.

What exactly do I want to know? Decide where your main interest lies. Is it in people, events, buildings or the origins of a place and how it has changed over time?

How much time can I put into the project? You might even end up writing a full-blown history of your area, village or city, but it is best to start with more limited aims and see where your research takes you.

What do I know already? Write down what you already know, listing any areas of interest that arise.

Looking close to home

Before launching into a wide-ranging enquiry, first explore what is nearest to hand. A trip to your local record office (see pages 18-19) should start to satisfy your curiosity.

Who lived in your home before you? Local archives will hold the answer or you may have a copy of the deeds.

How has your neighbourhood changed? Ask when a new estate was built, or when a factory or mine closed.

What are the main features of your landscape? Do you know the history of any nearby woods or fields? Comparing what is on an old Ordnance Survey (OS), tithe, enclosure or estate map (see pages 18-19) with the details on a modern OS one may tell you a great deal.

What tales do the locals have to tell? Ask others what they know about the area you live in. Start with your own family and neighbours, but be sceptical of romantic stories about the past. It could be a good idea to take a walk around the local streets first, noting down any features that you might want to ask questions about.
What might old pictures reveal? Look at old drawings, paintings and photographs (see pages 70-71). Ask when they were made and by whom. Can any of the people or places shown be identified? Take your own photograph of the same sites for comparison – ask what has vanished, what remains and what is totally new.

Keeping records

A systematic approach will save time and help you get the most from your research.

- Keep a series of different-coloured notebooks, one for each topic. Then regularly transfer information that you gather into larger files or a computer database.
- Your files or database should be flexible enough to include drawings and photographs.
- Keep a large-scale map of the area you are researching, to refer to and to scribble notes on.
- Make a full record of where you find your information. If it is from a book, write down the page number, title, author and publisher. If it is from a document, note its reference number and which archive it is kept in.
- Also note any documents that you have searched and found of no use. You do not want to go back to them by mistake.

A HELPING HAND

You may become so enthused by your initial research that you would like to discuss and compare your findings. It could also prove worth while to read what others have written on your local area, or on a subject of particular interest to you.

Local societies and classes Many places have a flourishing local history society. The British Association for Local History (see DIRECTORY) holds information on societies – see www.balh.co.uk for links to their websites. Your local authority or the Workers Educational Association (WEA) – see DIRECTORY – sometimes run local history courses.
Previous research Find out what has already been written about your community. The local studies section of your reference library (see page 18) should have indexes telling you what they hold in their archives and be able to tell you what is available elsewhere.
Journals and magazines You may come across articles relating to your area in *The Local Historian* (the journal of the British Association for Local History). Its sister publication, *Local History News*, lists events and exhibitions held nationwide. News, articles and listings are also found in *Local History Magazine* (see DIRECTORY) and *Ancestors* (the family history magazine of the National Archives – see page 12) often has useful material on community research.

LOCAL ARCHIVES

One of the most exciting parts of revealing the story of where you live will be discovering and reading original documents. The ones that are likely to be the most useful will be found in local archives: at your local reference library, or your city or county record office.

Getting to know your local resources

Documents relating to the key changes and events in the development of your area will be held in local archives. Make them your first port of call when you are researching the story of where you live.

Local reference libraries Many reference libraries have a local studies section, where copies of records such as census returns, registers of voters, old maps and photographs, as well as books and publications about the surrounding area, are kept. Their contact details will be in your phone directory or on your local council website.

English and Welsh record offices All counties and most large cities and metropolitan districts in England and Wales have offices where civic records, such as registers of births, marriages and deaths, are stored along with other documents relating to the area they cover. Addresses, phone numbers and websites are given in the DIRECTORY (pages 162-169) under city or county name.

Scottish record offices Local archive offices in Scotland generally cover larger areas than those in England and Wales. Also Scottish national archives (see page 13) hold more local documents than is the case in English and Welsh national archives. Contact details are in the DIRECTORY under city or region.

Internet service On-line links to local record offices and other useful archives throughout Britain can be found on **www.genuki.org.uk/big/**

What you can expect to find

Every city and county record office's archives hold collections of local records that cannot be seen anywhere else, as well as copies of important national records that relate to your district. Some offices produce booklets stating what is in their archives, or list such information on their website. The following is a list of what you are likely to find.

- Parish registers (see page 85) are held in all local record offices. Some offices also keep the archives of ancient dioceses, which include wills and probate inventories (see pages 154-155).
- Civic records, which include registrations of marriages, births and deaths in the area.
- Census returns (see pages 76-77) and the registers of those eligible to vote (see page 80).
- School and workhouse records (see pages 92-93 and page 85).
- Property records, which include deeds and planning applications.
- Papers that relate to court cases and disputes.
- Local council records, which include local tax and business registration documents.
- Manorial and estate documents (see page 152 and pages 148-149). Maps may be attached to many of these.
- Old maps, photographs and newspapers (see pages 72-73, 70-71 and 74)
- Collections of private letters and other personal documents are sometimes found in local archives.

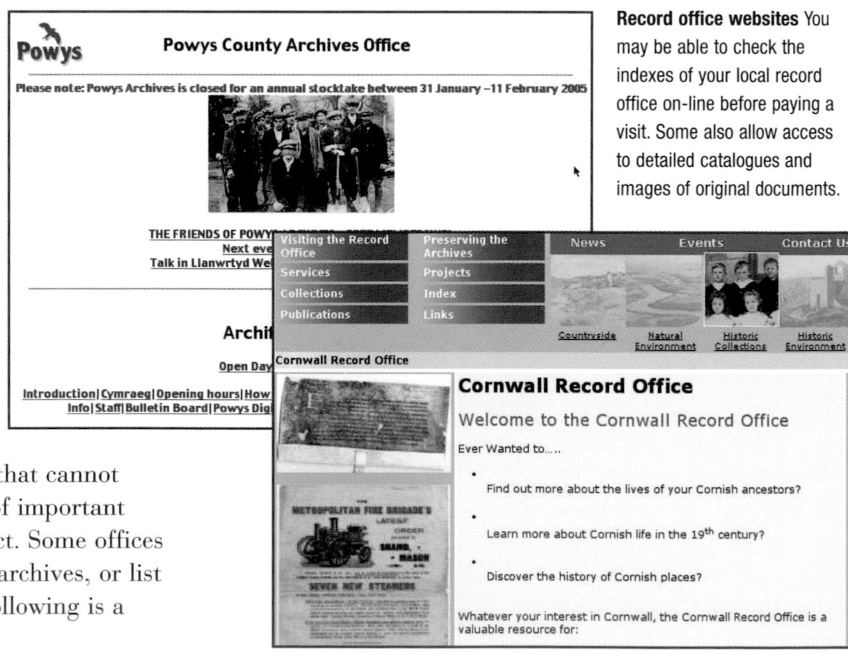

Record office websites You may be able to check the indexes of your local record office on-line before paying a visit. Some also allow access to detailed catalogues and images of original documents.

Using a microfiche reader

Looking in the indexes

Your first visit

Most record offices provide clear instructions on how to search for documents, and experienced staff will always be on hand to assist you.

Before you go

It will help you to make the most of your visit if you do a little groundwork before you go.

- Ring to check opening hours and to enquire about procedures, such as how to order documents, how long you may have to wait for them and whether they can be pre-ordered by phone. Ask if you need to book a microfiche reader (see above) or a computer terminal. Heavily used documents, such as census returns and parish registers, and those that are fragile, may only be available on microfilm or on-line.
- Bring a notebook and pencil (pens are not allowed). A laptop computer can sometimes be used, but check first.
- You will be issued with a reader's ticket, for which some means of identification, such as a driving licence, will be required. Some record offices will also ask you for a passport-size photograph.
- Arrive armed with any information you have already gathered and with any questions you hope to answer.

At the archives

Record centres house a wealth of documents, so you should enjoy a fruitful visit, particularly if you come armed with some of the advice given below.

- Be aware that coats and bags will have to be left in the cloakroom. Lockers are usually provided for valuables.
- Even if you think you know precisely which documents you wish to see, and have pre-ordered them, take some time to familiarise yourself with the index and catalogue files. It is likely that your local archive can fill in far more of the story of where you live than you thought.
- Start with the place-name indexes. These are a good place to search for documents on your community.
- Most record offices ask you to sign a different order slip for each document and allow you to request up to three at a time. Documents will be issued one by one and you will have to sign a receipt and return the document to the counter when you have finished with it. This is to limit the risk of irreplaceable documents going astray.
- Always note the reference number on any document you are given. You might want to see it again later.
- You can usually buy photocopies of documents and print-outs of microfiche or computer records. Do not spend time deciphering unfamiliar handwriting (see pages 14-15) when you can study it at leisure later.

MUSEUMS AND HERITAGE CENTRES

Documents, such as trade and property records, and artefacts and machinery relating to the history of your area, may also be found in local museums and heritage centres. Admission to any run by the local authority is usually free, but if you wish to search through private archives, such as those of a large country estate like Chatsworth in Derbyshire, you may be charged a small fee. Keep an eye open for courses or special events that museums might run, and remember that you may have to give advance notice if you wish to view material not generally kept on display.

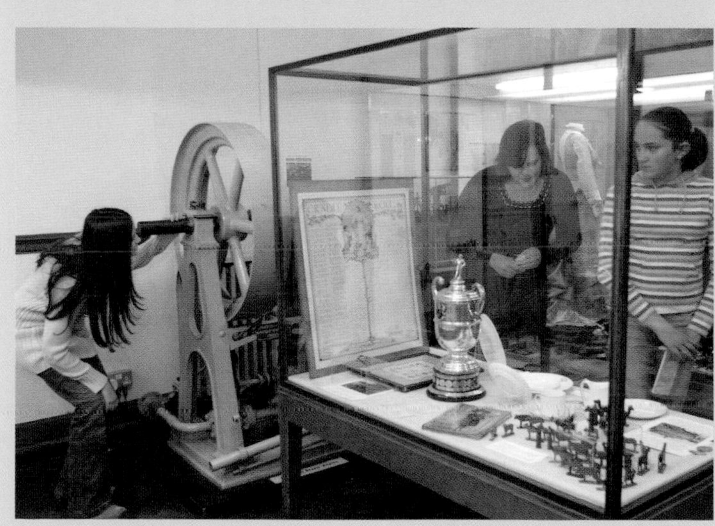

NATIONAL ARCHIVES

A visit to one of the national archives, of which Britain has some of the finest in the world, should help complete the story of your area. Records go back as far as the early Middle Ages: no other country has anything comparable with the 1086 Domesday Book.

England and Wales

Joint rule of the two nations goes back to the 13th century and most records of their shared history are held together.

The National Archives

The National Archives in Kew is the official record office for England and Wales (government records for the whole UK are also housed here). The name was adopted in 2003, upon the merger of the former Public Record Office (PRO) and the Historical Manuscripts Commission.

What it holds Among the thousands of documents, including Magna Carta and Shakespeare's will, there are many that should prove useful to a local historian.

- Lists of taxpayers range from those who paid poll tax in 1377-81 to those who were taxed on their hearths in Charles II's reign (see page 77).
- Legal documents include wills and probate inventories (see pages 154-155) and records of cases judged in the Courts of Chancery, Exchequer, Requests and Star Chamber (see page 161).
- Medieval records contain information about charters, local markets, deer parks and licences to fortify houses.
- Tithe awards and maps (see pages 18-19 and 73), Valuation Office surveys (see page 66), and the National Farm Survey of 1941-3 (see page 66) are among the many property documents.
- Military records, including millions of records of service, pensions and medals from the First World War.

Using the archives The reception desk staff will offer guidance and answer any questions. Leaflets are also available on the main classes of records that are held.

- There is no need to book and entry is free, but proof of identity is required to obtain a reader's card. This must be shown on every visit and is valid for three years.
- Many indexes of the collections are available on-line (see 'Practical information', opposite, for website). It may be useful to search through them before your visit.
- Up to three documents can be ordered in advance to be ready for viewing by phoning 020 8392 5200. The website will help you search for their reference codes. There are charges for photocopying.

The National Library of Wales

The archives kept at the National Library of Wales hold many valuable collections, ranging from manuscripts and maps to photographs, sound recordings and films. Here you will find many parish registers, all the diocesan records for Wales, pre-1858 wills, a full set of Welsh census returns (1841-1901), along with copies of old newspapers, maps and business records and directories. Proof of identity is needed to obtain a reader's ticket. The Library's website (see 'Practical information', opposite) includes a full on-line catalogue.

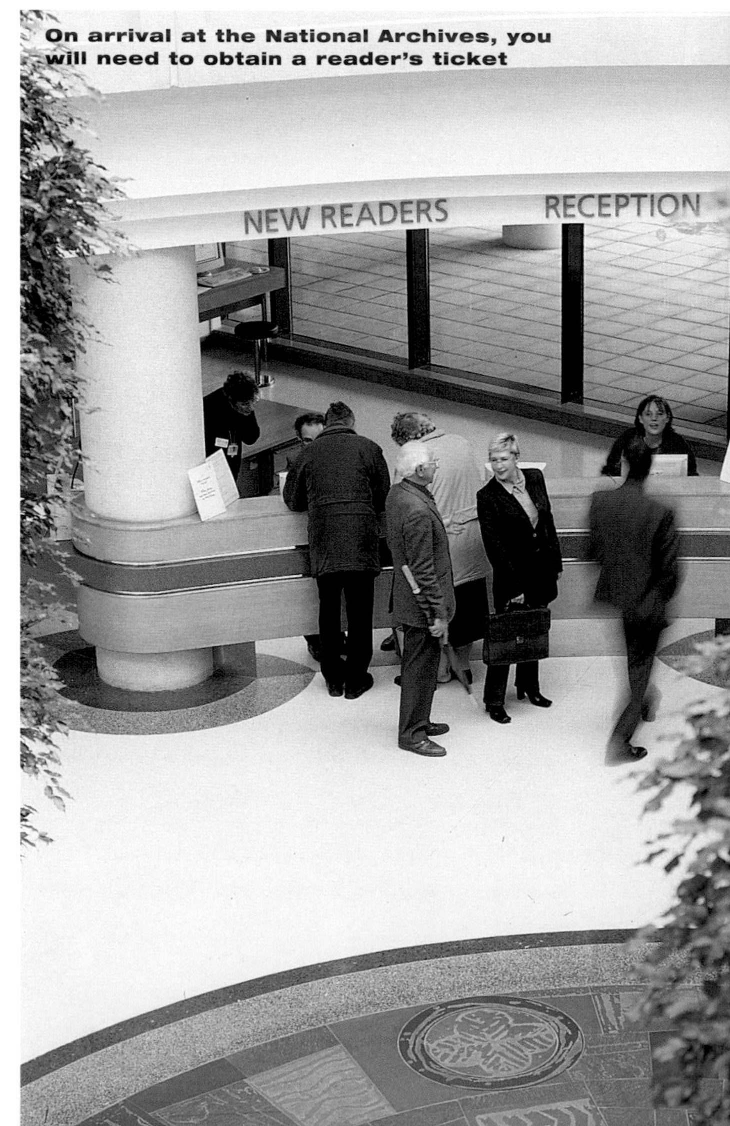

On arrival at the National Archives, you will need to obtain a reader's ticket

Background material Most of the archives not only provide extensive research services; they also publish a range of leaflets and books relating to the various records in their collections. Details are often given on the websites (see 'Practical information', below) and it may be useful to order and read some of them before your visit.

Scotland

Despite sharing a monarch with England since 1603 and the formal union of the two parliaments in 1707, Scotland has always maintained separate records of its distinctive history.

The National Archives of Scotland

The records at the National Archives of Scotland in Edinburgh (formerly known as the Scottish Record Office) date from the 12th century up to the present day.

- Details of documents held are given on the Archives' website (see 'Practical information', below). They include local authority and court records, registers of sasines (land transactions) and property deeds, as well as private and business papers.
- Contact the Archives before you visit to check the availability of documents you wish to consult. Some are not stored in the main building, and you may have to give several days' notice in order to view them.
- A number of records are not held in Edinburgh, but in the locality they relate to, often with local authorities or in universities and colleges. For information about such documents and where they can be seen, consult the Archives' website.
- Access to the Archives is free, but there is a charge for any documents that you wish to photocopy.
- A list of all private Scottish archives – the National Register of Archives for Scotland – is available on-site for reference. It details records held by individuals, landed estates, businesses, libraries, colleges and clubs.

General Register Office for Scotland

Parish and civil records of births, marriages and deaths, and census returns, are kept at the General Register Office for Scotland. Visits must be booked in advance and there is a search fee (see 'Practical information', right).

National Library of Scotland

Scotland's largest reference library houses an extensive collection of books, early manuscripts and maps (housed in a separate building). Details of how to obtain a reader's ticket are on the website (see right).

Family Records Centre

Although mainly of use to family historians, many of the documents held at the Family Records Centre are relevant to local history research. The archives include census returns for England and Wales (1841-1901), the records of births, marriages and deaths in England and Wales since 1837, indexes of adoptions in England and Wales since 1927, and registers of wills and death duties. An on-line link to the archives of the General Register Office for Scotland provides access to Scottish records, including census returns, registers of births, marriages and deaths, and parish records dating back to the 16th century.
The General Register Office for Scotland aims to open a Family Records Centre by the end of 2007.

PRACTICAL INFORMATION

- The National Archives, Ruskin Avenue, Kew, Surrey TW9 4DU, Tel. 020 8876 3444. www.nationalarchives.gov.uk
- The National Library of Wales, Penglais, Aberystwyth, Ceredigion SY23 3BU, Tel. 01970 632 800. www.llgc.org.uk
- The National Archives of Scotland, HM General Register House, 2 Princes Street, Edinburgh EH1 3YY, Tel. 0131 535 1334; and at West Register House, Charlotte Square, Edinburgh EH2 4DJ, Tel. 0131 535 1413. www.nas.gov.uk
- General Register Office for Scotland, New Register House, 3 West Register Street, Edinburgh EH1 3YT, Tel. 0131 334 0380. www.gro-scotland.gov.uk
- The National Library of Scotland, George IV Bridge, Edinburgh EH1 1EW, Tel. 0131 623 3700. www.nls.uk
- Family Records Centre, 1 Myddelton Street, London EC1R 1UW, Tel. 020 8392 5300. www.familyrecords.gov.uk/frc

OLD DOCUMENTS

Reading tax, legal and business documents, old letters and other texts could be part of your research. Whether the material has been printed or handwritten, you may need some help, as well as a little patience and practice, to decipher unfamiliar scripts.

Reading old text

When you delve into the archives for useful documents on your area or home, you may find you have some difficulty in understanding what you find. A few guidelines will help you on your way.

- Start with material written in the last 200 years and work backwards in time. You should be able to read most late-18th and 19th-century text quite easily, as modern 'copperplate' handwriting came into general use around 250 years ago.
- Another reason for not starting with early documents is that many were written in Latin. Except for the short period 1651-60, Latin was the language used for legal material, including manor court rolls (see page 152), up to 1733. An imperfect form known as dog Latin was often used in other documents, such as parish registers.
- Some spellings, even from as late as the 19th century, will surprise you. Once you get back to the 17th and 16th centuries, you will find that people generally spelt words as they sounded, with no regard for consistency.
- It helps to know the typical phrases that were used, so that you can anticipate what the document should be saying. For example, a will normally begins: 'In the name of God, Amen ...' and if the person who made it declares that he is 'seke in body but foole in mynd' this should be read as 'sick in body but full in mind'.
- Documents often include technical words, such as 'burgage' or 'appurtenances'. Inventories attached to wills (see pages 154-155) use many obsolete dialect words. You will need a specialist dictionary or glossary (see 'Find out more', opposite) to decipher these.

Interpreting a document

Do not think that because something is written down, it is an established fact. No single document can tell you the full story. It is just one version of what happened. Look at it critically, and compare it with related material.

- Enquire who wrote a particular document, when and why. You might not find precise answers, but posing the questions will put you in the proper frame of mind. Documents were not written for historians but for some immediate purpose, usually administrative or legal.

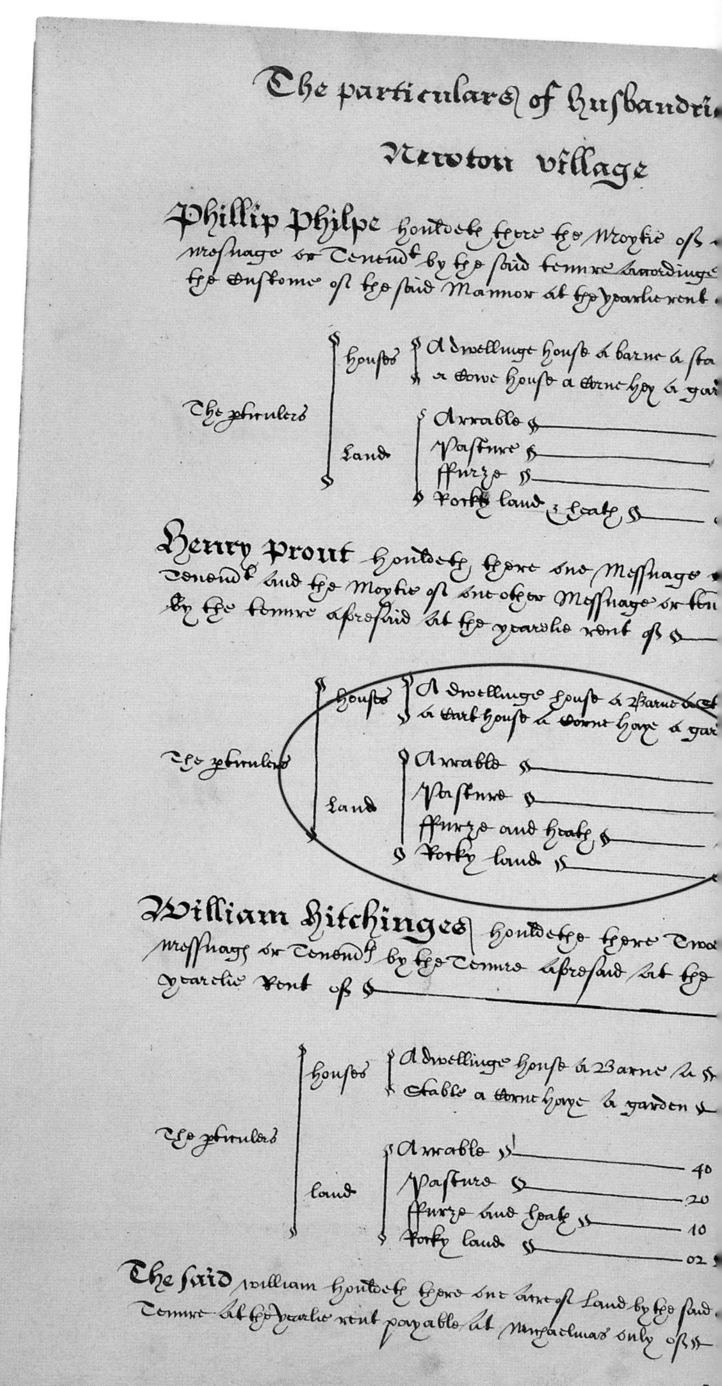

The particulars of husbandri[...]

Newton village

Phillip Philpe ...

Henry Prout ...

William Hitchinges ...

The said William ...

DECIPHERING SCRIPTS

When you first see a handwritten document from the Tudor and Stuart period (1485-1714), you may think that you will never be able to read it. Buy one of the packs on handwriting from different eras, which are usually on sale at your record office, and have relevant examples alongside you when going through your own document.

You will need to recognise the ways in which scribes tended to abbreviate words. A 'p' with a stroke through its stem was a common way of shortening 'par' (as in 'parish') or 'per' (as in 'person'). A wiggle over a letter 'm' signifies 'mm'. 'The' was generally shortened to 'ye', and apostrophes were widely used to indicate where letters had been missed out.

Some letters are harder than others to recognise, as they differ greatly from the way we write them today, or they have more than one commonly used form (see below). Capital letters are usually more difficult to decipher, as writers frequently used different styles, even in the same document.

's' at the beginning and in the middle of words usually looks like an 'f' without the crossbar.

'r' sometimes looks like a modern 'w', but can also be similar to an 'e' or even a 'z'.

A final 's' often looks like a number '6', leaning to the right.

'c' is generally written like a modern 'r'.

- You also need to analyse the information in a systematic way. A hearth tax return (see page 77) from the 1660s or 70s will list the householders and record the number of hearths on which they were taxed. From this, you can get a good idea of the social structure of a parish or township, based on the large numbers who paid for only one or two hearths, tapering upwards to richer families in larger houses with 20 or more. You might even be able to identify surviving houses and distinctive surnames. If you do this for the surrounding villages as well, you will see whether your community was different or typical.
- Some documents will be exciting finds, but most will merely add a little more to what you already know. Link the information from your document to what you have found in other sources. The people named in a tithe award (see pages 19 and 73) might also appear in a census return (see pages 76-77) or trade directory (see page 75). In this way, you will build up a broader picture of how your community grew and changed over time.

Working the manor In 1618, the rents paid by the tenants of the manor of Manorbier and Penally in Pembrokeshire were recorded (left). The resulting document not only tells us the names of the farmers and what they paid, it also gives us an idea of the property they held. Apparently one tenant, 'Henry Prout', rented 'A dwelling house, a barn, a stable, a cart house, a corn haye (a kind of enclosure) and a garden', along with 30 acres of arable land, 10 acres each of pasture and heathland (covered with 'furze', or gorse) and 5 acres of rocky land (see inset, above).

Letters of the law The various styles of lettering that made up the Court-hand alphabet (above) will be seen in 16th and 17th-century legal documents. Be aware that handwriting could be just as individual as it is today.

FIND OUT MORE

- *Reading Tudor and Stuart Handwriting* (L. Munby, S. Hobbs and A. Crosby, British Association for Local History, 2nd ed., 2002)
- *The Handwriting of English Documents* (L.C. Hector, Kohler and Coombes, 1988)
- *Oxford Dictionary of English* (eds. C. Soanes and A. Stevenson, Oxford University Press, 2002) Includes definitions of many now obsolete words.
- **http://yourhandwriting.ca/writing/oldhandwriting** Gives numerous links to useful websites offering assistance, with examples, on the reading of old documents.

THE INTERNET

Computers have made it much easier to research into local history. Useful websites are mentioned throughout this book and you can track down many more with a search engine. There are also some key sites that will provide you with helpful links and general advice.

General links

There are several websites that you are likely to refer to again and again when tracking down the details of the story of where you live.

- Links to the websites of most organisations involved in local history research in Britain can be found on **www.balh.co.uk** the British Association for Local History's site. Also, a visit to **www.humbul.ac.uk/topics/localhistory.html** will give you similar links, plus details of research projects, and access to an on-line course in reading and understanding old documents.
- Although mainly aimed at family historians, Genuki at **www.genuki.org.uk** is another excellent place to look for links to local history material. It has a page for every county in the British Isles, as well as pages on many individual towns and parishes.
- A good site for links to information on specific topics of history is **www.history.uk.com**

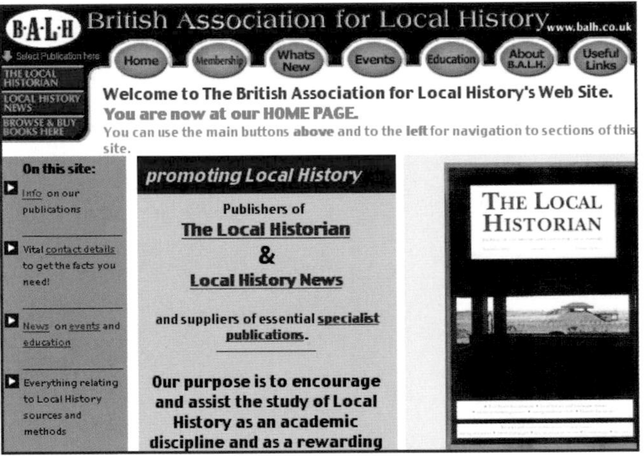

Record offices and libraries

The most useful archives for researching the history of a specific area are usually found at local record offices and libraries (see pages 10-11). Most have websites giving details of what they hold (see DIRECTORY, under the relevant city or county name, for contact details). You will also find links to such websites on the Genuki site (see above).

- At **www.archon.nationalarchives.gov.uk/archon** you can view the ARCHON Directory, a definitive list of local archives. It gives opening times and contact details for every repository of records in the British Isles.
- The A2A database at **www.a2a.org.uk** catalogues material held at English record offices, libraries, museums and heritage centres, while the Scottish Archive Network at **www.scan.org.uk** does the same for Scotland.
- Many public libraries in Britain have a local studies reference section. You should be able to find out about any of these and what they hold from your local authority's website, which can be accessed via links on **www.direct.gov.uk/D17/Directories/LocalCouncils.fs.en** Familia at **www.familia.org.uk** also lists public library records that are likely to interest local historians and genealogists.

On-line research

The volume of original material that you can view on the internet grows rapidly. You can find out what is available on your area by logging on to **www.enrichuk.org.uk** and selecting the Browse option, then the Geographic option.

Documents

Many archives and research institutes now publish some of their records on-line.

- Census returns (see pages 76-77) are one of the most useful research tools. Those for England and Wales from 1841 to 1901 are available on a variety of websites. The **www.scotlands-people.gov.uk** website has the Scottish census images and indexes online from 1841 to 1901, except for 1881 which has only an index. Note that not all census sites offer an address search, which makes looking for a specific street or house difficult.
- For the present day, the Office for National Statistics has data from the 2001 census on its Neighbourhood Statistics website at **www.neighbourhood.statistics.gov.uk**
- One of the most important local history publications is the *Victoria County History*, a project that aims to compile a detailed account of every county in England throughout history. Volumes are available in some libraries, and there is a project to create an on-line edition. See the website at **www.englandpast.net** for details.
- Another major project, covering the whole of England and Wales, is the Digital Library of Historical

Directories at www.historicaldirectories.org which offers access to a selection of trade directories for 1750-1919.

- In Scotland the Statistical Accounts provide summaries at a parish level of life in the 1790s and 1830s. They can be viewed on www.edina.ac.uk
- Many individuals, history societies, heritage centres and universities now place the results of any research they carry out on the internet. Genuki (see opposite) is one of the best places to find links to these documents.

Pictures

The internet is full of sites displaying photographs, paintings and prints of Britain's towns and villages that help reveal how they have changed over time.

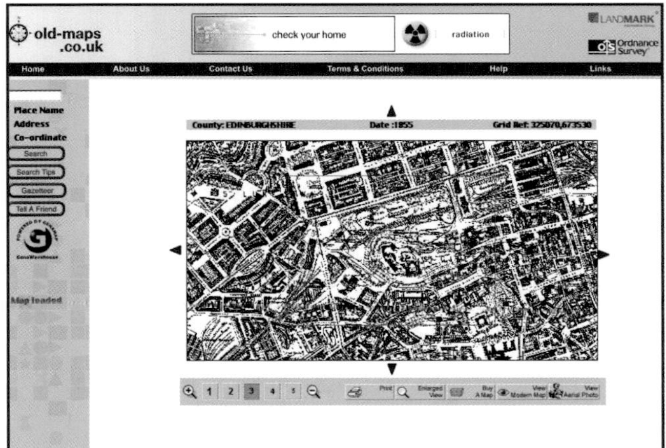

- Many local record offices and libraries have large collections, some of which can be viewed on-line (see 'Record offices and libraries', opposite, for details of websites).
- At viewfinder.english-heritage.org.uk English Heritage has assembled a large collection of photographs relating to local history in England, including pictures of buildings, industrial sites and community and social events from the 1840s onwards.
- One of the largest digital image collections is of works of art from the Guildhall Library's gallery and print room. More than 20,000 pictures, mainly engravings and paintings of London streets and buildings, can be seen by logging on to collage.cityoflondon.gov.uk
- Two useful sites for picture postcards are the Francis Frith Collection at www.francisfrith.com and PastPix at www.pastpix.com Both are designed to sell prints of old photographs, but small scans are available free.
- There are also several websites of modern photographs of old buildings. The largest of these is the Images of England site at www.imagesofengland.org.uk run by the National Monuments Register. It aims eventually to include a photograph of every listed building in Britain.
- The search engine Google also has an excellent facility for locating on-line photographs and pictures at images.google.com

Maps and plans

Tracing and viewing old maps on the internet can save a great deal of time, although in many cases digitised maps lack the clarity of the originals or of printed copies.

- The British Cartographic Society has a comprehensive on-line directory of British map collections at www.cartography.org.uk/Pages/Publicat/Ukdir
- Some of the best old maps are available on www.old-maps.co.uk which offers high-resolution scans of 6-inch Ordnance Survey (OS) maps (see page 18), from around 1870.
- The National Library of Scotland (see page 13) has an outstanding series of town plans in its on-line map collection at www.nls.uk/digitallibrary/map/townplans giving a high level of detail for 62 towns. It is also worth checking city and county record office sites (see above) for maps held in their archives.

Local history societies

There are countless local groups around Britain devoted to the study of their area and many have websites. A list giving full contact details is provided by *Local History Magazine* at www.local-history.co.uk/groups

If you want to get in touch with those who share your interests, there is bound to be a mailing list or on-line discussion group that covers the locality you are interested in. You will find links to a large number of these at www.genuki.org.uk/indexes/MailingLists.html

MAPS AND PLANS

By taking two maps of your area that were drawn at different points in history and comparing them, you will get an almost instant overview of how where you live changed during the gap in time that separates them.

Ordnance Survey maps

A modern Ordnance Survey (OS) map of your local area and the countryside and other settlements around it will place where you live in the context of its landscape. It should also help you to work out what it is you want to know about, such as street patterns, the relative size of communities, or what remains of past industries.

How to find OS maps The Ordnance Survey's website at **www.ordnancesurvey.co.uk/oswebsite/getamap** enables you to find and view a map from the current Landranger and Explorer series (see right) on-line. You can search by place name, postcode or OS grid reference. You can also buy a map from the on-line OS map shop.

Old OS maps The Ordnance Survey, Britain's national mapping agency, was founded in 1791 to map the south coast of England for defence planning. At the beginning of the 19th century, it turned its attention to general mapping, producing a series of 1-inch-to-1-mile maps – now known as the Old Series – that covered the whole of Britain. This was gradually replaced, from the early 1850s onwards, by the New Series of 6-inch-to-1-mile and 25-inch-to-1 mile maps, which was completed in 1897. In the meantime, extra information, such as new streets, factories and railway lines in areas not yet covered by the New Series, was added to fresh editions of the Old Series maps.

Walk with history Glancing at a copy of an early OS map as you walk your local streets may help to give you a sense of what it must have been like to live and work there just over 100 years ago.

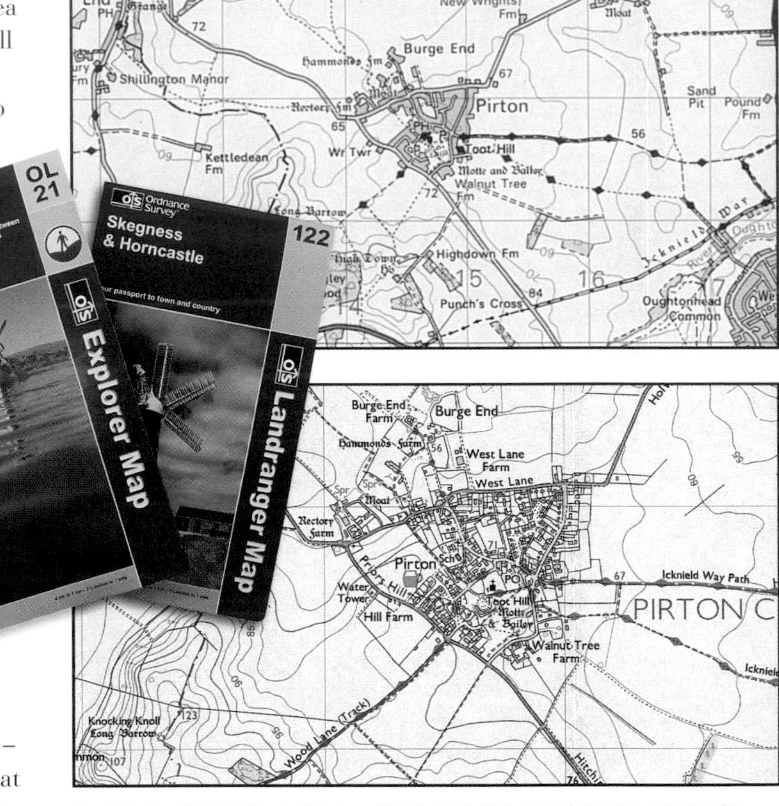

Lie of the land The Ordnance Survey publishes nearly 700 up-to-date maps covering the whole of the British Isles. Choose from their two main series, depending on how much detail you require. A Landranger map, drawn to a scale of $1\frac{1}{4}$ inches to 1 mile (top, above), will help show how your community fits into the surrounding area. Then you can zoom in for a closer view using an Explorer map (bottom, above) drawn on a scale of $2\frac{1}{2}$ inches to 1 mile.

How to find old OS maps The British Library holds the largest collection of OS maps in Britain (a catalogue of what is available is on **www.bl.uk/collections/map_os.html**). You can also order copies of all the Old Series and New Series maps on the Ordnance Survey website (see above). Other good facsimiles of these maps, some with a helpful commentary, include the Godfrey series (available from **www.alangodfreymaps.co.uk**) and around 90 of the post-1860, 1-inch Old Series maps. A large collection of 6-inch New Series maps for England, Wales and Scotland, dating from the 1850s to 1899, is available for viewing on **www.old-maps.co.uk**

Fixing rents The tithe award for the hamlet of Ramsden in the parish of Shipton-under-Wychwood in Oxfordshire, drawn up in 1838, includes a map showing clearly how the land at the time was farmed. As well as numbering all the plots to correspond with the owners and tenants listed on the tithe award, some field names and crops are also noted.

Tithe maps

The Tithe Commutation Act of 1836 changed the ancient system of all parishioners paying a tithe – a tenth of their produce or income – to the Church into a cash payment or rent-charge. It involved the making of an award, which identified landowners, their tenants and the land they worked. By 1852, about 86 per cent of England and Wales had been surveyed and awards, with accompanying maps, had been made for 11,395 parishes or townships.

What tithe maps tell you Tithe maps, dating from the mid 19th century, are often the earliest detailed maps of many parts of Britain. The awards list that accompanies each map identifies the owners and occupiers of every piece of property in the parish. These properties were numbered and plotted on the map.

Where to find tithe maps Three copies of each award and its map were made. One was deposited in the parish chest and will now be in the archives of the local record office (see pages 10-11); a second went to the local bishop and should be in the archives of the ancient diocese, or in the case of Wales at the National Library in Aberystwyth (see pages 12-13); the third, central government, copy will be in the National Archives at Kew (see pages 12-13).

Enclosure maps

Many English and Welsh parishes have a map attached to a parliamentary enclosure award, most of which date from 1750 to 1850. But some places had enclosed their fields and commons at a much earlier date. A private Act of Parliament was necessary where unanimity could not be reached, and the views of a minority were overruled. Altogether, 5341 awards were made for England and 229 for Wales. Most Scottish parishes were enclosed privately and few maps survive from that time.

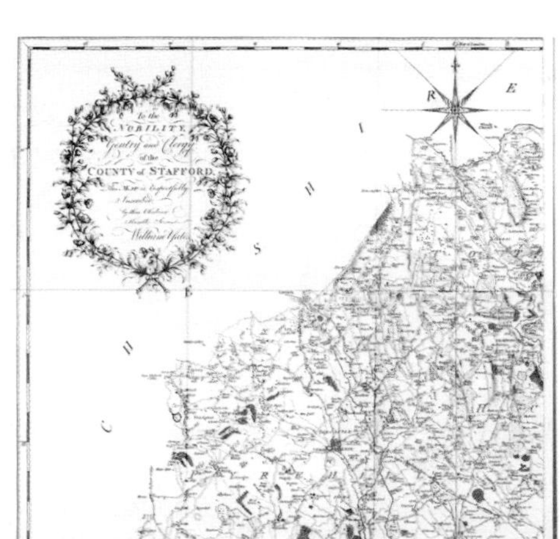

What enclosure maps tell you An enclosure map of a parish or township is likely to be the earliest one available of that particular place. Some, mainly those of upland districts, where only the parish commons and wastes were enclosed, do not include farmland. But those for areas where an open-field system was in use will give the owners and tenants of every piece of property.

Where to find enclosure maps Enclosure awards and their maps are kept in local record offices and reference libraries (see pages 10-11) and at the National Archives at Kew (see pages 12-13).

Estate and county maps

From the late 16th century, written surveys of manors or estates were often accompanied by a map, or 'platt'. The first, rather sketchy, county maps were being drawn up at around the same time, but it was not until the second half of the 18th century that a set of accurate 1-inch-to-1-mile scale maps of the English and Welsh counties was commissioned by the Royal Society of Arts.

What estate maps tell you You will discover how land was divided up and worked, as well as who owned and farmed it from an estate map.

Where to find estate maps The archives of national and local records offices, libraries, museums and heritage centres (see pages 10-11, 12-13) will include estate maps. Most date from the 18th or 19th century, but a few earlier ones survive: the National Archives (see page 12) holds around 60 pre-1603 maps for the Duchy of Lancaster.

What county maps tell you A sense of what the landscape was like before industrialisation can be gleaned from maps such as that of Staffordshire in 1775 (left).

Where to find county maps County record offices and reference libraries (see pages 10-11) hold copies. Some can also be viewed at the British Library (see DIRECTORY).

UNDERSTANDING PLACE NAMES

Every place has a distinctive name that tells you something about its past, whether it describes the landscape, a local industry, an ancient settlement or a feature, such as the Yarnbury Castle hill-fort in Wiltshire (above). Place names are perhaps the most telling records of Britain's history – Celts, Romans, Anglo-Saxons, Vikings and Normans have all left a mark on our maps. They tell a story of invasion, settlement, industrialisation and urbanisation – a story that continues right up to the present day.

Ancient names from the landscape Rivers were vitally important in the life of prehistoric settlers, and some of their names, thought to date back over 3000 years to pre-Celtic times, can still be found. Many simply mean 'river' or 'water', but the name of the River Dove (left), which runs through Staffordshire, Derbyshire and Yorkshire, means 'black', referring to the colour of the water.

The oldest place names were probably influenced by the Celts, the Iron Age people living in these isles two thousand years ago. They spoke two dialects: British, which later became Welsh and Cornish, and is thought to have included a variant spoken by the Picts (see opposite); and Gaelic (spoken in Ireland, north and west Scotland and the Isle of Man). With the arrival of the Anglo-Saxons and Vikings, the Celts in England for the most part stayed and learnt the languages of their conquerors. By contrast, in the extreme west around Cornwall, and in Wales and Scotland, Celtic languages continued to be spoken for centuries.

Many Celtic place-name elements bear a resemblance to Cornish and modern Welsh words, evidence of their linguistic links. For example, the Celtic word *penno*, meaning 'top', 'hill' or 'headland', is represented in both the Welsh and Cornish word *pen*. Examples are Penrith ('hill ford') in Cumbria, Pendleton ('farmstead by the hill') in Lancashire, Penzance ('holy headland') in Cornwall and Penarth ('top of the headland') in Wales.

CELTIC NAMES

The Celts were the native British people when the Roman conquered in AD 43-83. Celtic place names mainly describe landscape features such as hills and rivers, but there are also Celtic names for inhabited sites. Today, only a small proportion of Britain's place names have obvious Celtic roots, because many of the original names were replaced by the Anglo-Saxons.

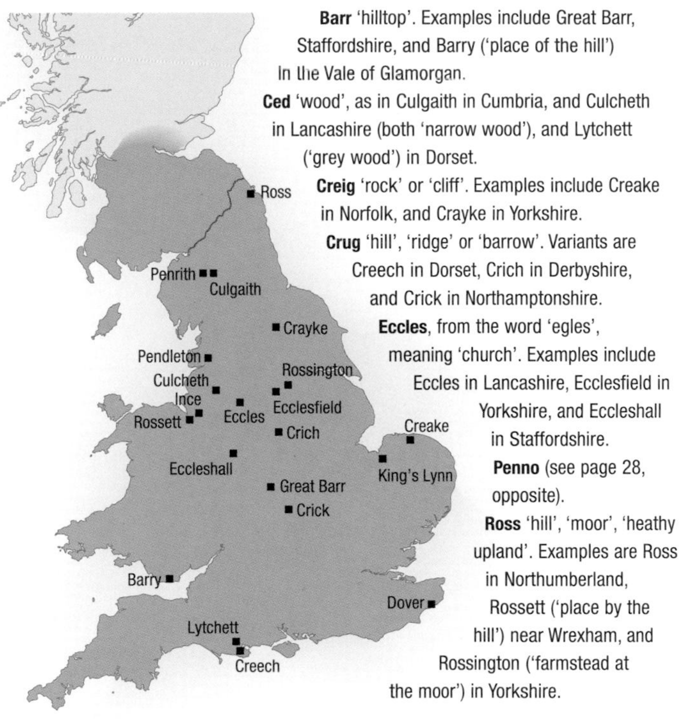

Barr 'hilltop'. Examples include Great Barr, Staffordshire, and Barry ('place of the hill') in the Vale of Glamorgan.

Ced 'wood', as in Culgaith in Cumbria, and Culcheth in Lancashire (both 'narrow wood'), and Lytchett ('grey wood') in Dorset.

Creig 'rock' or 'cliff'. Examples include Creake in Norfolk, and Crayke in Yorkshire.

Crug 'hill', 'ridge' or 'barrow'. Variants are Creech in Dorset, Crich in Derbyshire, and Crick in Northamptonshire.

Eccles, from the word 'egles', meaning 'church'. Examples include Eccles in Lancashire, Ecclesfield in Yorkshire, and Eccleshall in Staffordshire.

Penno (see page 28, opposite).

Ross 'hill', 'moor', 'heathy upland'. Examples are Ross in Northumberland, Rossett ('place by the hill') near Wrexham, and Rossington ('farmstead at the moor') in Yorkshire.

GAELIC NAMES

Many Scottish place names have Gaelic roots. Gaelic originated in Ireland and came to southwest Scotland in the 5th century AD with the Irish *Dál Riata* tribe, who the Romans called *Scotti*. Viking invasions later encouraged the Gaels to move east, where they supplanted the Picts.

Baile 'farm' or 'homestead', as in Ballindalloch ('meadow homestead') in Moray, and Balerno ('sloe-tree homestead') near Edinburgh.

Beinn 'mountain'. Examples are Ben Nevis ('mountain by the River Nevis'), and Benbecula ('hill of the fords') in the Western Isles.

Cill 'church', as in Kilmarnock ('church of my little Ernon') in Ayrshire, and West and East Kilbride ('church of St Brigid') in Lanarkshire.

Dun 'fortress', as in Dundee ('fort of Daigh'), and Dunkeld ('fort of the Caledonians') near Perth.

Drum 'ridge', as in Drummond ('ridge') and Drumnadrochit ('ridge of the bridge'), both in the Highlands.

Gleann 'valley', as in Glencoe ('valley of the River Coe') in Argyll.

Inbhir 'river mouth', as in Inveraray ('mouth of the River Aray') in Argyll, and Inverness ('mouth of the River Ness').

PICTISH NAMES

Little is known about the Picts, who occupied the northeast provinces of Angus, Atholl, Fife, Strathearn, Mar, Moray and Caithness until AD 844, when sovereignty of these territories was taken over by the *Dál Riata* Scots (see 'Gaelic Names', left). Place names in Scotland with a Pictish element date from the 3rd-9th centuries AD, although many have a second Gaelic element, which may have been added in the 9th and 10th centuries, when many of the people living in these areas would have spoken both languages.

The Pictish place-name element 'pit' is derived from 'pett', meaning 'a portion or share of land' and related to the English 'piece'. There are more than 300 examples in the northeast of Scotland, including Pitcairns ('portion of the mounds') and Pitlochry ('stony share') in Perth and Kinross; Pitcaple ('portion of the mare') and Pittendreich ('portion on the hill face') in Aberdeenshire; and Pittenweem ('share of the caves') in Fife.

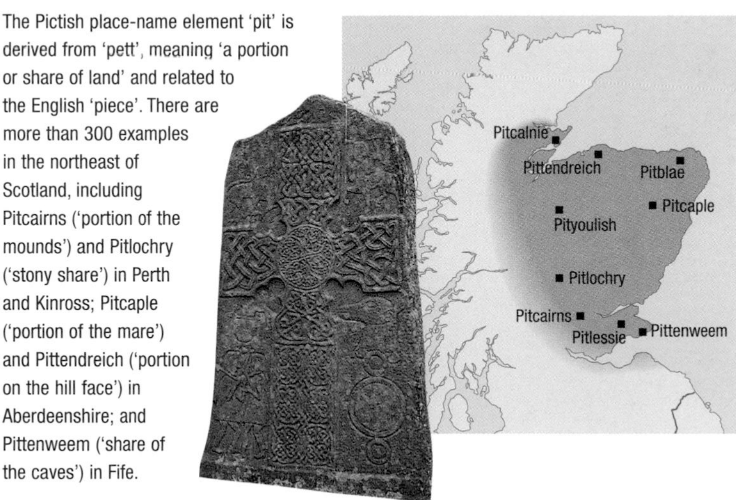

WELSH AND CORNISH NAMES

Welsh names can be found in English border counties such as Cheshire, Shropshire and Herefordshire, as well as in Wales. An example is Crewe, which means 'a ford' or 'stepping stones'. Nearly all Cornish place names have Celtic rather than Anglo-Saxon roots, because the English did not settle there until the 9th century.

WELSH

Aber 'mouth of a river', as in Aberdare ('mouth of the River Dar') in the Rhondda, and Abergavenny ('mouth of the River Gafenni') in Monmouthshire.

Caer 'fortress', as in Caernarfon ('fort in Arfin') in Gwynedd, and Cardiff ('fort on the river Taff').

Coed 'wood', as in Betws-y-coed ('chapel in the wood') in Conwy, and Coedpoeth ('burnt wood') in Wrexham.

Cwm 'valley', as in Cwmbrân ('valley of the River Bran') in Newport, and Cwmafan ('valley of the River Afan') in Neath.

Tre(f) 'farmstead', as in Trefeglwys ('farm by the church') in Powys and Tredegar ('Tegyr's farm') in Blaenau.

Llan 'churchyard', as in Llandudno ('church of St Tudno') in Conwy, and Llangollen ('church of St Collen') in Denbighshire.

Pen (see page 28, opposite)

Pont 'bridge', as in Pontypool ('bridge by the pool') in Torfaen, and Pontypridd ('bridge by the earthen house') in the Rhondda.

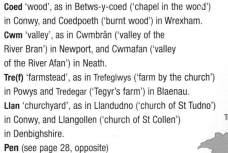

CORNISH

Pen (see page 28, opposite)

Porth 'harbour', as in Perranporth ('harbour of St Piran's parish') and Porthleven ('smooth harbour').

Tre 'hamlet' or 'farm', as in Tremaine ('hamlet of the stone') and Treneglos ('farm of the church').

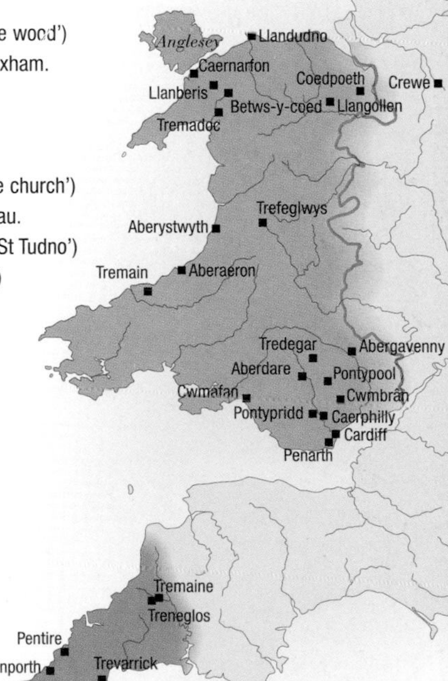

The arrival of the 'English'

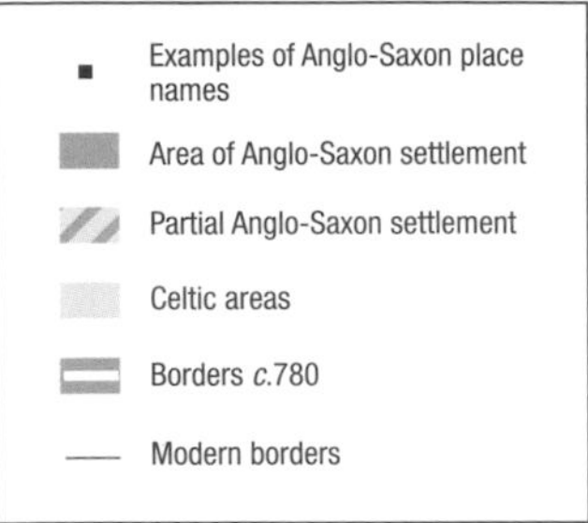

The Anglo-Saxons, whose language formed the basis of English, first came to Britain during the Roman occupation. But they did not put down roots until the 5th century AD – after rule by Rome had collapsed. As more of these migrants arrived, they gradually settled everywhere apart from Cornwall, Wales and most of Scotland, although you will spot some Anglo-Saxon place names, such as Hawick, Falkirk and Motherwell along Scotland's eastern border and in the Lothians.

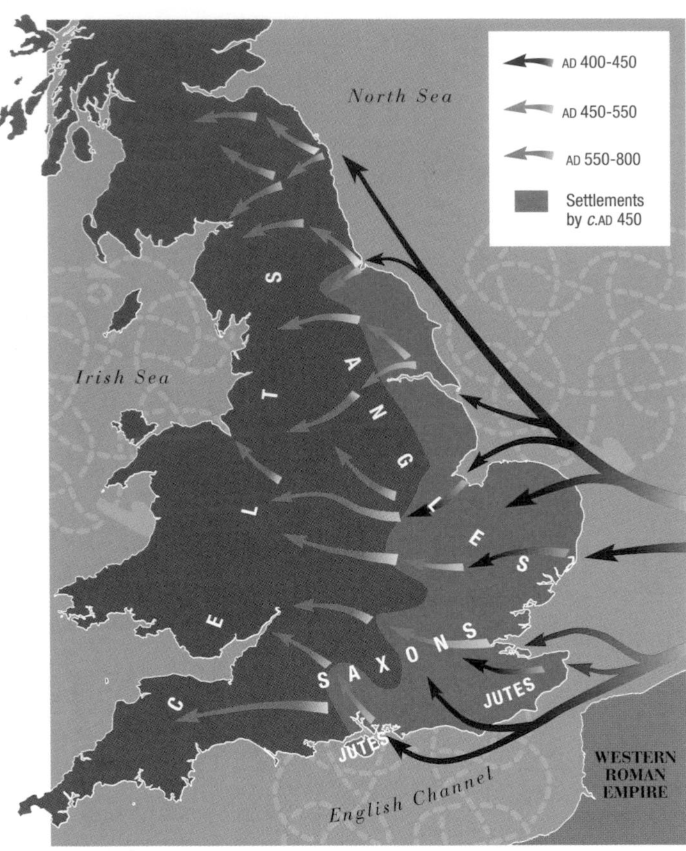

Anglo-Saxon migration Between AD 400 and 800, Britain was settled by various Germanic tribes. The Angles came from the Schleswig-Holstein peninsula, between modern-day Denmark and Germany, to settle in the east of England and what is now Northumberland, between the Humber and the Tees. Others came from farther south, from Saxony, settling first in southern England, then pushing across to the west.

THE FIRST ENGLISH NAMES

Most of the place names used in England today were coined by the Anglo-Saxons between the 5th and 11th centuries. Many include the name of a local lord. Alfreton in Derbyshire, for example, took its name from a man called Aelfhere, Brandeston in Suffolk from someone called Brant, and Menston in Yorkshire from a Mensa. But the majority of Anglo-Saxon place names describe landscape features such as hills, woods and valleys. Acton means 'a town set in oak woods' and 'Hooton', in the three south Yorkshire towns of Hooton Levitt, Hooton Pagnell and Hooton Roberts, means 'settlement on a spur of high ground'.

Ham 'homestead'. Examples include Amersham ('homestead of a man called Ealhmund') in Buckinghamshire, and Rotherham ('homestead on the River Rother') in Yorkshire.

Wic 'a Roman fort', from the Latin word *vicus*. Combined with 'ham' it means 'settlement alongside a Roman fort'. Examples include Wickham Market in Suffolk and Wykeham in Yorkshire.

Ing 'a group of people ruled by a tribal leader', from the Latin *ingas*. Examples of its use are Hastings ('Haest's people') in East Sussex, and Reading ('Reada's people') in Berkshire.

Ingham combines 'ingas' and 'ham' (see above), as in Birmingham ('estate of Beornmond's people') and Nottingham ('estate of Snot's people').

Barton 'outlying farm [where barley or corn is grown]' from the Old English *beretun*. Examples of its use include Mulbarton ('outlying farm where milk is produced') in Norfolk, Surbiton ('south farm') in Surrey, and Steeple Barton ('steep farm') in Oxfordshire.

Brough, burgh and **bury** 'fortified site'. Examples include Brough in Derbyshire, Bury St Edmunds ('fortified site or town associated with St Edmond') in Suffolk, and Iron Age hill-fort sites such as Almondbury, near Huddersfield in Yorkshire, Battlesbury in Wiltshire, and Danebury in Hampshire.

Dun 'hill'. Examples include Clevedon ('hill of the cliffs') in Somerset, and Durham ('hill island' or 'promontory').

Field 'large area of open land in a wooded landscape'. Examples include Lichfield ('open land near Letocetum') in Staffordshire, and Wakefield ('open land where wakes are held') in Yorkshire.

Ford 'a ford'. Examples include Oxford ('ford used by oxen'), Stamford ('stony ford') in Lincolnshire, and Stratford ('ford on a Roman road') in East London and in Warwickshire.

Haigh and **hale** 'nook' or 'corner'. Examples include Edenhall ('nook of land by the River Eden') in Cumbria, and Haughton ('farmstead in or by a nook of land') in Shropshire and in Staffordshire.

Hurst 'wooded hill', as in Ewhurst ('yew-tree covered hill') in Surrey, Chislehurst ('wooded hill with gravelly soil') in Kent, and Hurstwood ('wood on a hill') in Lancashire.

Ley 'woodland clearing'. It was often combined with someone's name as in Barnsley ('Beorn's woodland clearing'), Yorkshire, and Brackley ('Bracca's

ROMAN NAMES

In AD 43, four Roman legions and 20,000 auxiliaries landed on the Kent coast and defeated local British tribes in a series of skirmishes. It took more than 40 years for the Romans to establish their rule, and even then rebellious tribes in the north and west continued to put up strong resistance until the Romans left in the early 5th century. Somewhat surprisingly, this long occupation left little trace on English place names, as most Roman names were later replaced. The fact that the Celtic language survived throughout the occupation and for quite some time afterwards may also help explain this scarcity.

Evidence of a few Roman place names and settlements does remain. Some developed a more modern form, for example Lindum gradually became Lincoln and Isca became Exeter. The element 'caster', 'cester' or 'chester' in a name indicates the site of a Roman fort, as in Doncaster ('Roman fort on the River Don') and Chichester ('Cissa's Roman camp'). Also the Latin *portus*, meaning 'a port', finds its way into Anglo-Saxon names, such as Portsmouth.

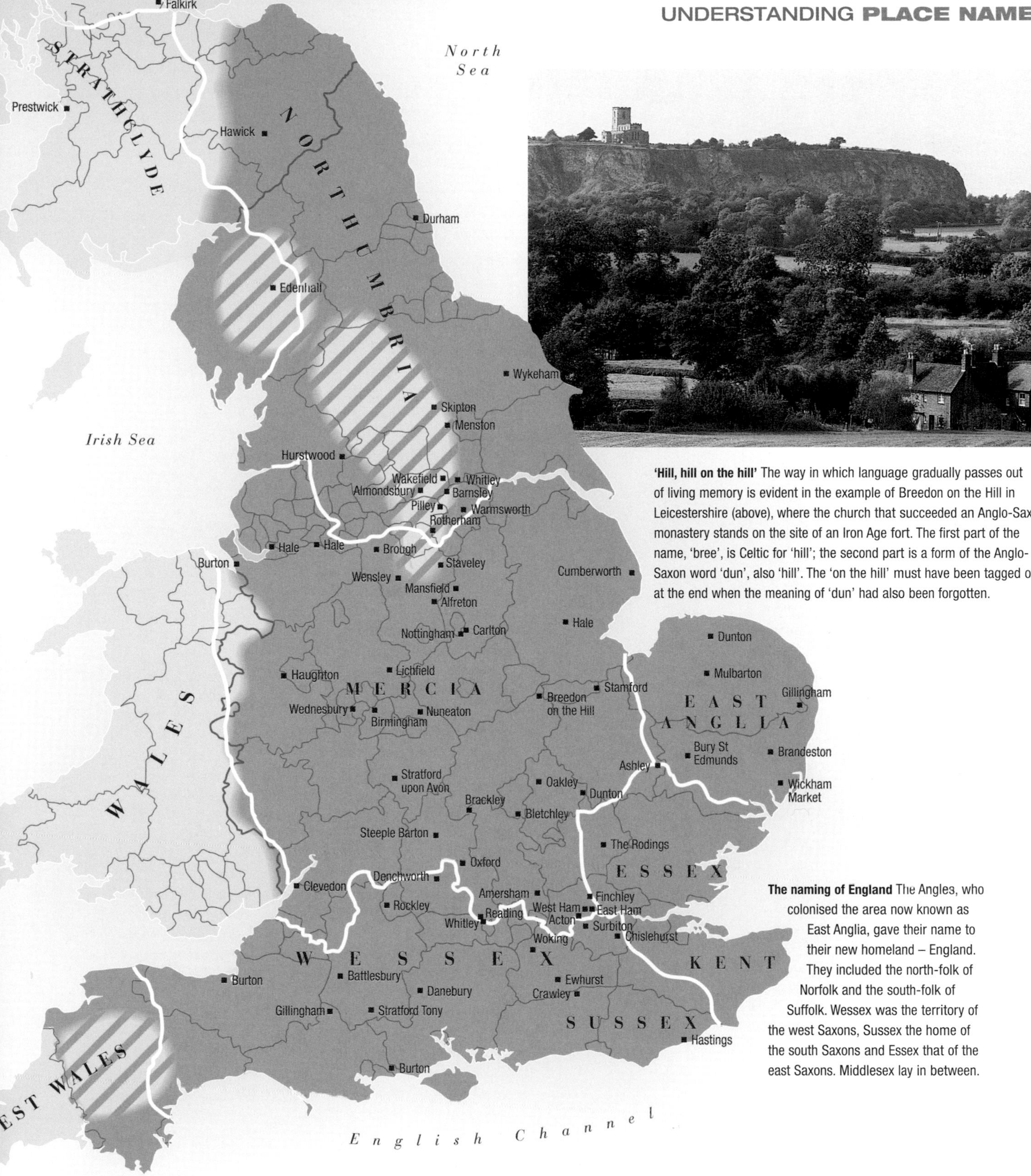

'Hill, hill on the hill' The way in which language gradually passes out of living memory is evident in the example of Breedon on the Hill in Leicestershire (above), where the church that succeeded an Anglo-Saxon monastery stands on the site of an Iron Age fort. The first part of the name, 'bree', is Celtic for 'hill'; the second part is a form of the Anglo-Saxon word 'dun', also 'hill'. The 'on the hill' must have been tagged on at the end when the meaning of 'dun' had also been forgotten.

The naming of England The Angles, who colonised the area now known as East Anglia, gave their name to their new homeland – England. They included the north-folk of Norfolk and the south-folk of Suffolk. Wessex was the territory of the west Saxons, Sussex the home of the south Saxons and Essex that of the east Saxons. Middlesex lay in between.

woodland clearing'), Northamptonshire. Sometimes the term is linked with the name of something found in the clearing, such as a type of tree, bird or implement. Examples of this usage are numerous and include Ashley ('clearing in an ash wood') in Cambridgeshire, Crawley ('woodland clearing where crows live') in West Sussex, Finchley ('woodland clearing where finches live') in north London, Pilley in Yorkshire and Staveley in Derbyshire (both 'woodland clearing where poles or staves are found'), and Whitley ('clearing with trees that have white bark or blossom'), near Reading in Berkshire.

Ton or **tone** 'enclosure', 'village' or 'farmstead'. Examples of its use include Carlton ('village of the freemen') in Nottinghamshire, Nuneaton ('the nuns' farm on the river') in Warwickshire, and Skipton ('sheep farm') in Yorkshire.

Worth also 'enclosure' or 'farmstead'. It was frequently combined with a personal name. Examples of this include Aldsworth ('enclosure of a man called Ald') in Gloucestershire, Denchworth ('enclosure of a man called Denic') in Oxfordshire, and Warmsworth ('enclosure of a man called Waermund') in Yorkshire. In southwest England, such place names often end in **-worthy**.

Raiders from the north

An attack in AD 793 by marauding Vikings on the monastery at Lindisfarne in Northumbria heralded a new era of conquest from across the North Sea. The Vikings were ruthless killers, but they were also farmers and traders who were keen to settle and make good use of the land they had seized. They were to dominate north England and parts of Scotland for nearly 300 years, but the Scandinavian place names they introduced have endured for far longer.

	The Five Boroughs of Danelaw
■	Examples of Scandinavian place names
	Area of Norse settlement
	Area of Danish settlement
	Ancient borders
	Border of Danelaw
——	Modern borders

THE LEGACY OF VIKING SETTLERS

The Vikings left behind many traces of their occupation in the areas where they settled: Danes in north and east England, Norsemen in north and northwest Scotland and along the Welsh coast. Fragments of the various Scandinavian languages and dialects crop up frequently in place names in these areas. Many describe natural features in the landscape, such as 'beck', 'dale', 'fell' and 'foss' (see 'Did you know?', right), but, as a testimony to Viking agricultural expertise, there is also a generous scattering of terms relating to farms and farming. Some of the most common are 'ing' meaning 'meadow', 'garth' meaning 'a grassy enclosure' and 'laithe' meaning 'barn'.

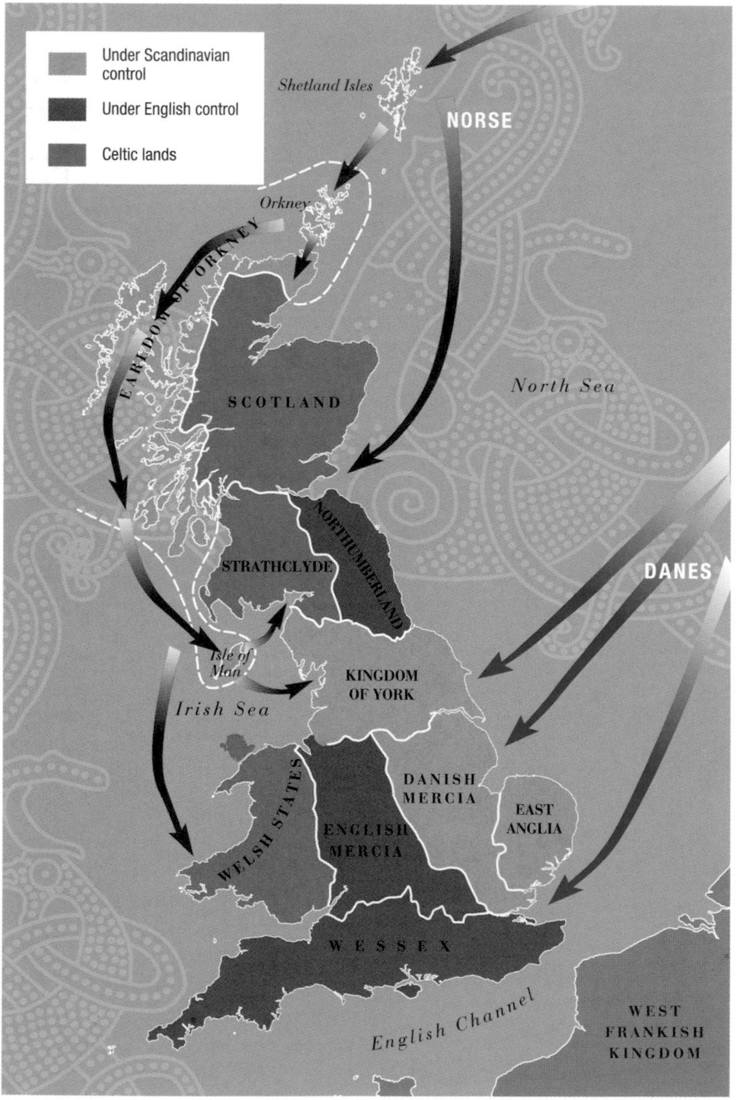

Viking attack Danish warriors plundered the east coast, while Norwegians raided the Orkneys, the Western Isles and Ireland, before settling in parts of northern England.

By 'farmstead' or 'village'. Examples include Coningsby ('king's village') in Lincolnshire, Ingleby ('village of the English') in Derbyshire, and Denaby ('Danes' village') and Selby ('village by willow trees'), both in Yorkshire.
Booth 'temporary shelter', often on a farmstead when combined with the ending 'by', as in Boothby ('farmstead with shelters') in Lincolnshire.
Kirk 'church', as in Romaldkirk ('church of St Rumwald') in Co. Durham, Kirby Bedon ('village with a church in the manor of the de Bidum family') in Norfolk, Kirkby Overblow ('village of the iron smelters with a church') in Yorkshire, and Kirton in Lindsey ('village with a church in Lindsey county') in Lincolnshire.
Scales 'a herdsman's hut'. Examples include several Scales in Cumbria, and Newton with Scales ('new village with a herdsman's hut') in Lancashire.
Thorpe 'outlying farmstead or hamlet'. Examples include Burythorpe ('hill hamlet') in Yorkshire, Grassthorpe ('grassy hamlet') in Nottinghamshire, and Gunthorpe ('Gunni's outlying farmstead') and Sculthorpe ('Skuli's outlying farmstead') both in Norfolk.
Thwaite 'clearing, 'meadow' or 'paddock'. Examples of its use include Armathwaite ('clearing of the hermit'), Braithwaite ('broad clearing'), and Seathwaite ('sedge clearing'), all in Cumbria.
Toft 'plot of land on which a homestead was built'. Examples of its use include Lowestoft ('Hlothver's homestead') in Suffolk, and Bratoft ('broad homestead') and Wigtoft ('homestead by a creek'), both in Lincolnshire.

DID YOU KNOW?

You are probably more familiar with Viking words than you think. They can be spotted in the names of numerous sites and landscape features across Britain:

Fell 'mountain', as used in the name of the Yorkshire peak, Fountains Fell.
Dale (from *dalr* or *dael*) 'valley', as used in Langstrothdale, one of the Yorkshire Dales.
Gill 'ravine'. An example is Scargill ('ravine where merganser seabirds are seen'), a village in Co. Durham.
Foss 'waterfall', as used in Janet's Foss in Yorkshire.
Keld 'spring'. Examples include the Yorkshire villages of Keld and Keldholme ('island or river meadow near the spring').
Carr 'marsh', as used in Carcroft ('enclosure near the marsh'), a village in Yorkshire.
Holme 'island'. Among many examples of its use are several villages in Yorkshire, East Anglia and the East Midlands, as well as a Sandholme ('sandy island') in east Yorkshire.
Lund 'wood'. Examples of it use include the two Yorkshire villages of Lund.
Scar 'cliff' or 'rock', as used in Newberry Scar near Middleton, in Teesdale.
Ey 'island' as in Anglesey (Ongull's island) and Swansea (Sveinn's island).
Ness 'headland', as used in Thorpeness ('a village near the headland') in Suffolk.
Beck 'stream'. An example is Troutbeck ('place by a trout stream') in Cumbria.

Peace agreement Most Vikings settled in the areas closest to their native shores – the coastal regions of east and northeast England. They became such a powerful force there that, in AD 886, Alfred the Great, King of Wessex, made a treaty giving them their own province, known as the Danelaw. The River Tees served as its northern border and a line drawn between London and the River Mersey as its southern boundary. Jorvik – present-day York – became the Viking's northern capital, but the Anglo-Saxon settlements of Derby, Lincoln, Stamford, Leicester and Nottingham also prospered. Refortified and extended, they were known as 'the Five Boroughs'.

FOLLOWING THE PLACE-NAME TRAIL

Current place names can give a clue as to where most Scandinavian farms in the Danelaw were. Along the western edge of the Wolds in Lincolnshire there is a line of 19 villages with names ending in 'by', meaning 'farmstead', but just four with totally English names. This suggests that these 19 were new settlements created by the Vikings on land that had not previously been farmed. In some Lincolnshire parishes, more than half the field names used in the 12th and 13th centuries are of Scandinavian origin. Norfolk, too, has many place names ending in 'by', such as Ormesby St Margaret, most likely sited on land that was farmed by a Viking called Ormr.

The stamp of the Norsemen
Viking invaders also left their mark on the map of Scotland. Their word for church, *kirkja*, is found in the names of many towns, such as Kirkoswald ('St Oswald's church'), Kirkcudbright ('St Cuthbert's church') and Kirkwall ('church bay') up in Orkney. Another example is the use of *vágr* or *vick*, both meaning 'bay', as in Stornoway ('steering bay') in the Hebrides, Lerwick ('mud bay') in Shetland and Wick ('by the bay') in the Highlands.

From the Normans to New Towns

The Norman invasion of England in 1066 added a liberal sprinkling of French words to the English language, but it hardly had any impact at all on place names. Later developments, such as the Industrial Revolution, were to be much more influential, although even from the Middle Ages onwards, a succession of new towns were being established, often taking their names from notable personalities and events of the time.

Gallic influence

The Normans brought a new social elite of nobles and church leaders to England's shores, extending into Scotland under David I a century later. Few settlers of more humble rank followed in their wake. The toilers and gatherers of society remained largely of Anglo-Saxon and Viking descent. So the Norman influence on place names was mainly confined to sites associated with the grand castles, cathedrals and monasteries that they built to help establish and defend their power. Towns with Norman French names, such as Beaumaris ('beautiful marsh') in Anglesey, Belper ('beautiful retreat') in Derbyshire, Devizes ('on the boundaries') in Wiltshire, Grosmont ('big hill') in Monmouthshire and Pontefract ('by a broken bridge') in Yorkshire grew up from the settlements centred around fortified Norman strongholds.

Double-barrelled place names in central and southern England are often Norman in origin too. They usually combined the old name of a manor with that of its new Norman owner. Examples include Kingston Bagpuize ('de Bagpuize's royal manor') in Oxfordshire, Wootton Bassett ('Basset's farmstead by a wood') in Wiltshire, and Thorpe Mandeville ('estate belonging to the de Mandeville family') in Northamptonshire.

Urban booms

Population increases in the 12th and 13th centuries led to the creation of many new towns in England and Wales, with a mass of Newports, Newtons and Newtowns appearing during this period. Flourishing commerce brought a flood of new market towns too, including Newmarket in Suffolk and Market Harborough in Leicestershire. More established places sometimes added the Old English word 'chipping', meaning 'market', to their original name to highlight their success. Among these are Chipping Norton in Oxfordshire and Chipping Ongar in Essex.

Industrialisation in the 18th and 19th centuries fuelled a further flush of urban expansion (see opposite), and in the 20th century, over-crowding and war damage triggered the creation of 28 planned new towns. Most simply took the name of a previous village or settlement on the same site. Milton Keynes in Buckinghamshire, for example, was first recorded in 1422 – Milton means 'farmstead' or 'estate' in Old English and Keynes refers to Lucas de Cahaignes, lord of the manor there in the 12th century.

The personal touch

In the 18th and 19th centuries, it became popular to name places after local landowners and captains of industy, as a mark of their importance or wealth. Arkwright Town in Derbyshire is named after the family of Sir Richard Arkwright, inventor of the

DID YOU KNOW?

Place names such as Blandford Forum, Lyme Regis and Chew Magna appear to have an obvious Latin derivation, but few actually date back as far as the Roman occupation. They were created in the Middle Ages, when Latin was the language used for administration by the Church and the educated classes. It became fashionable to use Latin words such as *forum*, meaning 'market', *magna*, meaning 'great', and *regis*, meaning 'king', to create the names for places that were considered to be of some importance.

Monastic influence French immigrants after the Norman conquest included Cistercian monks. Their wealth is evident even from the ruins of the magnificent abbeys they built, including Rievaulx (above). The name is a Normanisation of 'rye vallis' ('valley of the River Rye').

spinning frame, and Raynes Park in Surrey stands on estates owned by the Rayne family in the 19th century. A touch of romance lies behind the naming of Maryport in Cumbria. 'Mary' was the wife of Humphrey Senhouse, who built the harbour there between 1750 and 1760.

Several 20th-century new towns were also named in honour of illustrious individuals. The engineer Thomas Telford gave his name to Telford in Shropshire, while Peterlee in Co. Durham commemorates the local miner's leader during the 1930s, Peter Lee.

A princely plot Places such as Princetown in Devon (above) owe their names to Royal connections. The village was named after the Prince of Wales (later George IV, right) who owned Dartmoor and gave the land on which it, along with its famous prison, was built.

THE INFLUENCE OF INDUSTRY

The Industrial Revolution brought a crop of new towns named after the raw materials that drove the developing local industries. Coalport and Ironbridge (below) in Shropshire, Coalville in Leicestershire and Ironville in Derbyshire are examples. Some industrial communities, such as New Brampton in Derbyshire and New Lanark in Strathclyde, took their names from existing settlements. Many built on former common land took the name of an earlier settlement, as at Baddeley Green, Staffordshire, and Silkstone Common, Yorkshire.

Some 19th-century industrialists built their workers villages close to their factories. Port Sunlight in Cheshire was founded by William Hesketh Lever and named after a brand of soap he manufactured there. The Cadburys built a town for their employees on the old Bournbrook estate near Birmingham, changing its name to the more French-sounding Bournville because of the high quality of chocolate made across the Channel.

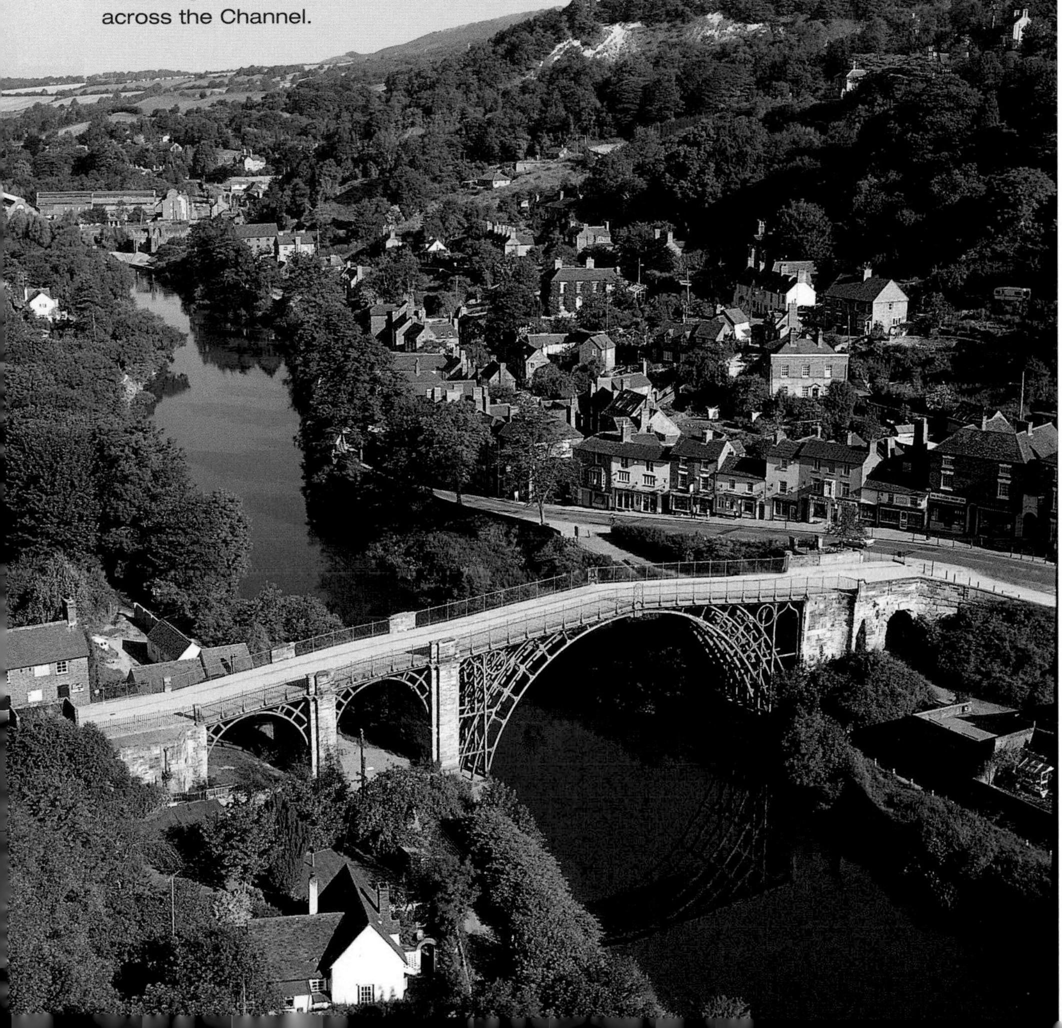

FIND OUT MORE

- *Signposts to the Past* (M. Gelling, Phillimore, 2nd ed., 1988)
- *English Place-Names* (K. Cameron, Batsford, 1996)
- *The Landscape of Place Names* (M. Gelling and A. Cole, Paul Watkins, 2000)
- *The Cambridge Dictionary of English Place-Names* (V. Watts, CUP, 2004)
- *The Oxford Dictionary of British Place-Names* (A.D. Mills, OUP, 2003)
- *The Penguin Dictionary of British Place Names* (A. Room, Penguin Books, 2003)
- *A Popular Dictionary of Cornish Place-Names* (ed. O.J. Padel, Alison Hodge, 1988)
- *Scottish Place-Names* (W.F.H. Nicolaisen, Batsford, 1976)
- *Scotland's Place-Names* (D. Dorward, Mercat Press, 1995)

EXPLORE YOUR LANDSCAPE

Trade, industry, transport of goods and essential supplies, field systems and enclosures – even the pursuit of wealth and power – all have left their mark on the layout of Britain's towns and countryside. Documents and maps can tell you much of the story, and may help to set you on the right track when you step out into the fresh air to explore your area on foot.

Making a start The countryside around you and the layout of your town or village may seem to be a stable backcloth to daily life, but it is likely to have undergone many dramatic changes over the centuries. Finding out when, how and why these occurred is both fascinating and fun.

- One of the quickest ways to get a good overall picture of how the landscape around you has developed is to consult maps of the area (see pages 18-19). Start with an up-to-date Ordnance Survey (OS) map, then compare it with earlier ones, which will probably be in your local reference library or record office (see pages 10-11). Make a note of the major changes that you spot.
- You can also find documents, such as planning applications and electoral rolls relating to features noted on maps you have consulted, in local reference libraries and record offices. Even a brief glance at these resources should help you to draw up a plan of action (see opposite).
- Keep a map, preferably a current OS one, with you as you walk around and make a note of what you discover. Also jot down any questions that arise, possibly to be answered by another search through the archives.
- Although focused just on England, a useful book that will help you to structure your exploration, no matter where you live, is *The Making of the English Landscape* (W.G. Hoskins, Penguin Books, 1991).

Field patterns Many of the stone walls that divide up the land in the Peak District follow boundaries laid down in medieval times.

Hidden past Signs of industry may be found even in the depths of the countryside. The long, grassed-over mound near the hamlet of White Coppice in Lancashire (above) is all that remains of an embankment constructed when quarrying was a major souce of income in the area.

Working out what you want to know

Before you set out on a journey of exploration, draw up a rough plan of action, including any questions you want answered. You may deviate from it as your knowledge expands, but it will give you a starting point.

Distinctive features Find out about special points of interest in your area, and focus your research, at least initially, on a particular topic. In the New Forest, you might try to identify the sites of cottages seen on a tithe-award map of the 1840s that were abandoned by the late 19th century. In northeast Scotland, you could survey the remains of the planned Victorian fishing settlement at Lybster. Every area will throw up something different.

Shape and size Why does the medieval parish church at Llandyfaelog in Carmarthenshire stand apart from the village inside a circular enclosure? Why do the central streets of Flint in north Wales form a grid pattern? Look at a current map of your town or village and see if anything stands out that you might investigate. Perhaps you live in open countryside. In that case, you could investigate if the present pattern of hamlets, cottages and scattered farmsteads is an ancient or fairly recent one by comparing it with what is featured on earlier maps.

Mysteries to solve What is the explanation for those curving ridge-and-furrow patterns in nearby pasture? Does an old map reveal a flourishing settlement or grand estate that has since completely disappeared? Attempting to answer such questions could lead you down an exciting path of discovery.

Some basic guidelines

Working through the material you gather in a methodical way will ensure you get the most from your research.

- Keep cross-checking visual and documentary evidence. If you spot the remains of a moated site, a search in local archives may reveal who constructed it and when.
- Your first interpretations may be wide of the mark. Be prepared to change them, as you uncover more clues.
- Comparisons with other places are essential to check how specific to your area a particular feature is. In rural Essex, you might check how many parish churches have a timber belfry or a Tudor brick porch.

FIND OUT MORE

- *Medieval England: An Aerial Survey* (M.W. Beresford and J.K.S. St Joseph, Cambridge University Press, 1979)
- *The History of the Countryside* (Oliver Rackham, Orion, 1986)
- *Rural England: An Illustrated History of the Landscape* (Joan Thirsk ed., Oxford University Press, 2002)
- *The Making of the English Village* (B.K. Roberts, Longman, 1987)
- *The Making of the Industrial Landscape* (Barrie Trinder, Sutton Publishing, 1988)
- *Trees and Woodland in the British Landscape* (Oliver Rackham, Orion, 2001)
- *The Harvest of the Hills: Rural Life in Northern England and the Scottish Borders, 1400-1700* (Angus Winchester, Edinburgh University Press, 2000)

Plotting the urban landscape

Until the Industrial Revolution of the mid 18th century, the countryside was still visible from most British town centres. Comparing maps down the ages will help you to discover how these green acres were swallowed up. Look for street names, such as The Meadows or Little Common, or for surviving pockets of woodland – all possible clues to a rural past.

How towns ate the land

Old maps enable you to get a good sense of the size and layout of your town or city at different points in time. By comparing them, you can see how and when the settlement grew beyond its medieval limits and, perhaps, how much the central street plan has changed, or to what extent property boundaries have altered. You will also notice how spaces have been filled and how paths across what were once fields and open countryside have evolved gradually into streets and alleyways.

The earliest town plans

At the beginning of the 17th century, John Speed (1552-1629) drew a series of county maps that he published in 1612 as the *Theatre of the Empire of Great Britaine.* Included were maps of the various county towns, many of which have been widely reproduced, particularly in the county histories that you are likely to find at your local reference library or record office (see pages 10-11).

- Note the position of the market place at the heart of the town and consider how its shape compares with today's.
- Look for the walls that enclosed most of the towns drawn by Speed and see if any of the streets were already spreading beyond them.
- Look for the names of the principal streets, then check to see how many of them survive.

Maps of the 18th century

English county maps of the second half of the 18th century (see pages 18-19), such as Hodskinson's 1783 map of Suffolk or Yates's 1786 map of Lancashire, sometimes have town maps as insets.

- The local record office or reference library will have copies of your county maps, including an 18th-century one. You should also ask whether it has been published, perhaps as a CD. Most English towns have at least one map from the 18th century, if not earlier, commissioned by the borough council or some other local body.
- Late 18th-century maps will show your town at the start of the Industrial Revolution, when it was beginning to grow rapidly. See how many ancient features are marked, such as remnants of town walls or castle ruins. Has the market place been encroached upon by shops and stalls? Have the livestock markets been removed from the central streets? Are there any planned developments of new streets beyond the ancient core?

Military outpost John Speed's map of Lancaster in 1611 shows a town dominated by its castle. Most other buildings sit along and around Market Street, with a few spreading out into the surrounding countryside along St Leonard's Gate and Penny Street.

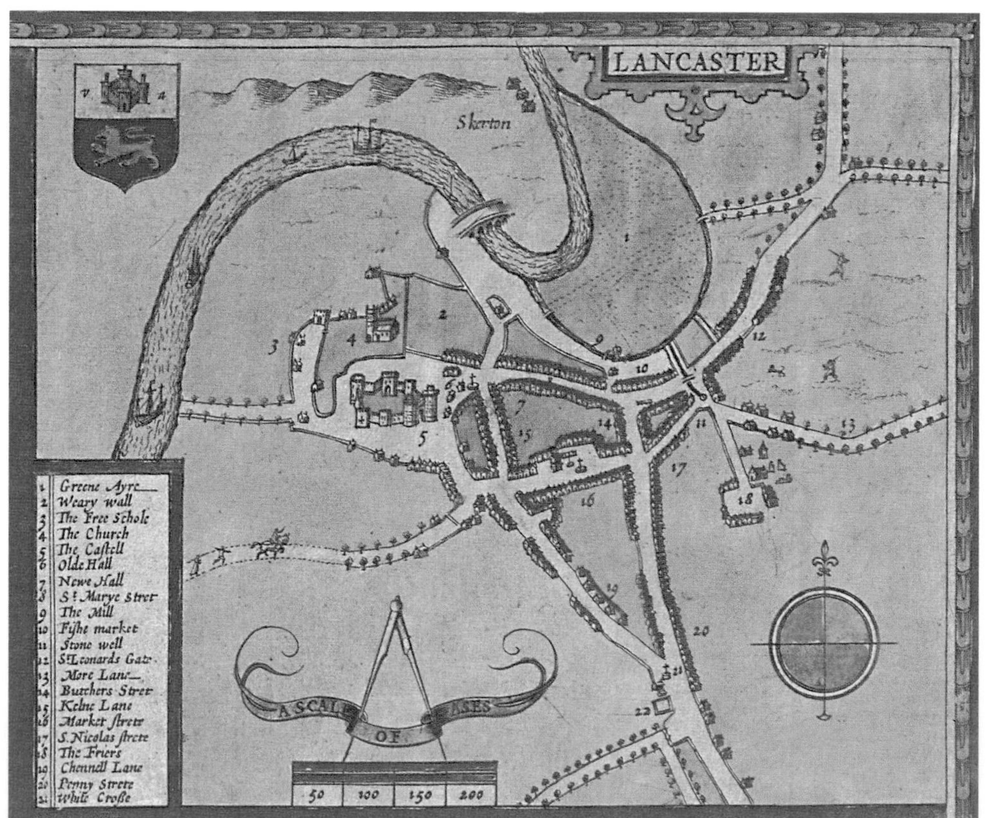

Maps of the 19th century

Your local record office or library is also likely to keep maps of your town that were commissioned by the local borough council or printed by local firms during the early 19th century. Compare these with Ordnance Survey (OS) maps (see pages 18-19) of the later 19th and early 20th centuries to find out

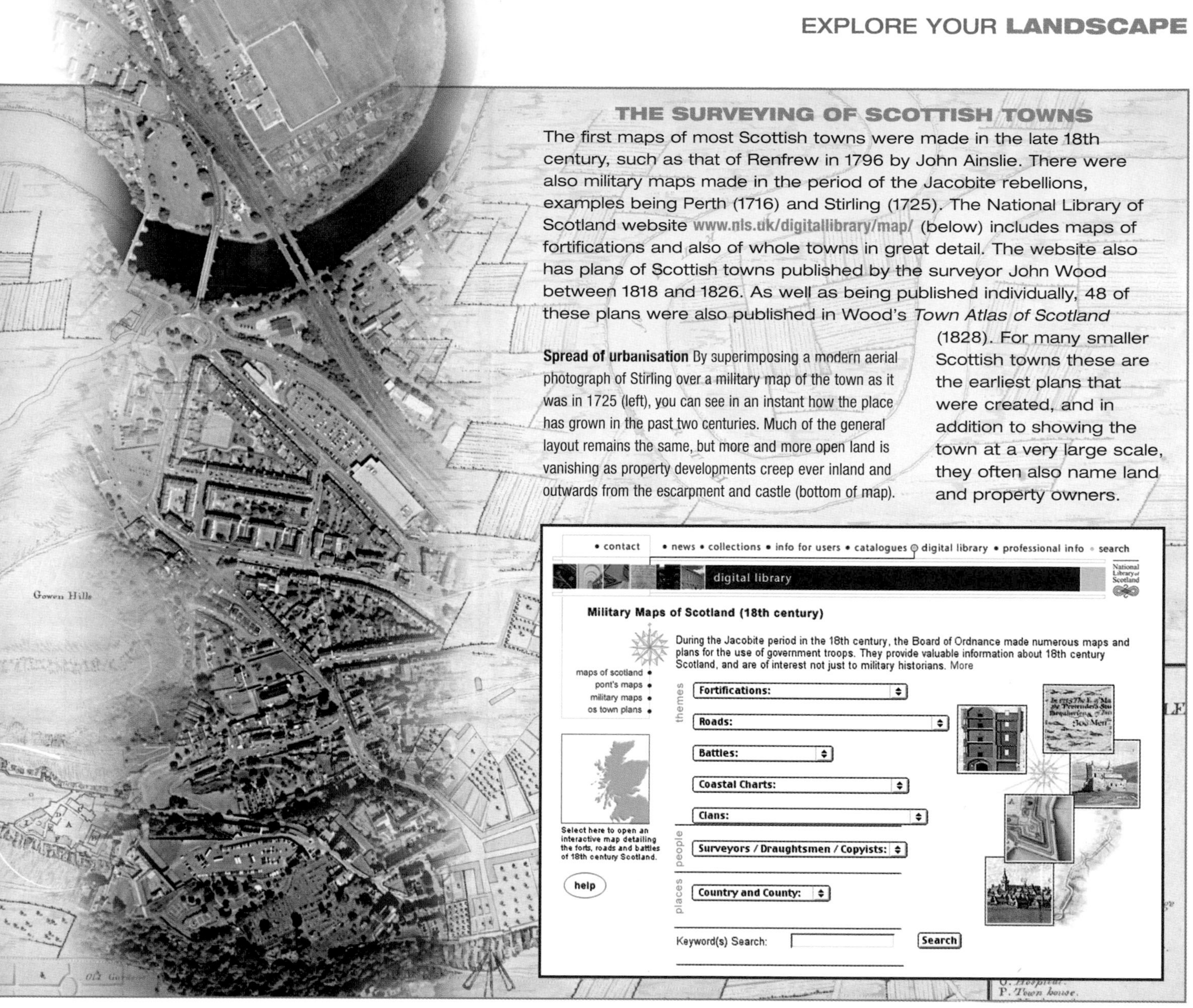

THE SURVEYING OF SCOTTISH TOWNS

The first maps of most Scottish towns were made in the late 18th century, such as that of Renfrew in 1796 by John Ainslie. There were also military maps made in the period of the Jacobite rebellions, examples being Perth (1716) and Stirling (1725). The National Library of Scotland website **www.nls.uk/digitallibrary/map/** (below) includes maps of fortifications and also of whole towns in great detail. The website also has plans of Scottish towns published by the surveyor John Wood between 1818 and 1826. As well as being published individually, 48 of these plans were also published in Wood's *Town Atlas of Scotland* (1828). For many smaller Scottish towns these are the earliest plans that were created, and in addition to showing the town at a very large scale, they often also name land and property owners.

Spread of urbanisation By superimposing a modern aerial photograph of Stirling over a military map of the town as it was in 1725 (left), you can see in an instant how the place has grown in the past two centuries. Much of the general layout remains the same, but more and more open land is vanishing as property developments creep ever inland and outwards from the escarpment and castle (bottom of map).

how your urban landscape developed in Victorian (1837-1901) and Edwardian (1901-10) times.

- Trace how the surrounding fields in the earlier maps became covered with streets, housing or industry.
- Note the names of new streets. They might suggest who the landowners or builders were, or help you to date them if they are named after a Prime Minister, such as Lord Palmerston (1855-8 and 1859-65) or a military victory, such as the Crimean War battle of Alma (1854).
- Look for the first appearance of churches, railway stations, sewage works and other public services.

Modern maps

Up-to-date town and OS maps are as valuable as older maps for understanding the story of urban growth in your area. Compare them with earlier maps and you will quickly spot the changes in layout and the evolving relationship with the surrounding landscape.

- See how much room is taken up by car parks, shopping precincts, industrial sites and other developments and ponder on when and why these sites were chosen.
- Notice the impact of ring roads and underpasses. Such developments have cut off the medieval castle at Carlisle in Cumbria and the parish church at Doncaster in Yorkshire from the historic core of these towns.
- Follow the growth of rail and road links with cities and other towns. Did these new routes of communication have an effect on the layout of your town?

FIND OUT MORE

- *The Cambridge Urban History of Britain* (P. Clark, M. Dauton and D.M. Palliser eds., 3 vols, Cambridge University Press, 2001)
- *The English Urban Landscape* (P. Waller ed., Oxford University Press, 2000)
- **www.getmapping.com** Detailed aerial photographs and mapping services for any area in Britain. Images can be downloaded directly to your computer.

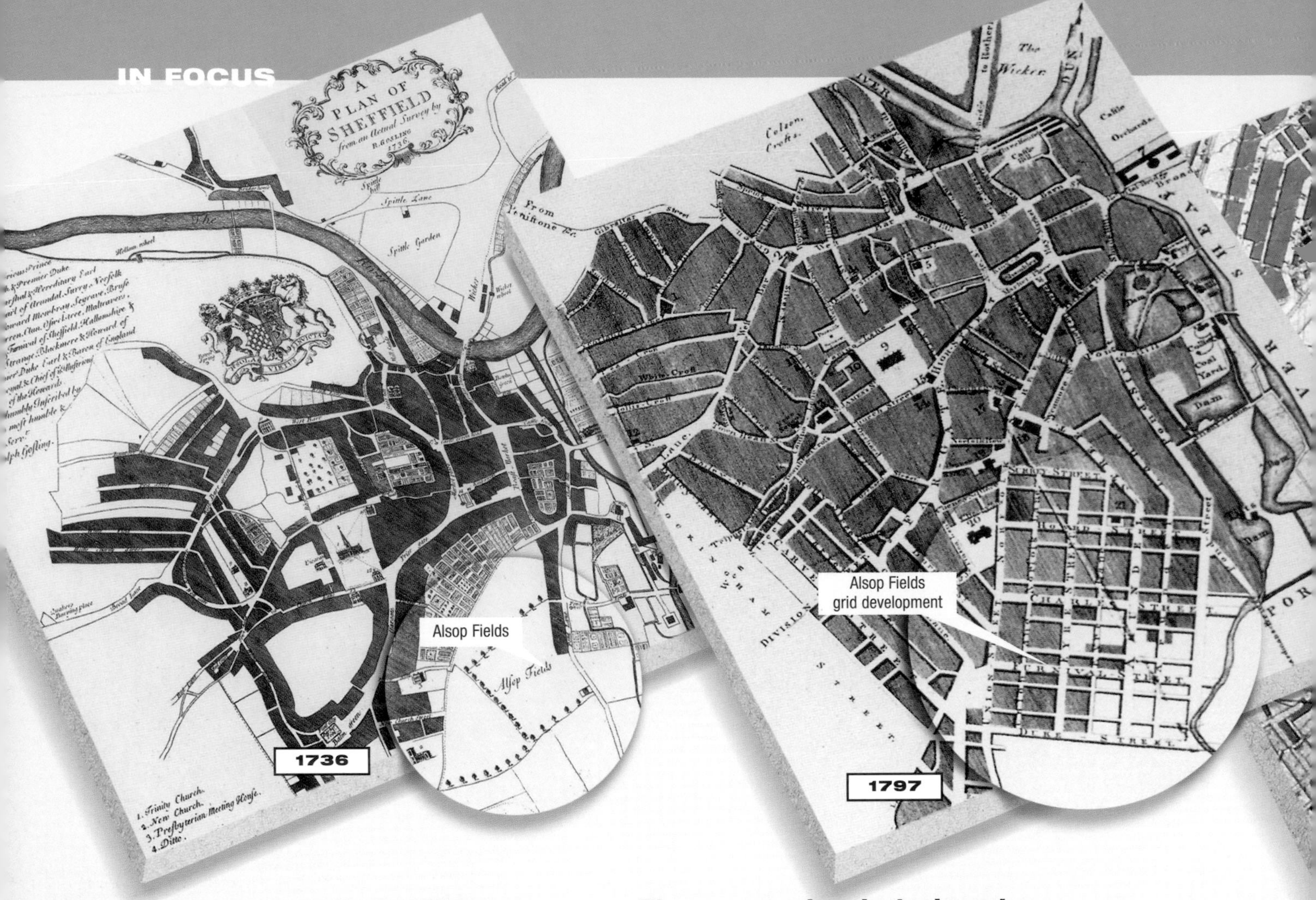

The market town gets smoky

The oldest surviving map of Sheffield (above), drawn by Ralph Gosling in 1736, shows the town just starting to spread beyond its medieval limits. Part of the lord's deer park is now a farm, known as Alsop Fields. Market Place and Beast Market still lie at the centre and many street names, such as Far Gate and Snig Hill, date from the Middle Ages. The site of the castle, demolished in 1649, is marked by Castle Hill and Castle Fould. There are just a few more recent buildings, north of the River Don. But the march of industry had begun. In 1726, Daniel Defoe described Sheffield as 'very populous and large, the streets narrow, the houses dark and black' – probably due to smoke from the growing number of cutlers' forges.

The seams begin to burst

William Fairbank's map of Sheffield in 1797 (above) shows a grid of new streets covering Alsop Fields. More buildings have also appeared in the northwest suburbs, although the town is still largely contained by its two rivers, the Don and the Sheaf.

The invention of high-quality 'crucible' steel in 1742 by a local manufacturer, Benjamin Huntsman, and that of Old Sheffield Plate in 1743, helped to create new industries and boost the more traditional one of cutlery manufacture. Improved transport and the opening of the River Don Navigation in 1751 widened the market. Sheffield, by 1764, was 'a town of considerable note for its manufactures'.

Watch the 'Steel City' grow

Sheffield was once a small medieval market town, dominated by the lord's castle and its huge deer park. But during the Industrial Revolution of the 18th and 19th centuries it expanded rapidly, eventually becoming one of Britain's largest cities, noted for its steel industry. By examining a succession of maps and paintings of the landscape made over this period, you can follow this transformation. You can chart the march of change in your own area by using the same method.

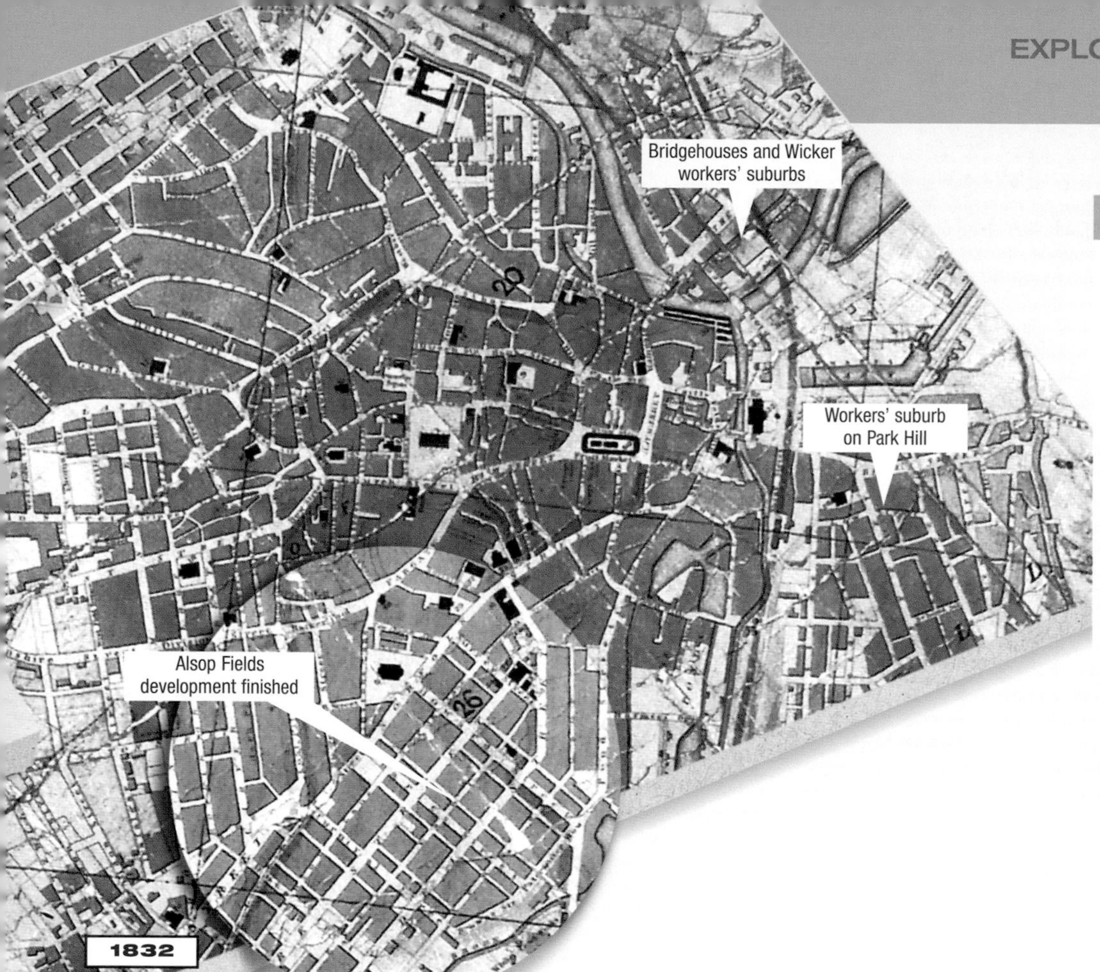

FIND OUT MORE

- Kelham Island Museum
On one of Sheffield's oldest industrial sites, displays tell the story of the people and machines from the city's industrial past.
www.simt.co.uk/kelham/kelham-html

Money-spinner In 1856, Henry Bessemer patented a cost-effective machine (above) for converting iron into top-quality steel. It helped turn Sheffield into a major industrial centre.

Expansion takes off

By 1801, the population of the parish of Sheffield was 45,755. Fifty years later it had reached 135,310 and the suburbs were spreading into the surrounding countryside. J. Tayler's 1832 map (above) shows buildings filling what were once the orchards, gardens and other open spaces of the old town. The Alsop Fields development is complete and a large estate for coal miners and other workers has risen on Park Hill, across the River Sheaf. Two other suburbs have evolved on former common land north of the Don: Bridgehouses and the Wicker, which are already starting to merge into one large enclave. Sheffield's social divide is becoming more marked as the middle classes move out into leafy suburbs along the new turnpike road to Manchester.

'Steel City' smothers the landscape

On early Victorian maps, Sheffield's suburbs gallop westwards, yet contemporary paintings show that the surrounding countryside could still be reached quickly on foot from the town centre. John McIntyre's view of Sheffield around 1850 (below), depicts a congested town, full of the new steelworks' chimneys, belching their smoke, but still framed by fields and moorland.

Over the next 50 years, as the population rose to over 400,000, 'Smoky Sheffield' grew into the 'Steel City', swallowing up great tracts of countryside. But amid all this expansion, the medieval pattern of its central streets remained constant at Sheffield's core.

Understanding village shapes

No two villages are alike. Some are small, neat and tidy, dominated by the manor house and the medieval parish church; others are large and sprawling, with petrol stations, builders' yards and perhaps an industrial estate on the edge. Some have kept their basic plan, others have been transformed. What can you deduce from the shape of yours?

A pattern of life Landscape can dictate the shape of a village. Kettlewell, Yorkshire (right), grew where the Cam Beck flows into the River Wharfe, but the steep slopes of the valley have prevented it from sprawling. A church was founded in the 12th century and terraced fields provide evidence of farming in Anglo-Saxon times. Later, villagers turned to lead mining. A corn market and cattle fairs were still being held here in Victorian times.

Signs of regular shapes

To find out why your village is shaped the way it is first look around to see if it has a regular plan. See if the properties fronting the street or village green have equal widths and stretch in parallel lengths to a back lane.

- Property boundaries tend to remain fixed over very long periods of time. Some of the houses will have disappeared and new ones will have been squeezed in, but the general pattern will not have altered a great deal.
- Some villages were planned in the 18th or 19th centuries by landowners or industrial entrepreneurs. Others date back further. County Durham, in particular, has a number of villages that were planned out in the Middle Ages.

Signs of irregular shapes

Planned villages are the exception. Many villages have an irregular shape and are often strung out along a street. If your village existed before the Industrial Revolution, its shape is likely to have developed since medieval times.

- Look for houses and cottages built in clusters. They may be gathered around the church or manor house.
- Early maps (see pages 72-73) may show the clusters more clearly. Have the gaps between been filled with new buildings?
- Follow the lines of the roads and lanes. What is now a long, curving street with houses might once have been broken up along smaller stretches. Or a road might twist and turn along the headlands of the blocks of strips in the former open fields. Look for clues in street names such as Westfield Lane or Longlands Avenue.

Learning from maps

Look at old maps (see pages 72-73) to find out whether the shape of your village has altered. Estate maps made in the 16th or 17th centuries show that many villages have kept the same shape over hundreds of years. Toddington, in Bedfordshire, expanded in the 20th century but is still recognisable as the village that was depicted on a map drawn by the Elizabethan map-maker Ralph Agas to accompany a survey in 1581.

If you look at maps made in the 18th or 19th century you can see the shape of your settlement before the ribbon development of modern times.

- If you live in a village rather than a district of scattered farmsteads, look for an enclosure or tithe award map.
- For tiny settlements, turn to the first edition, six-inch Ordnance Survey (OS) maps, made between the 1850s and the 1870s.

Deserted and shrunken villages

You might well find that your village had a larger population in the Middle Ages than it does now. Thousands of villages shrank or were completely

Village footprints Clues in the landscape, such as the ruined parish church of Godwick, in Norfolk, and an uneven field of earthworks – known to archaeologists as house platforms – indicate the site of a disappeared village. If there is an abandoned village near where you live, you will find it clearly marked on a local OS Explorer map (below left).

deserted in the centuries after the Black Death. The history of one village can be very different from that of its neighbour. At Foston, in Leicestershire, only the isolated church and Hall Farm survive, but across the parish boundary lies Wigston Magna, the largest village in the county.

- Look for rectangular-shaped grassy mounds, where buildings once stood, above the sunken tracks of former streets and lanes. They show up on aerial photographs, so check whether your local reference library has any.
- At the library, also look for the taxation lists, starting with the lay subsidies and poll tax returns of the 14th century, and compare them with the hearth tax returns of the 1660s and 1670s. Do the later lists have far fewer householders recorded?
- At your local record office look for any manorial or parish records, such as registers of baptisms, that may provide clues that the population level fell.

Abandoned markets

A large number of villages and towns acquired the right to hold a weekly market and an annual fair in the Middle Ages. Suffolk had more than 90 markets, including small places such as Bramfield, Kersey, Ringshall and Wissett. Many markets withered after the Black Death. Kelton not only lost the market and fair that was founded in 1292, it has completely disappeared and its site is known only from Joseph Hodskinson's 1783 map of Suffolk.

- Look out for a regularly shaped village green. It might have been a medieval market place.
- Notice any names that refer to former markets. In Norfolk, the village of Thorpe Market has a triangular space where a market was held in the 13th century.

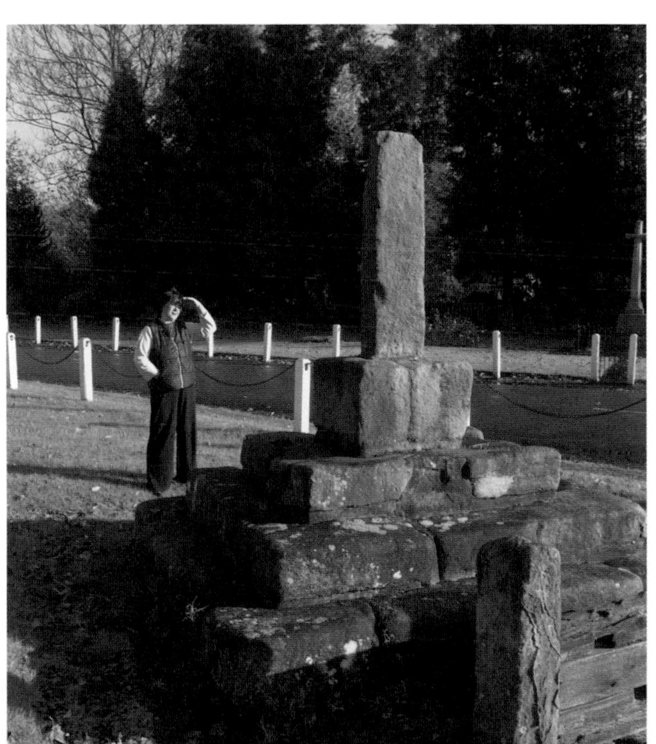

Villages in the 19th century

Many villages, especially those controlled by a squire, were smaller at the end of the 19th century than they were at the start, because country people moved to the towns to find work in the new industries that had developed. You can tell whether your village grew or shrank in Victorian times by looking at the population figures recorded in census returns (see pages 76-77).

Market days Look out for remnants of a market cross, perhaps on a village green, such as the 13th-century stump at Bolton-by-Bowland, Lancashire (left). The presence of a market in days gone by indicates that this was once a place of some significance. Many markets were abandoned after the Black Death.

FIND OUT MORE

- *Victoria County History*
An ongoing project to create an encyclopedic history of each county of England. If your area has been covered, there will be a record of whether a royal charter was granted to the local lord of the manor for a market.
www.victoriacountyhistory.ac.uk
- **www.nationalarchives.gov.uk/mdr/**
Contains details of the Manorial Documents Register for Wales, Cumberland, Hampshire, the Isle of Wight, Cumbria, Norfolk, Middlesex, Westmoreland, Surrey and Yorkshire are on-line. Court rolls, surveys, maps and documents are available.

Tracing the bounds of your parish

You may be only vaguely aware of the boundaries of your parish, but this old administrative unit is a key to the story of your landscape. Such knowledge was once vitally important for local communities who were dependent on their commons and wastes – the parish lands where they could graze livestock or dig peat for winter fuel. From the 16th to the 19th centuries parishes were also responsible for the poor, the highways, and petty law and order, so parish officers had to be certain which houses and cottages lay within their jurisdiction.

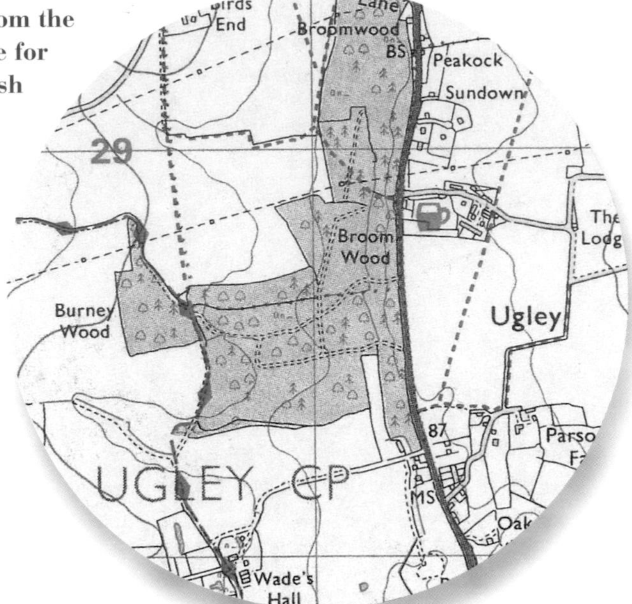

See how the land lies Your parish boundary will be marked on an OS Explorer map. A black dotted line along the road running north-south (above) shows the boundary for Ugley, Essex. The letters BS near the top indicate a boundary stone.

Parish shapes and sizes

Most rural parishes were formed by 1200. In much of lowland England their boundaries were usually the same as those of the manors of the local lords who had founded the church, but in some regions, such as Lincolnshire and Nottinghamshire, parishes were often formed from more than one manor.

The considerable variation in size and shape of parishes was dictated particularly by the quality of the soil, as well as by natural barriers such as woods and rivers and even ancient disputes with other parishes. In Lincolnshire, the compact parishes on the Wolds are very different from those that extend in narrow strips into the neighbouring Fens. The parishes of the Vale of Pickering stretch for miles onto the North York Moors. Some Welsh parishes were so large that they had to be divided into smaller units called townships, and then again into hamlets or quarters. This was also true of some lowland parishes in northern England, such as the parish of Great Budworth in Cheshire, which covered 35 townships. In south and west England the equivalent unit to the township was known as the tithing.

Manorial competition In medieval times Swaffham in Cambridgeshire was divided into two parishes: one belonged to the Prior of Ely who founded St Mary's Church (foreground), the other to three knights who built St Cyriac and St Julitta next door (background). The parishes were merged in the 17th century, with St Mary's Church becoming the parish church.

Boundaries on maps

It is easy to trace your present parish boundary – marked as a thin dotted line – on Ordnance Survey (OS) Explorer maps (see above). You can also spot minor place names that were derived from words for a boundary, such as Merebrook ('boundary stream') and Shirebrook ('county boundary stream'). Threap, meaning a dispute, occurs in names such as Threapland in Cumbria.

- At your county record office, follow the boundaries that were marked on the first-edition OS maps. These are the ancient boundaries before the changes of late Victorian times. Look for 'detached portions' that were tidied up by an Act of Parliament in 1894, when Urban and Rural District Councils took over many parish responsibilities. In Scotland there were similar local government changes, with elected county councils beginning in 1890.
- Tithe and enclosure award maps (see pages 18-19) are arranged by parish and bounded by parish limits. Estate maps often mark prominent boundary points, such as crosses or poles.

Consulting the records

Your local record office will hold a range of records that can tell you more about the size and shape of the ancient parishes around where you live. Start by looking

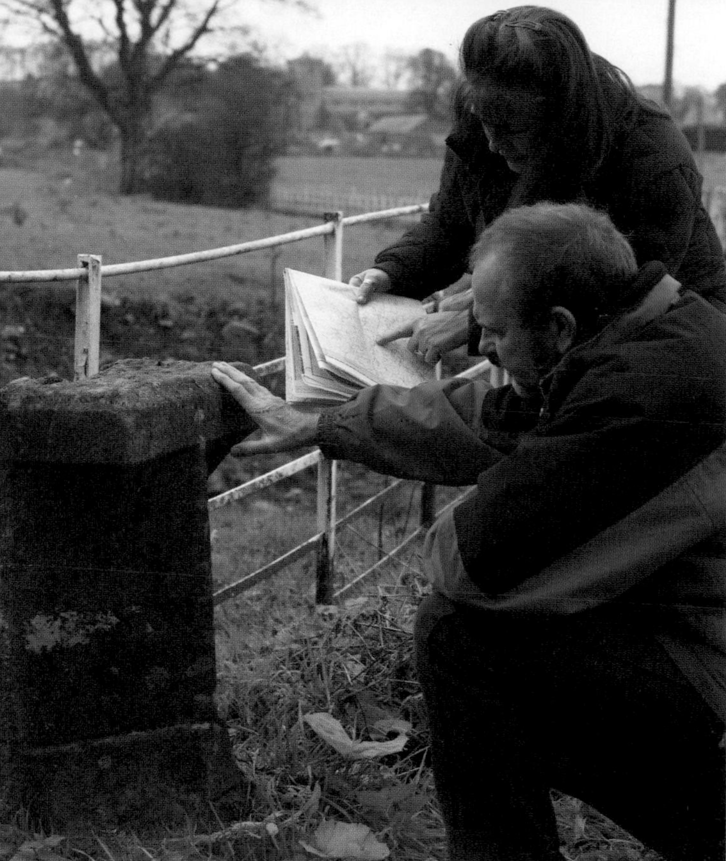

Inspecting the line Parish boundaries often run along the edge of fields, such as at Slaidburn, Lancashire (above). Boundary stones are clearly marked on OS Explorer maps, but may take some searching for if they have become hidden in undergrowth.

for names and descriptions of parishes in 19th-century directories (see pages 74-75).

- As the parish dictated the administration and work of the lives of most people, it was essential that they were reminded regularly of its boundaries. In estate papers and, less commonly, manor court rolls, you may find a written account from the 16th to the 18th centuries of a 'perambulation of the bounds' of your parish, when large crowds of parishioners walked all the way round the parish boundary at Rogationtide in early summer, with the minister leading the way and saying prayers at various points, such as a prominent tree – the Gospel Oak. Boundary landmarks were impressed on the villagers, such as a stream or a ditch, up to high points marked by a tree or a rock, or in featureless areas specially erected stones or poles marked with a cross and the initial letter of the parish.
- At your local library, look at the relevant volumes of the *Victoria County History* (www.victoriacountyhistory.ac.uk see page 35), to see if they contain information on the parish boundaries for your area.

Boundary stones

On an OS Explorer map, you can pinpoint the markers used to denote your parish boundary and then search for them on the ground.

- Boundary stones come in all shapes and sizes and might be found tucked half-hidden into the side of a country lane or rising plainly from the middle of open moorland.
- Stones that were shaped as a cross were often damaged during the Reformation in the 16th century.
- Chamfered edges to a base indicate that the stone is probably medieval.
- If you spot a date cut into a stone, it could be an inscription made during a Rogationtide perambulation rather than the year the stone was erected.
- If there is a stone with a particular name near where you live, such as White Cross or Lady Cross, you may find it mentioned as a boundary point in medieval charters or deeds kept at your local record office.

Parish perimeter If you spot a township boundary plaque, such as for Hopton and Coton (above), it denotes a subdivision of a large parish, usually in northern England.

Markers on the moors Boundary stones stand out clearly on moorland, where they often have a dual function as waymarkers, such as this stone on the route of the Cleveland Way and Lyke Wake Walk across the North York Moors.

Basic shelter A far cry from the dairy parlours of today, early cowsheds, like this bank barn in Patterdale, Cumbria, were simple constructions, made from local materials.

Buildings of the working countryside

In spite of the mechanisation of farming and the decline in traditional crafts, there are many centuries-old farm buildings to see beside modern replacements. They range from cowsheds and stables to windmills and maltings, many still in use.

The farmer's home and farmyard

Until Tudor times most farmhouses were thatched, with walls made of timber frames infilled with rubble, brick, or straw-and-mud 'daub' slapped onto a latticework of wattles. They were larger versions of the cottages of the farm's peasant labourers. In parts of Britain without local sources of building stone, such as East Anglia, this style persisted into Georgian times. In places like the Cotswolds, Yorkshire and the Scottish borders, the farmhouse was made from the locally plentiful stone, with a roof of stone or clay tiles. Such local styles using local materials persisted until the coming of canals and railways which allowed cheap bricks and slates to be moved easily and be used in buildings all across Britain.

Next to the farmhouse can often be found a large open working space, or farmyard, surrounded by the outbuildings, which may date back to the 19th or 18th centuries. Most farmyard buildings are still set fairly close together, for the farmer's convenience.

Farmyards dating from the 17th and 18th centuries might incorporate a dovecote, like the gabled and half-timbered example at Luntley Court in Herefordshire. A dovecote will often pre-date the farmhouse because it would have been built first to provide food while the more lengthy project of the house was underway.

Stables for farm horses have now become redundant. Many are riding stables, but they also have been converted into rural workshops and sales outlets, such as at Castle Ashby in Northamptonshire. Look out for less glamorous modern structures like the silage clamp, often banged together out of disused railway sleepers and covered in old tyres, and the slurry lagoon, a big storage tank for farmyard manure and other effluent.

The late medieval introduction of root crops and reliable hay storage meant that farm animals did not have to be slaughtered at the onset of winter, but could be kept alive until spring. They were generally housed on or near the farmyard in byres (cattle and sheep), sties (pigs) and coops (hens). Intensive animal farming has seen the spread of long, low buildings containing battery cages for hens, often forming enclaves away from the farmhouse and yard.

Roomy birdhouse The Luntley Court dovecote was built in 1673, a year before the house it served.

Cathedrals of the harvest

Barns for storing the harvested produce – mostly grain, hay and straw – were generally thatched wattle-and-daub constructions until medieval times, when the buildings became larger and more substantially built. Three superb examples in Essex are the 12th-century Grange Barn at Coggeshall and the 13th-century Wheat and Barley Barns at Cressing Temple nearby. Monasteries built huge tithe barns of stone to store their tribute and among the most impressive are the barns at Abbotsbury in Dorset,

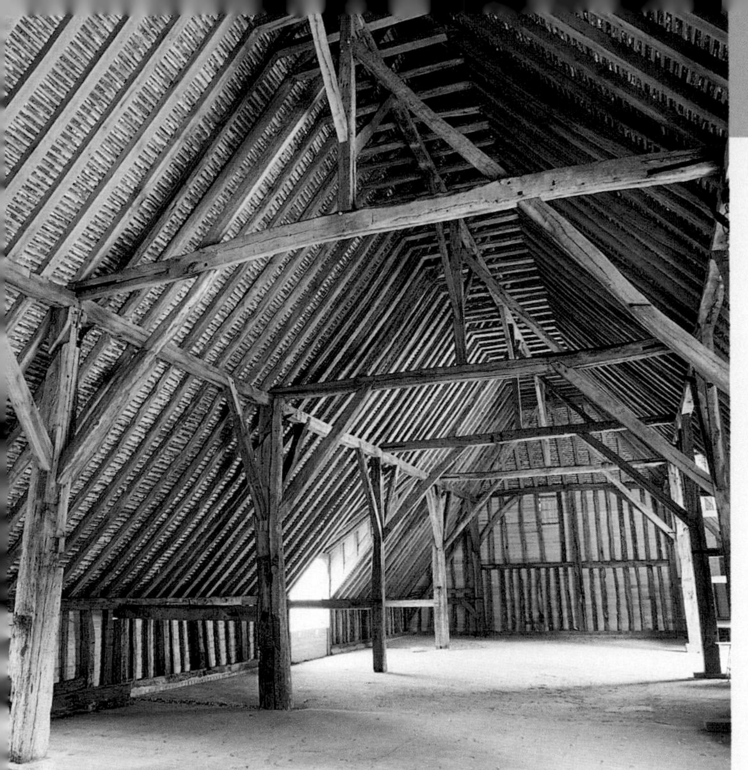

Storage on a grand scale Coggeshall Grange barn in Essex, built for a Cistercian monastery around 1140, is one of Europe's oldest timber-framed barns.

Ashleworth in Gloucestershire and Bredon in Worcestershire. Open-sided barns are a feature of many farms today, as are tall cylindrical silos for storing grain.

Other buildings to look for

Every village had a forge, and some will survive, perhaps as a house or pub, or even in working order, as at Branscombe in Devon. Big glass greenhouses dot the landscape in horticultural areas such as the Vale of Evesham and around Wisbech in Cambridgeshire, and the great pagoda-roofed hulks of maltings rise over barley country such as Suffolk and the lowlands of Fife.

FIND OUT MORE

Fine collections of historic agricultural buildings can be seen at locations across Britain.

- Auchindrain Township Open Air Museum Inveraray, Argyll. www.auchindrainmuseum.org.uk
- Avoncroft Museum of Historic Buildings Bromsgrove, Worcestershire. www.avoncroft.org.uk
- Chiltern Open Air Museum Chalfont St Giles, Buckinghamshire. www.coam.org.uk
- Museum of East Anglian Life Stowmarket, Suffolk. www.eastanglianlife.org.uk
- North of England Open Air Museum Beamish, County Durham. www.beamish.org.uk
- Ryedale Folk Museum Hutton-le-Hole, Yorkshire. www.ryedalefolkmuseum.co.uk
- St Fagans Natural History Museum St Fagan's, Cardiff. www.museumwales.ac.uk/en/stfagans
- Weald and Downland Open Air Museum Singleton, West Sussex. www.wealddown.co.uk

LOOKING AT MILLS

Away from the farm, the tall towers and crossed sails of windmills are highly visible features of the landscape. Look carefully and you will see that there are three basic types: tower, smock and post (see below). A good example of a tower mill, built in 1860, is the five-storey Billingford Mill in Norfolk, while Cranbrook Mill in Kent, built in 1814, is a fine smock mill. Outwood Mill in Surrey is the oldest working post mill in Britain and dates from 1665.

Faced with more efficient mechanical methods of milling flour, windmills ceased commercial production by the 1950s. Many were pulled down or converted into houses (see page 300); but some still grind flour, such as the mill at Wilton, near Marlborough, in Wiltshire.

Many watermills have also been converted for residential use, their huge wheels now still and merely for show. But some are open to the public, including Cotehele mill (National Trust) near Saltash in Cornwall, which continues to grind flour.

Tower mill Developed in the 18th century, these brick towers were designed so that only the top portion revolved. A series of gears transmits the movement from the sails to the millstones below.

Smock mill These 12-sided buildings were half brick and half timber. Like the tower mill, only the cap rotates with the sail. The miller could reach the sails from a gallery.

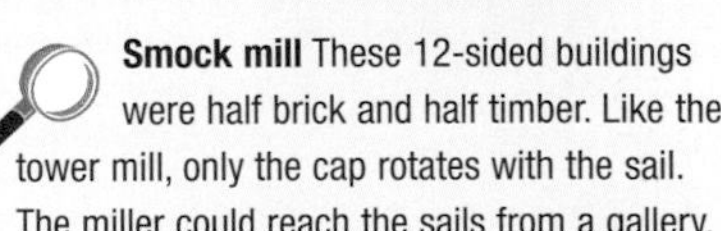

Post mill This is the oldest type of windmill, dating back to the 11th century. Massive oak beams support a large central post on which the whole mill rotates.

Water mill An undershot mill-wheel (above), where water flows through the vanes at the bottom, is less efficient than an overshot mill-wheel, where water strikes from the top, as it requires four times as much water volume to produce the same power.

Following the fields

The shape and name of every field tells a story. Fields with straight hawthorn hedges or stone walls were created when most communal open-fields and commons were enclosed by private Acts of Parliament, between 1750 and 1850. Small fields with irregular boundaries, twisting and turning up a hillside or around a wood, are likely to have been cleared of trees and rocks by medieval peasants or by their Elizabethan and Stuart successors. Field names will hold clues to how the land might have been used or to what crops it yielded.

Medieval farmers make a mark In some areas, such as near Tissington in the Peak District National Park, the medieval ridge-and-furrow pattern can still be seen clearly. You may find that the furrows often appear greener than the ridges. This is because they were used not just to divide the strips, but also for drainage. In winter they might be marked by settled snow or water, in spring by buttercups.

Patterns in the landscape

The neatly planned appearance of swathes of the English countryside, stretching in a broad band south from the River Tees in the northeast to Dorset in the southwest, contrasts with the randomly shaped fields of areas such as the Welsh Borders and the Weald of Kent.

In many parts of medieval England, the land of a parish was farmed in large communal open-fields. Much of this land has long since been converted to pasture, but the curving patterns of ridge-and-furrow (see main picture, above) can often be seen, providing evidence of ploughing. Large areas of ridge-and-furrow were obliterated in the 20th century by deep ploughing, but there are survivors, many of the best in Leicestershire and Warwickshire. Ridge-and-furrow patterns are much rarer in wooded, moorland or fenland parishes, which had only small open-fields.

Spotting ridge-and-furrow fields Look out for long, curving strips. They were shaped like an elongated 'S' to enable the plough-team of oxen to turn as they reached the end of the strip.

- Notice how the strip patterns follow the lie of the land, and blocks of strips, known in manor court rolls or deeds as furlongs or flatts, go off in different directions.
- See how the hawthorn hedges that define the present fields, created by the Enclosure Acts in the 18th or 19th centuries, often ignore the older pattern of ridge-and-furrow beneath. You may be able to follow the older patterns across several fields.
- If hedges or walls bound the earlier curving outlines of strips, they will be the result of enclosure by private agreements among farmers between 1500 and 1700.
- From medieval times up to the Parliamentary enclosure, farmers called their strips 'lands', a name that will be found in manor court rolls. At the end of a block of strips was the 'headland', allowing access and space for the plough-team to turn. Headlands were not ploughed and became raised by the accumulation of soil. Look for straight raised banks running across the landscape.
- Notice the deep boundary ditches that were dug to separate the open-fields from the commons or woods. Even if they have been partly filled in, you might be able to follow the boundary line (see pages 52-53).
- Not all ridge-and-furrow is medieval and associated with the strip system. New land that was taken in from the parish commons and wastes by the Enclosure Acts was often ploughed with straight narrow patterns of ridge-and-furrow to drain it. See how these patterns do not extend beyond the enclosing hedges or walls. They are common in hilly areas such as the Pennines.

Investigating field records

You can trace the history of local fields at your county record office. Look for old maps, mid 19th-century tithe awards and, to delve further back, manorial documents.

- Estate maps from the 16th to 18th centuries (see below) and enclosure award maps (see pages 18-19) show how open fields were divided into strips. There is often a precise match between the shape and sizing of the strips on a map and the ridge-and-furrow patterns on the ground (or seen in an aerial photograph).
- Tithe awards (see pages 18-19) in local record offices or the National Archives (see DIRECTORY), note whether fields were arable, meadow or pasture. From these you can see how land use has changed.
- Read the records of manor courts, which managed the open-fields. The jurors or 'homagers' of the court recorded 'paines', the penalties for breaking regulations. They were local men who made decisions on the best ways to farm, such as when to sow crops.

Old-time practices Manor courts appointed a pinder to put stray animals into a pinfold, or pound, until a fine had been paid. Has your village still got a pinfold, such as the one in Dalton-in-Furness, Cumbria (above), or perhaps a Pinfold Lane that might help you to identify the site?

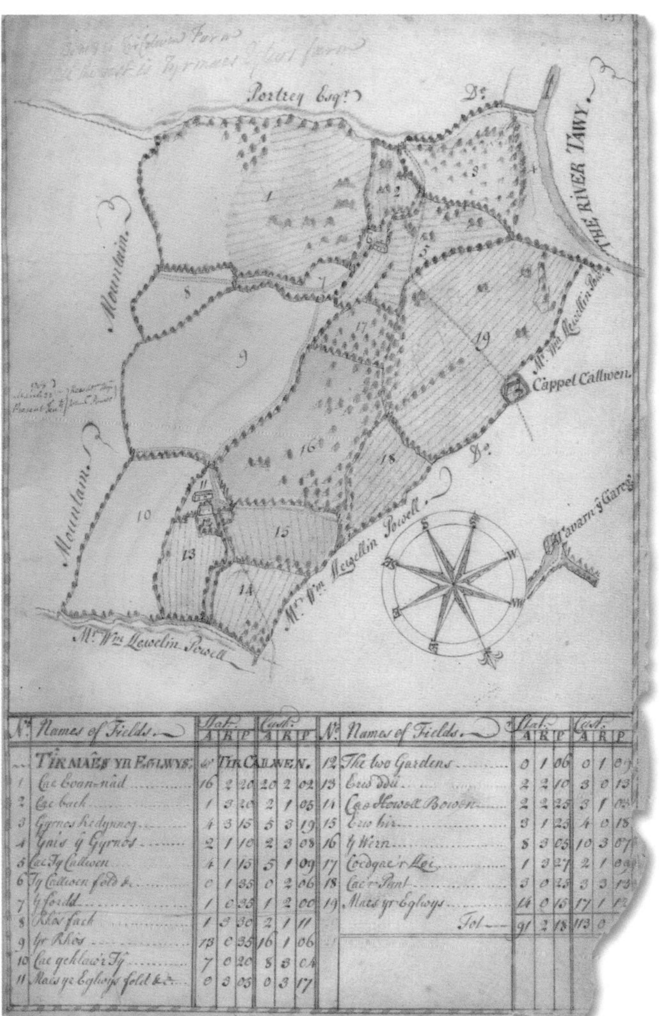

Charting the boundaries Old maps, such as the 1744 Blaen-Sawdde estate map, Carmarthenshire (above), show ancient field patterns and list field names and sizes. You may find some of these names repeated on later Ordnance Survey (OS) maps.

What's in a name? Field names will tell you how the land was once used. 'Wongs' were meadows, 'stubbings' were fields cleared from woods or scrubland, 'longlands' strips of arable crops in the open-fields. Other fields were named after the crops that were grown.

- You can collect all the field names of your parish from the Middle Ages to the present day by using manor court rolls, estate maps, tithe award and enclosure award maps, and any other documents that record field names incidentally. Those names that are noted in the latest county volumes of the English Place-Name Society (available in libraries and record offices) are a useful starting point. In some parishes modern field names differ from the old, but on the whole the names have remained remarkably consistent.
- You will probably come across examples of strange names such as 'catsbrain', meaning a soil where clay is mixed with pebbles. Welsh fields include both English and Welsh names and Scottish names may be in Gaelic, Scots or English. Names such as West Field, Town Field and Hall Flatt stem from the open-field system. Many meanings are straightforward, but be aware how names can be corrupted over time. For example, Sufferlong, recorded in Kibworth Harcourt (Leicestershire) in 1652, is probably a corruption of 'south furlong'.

FIND OUT MORE

- *A History of English Field Names* (John Field, Longman, 1993) Describes how field names came to be, and how even a modern street name can be traced to its rural roots.
- *Fields in the English Landscape* (Christopher Taylor, Sutton Publishing, 2000) Uses what can be seen in the landscape today to explore the history of the field.

Up among the hills and moors

Romantic writers and artists 200 years ago found inspiration in the aesthetic qualities of mountains and hills, yet earlier visitors described these landscapes as dismal and gloomy, and manorial surveys dismissed them as 'barren' and 'waste'. Meanwhile, farmers worked on regardless – grazing cattle and sheep, digging turf for fuel, using bracken for animal bedding and cutting heather to thatch roofs. Signs of their robust lives are all around.

Pattern of moorland life The grazing of sheep is typical of upland areas such as Ugborough Moor, Devon. Straight hedges mark the boundaries of enclosed pastures, cleared long ago from the moor, and small farmsteads dot the landscape.

The story of hamlets and farmsteads

In an upland area, you will see many more hamlets and scattered farmsteads than in the lowlands, where villages cluster around a church and manor house, surrounded by arable fields. In Wales, where about 60 per cent of the land is more than 152m (500ft) above sea level, isolated farmsteads are even more common than hamlets. In Scotland, farmsteads also abound, although pre-18th-century 'farmtouns' (see page 46) that once dominated the landscape can be traced by the suffix 'ton' in names such as Milton, Kirkton and Muirton.

Hamlets and farmsteads were the earliest forms of settlement, pre-dating the first Saxon and Viking villages. They are rarely recorded before the mid 13th century, when manor court rolls began to be kept. By this time the population was expanding rapidly and many new farms – the ones most likely to appear in the records – were being cleared from the moors and woods.

Tracing settlements You can find out about hamlets and farmsteads and how old they are by comparing old maps with new and tracing the names of the farms and their occupants through manorial records at your county record office. Many of the names will have changed over time, such as the Pennine farm known now as Belle Clive. It was recorded as Billeclif between 1208 and 1211 and means 'Billa's bank' from an Old English personal name.

- At your local reference library or record office ask whether the English Place-Name Society has published volumes for your county. These will show the earliest spellings of place names and explain their meaning. Some of the surnames recorded in manor court rolls and the poll tax returns of 1377-81 may derive from local

Family enterprises Most of the farms that were cleared from Dartmoor in medieval times were grouped in hamlets, perhaps as joint ventures by energetic young men. Some isolated farmsteads developed into hamlets when the sons of the first farmers built houses for themselves and their livestock. The foundations of a group of longhouses belonging to such a hamlet have been excavated at Hound Tor, at about 305m (1000ft) above sea level on the east side of Dartmoor (below). They appear to have been abandoned after the Black Death, when land was no longer scarce.

The unchanging face of upland farming

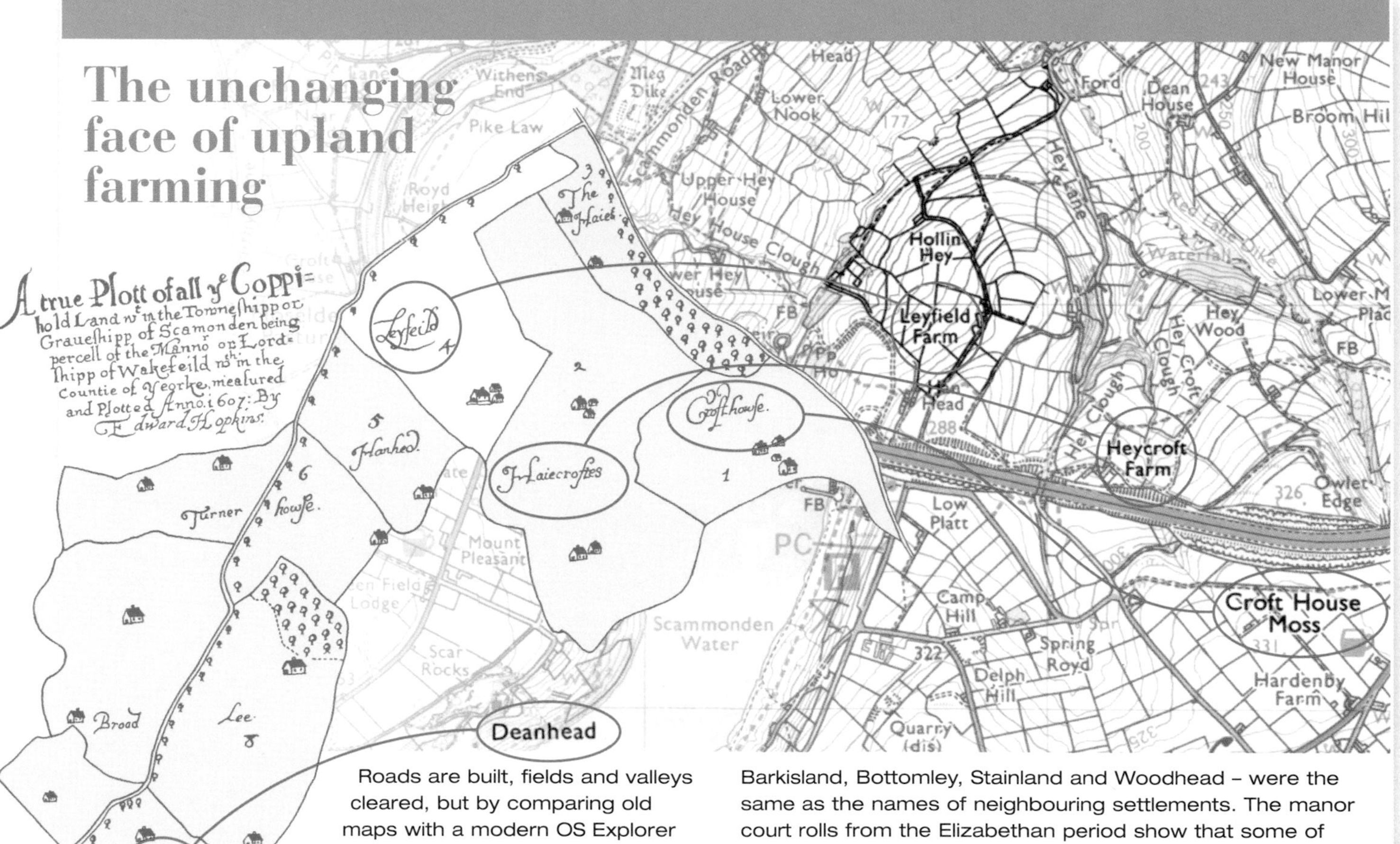

Roads are built, fields and valleys cleared, but by comparing old maps with a modern OS Explorer map you may be surprised to find how little the upland landscape has altered over the centuries. An estate map of 1607 of Scammonden, west of Huddersfield, Yorkshire (above left), records the farms in the township. Their names can be traced through references to them in manor court rolls, all the way back to the families who opened up this Pennine valley by clearing woods and moorland in the first half of the 14th century. They had not moved far as their surnames – Barkisland, Bottomley, Stainland and Woodhead – were the same as the names of neighbouring settlements. The manor court rolls from the Elizabethan period show that some of these farms were later sub-divided when the population began to rise, and wills from the same time reveal that many of the inhabitants of the farmhouses and cottages on the 1607 map were weavers as well as farmers.

Fast-forward 400 years to an OS Explorer map of today (above right) and there is still much to recognise in the landscape. Although the M62 motorway slices through Scammonden and a swathe of land has been swallowed by a reservoir, the farms still have much the same names and many of the old field boundaries can still be followed.

farmsteads – such as Broadbent, from a farmstead of the same name in the Lancashire Pennines.

- Ask to see transcriptions of any medieval charters, deeds and manorial records. Look for early references to farmsteads and hamlets and the clearing of new land from the woods and moors near where you live. These clearances will be named as 'assarts', 'intakes' and 'stubbings', or perhaps by dialect words such as the West Yorkshire 'royd'. Often, these words will be attached to a person's name, so you can tell that Gilroyd was 'Gilbert's clearance'. Typically, only one or two acres were cleared at a time, because the work was hard, and when the population increased rapidly in the late 13th century even smaller parcels of land were taken in from the parish wastes. After the Black Death the demand for new land ceased.

From hamlet to village Compare the pattern of settlement on 18th-century county maps and first-edition Ordnance Survey (OS) maps (see pages 18-19) to spot the many hamlets that did not appear until the 19th century, after the parliamentary enclosures of commons and wastes. Some of these places have industrial origins and grew into villages, such as the lead-mining community at Allenheads, Northumberland.

FIND OUT MORE

- *The Harvest of the Hills: Rural Life in Northern England and the Scottish Borders, 1400-1700* (Angus J.L. Winchester, Edinburgh University Press, 2000). A description of the relationship between people and the land, and the culture of rural communities.

Setting the boundaries of the land

From the earliest days farmers have looked for ways to prevent their animals straying, and to separate one type of crop from another. As notions of private property took hold it became important to separate roads from fields, and to distinguish a landowner's domain from his neighbour's. There are many kinds of boundary, from wire fences and earth banks to the water-filled ditches of wetland fields, but the most common are hedges and drystone walls.

Thin green lines

Hedges have existed since before the Romans. At first they were a line of portable hurdles that could be installed or removed at will. Some were strips of undergrowth left in place deliberately and then nurtured when a forest was cleared; others were newly planted. There were surges of hedge-planting when the Anglo-Saxons cleared forests and wildwoods for agricultural land, and during the enclosure of fields in the 18th and 19th centuries.

In the 1950s Britain had about half a million miles of hedges. Then landowners began to rip them out because they were too expensive and time-consuming to maintain, and hindered large modern farm machinery. Up to half the total mileage of hedges was destroyed in just 40 years, before people began to appreciate the ecological and environmental value of hedgerows. Today more hedges are planted (see left) than removed.

A reviving art Hedge-laying is an ancient method of maintaining hedges. The stems are allowed to grow, then cut half-way through near the ground and bent over at right-angles or diagonally. Vertical stakes rammed into the ground between the stems make a latticework frame, around which are woven the trailing twigs and shoots of the still-growing stems.

The traditional way to keep a hedge thick and in good shape is to trim, prune and cut it back by hand. The quicker way is to use a slashing machine. This leaves a splintered surface and also reduces the efficiency of the hedge, because unless the stems are regularly realigned horizontally they tend to grow vertically, destroying the inner framework and gradually reducing its effectiveness as a barrier.

Dating hedges

A rough-and-ready method for dating hedges is to take a 30m (100ft) stretch and count the number of tree and shrub species in it – discounting elder and bramble, which can appear and disappear quickly. Multiply that number by 100, and that is the age of the hedge in years. A more accurate method is to sample three stretches of the hedge and take an average. For example:

- Stretch A – oak, ash, hawthorn, blackthorn, rowan, holly = 6 species
- Stretch B – oak, ash, willow, dogwood, rowan = 5 species
- Stretch C – oak, ash, willow, hawthorn, holly, hazel, sycamore = 7 species

Average number of species = 6
6 × 100 = 600
Rough age of hedge = 600 years.

Barriers of water In the reclaimed wetlands of the Somerset Levels, man-made drainage ditches called rhynes demarcate the landscape.

Hedging and walling in action
When walking through dairy or sheep-farming areas you may be lucky enough to see a hedger or waller (below) in action. Demonstrations take place at various open-air museums around Britain. The National Hedgelaying Society and the Dry Stone Walling Association (see 'Find out more' below) are dedicated to the preservation and maintenance of hedges and walls. If you want to have a go yourself, contact the British Trust for Conservation Volunteers (see 'Find out more' below).

The old stone wall

Drystone walls have been built for more than 2000 years, mostly in upland areas where stone is plentiful. At first they were crudely constructed, of stones cleared from the land by hand. More sophisticated techniques evolved later (see right), as monasteries built them to enclose sheep pastures on far-flung fells. Walls around fields on lower-lying land tend to be older; they gradually crept further up the contours as higher, wilder common land was enclosed during the 18th and 19th centuries.

The walls are built on a foundation of small stones laid in a trench. The waller builds up the wall in layers, filling the centre with rubble. The whole structure is solidified by inserting a layer of through-stones half-way up the wall – these are large, shaped stones, laid across the grain of the wall. A layer of vertical or slanting stones tops the wall off.

Dating walls

Drystone walls are more difficult to date than hedges. The basic building method has never changed and so a recent wall can look as though it has been there for centuries. Manorial records (see page 152), estate records (see pages 49, 148-149) and enclosure awards (see pages 19, 73) may mention the putting up of walls between fields and so reveal when they were built. The following characteristics may also point to a wall built long ago:

- it surrounds small, irregular fields near a farmstead
- it separates the site of former Anglo-Saxon and Danish open fields from wetland or wasteland
- it is of irregular construction with some big boulders, with no through-stones or top stones
- if it does not change direction to avoid an obstacle, the chances are that it was built before the obstacle.

Patchy distribution Remnants of haphazard, irregular ancient field boundaries still exist in parts of Britain, including south Wales (pictured). But in the 25 years following the Second World War more than 150,000 miles of hedgerow were lost.

FIND OUT MORE

- www.hedgelayer.freeserve.co.uk Information about hedgelaying.
- www.britainexpress.com/History/english-hedges.htm The history of English hedges.
- www.hedgelaying.org.uk Website of the National Hedgelaying Society.
- www.britainexpress.com/History/drystone.htm Information on drystone walls in England.
- www.dswa.org.uk Website of the Dry Stone Walling Association.
- www2.btcv.org.uk Website of the British Trust for Conservation Volunteers.

On the trail of the lost highland and island folk

In the late 18th and 19th centuries entire working families in the north and west of Scotland, and its islands, eked out a living from a small agricultural holding known as a croft, supplemented by the cutting, collecting, drying and burning of seaweed ('kelp'). Evidence of these communities remains in many abandoned crofthouses, while unusual furrows and ridges in the landscape indicate earlier farming settlements. Records flesh out the lives of these hard-working people.

The changing scene

Life is very different today for the remaining 18,000 or so crofters of the highlands and islands, who have security of tenure, government grants and the right to buy their crofts. Before the Crofters' Holdings (Scotland) Act of 1886, tenants had few rights and landlords ruthlessly evicted thousands of crofters during the Highland Clearances. Visit the region's libraries and museums, and explore the abandoned settlements (see 'Find out more', opposite), and you can discover much about the crofting tradition.

The earliest settlements

Before the introduction of crofting in the 18th century, most people in the highlands and islands lived close together in communally run townships, or farmtouns. Small areas of arable land around the farmtoun were cultivated in strips in a common-field system known as 'runrig'. Each tenant or subtenant had grazing rights on the surrounding rougher land and on the shielings, the cattle's summer grazings, that lay beyond the township.

- Look for strip patterns, which can be seen as ridges and furrows, used to allow the land to drain. The ridges could be 1.8m (6ft) high and 6m (20ft) wide. Notice the thin grass boundaries between the strips.
- Visit the Auchindrain Township Open Air Museum (see opposite) to see a surviving old settlement.

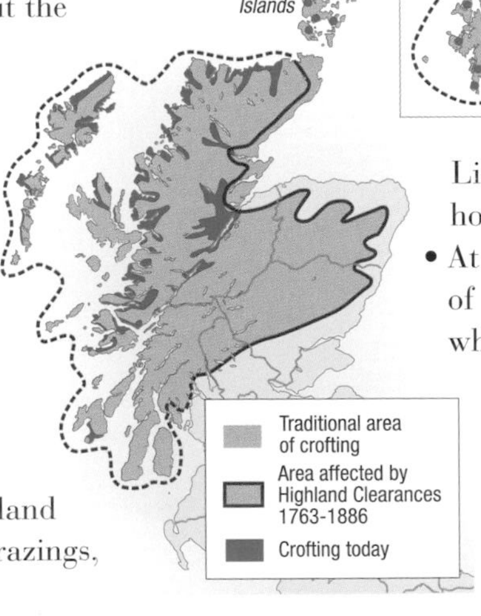

Crofters' territory You can find evidence of crofting from its heyday throughout the modern crofting areas of Orkney, Shetland, Ross, Caithness, Sutherland, Inverness, Argyll and the Hebrides. The effects of the Clearances were different in each region.

Understanding the life of crofters

When new industry and agricultural methods were introduced in the 18th century, highland and island tenants were shifted to the coasts and given crofts, or smallholdings. Here they had to learn to fish and provide the workforce for the kelp industry, as well as working what was often the poorest of land.

- Visit crofters' houses (see opposite). Note the use of local stone and clay for walls, and turf and heather for thatched roofs. The houses were single-storey and open to the rafters. Livestock was kept at the lower end of the house and wells were dug to supply water.
- At your local library look for collections of old photographs (see pages 70-71), which show crofters and their wives working side by side on their land. Notice how men used foot-ploughs to dig the rows for planting potatoes, while the women spread seaweed from the shore as fertiliser, which they carried in large wicker baskets on their backs. The women also used these baskets for carrying the peat that the men had dug for winter fuel.
- On the ground, look for 'lazybeds'. These were the small plots where crofters grew their crops of potatoes.

Lost way of life An abandoned crofting settlement near Lochgilphead on the west coast of Scotland is a poignant reminder of the people forced to leave Scotland during the Clearances.

Signs of the Clearances

The decline of the feudal clan system, which began in the 1730s, culminated after the battle of Culloden Moor in 1746. Many estates changed hands and the new landowners saw sheep farming, which required little labour, as the only profitable business. A trickle of emigrants that began around 1730 escalated after 1763, spurred on by generous land grants abroad. Between 1765 and 1777 about 20,000 people left the highlands and islands, followed by a further 15,000 in the next 30 years.

By the 1820s, most labour was surplus to requirements, and when, in 1846, potato famine came, most landowners saw eviction as the way forward. The later 19th-century clearances saw thousands shipped to Canada, New Zealand and Australia.

- On the ground, search for ruined walls enclosing abandoned fields and the foundations of derelict houses (see 'Find out more'), which show the scale of the Clearances.
- At the National Archives of Scotland (see DIRECTORY), see the Department of Agriculture and Fisheries records (AF 50/7 and AF 50/8). Each county volume for 1883 is arranged alphabetically by estate. The returns name the crofts, the tenants and the number of people living on each croft.

FIND OUT MORE

There are several sites on the Isle of Skye, on remote headlands or close to the sea, where the remains of crofts are visible. You can see the 12 dry-stone houses and outbuildings in the deserted village of Boreraig that were cleared for sheep farming by Lord MacDonald in 1853 and replaced by one shepherd's house. Lazybeds (see opposite) can be traced near Galtrigill.

- The Isle of Skye Museum of Island Life Housed in an atmospheric group of thatched crofthouses illustrating the crofter's daily life. www.skyemuseum.co.uk
- Auchindrain Township Open Air Museum An original highland township that survived the Clearances. www.auchindrainmuseum.org.uk

Harvest of the sea Crofters had to exploit what they could to boost their subsistence economy. Kelp gathered from beaches helped to fertilise their crops, but it was the landowners who benefited most, using the seaweed to produce potash for the manufacture of glass and soap.

Cutting Seaware, Skye

Viewing a great estate

The estates that Britain's biggest landowners built up from the late 17th to the 19th century still dominate many local landscapes. Even if your village did not form part of one, you may know villages nearby that did, and you rarely have to travel very far to come across grand houses and rolling parkland, dotted with temples, mausoleums, towers and other eye-catching follies.

CHATSWORTH IN 1870

The house and park at Chatsworth, Derbyshire, the home of the dukes of Devonshire, reached the height of their development in the late 19th century. It was one of many country estates that evolved with changes in landscape fashions and the fortunes of Britain's landed classes over three centuries. Characteristics such as 18th-19th century refashioning of the house, the splendid gardens with grand water features, the landscaped park and the discreetly sited workers' village are likely to feature on any great estate near to where you live.

Homes for the workers Many landowners rebuilt their estate villages in the 18th and 19th centuries to look as picturesque as possible. If a landowner owned all the properties, he could dismantle the old village and build a new one beyond the landscaped park and out of view of the house. The estate village of Edensor, on the opposite bank of the River Derwent to the great house at Chatsworth, was shifted to avoid 'spoiling' the view. Properties strung along the line of the village street well to the east of the present village were removed when Edensor was remodelled about 1840 (see illustration) for the 6th Duke to designs taken from architectural pattern books. The old Norman church was then replaced in 1866 by a huge Early English-style structure (see below), designed by Sir George Gilbert Scott. The former village street can now be picked out as a clear holloway (see pages 58-59).

Chatsworth House

River Derwent

Original site of Edensor

Edensor village

The changing house Like many great houses, Chatsworth, first built between 1687 and 1707 in grand Baroque style, replaced an earlier Tudor building. Its formal French-style gardens were then transformed by 'Capability' Brown, who completely re-moulded the immediate landscape, as he did at more than 200 other estates. Something of the formality of those earlier days was then restored with the glasshouses, including the majestic Great Stove, and spectacular water features of the Victorian gardener and engineer, Joseph Paxton (right), who was appointed head gardener in 1826.

Wandering the parks The fashion that began in the 1720s for rolling parkland, clumps of trees and stretches of water extending into the distance made an enormous impact on the landscape. At Chatsworth, the damming of lakes 122m (400ft) above the house provided the water to power the spectacular Cascade (above). Parks were also adorned with temples, obelisks and bridges to give the impression that the landowners were the enlightened successors of the ancient Greeks and Romans. Few of these follies served any purpose other than that of a summerhouse or perhaps a mausoleum. Look out for inscriptions on follies and monuments that may explain their use and give a date. You can use maps and prints at your local record office to trace what a park looked like at various times, then explore on the ground to see what features survive from each period.

Big house records

Architectural fashions changed over the centuries and you have to peel away several layers to discover how the styling of a house and its surroundings may have evolved.

- At your local library, look for descriptions of houses, their gardens and parks made by travellers such as Celia Fiennes (1690s), Daniel Defoe (1720s) and John Byng, Viscount Torrington (1780s and 1790s).
- Also at your local library, look for prints of houses, including those that have been demolished. To see houses and their formal gardens before they were remodelled into landscaped parks, look for the bird's-eye views drawn by Leonard Knyff and Jan Kip in *Brittania Illustrata* (1707).
- Look for 16th-19th century estate papers at the National Archives (see DIRECTORY) or your county record office. You may find plans of a house near where you live, changes made to the design during its construction, financial accounts, names of the craftsmen and masons, and the origins of the building materials.

The signs of estate villages

- You can spot estate villages by the uniformity of the house design. Many were built in Tudor or Jacobean styles, using traditional local materials for their walls and roofs. Others were given Gothic-style gables or Arts and Crafts bargeboards and decorative brick chimneys.
- Look for inscriptions on houses, such as the landowner's initials, and datestones that share similar dates. See whether any almshouses bear the name of the landowner.
- The neat, tidy cottages in estate villages were often of a higher standard than those in the sprawling villages that had no paternal landlord. Nonconformist chapels were allowed only if the squire was a Dissenter himself. If a pub was provided it usually bore the name of the family that owned the land.
- Look for surveys, maps, leases and annual accounts among collections of estate papers at county record offices. These may tell you tenants' names, the size of their farms and the rent they paid. Notice when farmhouses, cottages and barns were built, what types of livestock were kept, what crops were grown, and perhaps what new industrial enterprises were tried.

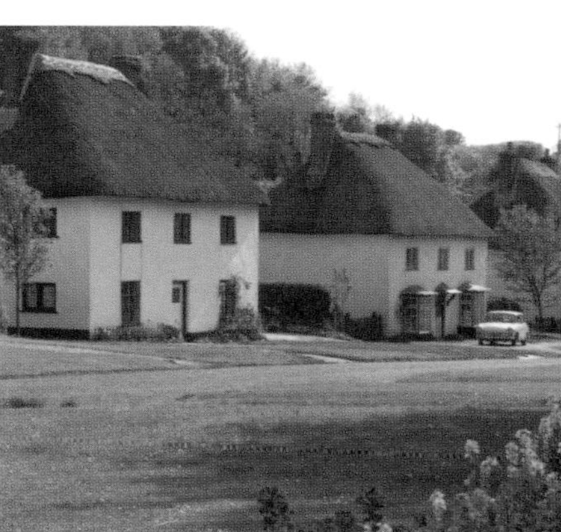

Moving houses It was not uncommon for landowners to shift entire estate villages to improve the view from the big house. At Milton Abbas, Dorset, Viscount Milton demolished the village in the 1770s, and built rows of identical cottages (above) well away from his house. The earthworks of the old properties are still visible.

Rediscovering rural life in old photographs

The rural landscape from the Victorian era up to the end of the Second World War is captured in countless old photographs, giving a vivid picture of life through the seasons in country communities of the time. They show a far more populated countryside than today, with men, women and children labouring in the fields at tasks that have now become mechanised. These images are readily available, often at your local library, museum or record office (see pages 70-71).

Don't believe everything you see

The paintings that hang in art galleries and country houses tend to show idealised landscapes, that reflect the standing and aspirations of the wealthy landowners who commissioned them. Their estate workers are usually out of sight or represented by mere dots in the background. Photography allowed for the creation of more realistic images, but take care when interpreting the scenes recorded in early photographs. Many were staged and often the photographer was trying to record working practices or fashions in dress that were disappearing at the time. If you look at a photograph of a shepherd wearing a smock or a team of oxen pulling a plough, do not assume that this was normal practice when the picture was taken.

Division of labour Some photographs may have been posed, but they still give a good idea of rural life. Women and girls had their own responsibilities, whether for farm produce (left, 1855) or looking after the poultry.

Tools of the trade The horse-drawn hay cart is a common sight in old photographs, but you may also spot unusual farming implements such as the long-bladed scythe with a swivel end (right, 1910), used for cutting meadow hay. Scythes usually had a fixed end.

Who did what?

Large numbers of people were employed on the land and you will see a wide range of tasks represented in old photographs.

- Look out for who was doing what. In Suffolk the most prestigious job was being in charge of the horses, especially the magnificent Suffolk Punches, but in East Yorkshire teenage boys who were hired as farm servants looked after the horses and did the ploughing, harrowing, muck spreading and harvesting with a binder.
- Note the specialist tasks being undertaken, such as hedging or shepherding, and the range of hand tools, including scythes, sickles, bill hooks and flails.
- Observe how the women played a full part in the running of a family farm. They can be seen milking the shorthorn cows and, wearing headscarves or bonnets and full-length dresses to keep out the sun, binding the sheaves of corn that stood among the stubble and earning a little extra by gleaning grains of ungathered

corn at harvest time. Photographs from the Second World War show land girls driving tractors and doing jobs usually performed by men.

- At harvest time everyone was expected to help. Notice that the landscape was full of children, either at work or at play.

Local brew Each region had its specialist activities. Kent was renowned for growing hops, which are used to flavour beer, and a huge number of London's Eastenders traditionally came to help pick them in late summer (above, mid 20th century).

Interpreting the images

Look out for photographs of the first tractors (see below). If they are dated they will help you to decide when the horse-and-cart era came to an end in your part of the countryside. On some farms it lasted until the 1950s or even later.

- Barns, stables and cowsheds still survive on many farms (see pages 38-39). Old photographs of them may help to show you how they were used and why they were designed as they were. They might help you to understand why such buildings are often ill-suited to modern farming, which could be the reason why so many have been demolished or neglected.
- You might find surviving sheep folds and the places where sheep were dipped to kill parasites or where their fleeces were washed. Some old photographs of rural life portray groups of men shearing sheep, driving flocks along a village street, or chopping turnips for winter feed. They may also show the importance of the family pig and the annual killing.
- Notice how the countryside was remarkably free of traffic before the advent of the car. Old photographs show that waggons, carts and sleds were used for transporting crops and manure. The isolation of rural farmsteads until the bicycle became widespread can be imagined from photographs of donkey carts, horse-drawn traps and buggies on unsurfaced lanes and roads.

Crafts of the countryside

The blacksmith or saddler often appear in photographs. They were focal points in village life. Look also for specialist crafts such as basket-weaving or the making of hurdles. If you see a saw pit, timber yard or corn mill, you might be able to find the site on a first edition Ordnance Survey (OS) map (see pages 18-19), and identify the owners in directories (see pages 74-75) and census returns (see pages 76-77).

FIND OUT MORE

- *The Museum of English Rural Life* At the University of Reading in Berkshire, the museum houses a comprehensive collection of artefacts, photographs, films and books that record the changing face of farming and the countryside. www.ruralhistory.org
- *The National Library of Wales* (see DIRECTORY) Holds a collection of 750,000 images from the early days of photography to the present, many of life in rural areas. www.llgc.org.uk
- *National Museum of Rural Life* Photographs in the museum's archive tell the story of Scottish country life from *c*.1750. www.nms.ac.uk/museumofrurallifehomepage.aspx

Modern methods The latest innovations were a popular topic for photographers. You may find images, such as harvesting by motor on a Lincolnshire farm (left, 1907), that record the gradual mechanisation of farming, although at first it did not appear to cause a reduction in the work force.

How ancient woods reveal their age

Britain's woodlands have been worked and nurtured for thousands of years, and have filled our imaginations with folk characters such as the Green Man and Robin Hood. By following a series of signs, you may well discover that there are remnants of ancient woodland closer to home than you think.

The remains of a landscape of trees

After the scouring of the last Ice Age, Britain grew thick with wildwood – trees such as oak, elm and lime have flourished here from around 7500 BC. Woodland was first deliberately planted about 400 years ago; any woods that predate 1600 are known as 'ancient woodland'. In spite of constant cutting and clearing throughout the centuries, much remains, such as the old beeches of the Savernake Forest in Wiltshire and the hornbeams of Epping Forest in Essex.

You can quickly learn to spot ancient woodland by studying Ordnance Survey (OS) maps and following clues on the ground. The irregular outlines, the boundary banks and the slopes and streams – look for these and other indicators to uncover ancient woodland.

Finding signs on a map
Although it is best to check out clues to ancient woodland by visiting the wood itself (see below), you do not necessarily have to. On a map, the outline of a wood, its name, the angle of the ground on which it lies, the presence or absence of a stream or a bank, even the shapes and names of the countryside round about, all present vital information as to whether that wood is a piece of ancient woodland or not.

The best maps to use are the OS Explorer series (see pages 18-19), which show field boundaries and plenty of other close-up detail, as in the example of Hagg Wood (right).

Other map indicators are the proximity of heath or common land, and the presence of a parish boundary (see pages 36-37) – parishes were created in medieval times or earlier, and their boundaries were often formed by woodland.

FOLLOW THE CLUES TO ANCIENT WOODLAND

Telltale plants Plants such as bluebells (below), dog's mercury, cuckoo pint, ferns, wood sorrel, marsh hellebore, enchanter's nightshade and meadowsweet are characteristic of ancient woods, where they have established themselves over hundreds of years.

Working the wood Coppicing, the harvesting of poles from coppice stools (the butts of trees, such as hazel, ash and beech, from which the poles grow), helps to maintain the wood and provide material for furniture making and other woodland crafts (see pages 54-55).

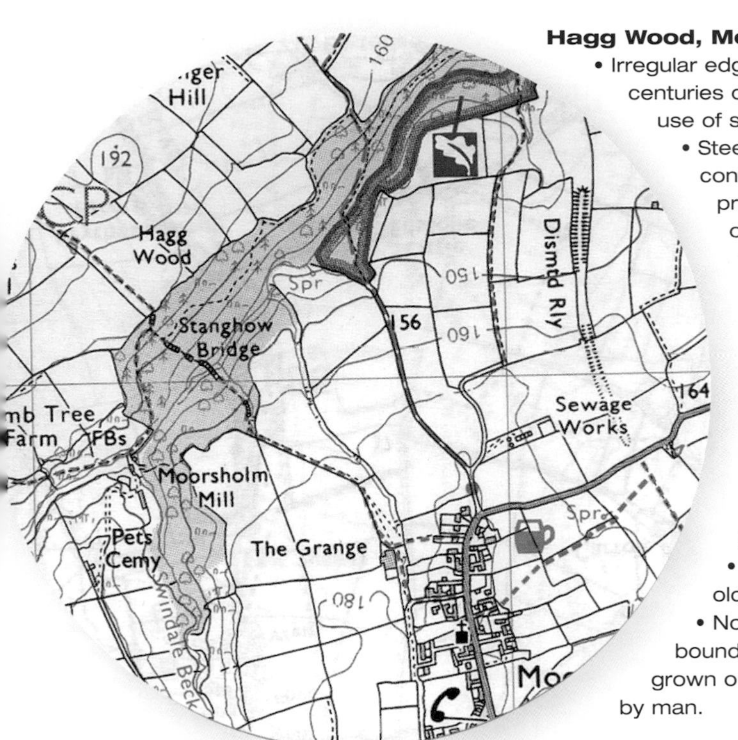

Hagg Wood, Moorsholm, Cleveland

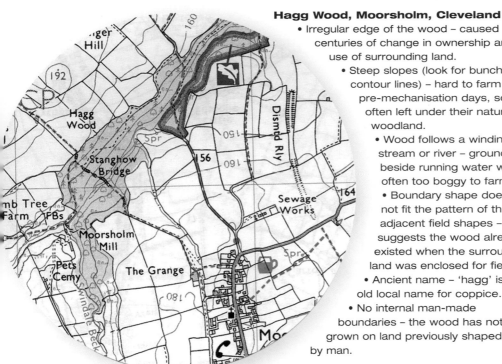

- Irregular edge of the wood – caused by centuries of change in ownership and use of surrounding land.
- Steep slopes (look for bunched contour lines) – hard to farm in pre-mechanisation days, so often left under their natural woodland.
- Wood follows a winding stream or river – ground beside running water was often too boggy to farm.
- Boundary shape does not fit the pattern of the adjacent field shapes – suggests the wood already existed when the surrounding land was enclosed for fields.
- Ancient name – 'hagg' is an old local name for coppice.
- No internal man-made boundaries – the wood has not grown on land previously shaped by man.

DID YOU KNOW?

Look at the name of a wood – it can be a clue to whether it is a piece of ancient woodland.

- Grove, lea, copse, thorns, hagg, hanger – old names for different types of woodland.
- Kiln Wood, Brick Copse, Tanner's Spinney – former industries that harvested the wood.
- Assington Thicks, Priory Grove, Grange Wood – names that reflect a nearby settlement.
- Ash Grove, Oak Spinney, Elm Hag, Beech Hanger, Hazel Copse, Maple Lea – names of long-established native tree species.

Lie of the land Stand back and take a look at a wood from a distance. An irregular edge, a steep slope and a stream gully are three good signs of ancient woodland.

Evidence of grazing Ancient woods will often have pollarded trees (below) at their edges. Pollarding the big boundary trees (cutting off their boughs several feet above ground height) allowed animals to graze common land right up to the edge of the wood.

Woodland limits Low, winding ditches and banks often mark the boundaries of ancient woodland. They were dug to prevent grazing cattle from entering the wood and damaging young coppices.

In search of woodland craft and industry

You are never far from woods in Britain: peaceful places, perfect for a quiet walk or nature ramble. Once they were hives of activity, worked for their supplies of wood and bark. Many woods have been cleared in recent years, but the remnants show signs of past industry, and old woodland skills are being revived.

Hidden hearths White coal pits, such as those in Holmesfield Park Wood in Derbyshire (above), can be spotted by the blackened earth beneath the foliage. They were used repeatedly to burn stacks of wood for days at a time to create white coal.

The importance of woods

Woods looked very different to our ancestors of a hundred or more years ago. Some trees were allowed to grow to full height before they were felled for timber, but most of the trees were coppiced (see pages 52-53) to provide wood for essential objects such as fences, hurdles, poles, gates, ladders, handles and furniture. Wood of only a few years' growth was cut into logs and faggots for industrial and domestic fires, and the twigs (known in the Midlands as 'rammell') were used for kindling. The bark was stripped and taken away by tanners to provide the tannin, or tannic acid, essential to the tanning process.

Charcoal - the all-purpose fuel

The ancient woods of Britain were once filled with the smoke rising from charcoal burners' kilns. Charcoal, made by burning the young wood of carefully managed coppices, was used for many different purposes. In particular, it was the main source of fuel for the water-powered blast furnaces of the 16th to 18th centuries.

- During the several days that the 'colliers' were making charcoal, they lived in temporary huts made of poles and covered with turf sods. A good example is preserved at the Weald and Downland Open Air Museum in Sussex (see DIRECTORY), or you can spot them in old rural photographs (see pages 50-51). Notice the coppiced wood stacked in hearths and covered with sods to exclude the air, so that the wood was charred slowly until all the moisture was lost.
- Former hearths, or platforms, in woods are often overgrown (see above). You can spot them by looking for blackened soft soils forming rough circles about 4.6m (15ft) in diameter. Rabbits tend to make burrows in them because of their softness. Elsewhere, you may see charcoal platforms forming terraces in a hillside.
- Lead smelters used a fuel known as white coal, which was charred to a lower temperature than charcoal. Hundreds of the white-coal pits or kilns, once covered with turf or bracken, survive in woods near old lead-smelting mills, particularly in Derbyshire and the Yorkshire Dales (see page 63).

Living on the job A charcoal burner would build a hut in the woods (below), where he lived while tending the kiln. A similar hut can be seen at Hestercombe Gardens, Somerset (right), as part of a re-created charcoal burner's camp.

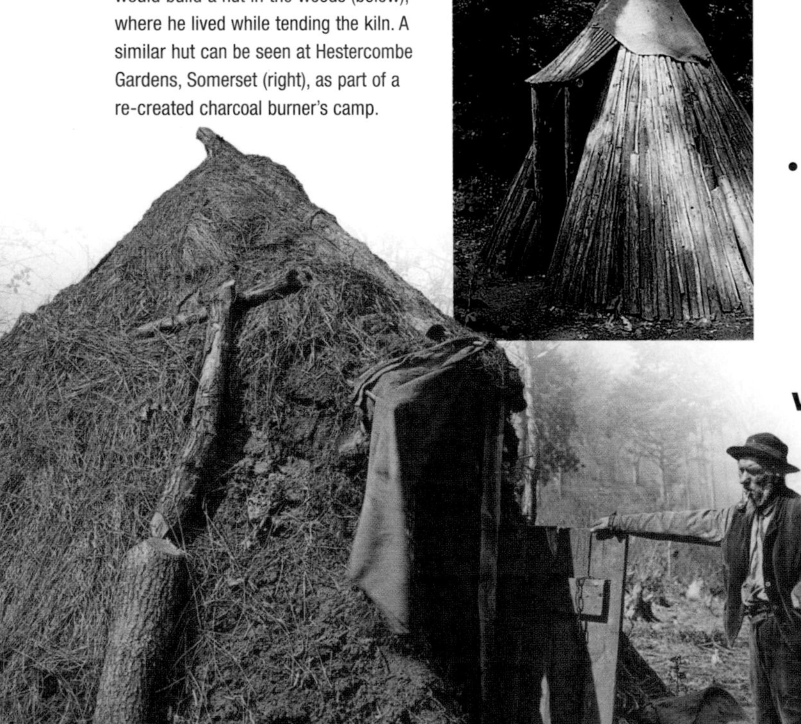

Woodland signs in the records

Most woods were privately owned. Manor court rolls and estate papers held in county records will mention woods and their management. You may find accounts of illegal fellings and the obligations of tenants to fence a wood to prevent the grazing of young shoots by livestock. The customs of some manors allowed tenants to graze cattle, horses and pigs at certain times of the year or to pollard trees (see pages 52-53) by lopping branches 2-5m (7-18ft) above ground.

- Look in the catalogues of estate papers for leases that allowed the 'coaling' of coppiced wood between the 16th and 18th centuries, the heyday of most coppiced woods when the iron and lead smelters paid high prices for charcoal. In 1653, George Sitwell of Renishaw Hall, a leading Derbyshire ironmaster, was allowed to fell 700 cords, or bundles, of oaks in the parish of Beighton and 'to convert the same to charcoal'.
- You may find references in estate accounts and leases to the transportation of charcoal and white coal by wheeled vehicles as well as packhorses.

Decline and recovery

The decline of Britain's woodlands began in the late 18th century with the replacement of charcoal by coke, derived from coal, in iron and lead smelting. The demand for charcoal fell and it became more profitable to convert coppice woods to timber growing, often with new species introduced, such as larch or sweet chestnut.

In 1919 the Forestry Commission was created and the change to conifer plantations was rapid. Between 1946 and 1976 about 30 per cent of Britain's ancient broad-leaved woods were destroyed by agricultural expansion or by replacement with conifers. But the tide has now turned, and the Woodland Trust, among others, is committed to preserving many old woods. Coppicing is undergoing a revival, particularly in southeast England.

- Spot the woods, or sections of woods, where the trees are different from those mentioned in leases and other records from earlier centuries. In woods in the north of England in the 19th century, beech trees – native in the south of England – were widely introduced.
- At your county record office, look at Victorian estate papers for 'woodwards' accounts' of what sort of trees were planted and felled. To date any changes, look at leases and bills of sale and old photographs.
- County reports known as *General Views of Agriculture*, from the 1790s and early 19th century, such as *General View of the Agriculture of Devonshire* by C. Vancouver (1808), have long sections on woods written at the time when many were undergoing change.
- If your local wood does not have any of the new species, and if the trees are mostly tall and thin, and competing for light, it may be that the old trees have not been coppiced since charcoal went out of fashion. Many old coppice woods have not been managed since the First World War.
- Compare the current Ordnance Survey (OS) Explorer map (see pages 72-73) of your district with first-edition OS maps to spot any changes. See how many woods preserve their original shape, even if the tree species are different. Notice whether any woods have been reduced in size or have disappeared altogether.

Practising an old skill A woodsman in Lancashire continues the tradition of coppicing, cutting trees to the ground for wood and to encourage new growth.

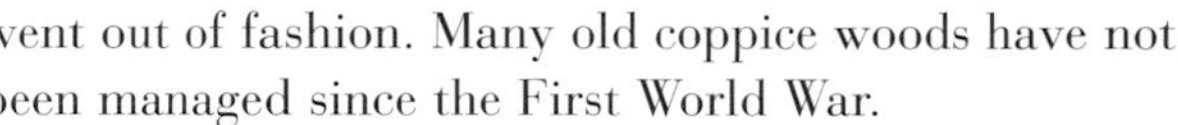

FIND OUT MORE

For further information about Britain's woodlands and ways in which you can become involved, contact the following organisations.

- **www.woodland-trust.org.uk** Find out where your nearest woodlands are located by looking at the Woodland Trust's on-line Directory of Woods. The Trust organises local talks, guided walks and volunteer work parties.
- **www.smallwoods.org.uk** The Small Woods Association aims to encourage the care and enjoyment of small woodlands and supports woodland crafts.
- **www.greenwoodtrust.org.uk** The Green Wood Trust works to regenerate broad-leaved woodlands by teaching traditional skills such as coppicing. It runs courses and offers opportunities for volunteer work.

Permission to work Estate accounts often hold leases concerning woodland activity. In 1682, the Duke of Newcastle granted a lease (below) in Derbyshire, which allowed two tenants, Thomas Starky and John Rogers, to make pits and kilns to convert wood into white coal and charcoal, to burn rammell (twigs), erect workmen's cabins and have free passage for oxen, horses, wains and carts to the nearest highways.

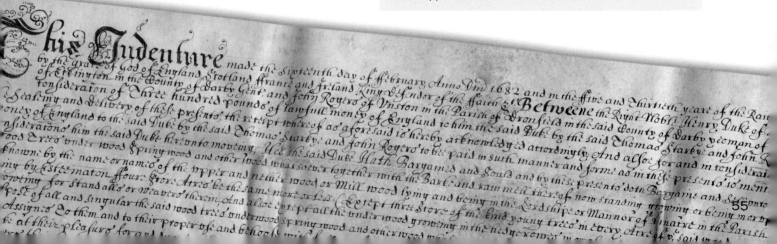

A nationwide view of England's trees

From 1924 to 2000 the Forestry Commission has regularly carried out county-by-county surveys of England to determine the extent and type of woodland cover. The fieldwork has resulted in the National Inventory of Woodland and Trees (NIWT), a rich resource of maps and statistics. Wherever you live in England, the inventory will give you a clear picture of the changing state of your county's woods and forests through time.

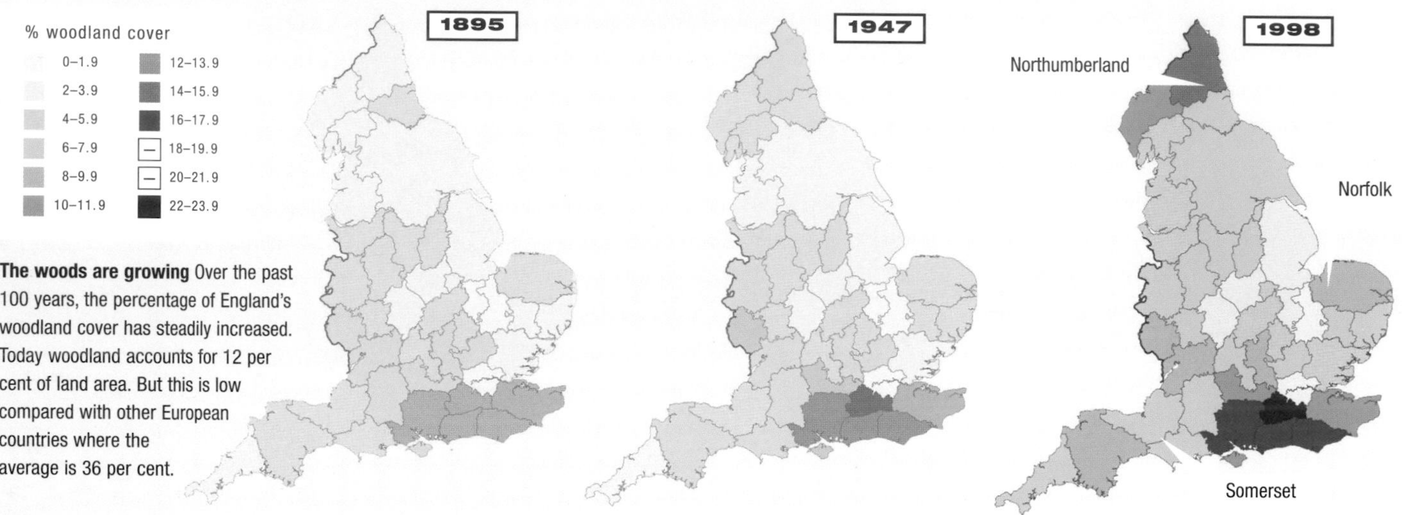

The woods are growing Over the past 100 years, the percentage of England's woodland cover has steadily increased. Today woodland accounts for 12 per cent of land area. But this is low compared with other European countries where the average is 36 per cent.

Somerset – land of oak and ash

The patterns of woodland change from county to county, shaped by each area's history. This is reflected in the NIWT, which has catalogued not only every swathe of woodland but also every lone tree. The 2002 survey shows Somerset to be a county with a surprisingly meagre covering of trees – about 7 per cent of the land area. In 1980 there was even less woodland – only 5.6 per cent. There are 1286 sizeable woods of 2ha (5 acres) or more, with an average area of 18ha (44 acres), and twice as many small pieces of woodland averaging just under half a hectare (1.25 acres).

As for the type of tree cover in Somerset, slightly more than half the woodlands are broadleaved, with oak and ash predominating. Conifers account for about a quarter of the woodland; most of them (17.5 per cent) are larch.

Norfolk – copses, clumps and pine plantations

In spite of its arable landscape, Norfolk has more tree cover, at 9.8 per cent, than Somerset, with 2191 woods of more than 2ha (5 acres). The woods' average area is 20.3ha (50 acres), which is comparable with that of the larger woodlands of Somerset.

Norfolk possesses a vastly greater number of small pieces of woodland – more than 16,000 compared with Somerset's 2478. This reflects Norfolk's historic status as a shooting county, where any landowner worth his salt planted copses to shelter game. The county is also low-lying and windswept, so every farm needed a sheltering clump of trees. Such windbreaks are more numerous than in Somerset – Norfolk has 42,900 narrow rows of trees and about 3000 classified as 'wide' (which are also useful as game cover). Norfolk has fewer free-standing trees than Somerset, numbering just under 4 million.

The proportion of broadleaved to coniferous woodlands in Norfolk and Somerset is roughly the same, with oak accounting for around a quarter of broadleaved trees in both counties. But Norfolk shows an overwhelming imbalance of species in its coniferous woodlands: four out of every five trees in these woods is a pine. This

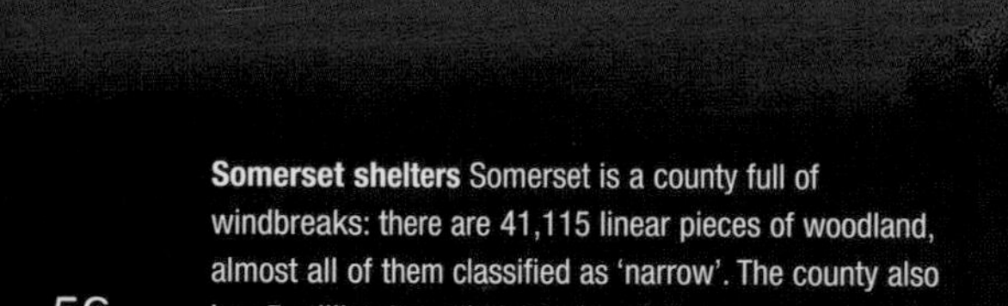

Somerset shelters Somerset is a county full of windbreaks: there are 41,115 linear pieces of woodland, almost all of them classified as 'narrow'. The county also has 5 million trees that stand on their own.

Norfolk plantings The Corsican pines at Holkham were planted on the dunes in the 19th century as a shelter belt. Pine trees dominate Norfolk's coniferous woodland – many were planted after the Second World War as sustainable sources of timber.

reflects the massive Forestry Commission plantings after the Second World War on the sandy Breckland heaths in the southwest of the county, where Thetford Forest covers around 21,000ha (51,900 acres).

Northumberland - the march of coniferous armies

An initial impression of Northumberland might be one of a county of treeless coasts and moors, but the NIWT tells a different story. In fact, Northumberland has more than twice as much land under trees (16 per cent of the county's total area) as Somerset (7 per cent).

Northumberland's trees are grouped differently from those of Somerset and Norfolk. The two southern counties both possess more small woods than Northumberland. Norfolk has more large woods, too; but the difference is that the Northumbrian woods, although fewer in number, are almost twice the average size – 38.1ha (94 acres) – of the East Anglian ones. The northern sportsmen and farmers seem to be able to do without windbreaks, since there are fewer than 2000 linear woodland features in the whole county. As for trees standing out on their own – blustery Northumberland with its cool temperatures can show fewer than a quarter of a million.

The biggest contrast between north and south is in the proportion of coniferous to broadleaved woodlands. Only 13.3 per cent of Northumberland's woods are broadleaved; the most numerous species (20 per cent) is birch, an early coloniser of post-Ice Age Britain. Three-quarters of the woods are coniferous, with sitka spruce – an introduced commercial forestry tree – representing 68 per cent of the species. That indicates just how important the Forestry Commission's presence is in Northumberland, another county that was high on the list for post-war commercial planting.

SPECIES OF TREES

Trees can be classified as native, naturalised or newcomers. Native trees have been here since before the last Ice Age, and include oak, ash, beech, birch, hazel, Scot's pine and elm. Trees that were introduced hundreds of years ago are said to have naturalised (sycamore, horse chestnut and Norway spruce). Newcomers have been introduced recently, mainly to produce timber (pine, larch, poplar and Douglas fir).

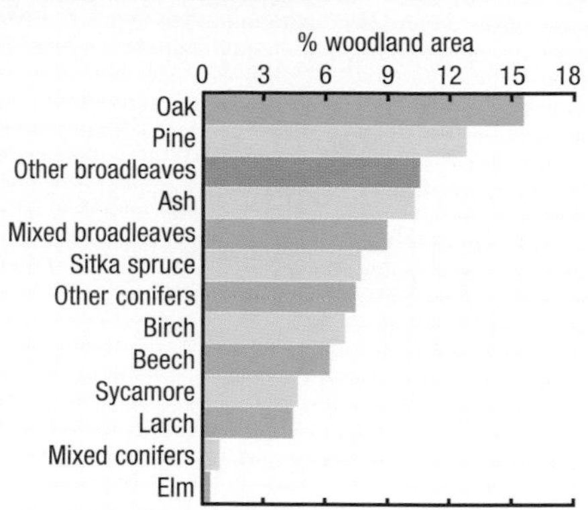

Mighty oak, tragic elm Long a symbol of England, the oak is still the dominant tree species (16.1 per cent). Pine is second due to large commercial forests, mainly in the north. The tiny presence of elm (0.4 per cent) reflects the devastation caused from the 1970s by Dutch elm disease, which killed some 80 per cent of mature trees.

Northumberland conifers Broadleaved species like silver birch (right) are outnumbered by huge expanses of conifer forests in Northumberland. The enormous Kielder Forest (below) is England's largest and most productive forest. It is owned by the Forestry Commission and consists of around 150 million trees, mostly Sitka spruce.

FIND OUT MORE

- *The Forestry Commission's National Inventory of Woodland and Trees* Available from Forestry Commission Publications, PO Box 25, Wetherby, West Yorkshire LS23 7EW
- **www.forestry.gov.uk/forestry/hcou-54pg4d** To access the inventory information on-line.

Travel on the rural highways and byways

Take a look at the road signs in your local area. You may spot some intriguing names, such as Salterway, Hollowgate or Packman Lane, which will set you wondering about their meaning. The roads, country lanes, footpaths and bridges in your area all have a story to tell about the local people, packmen and drovers who used them years ago. You can find plenty of clues that will explain their origins.

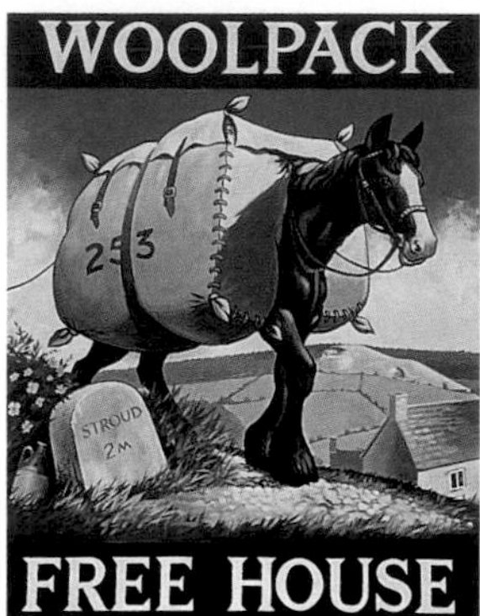

Watering holes Pub names, such as the Woolpack in Slad, Gloucestershire (above), the Packhorse or the Drovers' Arms, give clues to their history.

Drovers' network Look out for the old droving routes (above) – now often local walking trails – along which cattle, sheep, pigs and geese were driven across Britain to supply London and other fast-expanding cities from the end of the 16th century.

Routing for old names

In the 18th and early 19th centuries, the most important highways became turnpike roads (see pages 60-61), and country lanes were widened when the commons were enclosed. But many of the old names have survived.

- At your county record office, note the names on the 19th-century first edition six-inch Ordnance Survey (OS) maps, tithe award and enclosure maps, and any other local maps that are available (see pages 18-19). Then visit your local library and consult the county volumes published by the English Place-Name Society (see DIRECTORY). Look for the earliest references to these names and you may find explanations of their meanings.
- The word 'road' was rarely used before the late 17th century. The Anglo-Saxons used the term 'ways' and the Vikings 'gates'. Look for names such as Bradway ('the broad way') or Ridgeway, and Sandygate or Kirkgate ('the route to church'). In upland districts spot the Corpse Ways, which were the traditional burial routes from remote hamlets to the parish churchyard.
- 'Lane' had the same meaning as today, but dialect words such as 'sty' or 'rake' were also used for minor tracks or paths. Oxton Rakes in the Peak District commemorates the route by which oxen were driven to summer pastures.
- Find out what sort of traders might have used your local roads. The routes taken by packmen transporting salt from the Cheshire saltworks to Midland market towns can be followed on maps by looking for names such as Salters' Ford, Salters' Hill and Saltergate. The Salters' Closes provided overnight grazing.

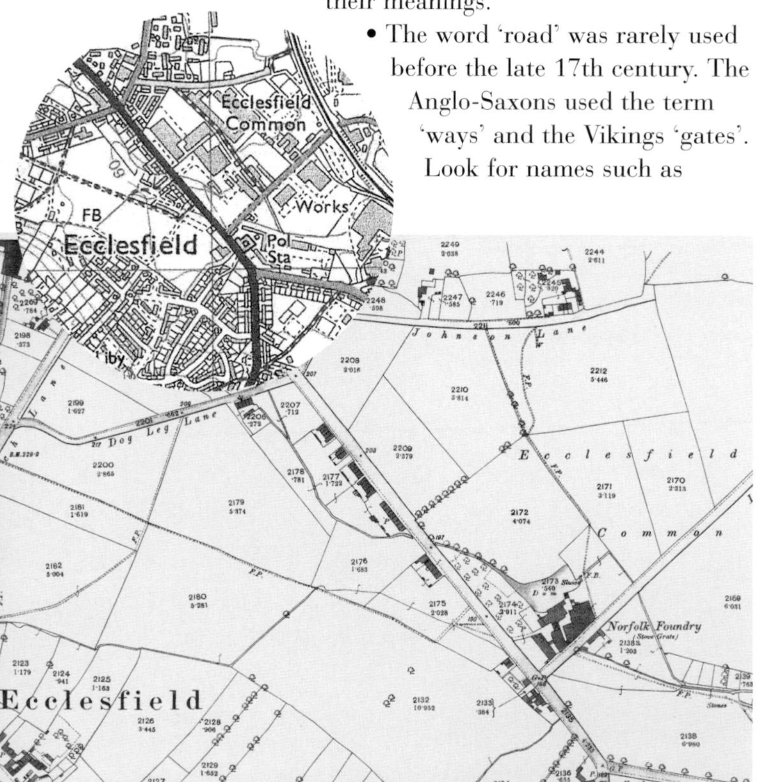

Changes on the ground Compare maps such as the first edition Ordnance Survey (OS) map from 1892 of Ecclesfield, Yorkshire (above), with a modern-day OS Explorer map (inset) and you will be able to see how lanes have developed into roads, where footpaths led to, and perhaps uncover the origins of a mysterious road or place name.

Following ancient tracks

See if you can find the old routes on the ground. Many of our roads have developed from the well-trodden paths of days gone by, but you may notice that some appear sunken with very steep banks.

Holloways The deep holloways or hollowgates (see right) were formed by the wear of wheeled traffic. In moorland areas, where tracks did not have to follow a definite line, notice how they fan out across the landscape to form a group of shallow holloways. The age of a holloway cannot be estimated from its depth because a sunken track could be produced in a few seasons of heavy traffic, but there may be other clues to help you to date them. For example, you might find deeply worn tracks leading to the site of a forge or furnace that was built in the 17th century and abandoned a hundred years later.

Bridges Look for sturdy medieval bridges with pointed arches, such as the bridge over the River Wye in Bakewell. These were wide enough to take wheeled traffic.

- At the county record office you can read the quarter sessions records from the 17th and 18th centuries to find out when bridges were repaired or enlarged by order of the Justices of the Peace (JPs).
- Check whether bridges near where you live were marked on the earliest county maps by Saxton or Speed (see pages 18-19).
- You may find a narrow packhorse bridge in your area, just wide enough to take a loaded horse. These bridges are most likely to be seen in upland districts, such as the Pennines, on routes that were never made into turnpike roads or widened for wheeled traffic. They date from about 1650-1750, when they often replaced wooden bridges. Their simple design should not mislead you into thinking that they are much older.

Local footpath features

Flagstones Look for lines of flagstones, known as 'causeys' or 'causeways', that were put down as footpaths or bridleways by parish authorities or landowners. Most surviving examples date from the 17th to the 19th centuries. Many are now overgrown or have been covered by modern surfaces.

Guide stoops If you live in Derbyshire, or the West and North Ridings of Yorkshire, look for early 18th-century waymarkers known as guide stoops (left). They helped to guide travellers across remote and featureless moorland, pointing the way to the nearest market towns and sometimes local villages and hamlets.

Finger posts Do any 'finger posts' made of cast iron (below), point directions in your parish? They date from the late 19th and early 20th centuries.

Stiles Are the stiles in your area all of the same design? The Peak District 'squeezers' (below) are two upright stones, splayed at the top to allow you to squeeze through. Also look out for any standing or recumbent stones with holes in them that once supported a gate hinge.

Making a deep impression You might find a sunken lane near where you live. Some of these byways can be more than 4.5m (15ft) deep, such as the aptly named Hollow Lane (left), leading from Montacute towards Ham Hill in Somerset. They became deeper as wheeled traffic gradually replaced packhorses between the 16th and 18th centuries.

FIND OUT MORE

- *Welsh Cattle Drovers* (Richard Moore-Colyer, Landmark Publishing, 1976). An account of the old droving routes.
- *A Dictionary of British Place Names* (A.D. Mills, Oxford Paperback Reference) Explains the meanings of place names.
- **www.st-andrews.ac.uk/institutes/sassi/spns** The Scottish Place-Name Society provides help on tracing the origins of names.

Where road, rail and canal cross the land

Turnpike roads, canals and railways revolutionised the transport system in the 18th and 19th centuries at a time when Britain's population and industries were booming. They made a huge impact on the local landscape, leaving a trail of evidence that you can follow on the ground and in records.

Looking for signs of turnpike roads

Britain's roads were in such a poor state by the late 17th century that Parliament introduced turnpike trusts to fund improvements and make the roads suitable for wheeled traffic. Many signs of the old turnpikes still exist, such as toll-keepers' cottages, milestones and bridges, trust records and surveyors' reports.

Pay as you go A toll-house (1824) on the cross-Pennine turnpike, now the A6033.

Tracing turnpikes Look along roadside verges for turnpike milestones and water troughs for the horses. Most early to mid 18th-century milestones are simple stone slabs with the mileage recorded on the side facing the road. Cast-iron plates were added in the second half of the 18th century, and milestones made entirely of iron date from around 1810 onwards. Fife in Scotland has some mile posts made at the Kirkcaldy foundry with precise mileages, sometimes in fractions of miles. One at Newport-on-Tay, near Dundee, erected in 1824, reads: 'Pettycur 33, New Inn 20, Cupar 11, Newport 0'.

- See if any original bridges survive or whether they have been widened for modern traffic. Sometimes, you can tell only by looking under the bridge for where the two structures were joined. Look for the dates or name of the turnpike trust on the bridges.
- At road junctions, look at the buildings to see if any were toll-keepers' cottages. Many are only one storey high and have large windows at both the front and sides to allow the toll-keeper to spot oncoming traffic.
- You may find a stretch of early turnpike road that was abandoned when a steep hill was by-passed. It will now be a grassy track, but will feature on early Ordnance Survey (OS) and county maps (see pages 18-19).

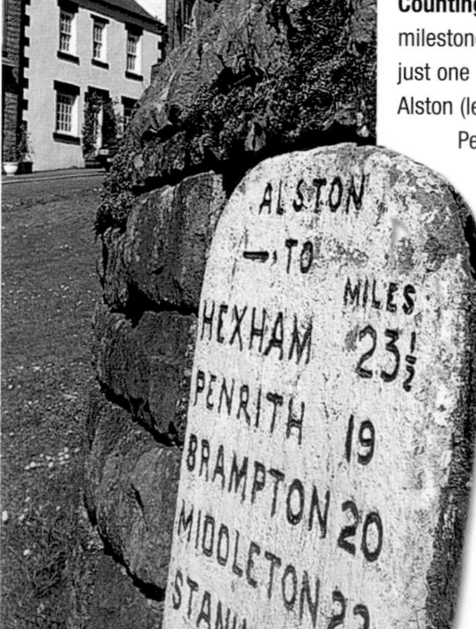

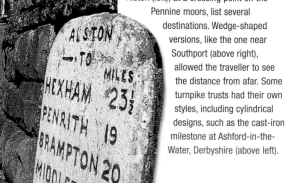

Counting the miles A wide variety of milestones can be spotted: some mark just one destination; others, such as at Alston (left), at a crossing point on the Pennine moors, list several destinations. Wedge-shaped versions, like the one near Southport (above right), allowed the traveller to see the distance from afar. Some turnpike trusts had their own styles, including cylindrical designs, such as the cast-iron milestone at Ashford-in-the-Water, Derbyshire (above left).

The high route Look out for disused railway tracks that have become walking routes. The Monsal Trail in Derbyshire crosses the old Midland Railway viaduct (left), built in 1863.

Turnpikes in the records At your local record office, look for turnpike trust minute books and for surveyors' reports and correspondence. Search early directories and local newspapers (see pages 74-75) for coaching and waggon services. Look for the principal stopping places, the names of inns that may still exist (see page 120) and the many service providers, such as the Breconshire Trust.

- Trace the course of early turnpike roads on late-18th-century county maps and compare with those seen on enclosure maps and first-edition six-inch OS maps (see pages 72-73). Make a note of any changes.
- Acts of Parliament setting up turnpike trusts are available from the House of Lords Record Office (see DIRECTORY). They give details of the type of traffic that used the road, the location of toll gates and the charges levied.

Navigating the canals

The canal system played a key role in transporting heavy goods such as building materials in the 18th and 19th centuries. You can follow disused stretches of canals along towpaths and under the bow-shaped bridges which allowed the horses towing the boats to cross to the other side. Spot the canal company's name on plaques found the on bridges.

- Look out for engineering feats, such as flights of locks, tunnels and aqueducts. You may still find signs of a lock-keeper's cottage or boatmen's pub beside a lock or at a canal junction (see page 107).

Canals in the records At your local county record office, you can identify the type of goods carried on a canal by looking at old photographs (see pages 70-71) and documents, such as the private Acts of Parliament that authorised the construction of canals.

- The 18th-century county maps (see pages 18-19) mark early canals, such as the pioneering Duke of Bridgewater Canal (completed in 1772) on Burdett's 1777 map of Cheshire. Compare these with the first-edition six-inch OS maps, which show the completed system.
- Look for prints and paintings of the waterways in your local record office or museum.

On the track of railways

Evidence of Britain's extensive railway network – before it was severely pruned in the mid 20th century – can be seen across the countryside. If there is a disused line near where you live, note how bridges, viaducts, cuttings, embankments, tunnels, sidings and signal boxes have made an impact on the landscape. If you find a bridge over a wide grassy track, see whether it matches up with a 'dismantled railway line' marked on the current OS map. Some lines have been converted into footpaths and cycle tracks.

Railways in the records At your county record office, look at large-scale OS maps from the mid-Victorian period onwards to see how the railway system developed and to spot branch lines that have since been abandoned.

- Images of steam locomotives have been captured in many books of old photographs (see pages 70-71).
- Records of former railway companies, including maps and plans, staff records, reports and accounts are held at the National Archives in Kew and Edinburgh, and the House of Lords Record Office.

Country halt Look for signs of disused stations, such as Hatton, near Lancaster (below). Platforms often remain, but the buildings may have been converted to another use. Some former steam train lines have been restored by local groups of enthusiasts, and both these societies and railway museums often hold excellent collections of railway memorabilia, including timetables such as for the Lancashire and Yorkshire Railway, 1910 (above).

FIND OUT MORE

- *National Railway Museum* Vast collection of rolling stock and historic documents (see pages 252-253). www.nrm.org.uk
- *National Waterways Museum* Archives of the early canal companies. www.nwm.org.uk
- *Nicholson Guides to the Waterways* (OS-Nicholson, 2000-2003) A comprehensive series of guides to the canal network.

Looking for signs of rural industry

The story of where you live might begin with an iron works, a mine or a slate quarry that was set up deep in the countryside. For centuries, rural people have earned their living from many industries, not just farming. You will find signs of these activities on moorland, in woods, on the coast and beside rivers.

Monuments to tin The ruins of the once lucrative tin-mining industry litter the Cornish landscape, such as the pumping engine house at Wheal Coates, St Agnes, built in 1872. Workings extended deep under the sea.

Uncovering the evidence

The countryside has hummed with industrial activity since prehistoric times. There are signs of ancient flint mines at Grimes Graves in Norfolk and copper mines at Llandudno in North Wales. But the greatest surge in rural industry took place in the 18th century.

To find out about the industries in your area, talk to older members of your community, such as former tin miners. At your local library and record office, search for old illustrations and photographs (see pages 70-71) of industrial landscapes, and look for documentary and map evidence. You might find a lease for a coal mine among estate papers or see that a quarry was still being worked at the time of an early Ordnance Survey (OS) map (see pages 18-19). These might explain physical features that can be seen in the surrounding landscape such as overgrown workings or derelict dams.

Countryside clues First-edition OS maps often mark the sites of former industries, such as Rainstorth Colliery, near Sheffield (1892, left). Visit the area now, and you might spot some remains.

Following an industry

Many industries were specific to certain areas. The local geology often played a key role in their location.

The early iron industry Mining for iron ore took place across much of Britain from the Weald in Kent through the Midlands and south Wales, north to Yorkshire. You can spot the sites by looking for the abandoned bell pits of the ironstone miners. They often appear in woodland as water-filled depressions up to 2m (6ft) in diameter and 6m (20ft) deep. Look for traces of charcoal blast furnaces and forges, wheel pits and the outlines of dams.

- You can identify old iron-working sites through names such as Cinder Hill or Smithies on OS maps. At your local reference library or record office, consult the volumes of the English Place-Name Society or the *Victoria County History* (see 'Find out more', page 35) for any mention of them in charters and leases. Many sites were worked by monks and are mentioned in the ecclesiastical records.
- At your reference library, refer to British Geological Survey maps, which mark outcrops of ironstone and coal. Then, at your record office, turn to 18th-century county maps to spot the 'fire engines' that pumped the water out of mines. Landowners were keen to exploit mineral deposits – look for evidence in estate papers.

Cornish tin mines Tin was mined in Cornwall from prehistoric times. The greatest period of activity was in the late 18th and 19th centuries, when beam engines were

Walking into history Even on a family walk in local countryside, you might come across signs of an industrial past. A millstone lying in open moorland at White Coppice in Lancashire (above) provides a clue to past activities in the area.

used for pumping and winding, and for crushing ores. Mineral railways took the tin from smelting works to the ports on the coast. Foreign competition brought most of the industry to an end in the Victorian period.

- Look for the remains of engine houses, chimney stacks, wheel pits and winding gear. Many mines, such as those at Botallack, near Land's End, are perched precariously on steep cliffs overlooking the sea.
- At your county record office and library look for old photographs of mines and mining villages. Note their layout on first-edition, large-scale OS maps. Search surviving company records for maps, reports, accounts and correspondence.

Millstone-making The entrances to the Peak District National Park are marked by a distinctive sign in the shape of a millstone. Hundreds of millstones, in various stages of manufacture, litter former quarries on the park's gritstone edges and on adjacent stretches of moorland. The heyday of this ancient industry was from the 16th to the 19th century.

- Abandoned millstones that were intended for corn-milling have a flat side for grinding, a convex top, and narrow, rounded edges. They commonly had a diameter of 152-178cm (60-70in). Most of the remaining stones were used for pulping wood into paper or for grinding paint. They come in different sizes, are flat on both sides, and have sharp, right-angled edges.
- Look for the levelled tracks and holloways (see pages 58-59) leading from the quarries. The millstones were moved along these on sledges.
- At your local record office, search for millstone hewers in the census returns and for the names of quarry owners in trade directories (see pages 75, 76-77). Information on the running of the industry may be found in account books, leases and correspondence. Early editions of OS maps will show you which quarries were in production and when.

Swaledale lead mining Lead mines were associated with limestone districts, such as the Yorkshire Dales, the White Peak of Derbyshire and the Mendips in Somerset. The industry goes back at least to Roman times and flourished until the late 19th century. When the lead mines of Swaledale in the Pennines became exhausted, the local population fell by 50 per cent between 1871 and 1891.

- On the ground, look for deep grooves in the hillsides, known as 'hushes', which were made by damming a stream to uncover the veins of lead. Search for the drainage channels of the deeper mines, which appear as stone-built tunnels in the hillsides. Find the ruins of former smelting mills, such as Old Gang Smelt Mill, near Reeth, whose chimneys and ruined buildings are surrounded by heaps of debris.
- At your local record office, spot the mines and smelting mills on early OS maps and in old photographs. Search for the leases and business records of mining companies.

Explosive material An accident at the Chilworth gunpowder works (left), which killed six men, is recorded in a 1901 edition of the *Surrey Advertiser*. Old newspaper reports (see pages 74-75) such as this can highlight former industries where you live.

FIND OUT MORE

- *The Making of the Industrial Landscape* (Barrie Trinder, Weidenfeld & Nicolson, 1997) Describes rural industry in the 18th and 19th centuries.
- Great Orme Mines Llandudno, north Wales. Explore the tunnels of a copper mine that dates back to the time of the Bronze Age. www.greatorme.freeserve.co.uk
- Geevor Tin Mine Pendeen, Cornwall. Work ceased at Geevor in 1990 and the mine is now open to the public. www.geevor.com

Rips and repairs in the landscape

For better or for worse, the stamp of heavy industry on the landscape can be jaw-droppingly spectacular. Even in places where the effects seemed irreversible, ingenuity, energy and money have helped to remedy the deepest scars.

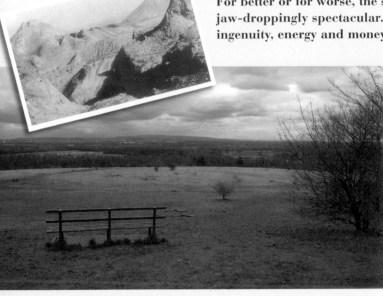

Before and after The three huge slag heaps (top) left by Garswood Hall Colliery in Ashton-in-Makerfield, Lancashire, used to be known as The Three Sisters. Today the spoil heaps have been transformed into the Three Sisters Recreation Area, set among ponds, woodland and open fields.

Mining heaps

Perhaps the most spectacularly visible industrial devastation of the landscape took place in the 19th and 20th centuries as a result of coal mining in south Wales, Lancashire, Yorkshire, County Durham, Lanarkshire and Lothian. Ugly pithead winding gear and mine buildings dotted the landscape, while red-brick colliery villages sprawled over the once-green countryside. Towering menacingly over the scene were the great black spoil tips or slag heaps.

But this is not the story today in the former coal-mining towns. Most of the industry has gone and the landscape is being transformed. Nearly all the colliery heaps have been reclaimed. Seeded with grass and trees, the scenic hillocks, such as those at Ebbw Vale in south Wales, look as though they have always been there. Many are now incorporated into parkland, the heavy industry of the past giving way to a new industry of leisure, as in the Three Sisters Recreation Area in Lancashire (above).

Big holes in the ground

Industry did not make these huge spoil heaps without creating equally large holes. Perhaps the best-known post-industrial hole is the 60m (200ft) deep pit at Bodelva near St Austell, where china clay had been dug since 1830. It was acquired by the Eden Trust in 1998 and turned into the Eden Project botanical garden.

Digging for gravel across central and southeast England to help fuel the post-war boom in road and house building has produced many wide, shallow holes. When the gravel is exhausted, the problem of what to do with the pits has often been solved by turning them into watersports and leisure parks. Cotswold Water Park in Gloucestershire consists of 133 lakes that have formed from the extraction of the rich gravel deposits of the Upper Thames Valley. The park, covering an area 50 per cent larger than the Norfolk Broads, has metamorphosed into a haven for wildlife such as otters and the rare water vole, as well as hosting 20,000 wintering wildfowl such as pochard, gadwall and tufted duck.

Flooded pits are also a feature of abandoned quarry workings, and many have become fishing lakes and diving centres. Stoney Cove's granite works in Leicestershire

From industry to fun The flooding of more than 100 gravel pits over an area of 40 square miles has created an ideal watersports venue at the Cotswold Water Park. With gravel extraction still going on in the area it is still set to expand.

Man-made peaks The processing of china clay at St Austell is Cornwall's largest industry. It has produced huge waste heaps, white and grey mini mountains of spoil known locally as the 'Cornish Alps'.

were active in the first half of the 20th century, but when work stopped in 1958, the quarry filled with natural spring water. With its terraced depths of 6m (20ft), 20m (66ft) and 35m (115ft), it is an ideal setting for the sport of diving.

Where quarries are still active, the holes remain. Whatley Quarry in the Mendip Hills of Somerset, worked for its limestone, ground up for the building industry, has produced a hole 1 mile long, 91m (300ft) deep and still growing. The Delabole slate quarry in Cornwall, active since at least the early 17th century, plunges 130m (425ft) below ground level, and has a circumference of 1½ miles. The Delabole Slate Company continues to remove 120 tons of slate block per day, but modern mining techniques have improved quarrying efficiency, ensuring that waste mountains are a thing of the past.

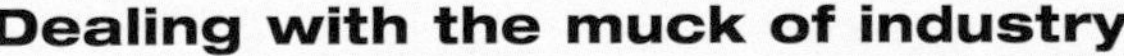

Dealing with the muck of industry

Although heaps and holes are immediately apparent, in some places the mark left by industry has been more insidious, the damage done in the days when there was nothing to stop the poisoning and polluting of the land. County Durham's coastal coalmining communities devastated their cliffs, beaches and sea by tipping colliery waste and raw sewage. But the beaches have been cleaned and the coal tips cleared and landscaped.

Particularly badly hit was the lower Swansea Valley, one of the largest areas of industrial dereliction in Europe, crowded with industrial plants that processed coal, zinc, tin, lead, steel and copper. In the 1960s a project was initiated to clean up the valley, and 20 years on the derelict buildings had gone and the soil cleaned of pollutants so that trees could be planted. Today the site is transformed – a landscaped mix of light industry, shopping centres and outdoor recreational facilities.

Live and let live In spite of the chemical works that dominate the horizon at Seal Sands, Teesmouth, the extensive mud flats form part of a National Nature Reserve, renowned for its waterfowl and seal species.

FIND OUT MORE

- *How Green Was My Valley* (Richard Llewellyn, Penguin Books, 1939).
- Dinton Pastures Country Park Gravel pits turned into lakes and islands. www.wokingham.gov.uk/leisure/parks-open-spaces/parks-open-spaces/dinton-pastures
- Stoney Cove National Diving Centre Story of the granite works. www.stoneycove.com
- Cotswold Water Park Information on leisure activities and wildlife. www.waterpark.org
- Delabole Slate Quarry Information on the quarry and its products. www.delaboleslate.co.uk
- Durham Heritage Coast Story of the coast's clean-up. www.turning-the-tide.org.uk
- Lower Swansea Valley Story of post-industrial transformation. www.swanseaheritage.net/themes/industry/index.asp

Seeing how the modern countryside has changed

If you were to travel back only about 70 years, much of the countryside would appear very different. You would see more hedges, more meadows and more people. The results of two remarkable surveys will help you to create a vivid picture of what rural life was like before intensive farming transformed the British landscape.

The National Farm Survey

A good way to capture the old pattern of farming before the days of mechanisation is to consult the National Farming Survey of 1941-3 (see also page 134). The wartime government, concerned to ensure the efficient production of food, investigated every farm of more than five acres – nearly 300,000 in all. Each farm was graded A, B or C, according to the competence of the farmer. You can find the records of this extensive survey at the National Archives at Kew and Edinburgh (see DIRECTORY).

- Look at the forms completed by the farmers, recording the size of the farm, the number of tractors, working horses and full-time staff, including land girls, the acreages devoted to cereals, root crops and grassland. By studying all the returns for your village or parish you can obtain a clear picture of local farming practices and management at the time.
- By reading the answers on the forms you will be able to see who had a water supply to the farmhouse, farm buildings and fields, whether electricity had been installed, and whether the farm was infested with rabbits, rats and mice, or wood pigeons.
- Look at the maps, based on the Ordnance Survey (OS), which were colour-washed to show the extent of each farm and its field boundaries. These will enable you to check for change or continuity with the present day.

The Valuation Office surveys

After the 1910 Finance Act, the Inland Revenue carried out surveys and valuations of all the land and property in Britain (see also page 140). Records for England and Wales are held at the National Archives at Kew (series IR 58, IR 121, IR 124-35). Those for Scotland are in the

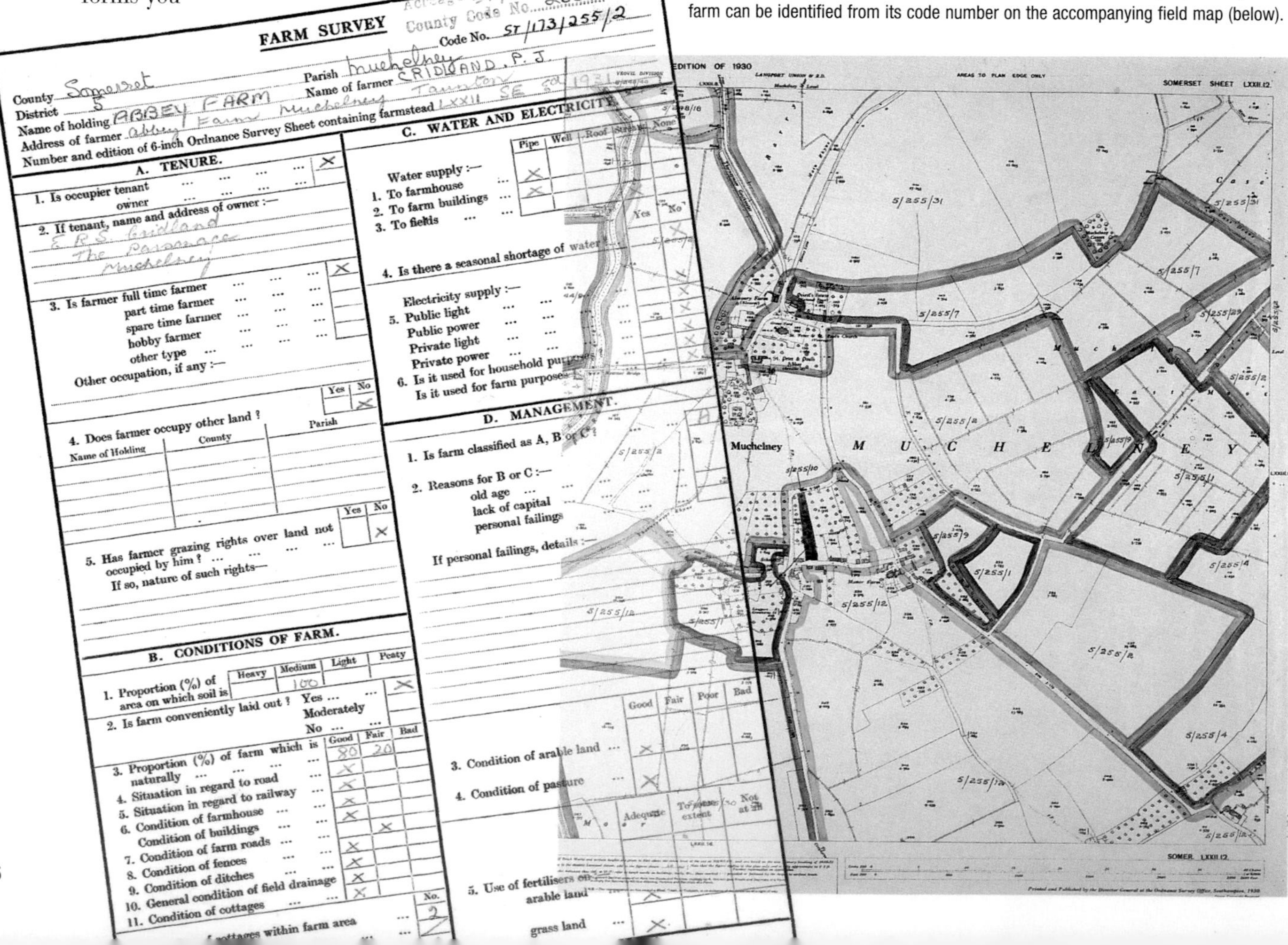

FARM SURVEY

Acreage = 196
County Code No. 255
Code No. ST/173/255/2

County Somerset
District 5
Parish Muchelney
Name of farmer CRIDLAND, P. J.
Name of holding ABBEY FARM
Address of farmer Abbey Farm Muchelney
Number and edition of 6-inch Ordnance Survey Sheet containing farmstead LXXII SE

A. TENURE.

1. Is occupier tenant ... X
   owner
2. If tenant, name and address of owner :— E. R. S. Cridland, The Parsonage, Muchelney
3. Is farmer full time farmer ... X
   part time farmer
   spare time farmer
   hobby farmer
   other type
   Other occupation, if any :—
4. Does farmer occupy other land ? Yes / No: X
   Name of Holding | County | Parish
5. Has farmer grazing rights over land not occupied by him ? Yes / No: X
   If so, nature of such rights—

B. CONDITIONS OF FARM.

1. Proportion (%) of area on which soil is — Heavy | Medium: 100 | Light | Peaty
2. Is farm conveniently laid out ? Yes ... X / Moderately / No
3. Proportion (%) of farm which is naturally — Good: 80 | Fair: 20 | Bad
4. Situation in regard to road — Good: X
5. Situation in regard to railway — Good: X
6. Condition of farmhouse — Good: X
   Condition of buildings — Fair: X
7. Condition of farm roads — Good: X
8. Condition of fences — Good: X
9. Condition of ditches — Good: X
10. General condition of field drainage — Good: X
11. Condition of cottages — Good: X
   No. of cottages within farm area — 2

C. WATER AND ELECTRICITY.

Water supply :— Pipe | Well | Roof | Stream | None
1. To farmhouse — X
2. To farm buildings — X
3. To fields
4. Is there a seasonal shortage of water — Yes | No: X
   Electricity supply :—
5. Public light — X
   Public power — X
   Private light — X
   Private power — X
6. Is it used for household purposes — X
   Is it used for farm purposes — X

D. MANAGEMENT.

1. Is farm classified as A, B or C ?
2. Reasons for B or C :—
   old age
   lack of capital
   personal failings
   If personal failings, details :—
3. Condition of arable land — Good: X | Fair | Poor | Bad
4. Condition of pasture — Good: X
5. Use of fertilisers on: Adequate | To some extent | Not at all
   arable land
   grass land — X

Top marks Answers on National Farm Survey questionnaires tell you who owned and worked a farm and how well it was run. At Abbey Farm in Muchelney, Somerset, the tennant farmer in 1942, a Mr Cridland, apparently did an excellent job (see left). The farm can be identified from its code number on the accompanying field map (below).

National Archives at Edinburgh (RS 51-88, IR 101-33). Local records may survive at your county record office.

- The records include the surveyors' field books and forms that were filled in by property owners. Farms and other properties referred to in the field books are identified on accompanying OS maps.
- Compare both 20th-century surveys with the tithe awards and maps of the 1830s and 40s (see pages 18-19) to see whether farms changed size and shape. Compare the amount of arable, meadow and pasture in the 1910s and 1940s with the same figures recorded a century earlier.

The look of farming today

Farming has altered radically since the Second World War. Food production has increased, yet fewer people are employed on the land – one person on a tractor can do the job of many agricultural labourers. Yet the rural landscape still hums with life that you can discover.

- Look out for newspaper reports about diversification, such as the growing of coriander in the Pennines for the Asian market in west Yorkshire, the construction of trout farms, the rearing of pheasants, or the setting up of farmers' markets for local food producers.
- At your local library or record office search for newspaper reports (see pages 74-75) and the archives of conservation bodies, such as the Council for the Protection of Rural England (see DIRECTORY).
- Look at how the countryside today is catering for leisure pursuits and tourism. Has rambling, climbing and cycling affected the local economy and the appearance of the landscape, with campsites, signposted paths, or farmhouse bed-and-breakfast and self-catering facilities? These are all part of the continuing evolution of our countryside.

Charting changes Notice how old farmhouses, outbuildings and field walls were constructed of local materials that blend into the landscape (see pages 38-39). Contrast these with the large modern farm buildings (above) that often look out of place. What has happened to the old outbuildings? Were some converted into housing? Talking to farmers and farmworkers is a good way of finding out about the huge changes that took place in the 20th century. You might discover why hedges were destroyed and what effect it had on bird and mammal populations; when silos replaced traditional haystacks; and what happened to the stables when horses were replaced by tractors.

Shot into shape If you live in an upland area of Britain, you may notice the distinctive patchwork appearance of local moors. This is because they are used for shooting grouse, and every 10-12 years stretches are burned to ensure a fresh supply of heather for the birds. Grouse moors in Britain (marked as squares on the map above) are shot less intensively than in their late-Victorian and Edwardian heyday (above right). Look for old or ruined shooting butts and cabins. At your county record office, search for enclosure awards and maps, and estate papers (see pages 18-19), which may reveal when a grouse-shooting moor came into being and how many birds were shot in a season.

EXPLORE YOUR COMMUNITY

The people, the streets, the churches, the workplaces, the shops and the public buildings – there are so many aspects to your village, town or city to explore. You can take to the open air, walk the pavements and look at the many clues all around you. Then search your local archives, where the many layers of your neighbourhood's story lie waiting to be discovered.

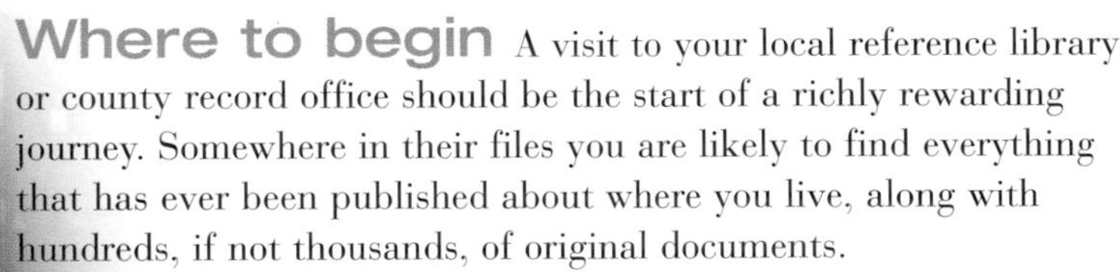

Where to begin A visit to your local reference library or county record office should be the start of a richly rewarding journey. Somewhere in their files you are likely to find everything that has ever been published about where you live, along with hundreds, if not thousands, of original documents.

- You could start by unearthing all you can about eminent local people, the sort that the Victorians would have called 'local worthies'. For details of those who achieved national fame, you should also look in *The Dictionary of National Biography* (60 vols, OUP, 2004; and on-line by subscription – see **www.oup.com/oxforddnb/info/**).
- Or you might be more interested in an infamous person like Spence Broughton, the highwayman whose gibbet stood in what is now Broughton Lane, Sheffield, for 35 years after he was hanged there, as a ghastly warning to wrongdoers. Local newspapers, prison records and court records will reveal those who strayed on to the wrong side of the law.

Doing some groundwork Before you tackle the reference libraries and record offices, see what you can find out about your area by walking around it and looking for clues to its history. Strolling through ancient streets, or around a market place or beside a canal, can often give you a better sense of the place than hours of pouring over documents.

Building up clues

Look closely at the architecture of your town or village. The design of a building and the material used to construct it can usually tell you much about its age and original use.

Easy dating Remember that many buildings have a datestone, possibly over the front door or up in the gable.
Mixed styles Buildings have often been altered or modified at different times. That smart Georgian front may be covering up an older timber-framed structure.
Names House names can hold clues to age. The Red House is likely to be an early brick building, and houses in Alma Street probably date back to around the time of the Crimean War battle of that name, fought in 1854.
Change of use Many buildings no longer serve their original purpose. A worn inscription might tell you that a house was once a school or the bingo hall was a cinema.

The working life

Some places have, or had, links with a particular trade. Look for any signs of this, which you could use along with old records to unravel the story of local industry.

What to ask Set out the questions you want answered before you start. When and why did an industry or activity begin? When was its heyday? When were factories or other work places abandoned?

Finding key features

A good way to start your research is to focus on an aspect of your town or area that gives it a distinctive identity. This could be a town square, a church or a river crossing.

What to ask Which is the oldest part of the town? Did the town grow continuously or were there periods of decline, followed by renewed growth? Are there landmarks to see, or documents to discover, that will provide clues to the town's early history?

Working backwards

To discover the origins of the place where you live, it is often easiest to begin with the well-documented 20th and 19th centuries and work backwards.

Easy start Be realistic and begin with topics that are the most likely to yield information quickly. Key records, such as census returns, tithe award maps and manor court rolls, are usually easily accessible at your local reference library or county record office (see pages 10-11).
Visual approach Old newspapers and parish magazines may contain photographs of significant events. A street party celebrating VE Day in 1945, or perhaps the opening of a factory or sinking of a mine shaft, could have been captured on camera. Local newspapers often have their own archives, but you could also look in the local library or British Library Newspapers (see DIRECTORY).

Window on to the past Old photographs can help you to step backwards in time. You may have family albums lurking in the attic, or you could search the archives of local newspapers, which are bound to have recorded major events, such as the procession in Wandsworth, London (below), to mark Edward VII's coronation in 1902.

FIND OUT MORE

- *Researching and Writing History* (David Dymond, British Association for Local History, 1999)
- *English Local History, An Introduction* (Kate Tiller, Sutton, 2002)
- *The Oxford Companion to Local and Family History* (David Hey ed., OUP, 1998)
- *The English Town* (Mark Girouard, Yale University Press, 1990)

Old photographs and oral history

Old photographs grab our attention and help us to pose questions that will unravel the past. Who are these people and what are they wearing? Where exactly was that building? Some answers may lie in local archives, and you might find that talking to an elderly relative or neighbour helps too.

People and places caught in time

The new art of photography developed quickly in the early years of Queen Victoria's reign. Enthusiasts began to use the new medium in the 1840s and 50s to create a visual record of where they lived. You might well find a photo of the parish church before the graveyard was tidied up or extended, or a view of labourers digging a railway cutting, or a shot of that new form of public transport: the horse-drawn omnibus.

Ordinary people, who could not afford painted portraits, were now able to have an accurate likeness recorded cheaply at the photographer's studio. The Victorians often appear so serious in those early shots, but that is often just the result of holding a smile for the long exposures required – usually several minutes – while a clamp was used to keep the head still. Spontaneous family 'snaps' only started to appear with the arrival of the Kodak Box Brownie camera, around 1900.

Civic pride Judging by the horse-drawn cab to the left of the picture and the fashions worn by the light scattering of people shown, the picture-postcard of Hereford High Street (above) was probably taken just before the First World War.

Picture-postcards The heyday of the picture-postcard was between 1900 and 1920, when cuts to working hours gave people more time to go on holiday or visit friends, and the speed of the railways meant the swift delivery of posted messages. People took pride in sending friends and family an image of their town square or parish church.

The Postcard Traders Association on **www.postcard.co.uk** can help you to find and date picture-postcards, and many are included in the books and archives given below.

WHERE TO FIND OLD PHOTOGRAPHS

The invention of photography has bequeathed to us a detailed visual record of the years from the mid-19th century onward.

The local bookshop Towns and villages throughout Britain have been chronicled in books of old photographs. These often form part of a series, such as 'Britain in Old Photographs', published by Sutton (far left) or 'Images of England', published by Tempus (left) perhaps in co-operation with a local history society. Each book serves as a complete pictorial 'essay' on a community, and will include street and workplace scenes, records of special events such as coronation celebrations, Whitsuntide processions, Sunday School outings, annual fairs and weekly markets, and snaps of football teams, brass bands and church choirs. The best have informative captions.

Libraries and museums Most public reference libraries and some museums have large collections of local photographs. Some of these images are now available on-line (see page 17).

The National Archives at Kew (see DIRECTORY) An extensive collection, dating from 1842 to 1912, is catalogued at the National Archives in a series known as COPY 1. Other important collections are in the National Museums of Scotland and the National Library of Wales, Aberystwyth (see DIRECTORY).

The Rural History Centre Around 750,000 images of all aspects of rural life (particularly in the south of England), from the mid-19th century to the present, is stored in the Centre's archives, which are housed at the University of Reading in Berkshire (see DIRECTORY). See also 'Rediscovering rural life in old photographs' on pages 50-51.

Using oral history

Valuable information about the lives of ordinary citizens in the past was rarely written down and can be recovered only from talking to old people. George Ewart Evans was the first person to use this 'oral history' technique in a systematic way. He wrote a series of books, starting with *Ask the Fellows Who Cut the Hay* (Faber, 1956), which he based on the memories of men and women who were born in the last quarter of the 19th century and had lived and worked most of their lives in the Suffolk village of Blaxhall. His final book, *Spoken History* (Faber, 1987), is a summary of his work.

Evans showed that what had previously been dismissed as 'mere hearsay' was an invaluable, detailed explanation of a former way of life that was hardly mentioned in documentary sources. Oral history can give a realistic account of daily life, household arrangements and working practices. This is often the only way to learn how, for instance, hand-tools were used or meals were cooked.

- Record your own memories first. This will alert you to what questions to ask and may be useful to others.
- When you first visit someone whose memories you want to record, take along some old photographs to get them talking.
- *Oral History for Local Historians* (Stephen Caunce, Longman, 1994) is packed with good advice on interviewing techniques.

A way of life preserved One of the most widely acclaimed of the early photographers was Frank Meadow Sutcliffe. He moved to Whitby on the north Yorkshire coast in 1870 and over the next 40 years took hundreds of vivid and detailed photographs of the port and its people, leaving to posterity a unique record of the fishermen and their families.

Reading the images Few old photographs have names or dates on them, so you may have to learn to spot the visual clues they hold. Postcards can be easier to place, because there is often a dated message on the back. The following pointers should help guide you on your way:

- Look at buildings in the background that can be dated.

- Look at hairstyles and dress, which may also suggest a date.
- Ask why a photograph may have been taken, and by whom.
- Be aware that any customs, crafts or activities recorded may have been curious survivals rather than typical of the time.
- *Family Photographs 1860-1945* (Robert Pols, The National Archives, 2002) is a useful guide to interpreting old images.

FIND OUT MORE

Many books of personal memoirs give accounts of local communities in the fairly recent past. Some fine examples are:

- *Lark Rise to Candleford* (Flora Thompson, OUP, 1945) Rural life in 19th-century Oxfordshire.
- *Speak for England* (Melvyn Bragg, Secker & Warburg, 1976) Reminiscences of people in Wigton, Cumbria.
- *A Woman's Place: An Oral History of Working Class Women, 1890-1940* (Elizabeth Roberts, Blackwell, 1995).
- *Yorkshire Fisherfolk* (Peter Frank, Phillimore, 2002) Illustrated by numerous old photographs.
- *A Local Habitation: Life and Times, 1918-1940* (Richard Hoggart, OUP, 1989) A working-class childhood in early 20th-century Leeds.
- *The Road to Nab End* (William Woodruff, Abacus, 2002). Growing up in a Lancashire cotton-mill town just after the First World War.

A selection of good on-line sources of old photographs (including picture-postcards) is given on pages 16-17 in the 'Getting started' section.

Maps and plans

Unfold a map of your district and you immediately start to ask questions. Why is my village no more than a church, a farm and a few cottages, when its neighbour is large and sprawling? Why is the railway so far out of town? Why do some areas, such as the parish of Sandal Magna in Wakefield, Yorkshire, have such ancient-sounding names, while districts close-by have more modern names? A map can give you a feel for the distinctive character of a place.

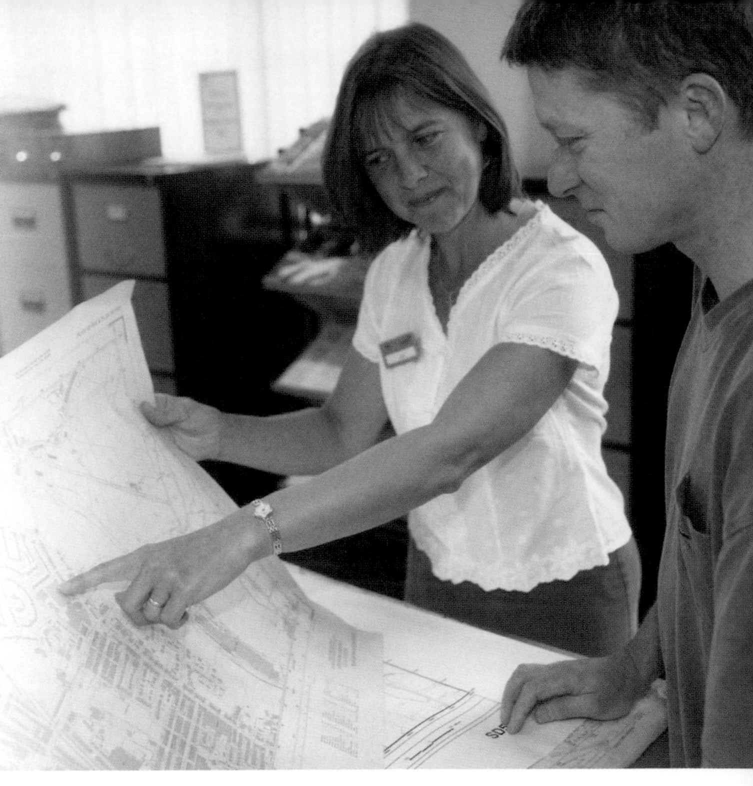

Forward thinking Make the most of any archive by phoning ahead to explain the purpose of your visit and, if possible, to enlist some expert help. You will be amazed at how much information you gather in a short space of time with such assistance.

Mapping out the past

Old maps can provide snapshots of an area at various points in its history. Compare them with modern aerial photographs to see if medieval features, such as moats and castle mounds, can still be identified on the ground and to judge how a place has grown, or perhaps shrunk. Look at other records from about the same date as your maps. There should be a census return (see pages 76-77) recording the inhabitants of your town or village at about the time the first Ordnance Survey map (see below) of the area was drawn up, or a directory (see pages 74-75) listing the various types of tradesmen. Try placing these people in the houses shown on your map.

Ordnance Survey maps

One of the best starting points for exploring the history of your community is an Ordnance Survey (OS) map. They are readily available, cover the whole of Britain and take you back quickly and easily from the present day to well into the 19th century (see page 18). Comparing OS maps of Barlow in Derbyshire (below) shows how they can provide a broad framework of developments in a community over the last two centuries, raising questions, possibly about changes in employment or the origin of place names, that can be answered by looking elsewhere.

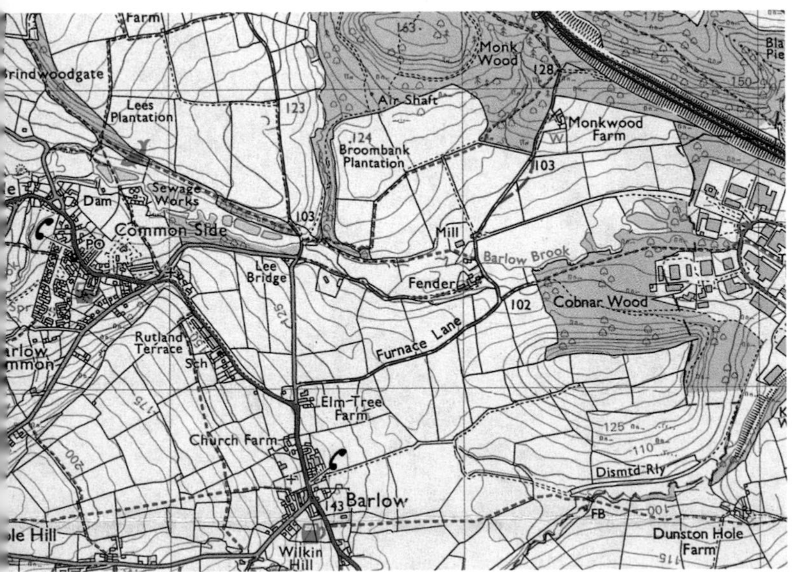

The here and now The up-to-date OS Explorer series map (see page 18) shows that the parish of Barlow has the small village of Barlow at its centre with a larger settlement, Common Side (likely to be the site of former common land), half a mile to the north. A row of houses called Rutland Terrace stands in between, and there are numerous scattered farms and extensive woods, including Monk Wood (bisected by the A61 trunk road) and Cobnar Wood, which is encroached upon by a trading estate.

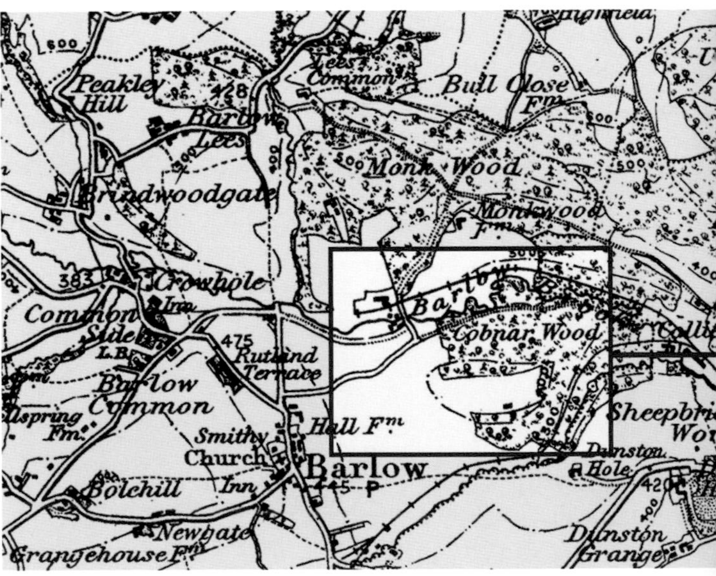

Looking back On the 1-inch OS map, published in 1907, no trunk road or trading estate is present, but a railway line passes through the lower part of Cobnar Wood towards a coal mine and an ironworks (Sheepbridge Works). Rutland Terrace is marked and Common Side is smaller than today. An earlier first edition 1-inch OS map of the area, based on a survey of 1837-9, shows no Rutland Terrace and few houses at Common Side, but the same underlying pattern of farms, fields and woods.

Tithe-award maps

You might be able to follow your community farther back in time using a tithe award and its map from your local archives (see page 19). These were drawn up between 1836 and 1852 for 11,395 parishes, listing all the properties in each area, which were plotted on the map and numbered. The size and use of each property is given, along with owners' and tenants' names.

- A tithe-award map, drawn on a large but not uniform scale, is often the earliest detailed map available of your parish or township. Compare it with a first edition six-inch OS map (see page 18) of the area, which is likely to have been drawn several decades later. Check whether features such as a railway or an industrial site marked on the OS map were there at the time of the tithe award.
- See if you can match families recorded in the 1841 and 1851 census returns (see pages 76-77) for your area to names of owners and tenants listed in the tithe award and to the farms and cottages on the map.

Dividing up the community Beedon in Berkshire was granted its first enclosure award in 1843 (inset), which lists the distribution of parcels of land around the village, including those given to Queen's College, shown on the attached map (above).

Enclosure-award maps

Many English and Welsh parishes have a parliamentary enclosure award with a map attached, usually dating from between 1750 and 1850. Altogether, 5341 awards were granted for England and 229 for Wales. The enclosures in Scotland were mostly private and few maps survive.

You can view enclosure awards and their maps at the National Archives (see DIRECTORY), or you could try your local record offices (see pages 10-11).

- Note how the land was distributed by an enclosure award: how much was allotted to the local lord, the church or the poor, or perhaps as a quarry or gravel pit for maintaining the highways (see pages 60-61).
- Look for the letter 'T' next to a field boundary. It tells you that the owner of the land on which it is marked is responsible for maintaining the wall or fencing along that boundary. Awards also set out rights of way along footpaths and mark public roads and watercourses.

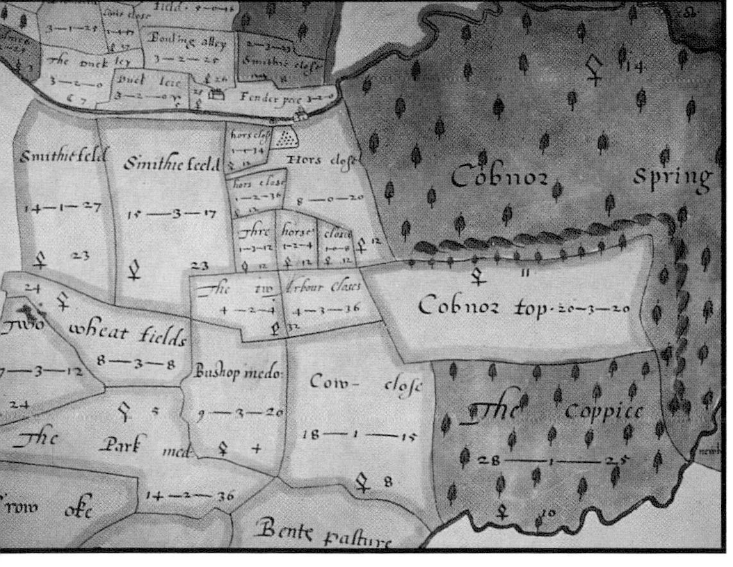

Marking territory In 1630, the land around Barlow was mapped out on behalf of the Cavendish family, who held estates there until 1813, when they passed to the Dukes of Rutland (note Rutland Terrace on the OS maps, left). These maps tell you that by this date only one cottage had been erected at Common Side and that Cobnar (spelt 'Cobnor') Wood had much the same shape as it does today. The present pattern of farmsteads, fields and woodland appears to have been well established.

Estate maps

You may strike lucky and find that your area appears on a map, or 'platt', that accompanied a survey of a manor or estate dating as far back as the late 16th or 17th centuries. These estate maps (see page 19) are mainly concerned with establishing boundaries and ownership, field names and, in a few cases, land-use. You will find them at both national and local record offices, mostly dating from the 18th and 19th centuries. Some of the earliest ones, including around 60 maps of the Duchy of Lancaster from before 1603, survive in the National Archives (see DIRECTORY).

FIND OUT MORE

- Current OS maps can be found on www.ordnancesurvey.co.uk
- *Reproductions of the First Edition One-inch OS Maps of England and Wales* (J.B. Harley ed., David and Charles, 1969-71)
- The Godfrey Edition, a series of reprints of more than 1700 old maps. www.alangodfreymaps.co.uk
- The complete collection of six-inch OS maps, 1846-99 can be viewed on www.old-maps.co.uk

Newspapers and directories

You can learn all sorts about your neighbourhood and its former inhabitants from old copies of local newspapers. They are crammed with information: announcements of births, marriages and deaths; lengthy obituaries of prominent local people; advertised businesses and sales; court cases and bankruptcies; sporting and social events. Consulting gazetteers or trade directories should fill in many of the gaps and answer questions raised by your research, helping you to forge a vivid impression of your community's past.

Where to find newspapers

Most local reference libraries hold old copies of local newspapers, and sometimes local record offices (see pages 10-11) keep them too. They are usually available only on microfilm, because they tear easily. The following places are also good sources.

- British Library Newspapers (see DIRECTORY), in Colindale, north London, houses back copies of every British newspaper, national and local. A catalogue and details of opening hours and facilities can be viewed on **www.bl.uk/collections/newspapers.html**
- The National Library of Wales (see DIRECTORY) and the Bodleian Library, Oxford (see DIRECTORY), also hold large newspaper collections. Many Scottish newspapers are held on microfilm at county record offices.
- *Local Newspapers, 1750-1920* (J. Gibson, B. Langston and B.W. Smith, 2nd ed., Federation of Family History Societies, 2002) tells you which local newspapers are kept where, throughout Britain.

Using newspapers Although your search is likely to require a long session at a microfilm reader, your efforts should be well rewarded. You may also find that the newspapers you want to look at have been indexed.

- Allow yourself time to become familiar with the format of a newspaper. You will soon get to know which sections to look at carefully and which to skip.
- Read the advertisements – they can be as informative as any news article, telling you about local business and what was for sale. You may learn when gas burners were first installed in local kitchens or when new fashions caught on in your area.
- If you are interested in entertainment and sport, newspapers are one of the richest sources of information, from details of weekly whist drives to the achievements of the local football and cricket teams.

Gazetteers

During the 19th century, several dictionaries of British places, or gazetteers, were published. The following are most likely to offer information on your area.

- Samuel Lewis's 'Topographical Dictionaries' for England, Wales and Scotland, with an atlas, appeared between 1831 and 1849. They contain brief histories of towns and villages with population figures and notes on businesses and local institutions. Copies are available at large reference libraries and at the British Library (see **www.bl.uk/collections/map_gazetteers.html** for details). A CD of them can be ordered from **www.genealogy.com**
- J. M. Wilson's *The Imperial Gazetteer of England and Wales* (1870) and *The Imperial Gazetteer of Scotland* (1882) give more detailed information. Again large reference libraries usually hold copies.

BRIGHTON & HOVE HERALD 22/4/44

YOUR TRUSTEE SAVINGS BANK is at 30, NEW RD., BRIGHTON 128, CHURCH RD., HOVE

BRIGHTON AND HOVE HERALD

DRINK AND ENJOY KEMP TOWN BREWERY I.P.A. Brighton's Best Bitter

Registered at the G.P.O. as a Newspaper. Telephone: BRIGHTON 6001 (3 lines).

SATURDAY, APRIL 22, 1944

POSTAGE: Inland 1½d. Foreign and Colonial, 1d. H.M. Forces and Ships Abroad, 1d.

PRICE THREEPENCE

No. 7189

Nazi Night Raider Crashes in Churchyard of South Coast Town

NO CASUALTIES: BUT HOUSES EVACUATED

Dead Pilot Was Wearing Iron Cross

BELIEVED to have been hit over London, a Messerschmitt fighter-bomber, attempting to return to its base, crashed early on Wednesday morning in a South Coast town. The crippled plane fell in the roadway and crashed through a wall into the churchyard of an ancient and historic church, the "mother church" of the town.

The pilot—who was wearing an Iron Cross—was killed, his body being found hanging with his parachute on the branches of a tree on the opposite side of the road. Fortunately there were no civilian casualties, though a number of residents in the district were temporarily evacuated from their homes owing to the presence of one or more unexploded bombs.

N.F.S. and wardens were quickly on the scene, and firemen fought the flames despite the danger of exploding ... Flares carried by the plane also ignited. The ... lamp standard, which was bent in the ... into the wall ...

Another view of the wreckage of the Nazi raider brought down in the early hours of Wednesday, showing an unexploded bomb lying in the crater made by the plane just inside the churchyard.

The tall and part of the fuselage of the Messerschmitt fighter-bomber after it had crashed in a churchyard of a South Coast town in the early hours of Wednesday.

Absent From Duty

CIVIL DEFENCE NURSE FINED

A NURSE formerly attached to a mobile first-aid party in the Portslade Civil Defence Service figured in a case before the Hove County Magistrates on Monday, when she was alleged to have absented herself from Civil Defence duties.

The defendant was Constance Kirby, a married woman, whose ... was given as Lockbridge- ...

Young Lecturer's Tragic Death

"SENT TO BRIGHTON AGAINST HIS WILL"

THE circumstances which led a young man—a B.Sc. and lecturer on civil engineering at Brighton Technical College—to take his life were not fully established at the inquest held yesterday (Friday) on Arthur Henry Williamson, aged 20, of Maldon-road, by the Borough Coroner (Mr Charles Webb).

It was stated that deceased had been refused permission by the ...

SIX MONTHS FOR PACIFIST

Lover Of Freedom Who Said "No" To Medical

A 19-YEAR-OLD Crowborough pacifist, Anthony Peter Harry Whittam, son of a Royal Air Force officer, was sent to prison for six months with hard labour at Brighton on Thursday. He failed to comply with an order to submit himself for a medical examination.

Whittam, described by his mother as "a great lover of freedom and justice," was before the Court the previous day, when he ... to submit himself ... he refused ...

New Principal Of Technical College

DR. G. E. WATTS

THE new head of Brighton Technical College is Dr. Gordon Edward Watts. He is M.A., Ph.D., B.Sc., F.R.I.C., and has been vice-principal since 1936.

Dr. Watts' appointment was this week approved by the Education Committee.

"I am looking forward to the work ahead," he told a *Herald* reporter, "and particularly to the opportunity we shall have for further development in the post-war period. We look for very great expansion in several directions."

Dr. Watts has been at the college since September, 1930, ... appointed a lecturer ...

BRIGHTON AND HOVE'S "SALUTE" WEEK

£1,500,000 in Sight

BUT STRENUOUS EFFORTS NEEDED TO-DAY

BRIGHTON and Hove's spectacular "Salute the Soldier" Week closes to-day (Saturday). The ambitious target of £1,500,000 is in sight, but strenuous efforts will be needed in the final effort to-day if success is to be achieved. Figures at the close of each day of the campaign so far have been:

Saturday	£231,303
Monday	£401,008
Tuesday	£601,239
Wednesday	£779,284
Thursday	£1,000,789

Complete figures for yesterday (Friday) will not be available until this morning, but the *Herald* was informed that by the afternoon the total was approaching £1,200,000 ... This means that the last day will have to be the biggest of the Week.

Some £300,000 is still required if the million and a h... is to be reached. It is a stiff challenge, and only a determi... effort by large and small investors alike will bring success.

From the opening by Field Marshal Sir Cyril Deverell ... the impressive drumhead service at the Dome on Sunday ... "Salute the Soldier" Week has proved a great stimulus to ... Savings movement in the two towns. All sections of the ... munity have made their daily "salute," and to-day the ... closes on a final note of pageantry—a triumphant note, ... confidently hoped—with "Mayor's Salute."

IMPRESSIVE OPENING PAGEANT

"MAYORS' SALUTE" TO-DAY

A step into history
Reading a wartime newspaper (right) can be one of the best ways of understanding the details of day-to-day life at the time. D-Day was less than six weeks away when this Brighton paper was published.

Community 'portraits' The earliest trade directories appeared in the late 17th century, listing useful addresses for merchants and businessmen, but the more detailed ones, likely to be of most value to you, date from the 19th and early 20th centuries. The first national series was published by James Pigot between 1814 and 1853. William White was another notable mid-19th-century directory publisher, but the best-known is Frederic Kelly, whose first directories appeared in 1845. Kelly's directories dominated the market right up to the early 1970s, when they finally ceased publication, superseded by the Telephone Directory and Yellow Pages.

Trade and commercial directories

The sense of what a town or district was like to live in at a particular time is often captured in its trade directories. They identify the main property owners ('principal inhabitants'), name the shopkeepers, and list the various tradesmen who helped to give a place its unique character.

Some cities, such as Birmingham and Sheffield, have directories dating from the late 18th century. Soon after, smaller towns were being covered and by the 1830s the first county directories appeared. Within a decade, trade directories for all parts of Britain were being issued every couple of years.

Where to find directories Reference libraries and record offices have large collections of local directories on their shelves. Pages can usually be photocopied.

- The Family Records Centre (see DIRECTORY) has several hundred English and Welsh directories on computer.
- The London Metropolitan Archives (see DIRECTORY) has a set of London directories on microfilm, but the largest London collection, as well as a major national one, is housed at the Guildhall Library (see DIRECTORY).
- Directories for many counties have been published on CD. A full list is available on **www.genealogysupplies.com**

What you will find in directories Most directories from the mid 19th century onwards will contain the following:

1 A long (though often unreliable) account of the history, topography and economy of the county or district.

2 A list of important towns, followed by their surrounding villages. Some late Victorian directories divide the entries for towns into street sections, which are accompanied by detailed pull-out maps.

3 Local administrative units, such as parishes, townships and manors, are named and described, giving an insight into how your community was organised in the past.

4 An introduction to each group of settlements, covering local history, land ownership and tenures, and the nature of the economy. The population figure from the most recent census is also noted.

5 Names, addresses and occupations of 'principal inhabitants' and classified entries for various tradesmen, arranged alphabetically.

6 Details of railways, coaches and other transport services.

Directory. North Wales.

BALA AND NEIGHBOURHOOD.

BALA is a small market town, township and borough, by prescription, in the parish of Llanycill, hundred of Penllyn, county of Merioneth; 198 miles N. W. from London, 12 S. W. from Corwen, and 18 N. E. from Dolgelley; seated on level ground, near to the lake of Bala, from which the name of the town is derived, as well as the chief celebrity that belongs to it. This lake, a fine expanse of pellucid water, is about ten miles in circumference, four in length, in some parts one mile across, and more than one hundred feet in depth; surrounded by hills and well stored with fish, among which are found the char and the gwyniad; the latter resembling the salmon in shape, and the trout in flavour. The use of nets is strictly prohibited, but angling freely permitted; and in the proper season the water is much resorted to for that purpose. The river Dee, which has two spring heads in the eastern part of Merionethshire, after uniting, are supposed to pass through this pool,—without mixing its waters with those of the lake; after leaving which it runs into Denbighshire, when, turning north, it washes the walls of Chester, and falls into the Irish sea. Bala is entitled to the rank of a corporation town, and, formerly, it is said to have enjoyed some valuable privileges, which have nearly—if not altogether—become obsolete, and its municipal consequence has gone much to decay: the spring assizes for the county are, however, still held here. The manufacture of flannel and hosiery, together with tanning and wool-stapling, are now the principal branches of trade.

The places of worship are the chapel of ease to Llanycil, and one each for Calvinists, Independents and Wesleyan Methodists. Here is a free grammar school, the patronage of which is in the principal and fellows of Jesus' College, Oxford. Near the town are the remains of three Roman camps, supposed to have been used as exploratory stations, before the Ordovices were subdued. The market is held on Saturday; and there are four fairs for cattle, viz. 14th May, 10th July, 24th October, and 8th November, that on the 10th of July is also for lambs. The township of Bala contained, in 1821, 1,163 inhabitants; in 1831 the population was returned with the parish;—and in 1841 it numbered 1,255. The entire parish of Llanycil contained, at the last-named period, 2,467 persons.

POST OFFICE, Chapel-street, Samuel Thomas, *Post Master.*—Letters from LONDON and all parts (DOLGELLEY and BARMOUTH excepted) arrive every afternoon at thirty-seven minutes past one, and are de- patched every morning at nine.—Letters from DOLGELLEY and BARMOUTH arrive every morning at a quart before nine, and are despatched every afternoon at two.

GENTRY AND CLERGY.
Anwell Rice, Esq. Vron Dderw
Anwill Robert, Esq. High st
Davies John, Esq. Vronhenlog
Edwards Rev. Lewis, High st
Evans Samuel, Esq. magistrate, Bodweni
Greenwood Thos. Esq. Brynraber
Griffiths Edward, Esq. Grien yn
Griffiths Rev. Thomas, Vicarage
Harrop Jonah, Esq. Aberhirnant
Hopwood Capt. Edward John Gregg, Fachdeiliog
Jones Rev. Hugh, Llangowen
Jones Rev. John, Bryn derfel
Jones Mr. John, the Lodge
Jones Miss Margaret, High st
Lloyd Rev. David M. Pale
Lloyd George Price, Esq. magistrate, High st
Price Rev. Peter, Rectorage
Price Richard Watkin, Esq. magistrate, Rhiwlas
Thomson Rev. William, High st
Williams Rev. John, Glanhirnant

ACADEMIES AND SCHOOLS.
CHARITY SCHOOL, Chapel street—Robert Lewis, master
Edwards Rev. Lewis, High st
FREE GRAMMAR SCHOOL, High st—David Edwards, master
Maddocks Elizabeth (ladies' boarding), Pen y bont
NATIONAL SCHOOL, Llanawr—Jos. Jones, master

BOOT AND SHOE MAKERS.
Davies Hugh, Chapel st
Davies John, Chapel st
Davies Morris, High st
Hughes David, Llanawr
Jones Jacob, High st
Jones John, High st
Jones William, Llanawr
Roberts Moses, High st
Roberts Richard, Plassa
Thomas John, Chapel st

BUTCHERS.
Roberts Cadwallader, High st
Rowlands Thomas, New Chapel st

CHYMISTS AND DRUGGISTS.
Jones Thomas, Chapel st
Jones Wm. (and ironmonger), High st

CURRIERS AND LEATHER SELLERS.
Hughes William, High st
Roberts Edward, Chapel st

EARTHENWARE DEALERS.
Richards John, High st
Richards Thomas, Chapel st

FIRE, &c. OFFICE AGENTS.
CROWN (life) AND FARMERS' AND GENERAL, Isaac Gilbertson, High st
PALLADIUM (fire and life), John Jones, Chapel st

FLANNEL MANUFACTURERS.
Jones Robert (and grocer & draper), High st [Plassa

INNS AND PUBLIC HOUSES
Bull's Head Inn, Jane Davies, High
Eagles, Margaret Jones, High st
Goat, Edward Rowlands, High st
King's Head, Hugh Hughes, High
White Lion Hotel (& posting hous and excise office), William Jone High street

Retailers of Beer.
Evans Peter, High st
Jones Robert, Llanawr
Jones Thomas, High st
Lewis Margaret, High st
Owens Owen, High st
Parry Thomas, High st
Roberts John, Chapel st
Rowlands David, High st
Rowlands John, High st

LINEN DRAPERS.
See under the head Grocers,

MILLINERS & DRESS MAKRS.
Evans Catherine (and straw hat maker), Mount st
Pugh Catherine & Lucy (and straw hat makers), Chapel st
Saunderson Sarah, High st

SADDLERS.
Evans Thomas, High st
Jones Griffith (and fishing tackle maker), High st

SHOPKEEPERS & DEALERS IN

Who was who A Victorian trade directory, like the one for Bala, north Wales (right), may offer more than just information about the structure of your community at the time. You might discover something new about an ancestor or a local notable.

WATCH OUT

Do not expect a directory to list everyone living in an area at the date given. It will not record those of humble status, such as servants and labourers.

FIND OUT MORE

- **www.archivecdbooks.org** A range of reproduction copies and CDs of old British journals and newspapers can be ordered from the on-line catalogue.
- **www.historicaldirectories.org** An on-line library of English and Welsh trade directories, dating from 1750 to 1919.

Census returns

The census books for 1801 to 1901 provide a decade-by-decade review of Britain in a century of unprecedented change. Find out the names of the people who once lived in your street or village, how they earned a living, and even where they were born. By working through the returns you can build a clear picture of how your community has evolved.

A glimpse into the past An 1891 census return for Zetland Road in Bristol shows a street of villas inhabited by the families of middle class tradesmen, including a commercial traveller and sugar broker. The households were small and each had one or two servants.

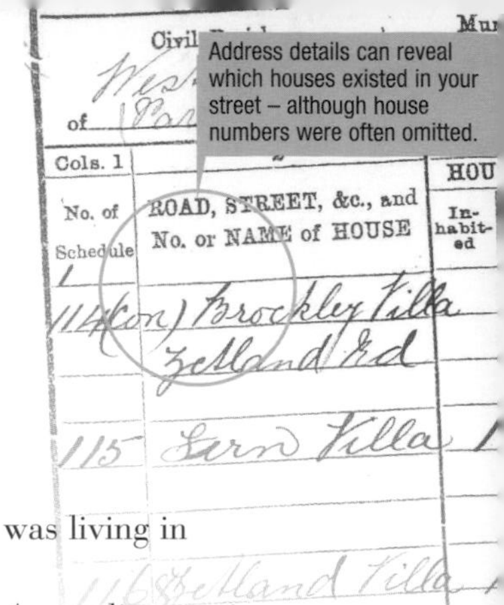

Address details can reveal which houses existed in your street – although house numbers were often omitted.

What the census can tell you

The first census was taken in 1801, but the enumerators' returns, which give personal details, do not survive before the census of 1841. With each census the returns gave more information, recording age, gender, birthplace and occupation. Census surveys are closed for 100 years, so the most recent survey that you can access is the 1901 census. Start your research here and work backwards to piece together the story of your community.

The 1901 returns These are the easiest records to access and use. They are available on-line (see below) and are fully indexed so you can search by street. Simply type in your address to find out who was living in your street in 1901.

The 1891 and 1881 returns An on-line service provides access to the 1891 and 1881 census records via the National Archives' website and other websites (see below). Although designed primarily for family history research, you can browse the records to find your street. Records are grouped by county, then by parish and then by enumeration district – the area that a census worker, or enumerator, could cover in a day. Click on the links next to the district numbers to see descriptions of the areas covered. When you have located your street, click on the link for the relevant district number to see the record. You can also view census returns at your local records office or the Family Records Centre in London (see below), who will give advice on how to use them.

WHERE TO FIND CENSUS RECORDS

The easiest way to access the returns is on the internet but they are also available at many record offices.

FOR ENGLAND AND WALES

On-line records for the 1901 census are available on a pay-per-view basis at **www.1901census.nationalarchives.gov.uk.** All census records from 1841-1891 can now be viewed on-line at **www.nationalarchives.gov.uk/census/.** There is a fee to download information and images from a census entry. You may access the 1841, 1851, 1861, 1871, 1881 and 1891 on-line census records free on site at The National Archives in Kew and the Family Records Centre in Islington, courtesy of Ancestry.co.uk.

In addition to the National Archives, other principal providers for the census returns for England and Wales are:

1841 www.ancestry.co.uk; www.britishorigins.com
1851 www.ancestry.co.uk
1861 www.ancestry.co.uk; www.findmypast.com
1871 www.ancestry.co.uk; www.britishorigins.com
1881 www.ancestry.co.uk
1891 www.ancestry.co.uk
1901 www.ancestry.co.uk

Local record offices and city reference libraries normally have copies of census returns on microfilm or microfiche for the relevant county.

The Family Records Centre (see DIRECTORY) holds census records for 1841 to 1891 on microfilm and the 1901 returns are stored on microfiche.

The National Archives (see DIRECTORY) has microfiche copies of the 1901 census returns.

The National Library at Aberystwyth (see DIRECTORY) has copies of all Welsh records and those for the border counties of Cheshire, Shropshire and Herefordshire.

FOR SCOTLAND

Libraries and county record offices hold copies of local returns.

The National Archives of Scotland (see DIRECTORY) holds returns for 1841-1901 on microfilm or microfiche.

On-line returns for Scotland from 1841-1901 are available at **www.scotlandspeople.gov.uk.** Images and indexes are available for all years with the exception of images for 1881 which are not available.

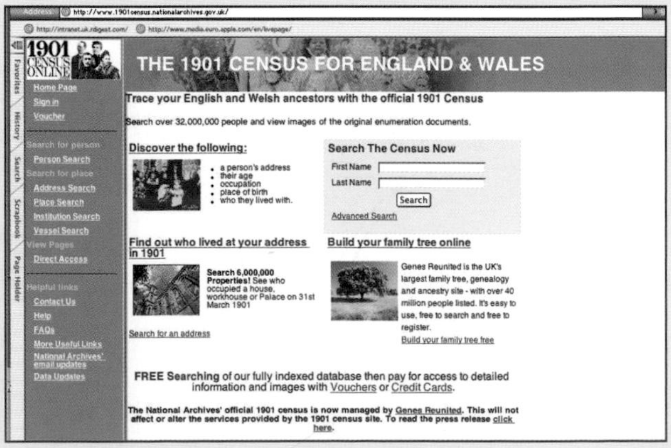

Occupations such as weaver, miner or shepherd give a good indication of the main industries and jobs in the area at the time.

Birthplace details can highlight patterns of migration as people were often forced to leave home to find work elsewhere.

Names of people living in your street or village can tell you who the long-standing families in the local community were.

Returns from 1841 to 1871 These are now available on-line. The more recent the returns the more informative they are. The earliest survey to include personal details was the 1841 census but the information is not detailed.

- Relationships between household members are not given.
- The returns record the ages of children under 15 but round all other ages down to the nearest 5.
- Birthplaces are not recorded. People were simply asked if they were born in the county of their current address.

The census pitfalls

Census records are a mine of useful information but there are certain drawbacks that you should bear in mind.

- The reliability of the information depends on the statements given by householders and the accuracy of the copies that were made.
- There are sometimes discrepancies in details such as age and place of birth from one census to the next.
- Entries for occupations may appear to be inconsistent. A man might have been recorded as a weaver when he also had a small farm. Agricultural labourers often took on other jobs, especially during the winter.

FIND OUT MORE

These sources offer helpful information on finding and using census records.

- *Making Use of the Census* (Susan Lumas, PRO Publications, 2002)
- *Using Census Returns: A Pocket Guide to Family History* (PRO Publications, 2002)
- *The Genealogist's Internet* (Peter Christian, The National Archives, 3rd edition, 2005)
- **www.genuki.org.uk/big/census_place.html** A searchable database of places in the 1891 census.
- **www.nationalarchives.gov.uk/pathways/census/** An on-line exhibition shows how the 1901 census records have helped to reconstruct the history of four communities.

Hearth tax returns

To build up a picture of the people who lived in your community before the 19th century, consult the 17th-century hearth tax returns. These list the heads of households who were liable to pay a tax on chimneys and provide information on their occupations. The tax was collected twice yearly between 1662 and 1688 in England and Wales, and returns survive for the years 1662-6 and 1669-74. Hearths in Scotland were taxed between 1691 and 1695.

- The number of hearths on which tax was paid reflects the size and comfort of the house and can give a good idea of the owner's social standing in a community.
- They also show the distribution of surnames: many distinctive names were still confined to the places where they originated.

WHERE TO FIND HEARTH TAX RETURNS

- The original returns are stored at the National Archives in Kew and the National Archives of Scotland (see DIRECTORY).
- Returns survive for half of the English counties and Glamorganshire. Enquire at your record office if anything has been published for your county.
- A project based at the Roehampton University (see DIRECTORY) aims to make available microfilm and printed editions of returns for all counties.

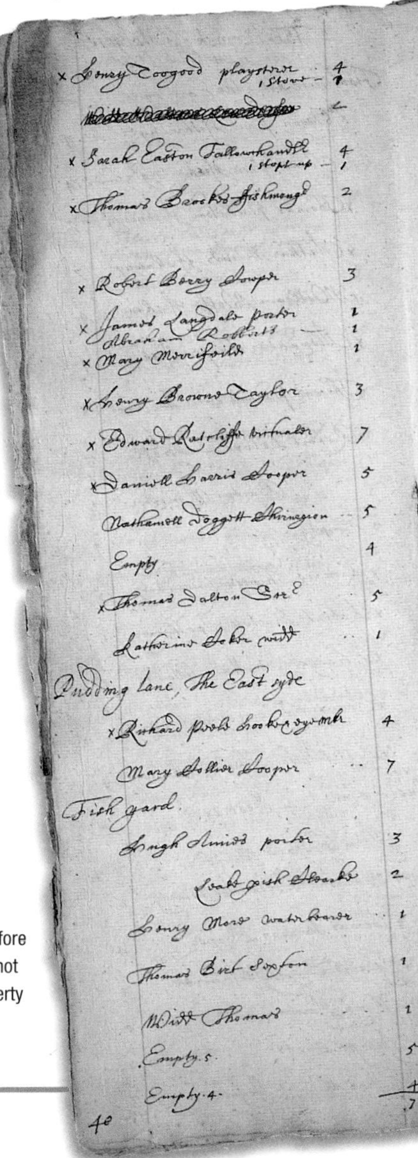

A wealth of hearths A tax return for Pudding Lane, London, in 1666 – just before the Great Fire broke out there – reveals not only the number of hearths in each property but the occupations of the tradesmen, including a fishmonger and a draper.

The records of Scotland

Before 1603, when James VI of Scotland also became James I of England, the Scots had a history that was totally separate from that of England and Wales. Even after that date, despite the union of the two parliaments in 1707, they followed a path of their own in many respects, particularly in relation to law, education and religion. You will therefore come across many records that are unique to Scotland.

A local start

As in the rest of Britain, the best place to begin your search is likely to be on home ground – at your local history centre or reference library. Many will hold treasure troves of material on your town or village, including old maps, indexes of newspapers and census records. You usually have to visit to find out exactly what is available, as few have catalogues on-line. Look in the phone directory for addresses and other contact details.

Scotland on-line The Scottish Archive Network (SCAN) is a useful tool for researching the story of almost any locality in Scotland. The website at **www.scan.org.uk** gives details of what is held in all of the country's archives, along with their addresses, phone numbers and opening hours.

A fragmented Church

Before the Reformation of the late 16th century, Scotland was a Roman Catholic country. Episcopalianism then became the dominant form of Protestantism until 1690, when Presbyterianism was embraced by the Church of Scotland. In the 19th century, many more expressions of faith emerged including the foundation of the Free Church of Scotland in 1843.

This history manifests itself in the abundance of ecclesiastical buildings seen in most Scottish towns and cities, even in small settlements (see pages 90-91). It was common for competing ministries to build churches next to each other, each of which would keep its own records (kirk session minutes). The earliest date from 1553, later than in England and Wales, where it became mandatory to keep records in 1538.

Education and law

In 1696, laws were passed that led to the establishment of a national education system for Scotland. Provision was patchy at first, but by the early 18th century, every parish had its own school, offering a basic education, though usually only for boys. It was not compulsory and it was not free, but it was cheap and of a high standard. Records on schooling in Scotland (see page 93) therefore relate to nearly all social classes in a community from a much earlier date than similar documents covering England and Wales.

Scotland has its own separate legal system, which will particularly affect any research you do into property transactions. Details of such dealing in Scotland have been recorded since 1617 in the Registers of Sasines (see page 148). They can be seen at the National Archives of Scotland (see DIRECTORY). Use of sasine registers is gradually being replaced by the Land Register, set up in 1979. It can be consulted on-line at **www.ros.gov.uk**

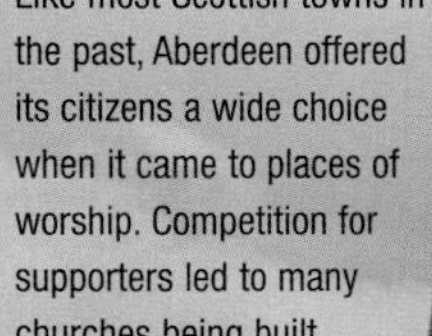

Aberdeen's churches
Like most Scottish towns in the past, Aberdeen offered its citizens a wide choice when it came to places of worship. Competition for supporters led to many churches being built almost side by side. The Belmont Relief Chapel (below, left), later known as the South Parish Church, was built within yards of the medieval Kirk of St Nicholas (right) in the 18th century.

Other useful legal records are those of the Dean of Guild Courts, containing information about buildings in the various burghs; sheriff court records, which provide evidence of disputes and criminal cases; and Justice of the Peace records, which reveal instances of minor local misdemeanours. All of these documents are held by the National Archives of Scotland (see DIRECTORY).

Government in action

Parliamentary Papers will include specific 'Scotland' reports, which have much information about particular parishes. One, dated 1844, on the 'Poor Law Inquiry, Scotland', reveals that in Prestonpans parish, East Lothian, there were 144 paupers; women and children earned 8d a day for field labour; 19 pubs sold spirits and 11 shops sold alcohol. Parliamentary Papers are held by the legal deposit libraries, which include the National Library of Scotland (see DIRECTORY), the British Library (see DIRECTORY) and the National Library of Wales (see DIRECTORY), and by many university libraries, which usually charge a consultation fee.

Statistical accounts

Scotland is also fortunate to have reports giving detailed statistics on its various communities and their inhabitants, dating back to the late 18th century. Contents vary from place to place, but generally the topics covered include geography and geology, industry, agriculture, markets, populations, incomes, prices of goods, curiosities and antiquities, eminent citizens, churches and schools.

The two earliest sets of reports can be viewed at **edina.ac.uk/stat-acc-scot** You will also find the *Third Statistical Accounts* for some places giving information up to the mid 20th century, and there are accounts for Midlothian and East Lothian up to 2000, which are usually available at local reference libraries (a CD of the Midlothian report can be bought from **www.midlothian.gov.uk/library**).

Maps

Much of the National Library of Scotland's map collection can be seen on-line at **www.nls.uk/collections/maps/index.html** It includes the first detailed maps of Scotland, created by Timothy Pont (*c*.1565-1614). He travelled the country during the 1580s and 90s, surveying and making copious notes. The maps he drew formed the basis of the first atlas of Scotland, published in 1654 by Joan Blaeu as part of a monumental world atlas, the *Atlas Novus*.

Pont maps The 77 surviving maps created by Timothy Pont (see below) are a rich source of information on life in 16th-century Scotland. Some focus on individual places, such as Dundee (above), while others cover swathes of countryside.

Burgh Surveys More than 70 Burgh Surveys have been produced and published by Historic Scotland (see DIRECTORY). These reports bring together current archaeological and historical research to provide a wide-ranging picture of the past. Each one includes a description of the geography and physical setting of a particular burgh together with a review of its history from prehistoric times to the present day.

FIND OUT MORE

- *Scottish Local History: an introductory guide* (D. Moody, Batsford, 1986)
- *Exploring Scottish History* (M. Cox, ed., Scottish Library Association, Scottish Local History Forum and The Scottish Record Association, 1999)
- *Tracing Scottish Local History* (C.J. Sinclair, National Archives of Scotland, HMSO 1994)
- *Tracing Your Scottish Ancestors: the Official Guide* (National Archives of Scotland, HMSO, 2003)
- *East Lothian Fourth Statistical Account 1945-2000, Vol. 1* (S. Baker, ed., East Lothian Council Library Service, 2003)
- *The Nation Survey'd: essays on late sixteenth century Scotland as depicted by Timothy Pont* (I.C. Cunningham, ed., Tuckwell Press/National Library of Scotland, 2001)

Meet the people of your street

Do you ever wonder who lived in your street before you, how large their families were and what they did for a living? A few visits to your local city or county archives should bring you the answers to these questions, and some of your neighbours can probably give a lively account of all the comings and goings.

Ask the neighbours

The best way to start your research on the people of your street is to talk to long-term residents. People usually love talking about their family history. Start by asking them how long have they been there. Where did the family come from? Why did they choose to move to your town or village? And why this house in this street? If you ask everyone the same questions, you will quickly get a broad overview of the lives unfolding around you.

Soon you will need to flesh out the information you have gathered with a visit to your local reference library and then, perhaps, to the city or county record office to track down any documents about your street. Always work back in time from what you already know.

Electoral registers and directories

Your local record office (see pages 10-11) will have a collection of electoral registers, giving the names and addresses of everyone who was entitled to vote in national and local elections from 1832 to the present day. Trade and commercial directories (see page 75) may take you back further. But neither source will give a complete picture, as universal suffrage for men was not granted until 1918 and for women until 1928, and the directories only list leading tradesmen and the better-off citizens.

Be alert to the fact that a street name or the house numbering may have been changed. Houses in many streets were not given numbers until well into the latter half of the 19th century.

The Burgess Roll of THE BOROUGH OF BIRMINGHAM.

LADY WOOD WARD.

High society Mention of your street in a 19th-century electoral register (left) will tell you that it was home to some of the area's leading citizens. For much of the century the right to vote was restricted to a moneyed, mostly male, elite. Qualification for the franchise – usually property ownership – is stated.

Soho street, Smethwick, Six ways to Rabone lane. MAP C 1.

WEST SIDE.

1 Shaw Jesson & Harry, grcrs
2 Gosling John & Sons, butchrs
3 Thornburn John, boot ma
4 Hinton Jn. Wilfred, tbccnst
5 Beehive Co. clothiers
6 Adams Edwin, grocer
8 Freeman, Hardy & Willis Limited, boot makers
9 Dexter Charles, baker
10 Butler George, hair dresser
11 Edwards Miss Annie, fancy draper
12 Jesson David, confectioner
13 West Herbert, hatter
14 Green Alfred, dining rms
15 Hadley Chas. furniture dlr
27 Round Geo. beer retailer
36 Churchill Joseph Henry, hair dresser
37 Waterhouse Wm. tobcconist
38 Saunders Thomas, boot ma
39 Ray [illegible]ancis, greengrocer

Face-to-face A street directory for Smethwick (right) tells you much about the prosperity of the area, but snaps, such as that of a street party held for George V's Silver Jubilee in 1935 (below) breathe life into such lists.

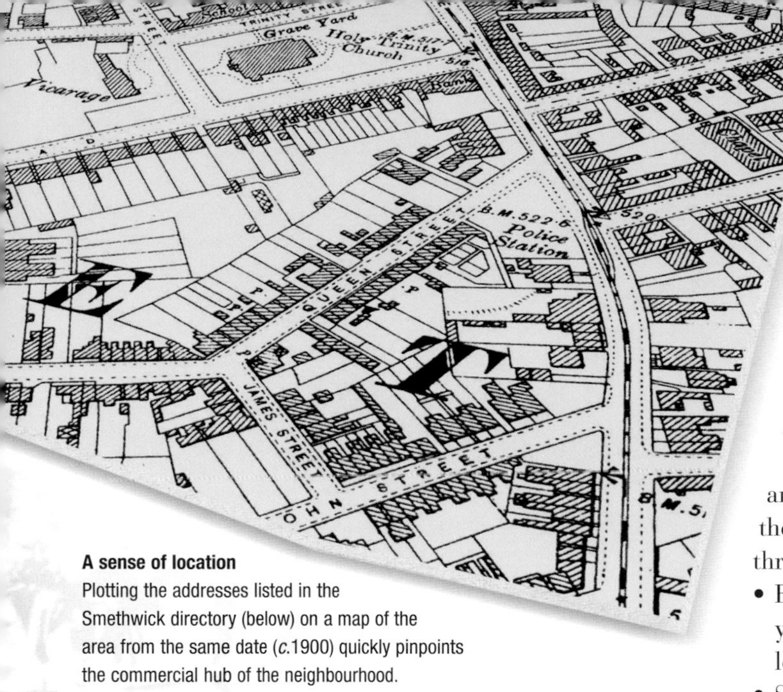

A sense of location
Plotting the addresses listed in the Smethwick directory (below) on a map of the area from the same date (*c.*1900) quickly pinpoints the commercial hub of the neighbourhood.

Putting your street on the map

Reference libraries usually keep local maps, including larger-scale Ordnance Survey (OS) ones (see page 18). It might be useful to look at a map from the same period as any directory or electoral register you have been searching through. See how many houses, shops and other buildings listed in the directory or register you can locate. This may provide you with a useful framework of information for when you turn your attention to census returns.

What the census reveals

Your library or record office will have a complete set of census returns for your district from 1841 to 1901. Most will also have a catalogue to guide you to your street, but be prepared to search in more than one place. Be aware that the boundary of a census enumerator's district might go down the middle of a street, or swing round a corner, so that your street might be in more than one district (see also 'Census returns' on pages 76-77).

At first glance census returns can appear to contain an overwhelmingly large amount of information, but these guidelines should help you to work your way through it all.

- Begin by looking at the census return for a period that you have already done some research on, perhaps by looking at a trade directory or map.
- Start by noting down all the families who were living in your street in a particular year, then check how many were there in earlier and later census returns. This will give you an idea of who the 'core families' that stayed put were and who came and went within a few years.
- From the 1851 census onward, the birthplace of each person was noted. Although this information is not always accurate, you could still use it to work out a general pattern of migration from around Britain.
- Look especially at the birthplaces of the children within one family. If they are different, they may indicate the approximate dates of the movements of a family before they arrived in your street. On the whole, people moved within the neighbourhood with which they were familiar, but the rapid growth of industry in many towns during the 19th century attracted people from further afield in search of work.
- Census returns can give an indication of the economic status of a community by revealing how people earned their living. Look first at the work done by the men, noting the occupations of all the heads of households, then those of the young men and boys. Next turn to the women, but remember that many of them did jobs that were part-time and not usually recorded.

Searching earlier records

The further back in time you go, the more difficult it is to find detailed documentation. But the familiarity with your local archives that you will gain by searching through the more recent first, should prove useful when hunting for the older, more obscure material. Look for any mention of your street or district in the catalogues of manorial and parish records (see page 85), for any references to old maps – especially tithe-award ones (see page 19) – that you are able to examine, and enquire about published sources of information, such as hearth-tax returns (see page 77).

The naming of our streets

Most of us live on a street and in a community full of streets, with names that we probably take for granted. But there is a reason for every road name, and many are associated with intriguing stories. The word 'street' itself originates from the Anglo-Saxon 'strete', which refers to a paved road as constructed by the Romans.

A meaning lost in time The shortest street in York has the longest name: Whip-ma-whop-ma-gate. It has changed over the years from the medieval 'Whitnourwhatnourgate', meaning 'what a street' – a street that is so short it can scarcely be called one. The new name seems to reflect an association with beating or whipping. But was that, as some claim, the siting of a whipping post nearby for chastising beggars and rogues, or was it the more esoteric practice of whipping dogs called whappets there on St Luke's Day? The question continues to baffle historians.

WHIP - MA - WHOP - MA - GATE
The shortest street in York. Known in 1505 as Whitnourwhatnourgate (and meaning 'what a street !') it was changed later into its present name.
The footpath was paved in York stone by York Civic Trust in 1984.

Pathways into the past

Some of Britain's roads have their origins as ancient trackways used by travellers and tradesmen long before cars were invented. These old roads usually retain the word 'way' in their names. The Harrow Way is the oldest road in Britain, and it keeps its name for much of its route from Folkestone to Stonehenge. The old trackways are often sunk into the landscape, with high banks on either side, or they may follow a natural ridge. Names like Holloway Lane and Ridge Street reflect this.

Roman roads such as the Fosse Way and Watling Street tend to keep their names as they pass through towns. They are typically straight, joining two places by the most direct route. Latin elements in some street names can still be made out through the fog of two millennia. Chesterton Lane in Cambridge dates back to the remains of the castrum or Roman camp ('Chester') to which the lane led, noted by the Saxon farmer who established his tun or farmstead there ('-ton').

Danish street names are common in the north of England, especially 'gate'. The Danish 'gata' and Anglo-Saxon 'geat' both meant a thoroughfare, not an opening in a wall. Once you understand this, the York street names of Castlegate, Coppergate, Fossgate and Stonegate make more sense – they are ways through the city that do not necessarily pass through any gates.

Medieval markets and mysteries

Street names can reveal the medieval origin of a town layout, and even who was selling what and where. In Salisbury in Wiltshire streets around the centrally placed Poultry Cross (right) have names such as Butcher Row, Fish Row and Salt Lane. Other names may not be as obvious. York's famous street of leaning old houses called The Shambles was the butchers' quarter in medieval times and takes its name from the 'shammels' – the shelves that butchers used to display their meat.

Medieval market square The medieval layout of Salisbury can be seen in the old market square's central Poultry Cross and appropriately named streets nearby such as Butcher Row and Fish Row.

Follow the signs Kirkgate in Ripon, North Yorkshire, literally means 'church way', and with the magnificent Ripon Cathedral in the background it is quite obvious why it was so named. The street name is likely to be very old indeed since there has been a church on the site since St Wilfred built one there in the 7th century.

Military victories Sebastopol Road in Aldershot (top) is one of many throughout Britain, all likely to have been built in the mid 19th century and named after the great siege in the Crimean War (1853-6).

Pride of the Empire

In the 19th century huge movements of people from the country into the towns and from town centres outwards led to the creation of numerous suburbs to accommodate them. Thousands of new roads had to be named. Fortunately the street namers were not short of material. Britain was full of her own importance as an imperial power and so many of the names had a colonial flavour – Bombay Street, Jamaica Street, Tobago Street – or commemorated battles and martial heroes – Waterloo Road, Wellington Parade, Havelock Road.

If a town had particular associations, it generally wanted to draw attention to them when naming its streets. In an army garrison town such as Aldershot, it is no surprise to find mention of Crimean War commanders and battles – Alma Close, Raglan Close, Redan Gardens, Sebastopol Road – or Nelson Road, Victory Stadium and Trafalgar Place in Portsmouth, home of the Royal Navy.

Local heroes

Some streets are named after famous people from the locality. In Hereford there is a Gwynne Street where Nell Gwynne, mistress to Charles II, was reputedly born. It would be astonishing if Liverpool had not honoured the Beatles by naming Paul McCartney Way, George Harrison Close, John Lennon Drive and Ringo Starr Drive after its very own Fab Four.

Other names commemorate people held in high regard by the community but unknown outside it. In Ammanford, south Wales, a 1970s estate road is called Stewart Drive. It is named in honour of local doctor Donald Stewart, a much-respected Scotsman who came to Ammanford as a young practitioner in 1909 and served the town for the rest of his working life.

PUTTING A GLOSS ON A NAME

When looking at street names do not overlook the endings. Victorian street namers opted for endings that might lend a touch of class such as Mill Avenue or Mill Promenade, which sound grander than Mill Street, even if the road is an urban back street rather than a broad avenue lined with trees. The Victorians also took the opportunity of urban expansion to 'clean up' some names they saw as vulgar. Love Lane was acceptable but the examples of Grope Lane were changed. One of the few survivors may be Grape Lane in York, which probably has little to do with the fruit.

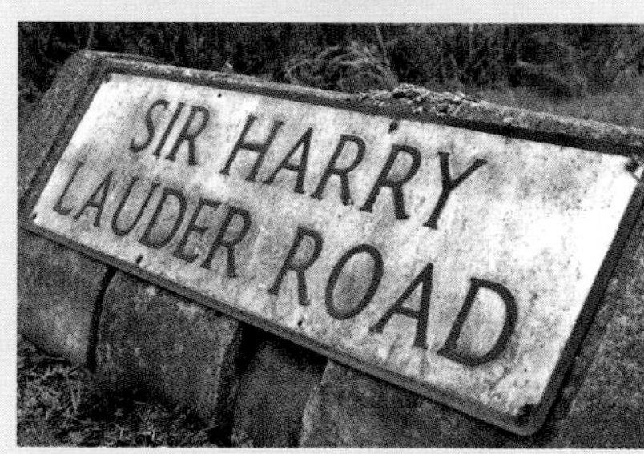

Always remembered Street names can be a lasting record of a local celebrity. Harry Lauder may not be as famous as he was in his music-hall heyday, but the singer's name lives on (above) in his native district of Portobello in Edinburgh.

FIND OUT MORE

- *The Street Names Of England* (Adrian Room, Paul Watkins Publishing, 1992)
- **www.thepotteries.org/focus/002.htm** Street names in The Potteries.

Getting to know the people of your whole community

Once you know your street, you can see how it fits into the community as a whole. Again look closely at directories, maps, electoral rolls and census returns. What similarities and differences are there between your street and others close by? Are more people moving into or out of the area? What job do they do and how has this changed over time? Perhaps you will discover where someone famous, or infamous, lived.

Finding the local celebrities

Wherever you live, some son or daughter of the place will have made their mark on society.

Wall plaques Look out for a blue English Heritage or similar plaque on the walls of houses, commemorating an illustrious member of your community.

Street names Walk around and check on maps to see if any streets or public buildings are named after a local worthy.

Famous son Signs of celebrity may be anywhere. A tiny terraced house in Ulverston, Cumbria, similar to the others crammed around it, is marked out as the birthplace of Stan Laurel (above), while his statue (left) graces a corner of North Shields where he lived as a child.

Local newspapers At your local record office (see pages 10-11) you will find a mine of information in old editions of local newspapers (see pages 74-75). Events such as royal visits and the openings of major public buildings were probably attended by the local celebrities of the time. Their political actions and business affairs will also have been extensively reported, and there are likely to be lengthy obituaries of most leading inhabitants.

Older local histories Ask at your local reference library if they keep copies of any older, published local histories. These frequently contain biographies of notable members of the community, which are often accompanied by photographs. Some, with such splendid titles as 'Accrington Captains of Industry' or 'Hallamshire Worthies', deal exclusively with the illustrious.

Uncovering the bad apples

Criminals are just as likely to be well recorded as the great and the good. Some areas may even have had a reputation for crime and disorder, especially at certain times of the year, such as when annual fairs like the Nottingham Goose Fair were held.

- Court cases were reported at length in local newspapers and the more sensational crimes frequently became part of local folklore.
- Prisoners are well documented from 1877, when the Home Office took over responsibility for prisons. Prison registers going back a hundred years and sometimes more are held at the National Archives at Kew (see DIRECTORY). These note the age of a convict, his or her physical appearance (accompanied by a photograph), place of birth, marital status and occupation.
- The inmates of prisons are listed in census returns (see pages 76-77), although in some cases they are recorded only by their initials.
- From the 16th century onwards Justices of the Peace tried many offences at meetings known as quarter sessions. Their records are kept in the archives of county record offices (see pages 10-11).

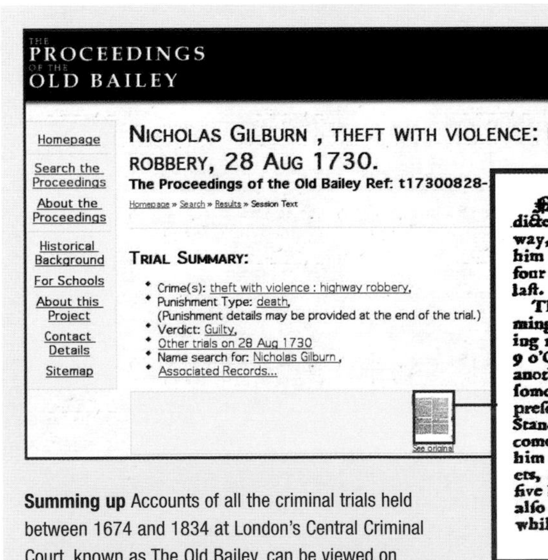

THE PROCEEDINGS OF THE OLD BAILEY

Homepage
Search the Proceedings
About the Proceedings
Historical Background
For Schools
About this Project
Contact Details
Sitemap

NICHOLAS GILBURN , THEFT WITH VIOLENCE: HIGHWAY ROBBERY, 28 AUG 1730.

The Proceedings of the Old Bailey Ref: t17300828-

Homepage » Search » Results » Session Text

TRIAL SUMMARY:

- Crime(s): theft with violence : highway robbery,
- Punishment Type: death,
(Punishment details may be provided at the end of the trial.)
- Verdict: Guilty,
- Other trials on 28 Aug 1730
- Name search for: Nicholas Gilburn ,
- Associated Records...

See original

Summing up Accounts of all the criminal trials held between 1674 and 1834 at London's Central Criminal Court, known as The Old Bailey, can be viewed on **www.oldbaileyonline.org**. There are images of around 66,000 original pages of proceedings and lists of prisoners, giving names, ages, crimes, and usually verdicts and sentences.

The all-encompassing parish

Records of key events in parishioners' lives were once kept in the parish chest inside a church, but are now housed in local record offices. They deal not only with spiritual concerns, but also with secular matters. From the 16th to the 19th century, the parish was responsible for appointing constables to enforce law and order, for maintaining the highways (see page 106), and for looking after the poor and needy.

Reading the registers Among notes on parish business and accounting, you will find details of baptisms, marriages and burials in your community possibly going back as far as 1538, when each church was ordered to record such rites of passage.

- Use the information to get an idea of how long some families have been in the area. Adding up the annual totals of baptisms and burials will show you whether the population was rising or falling at different periods of time. A sudden increase in burials might indicate a visitation of the plague or other deadly epidemic.
- Some parish registers note a man's occupation, (although they are rarely consistent in this before 1813), which will give you some sense of what the people in your community did for a living. Compare this with occupations noted on census returns from 1841 onwards.

Poor relief From the beginning of the 17th century, parishes levied local rates to provide money for the 'deserving poor'. Parish archives will also contain a record of this work.

- Money, clothes and shoes were doled out on a regular basis. The names of recipients are often recorded.
- Fathers of 'bastards' were identified and their names listed, with the sum they were required to pay for their child's upkeep recorded.
- Paupers originally from another parish were frequently sent back there, so as not to be a burden on their adopted community. 'Settlement papers' recording disputes taken before a Justice of the Peace give brief accounts of the movements and distress of abandoned wives and children, the infirm and the disreputable.
- Some parishes built poor houses to look after the most needy and provide work for the able. The workhouses erected after the Poor Law Amendment Act (1834) were the result of a new national system of unions of parishes. Any surviving workhouse records, such as admittance registers, will be found at county record offices, and the inmates are listed in the census returns of 1841-1901.

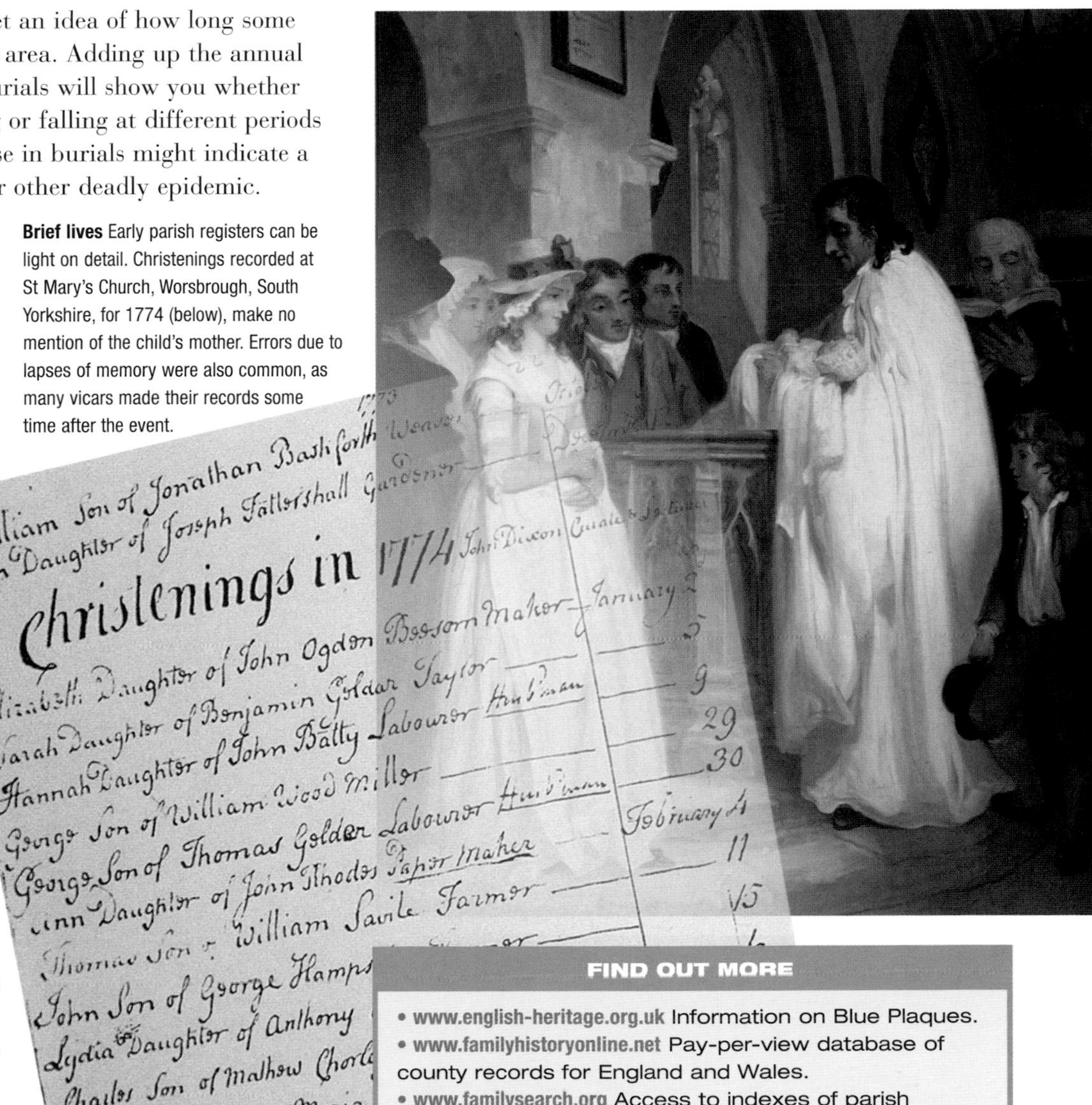

1773
William Son of Jonathan Bashforth Weaver
Ann Daughter of Joseph Fattershall Gardener

Christenings in 1774 John Dixon Curate

Elizabeth Daughter of John Ogden Beesom Maker January 2
Sarah Daughter of Benjamin Goldar Taylor 5
Hannah Daughter of John Batty Labourer Husbandman 9
George Son of William Wood Miller 29
George Son of Thomas Golder Labourer Husbandman 30
Ann Daughter of John Rhodes Paper Maker February 4
Thomas Son of William Savile Farmer 11
John Son of George Hamps...
Lydia Daughter of Anthony ...
Charles Son of Mathew Chorl...
Martha Daughter of Maria ...
Sarah Daughter of Thomas ...
James Son of Joshuah ...
Anne Daughter of John ...
George Son of George ...
Hannah Daughter of David Frost 14
Hannah Daughter of William Goldar 15
... Jonathan Rushley Paper Maker October 9

Brief lives Early parish registers can be light on detail. Christenings recorded at St Mary's Church, Worsbrough, South Yorkshire, for 1774 (below), make no mention of the child's mother. Errors due to lapses of memory were also common, as many vicars made their records some time after the event.

FIND OUT MORE

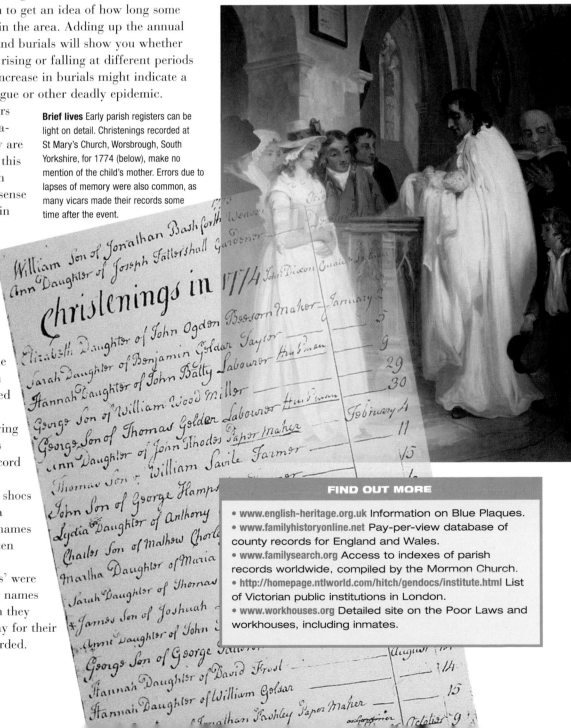

- **www.english-heritage.org.uk** Information on Blue Plaques.
- **www.familyhistoryonline.net** Pay-per-view database of county records for England and Wales.
- **www.familysearch.org** Access to indexes of parish records worldwide, compiled by the Mormon Church.
- **http://homepage.ntlworld.com/hitch/gendocs/institute.html** List of Victorian public institutions in London.
- **www.workhouses.org** Detailed site on the Poor Laws and workhouses, including inmates.

Looking at your parish church

Your parish church is possibly your neighbourhood's oldest building, for centuries the focal point of local life. A close look at it, starting with the churchyard and exterior of the building, will reveal not only its history, but also much about your community, its times of feast and famine and the identity of important local families. Rich and poor alike will have taken pride in maintaining, enlarging and embellishing the church, and it is not difficult to unearth the evidence from what you see and from the parish records.

Clues in the churchyard

Before you go inside a church, look around the churchyard. The present appearance, with lych gate, paths and trees, probably dates from the Victorian period, but you will reach further back in time by studying the gravestones. You may find some graves from the 17th century; before then, they were marked with a simple wooden cross.

Who lies where? Look near the main door on the south side of the church for the earliest gravestones. Until the 18th or 19th century, the north side was regarded as the devil's side, where excommunicates, the unbaptised and suicides were buried. Churchyards are normally larger on the south side than the north, although later additions to their land may have obscured this arrangement.

Spot the names Only the better-off families in the 17th century erected gravestones, but by the 18th century the fashion had spread to most households. The poorest people might not have had gravestones even in the Victorian period, when some of the richer locals were commemorating their dead with elaborate memorials.

- Look for groups of gravestones with the same surname. These are likely to belong to long-resident families of your community. You may find their names appearing again in parish and census records (see pages 80-81).
- If the local stone has weathered badly and the wording is unreadable, check at the local record office to see if a family history society has made a 'monumental inscriptions' survey to record all the details.

Outer appearances

Stand back from your local church and observe the way in which it has been built. You may be surprised at the number of contrasting styles. This is partly because in the Middle Ages the rector, in return for receiving tithes from the parishioners, was responsible for building and maintaining only his part of the church, which included the chancel at the east end where the high altar is sited (see pages 88-89). The parishioners looked after the nave, aisles and tower, and often restyled their part of the church, while the rector's end remained untouched. Architectural variety also came about when parishes could not afford to rebuild, but just added a few features in a new style. This piecemeal work makes parish

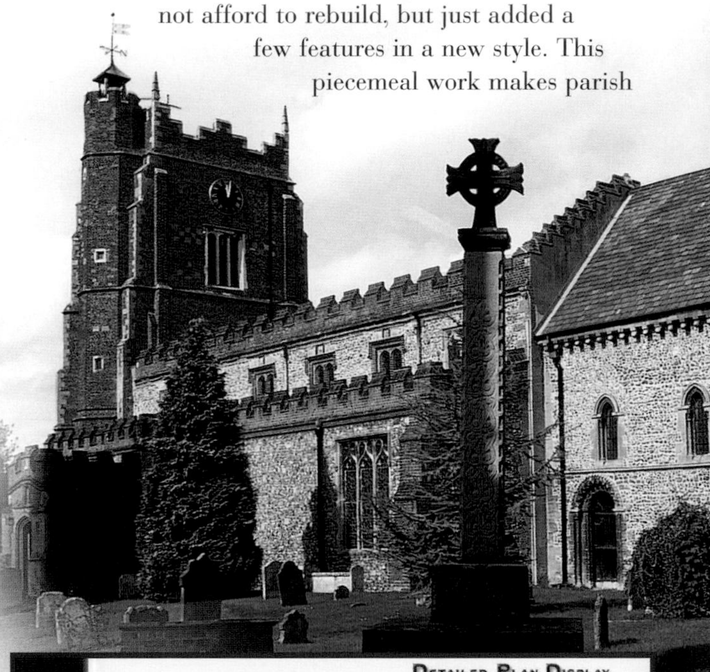

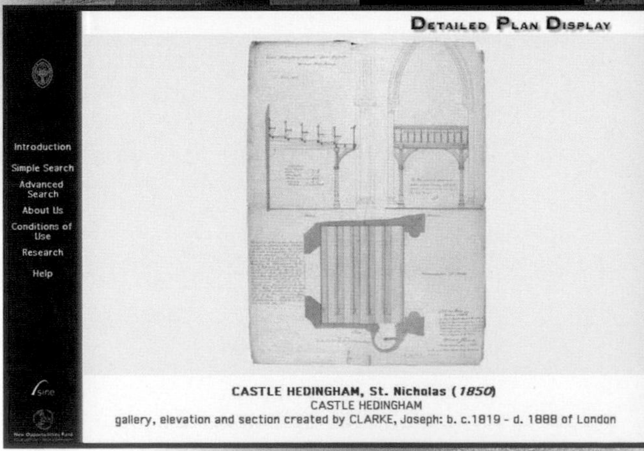

churches all the more interesting to examine. Even if they appear to be of one era from the outside, it is often possible to find earlier work inside (see pages 88-89).

Style pointers Try to fit the architectural styles of the church to booms and slumps in the local economy. The tower at East Bergholt, Suffolk, was not completed because of the collapse of the woollen cloth trade in the 1520s.

- Look for private chapels, known as chantries, built by parishioners or local guilds. The most convenient space for them was beside the chancel.
- Churches were dependent on fund-raising events, such as the May games. You may see an inscription like the one at Long Melford, Suffolk, praising the contributions of 'all the well-disposed men of this town'.

The story in the stones

Look at the materials that were used to build your church for clues about how it was constructed and even paid for.

Recycled materials Early medieval masons used whatever local materials were at hand, including bricks and stones from Roman forts or boulders and pebbles from the fields.

- Humble materials could also be used to construct very fine buildings. In East Anglia the great churches that were built out of the profits of the cloth trade, such as Southwold and Stoke-by-Nayland, were constructed of rubble, with a veneer of knapped flints. A clue to the expense that was lavished on the construction of these churches is the imported limestone used for the corner stones and window frames.
- A church built entirely of the finest imported stone will suggest a parish that had become wealthy in the later Middle Ages. Such places are often on the coast or a river, where the stone could be easily landed.

Extending through the ages St Nicholas Church at Castle Hedingham in Essex (above) has, like many English churches, been restyled and added to over time, perfectly encapsulating the history of the area. The Norman 'wheel' window in the chancel dates from the 12th century; the tower is 17th-century, but was built with reused bricks from the nearby castle; and work on a gallery was carried out from 1850 (see plans, left). You may be able to trace alterations and restoration work to your church – **www.churchplansonline.org** gives on-line access to the Incorporated Church Building Society's archive of plans for new and existing churches from 1818 to 1982.

WHEN WAS YOUR CHURCH BUILT?

You can often date your church from architectural details, such as the shape of the tower or the size and decoration of the windows.

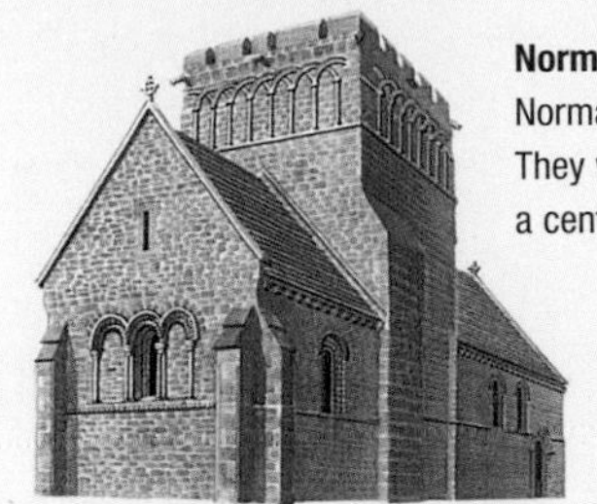

Norman Following their conquest of England in 1066, Norman barons built numerous small stone churches. They were planned in the shape of a cross and featured a central tower, round arches and small windows.

Early English The Gothic style, characterised by steeples, pointed arches and rib vaults, came to England via France around 1175. The design was more elegant than the Norman churches, with thinner walls and larger windows.

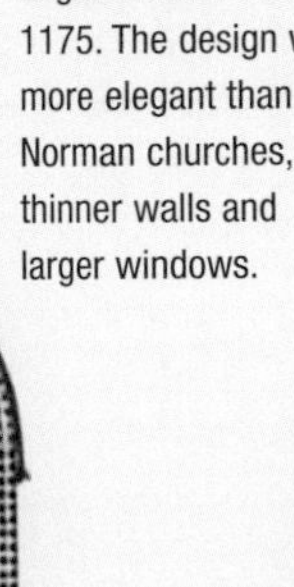

Decorated Gothic From around 1250, stonemasons unleashed their creative talent. Windows were divided by vertical mullions and embellished with complex tracery. Arches and gables were decorated with stylised leaves.

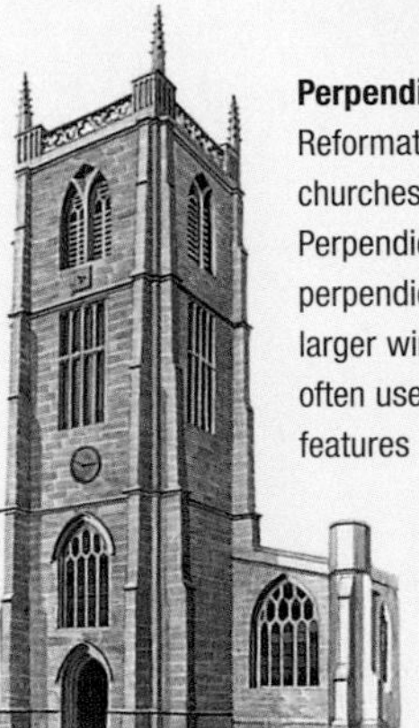

Perpendicular Gothic From 1350 to the Reformation in the mid-16th century, churches were built in a late-Gothic or Perpendicular style, named after the perpendicular lines of the mullions. These larger windows were filled with stained glass, often used to tell Biblical stories. Other features included flat lead roofs hidden behind battlements and pinnacles, carved wooden ceilings, long ranges of windows and fan vaulting. The sturdy towers are the glory of these churches.

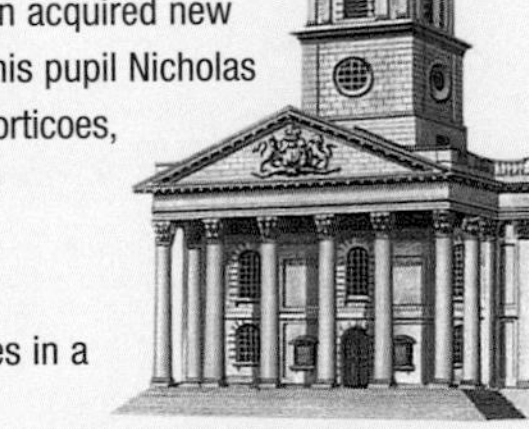

English Baroque After the great fire of 1666, London acquired new churches, many designed by Christopher Wren and his pupil Nicholas Hawksmoor in the classical English Baroque style. Porticoes, graceful spires and internal galleries were among the features, such as at Hawksmoor's Christ Church, Spitalfields. In the 18th century the parishioners of expanding towns and rural landowners built churches in a more restrained classical style.

FIND OUT MORE

- **www.church-search.com** A database of Church of England parish churches.
- **www.genuki.org.uk/big/parloc/search.html** A database giving locations for parish churches.
- **www.visitchurches.org.uk** The website of The Churches Conservation Trust.
- **www.britainexpress.com/History/english-parish-churches.htm** The history of English churches.
- **www.newadvent.org/cathen/15653b.htm** 'Windows in Church Architecture' (from the Catholic Encyclopedia).
- ***England's Thousand Best Churches*** (Simon Jenkins, 2000, Penguin Books)

Inside your parish church

Your parish church is a time capsule of local history. Inside you will find effigies, monuments and brasses, sculptures and portraits, gravestones and plaques dedicated to past members of the community. If you trawl through the parish records at your county record office, you may find churchwardens' accounts going back hundreds of years detailing day-to-day transactions, who cleaned the church and when alterations took place.

Memorials to local worthies

To find out who were the movers and shakers of your parish, step inside your church and you will see a range of memorials to local people, from medieval effigies to lists of those who died in the First and Second World Wars. Some names will provide links to other local families who you may encounter elsewhere in your research.

Effigies, monuments and brasses Look at the inscriptions to discover who was important and why.

- If you see a stone carving of a man in a reclining position, clad in armour, often with his feet resting on an animal, and perhaps with his wife at his side, it is probably a local lord dating from the 13th to the early 16th centuries.
- Elizabethan and Stuart effigies were in Italian Renaissance style and made of polished alabaster. They often show a man and his wife kneeling or seated in prayer. In the later 17th and early 18th centuries, effigies became grander and more Baroque in style and featured family groups. Also popular at the time were lifelike classical busts or full figures, carved in marble.
- Look out for memorial brasses. They were popular from the 14th to the late 16th century, and again in Victorian times, but were not intended to be accurate portraits.
- If you study the gravestones inside the church and wall-mounted memorials, you will discover the names of the better-off parishioners.
- You may see charity boards, which recorded any charitable endowments to the church.

THE ANATOMY OF A CHURCH
However much your parish church has been altered and whatever its size, you will still be able to identify the most common features, such as the chancel, nave, pulpit and font. The Georgian box pews may have been removed by the Victorians, and the rood screen might be missing, but you may find an old painting or photograph in the church showing how it once looked.

Local knight Tombs such as that of Sir William Martyn (d.1503) at St Mary's, Puddletown, Dorset (above), will reveal the identity of local prominent citizens, whose names may also appear in church documents. The box pews at St Mary's survived Victorian 'improvement'.

Symbolic clues Parish churches were a riot of colour in medieval times before they were whitewashed during the Reformation in the 16th century. But you will still find them adorned with carvings of Christian symbols. The eagle is the symbol of St John the Evangelist and is commonly found on the lectern from where the Gospels are read. Look for the symbol of the saint to whom the church is dedicated, such as the lion of St Mark. You may see a fish, the early Christians' symbol of Christ from the story of the feeding of the five thousand; a dove represents the Holy Spirit; a lamb, the Redeemer; wheat heads, the 'bread of life'.

What to find in the records

The parish records in your county record office will record key changes and the day-to-day life of your local church.

Medieval wills These may contain bequests to finance new work in your local church, such as the insertion of windows, the heightening of the tower, or the addition of a chantry chapel.

Diocesan archives Look for licences, known as faculties, granted by a local bishop in the 19th and 20th centuries to authorise your church to make structural changes to the building.

Churchwardens' accounts Look out for details of expenditure on maintenance, cleaning and decoration. Some accounts survive from the Reformation and often provide information about alterations made to churches. An account for a York parish reveals that in 1547 a labourer was paid twopence for removing dirt from St Michael's, Spurriergate, at the time 'the seyntts [saints] was takyn down'. The accounts will say when the church-wardens paid the bell-ringers for celebrating major events, such as a coronation, and when parishioners were paid to shoot birds and vermin.

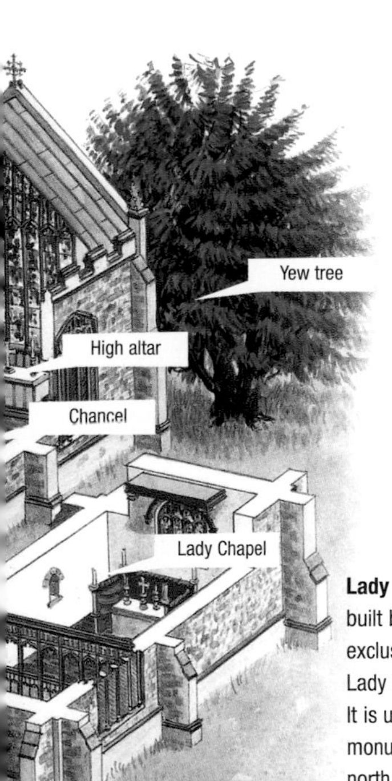

Chancel The east part of the church, known as the chancel, belonged to the rector. The high altar could be seen dimly through the rood screen that divided the nave, and the parishioners, from the chancel. Look out for slots in the walls, where the screen was once fixed, and for a blocked staircase that once led to the large crucifix and the carved figures of the Virgin Mary and St John on top of the screen. Outside in the churchyard you may see a yew tree, a symbol of immortality.

Lady Chapel Today, the former chantry chapel, built by a wealthy parishioner or guild for their exclusive use (see page 87), is often known as the Lady Chapel, regardless of its original dedication. It is usually open for private prayer. Look for a monument or plaque to its original benefactor. If the north side of the church had a chantry chapel, the space is now sometimes occupied by the organ.

Nave The main body of the church is known as the nave. This was the parishioners' part of the church, where, during services, the congregation stood. If your church has a stone bench around the wall, it was intended for the old and infirm, hence the expression 'the weak to the wall'. In the Middle Ages the nave was also used as a village hall and meeting place. Pews may bear the names of wealthy local families.

PEW BELOW.

I John Freeman the present Senior Churchwarden of the Parish of St. James, within the Liberty of Westminster, do hereby (with the Consent and Allowance of the Vestry of the same Parish to me in that behalf given) Dispose of and Let to Mr T. Cooper an Inhabitant of the same Parish, the free Use of the Pew Numbered 26 in the North Aisle of the Parish-Church of the said Parish; to hold and enjoy the same at all seasonable Times for hearing Divine Service in the said Church, from henceforth until the 25th Day of December 1811 Provided the said Mr Cooper do, on Production and Delivery hereof unto him pay or cause to be paid unto Mark Klyne the Collector legally appointed to receive the same, the Sum of Four pounds sixteen shillings On Payment and Receipt whereof, the said Collector is required and directed to sign and deliver to the said Mr Cooper the Receipt at the Foot hereof. Witness my Hand this 25th Day of D

Received of the above-named the above-mentioned Sum of as Witness my Hand this 12 D

H. Reynell, Printer, 21, Piccadilly, London.

Pews for rent Well-to-do parishioners used to rent private pews by the year. Among your parish records at the county record office you might come across a document such as this pew rent receipt dated 1810 for St James's, Westminster.

FIND OUT MORE

- www.kencollins.com/glossary/architecture.htm A glossary of church architecture.
- www.ecclsoc.org/main.html Information on church architecture and furnishings.
- www.britannia.com/church/studies/index.html Historical articles on many parish churches.
- *Buildings of England* (Nikolaus Pevsner, Penguin Books). Accounts of parish churches by the architectural historian. www.pevsner.co.uk

Recognising other houses of God

Walk around your town or village and you may find a variety of places of worship, not just the parish church. A town will probably have Baptist or Presbyterian chapels, a Catholic church, a Quaker meeting house and perhaps a synagogue, mosque or Hindu temple. Even a small village may have a Methodist chapel. These places of worship all hold clues to the character of your community.

Nonconformist churches

A Nonconformist or Dissenter was someone who refused to conform to the Church of England as it was re-established after the restoration of Charles II in 1660. Baptists, Congregationalists, Presbyterians and Quakers were the main groups to emerge in the 17th century, although at this period Nonconformists numbered only 4 per cent of the English and Welsh population. One of the largest groups were the Methodists, whose first national conference was held in 1744.

The first Nonconformist meeting houses were built by Puritan landowners in the 17th century. They were known as chapels, because they were similar in style and simplicity to chapels erected in the Middle Ages in remote places far from the parish church.

Where to look

If you live in a town, venture down the side-streets to look for chapels. The main streets were often too full to build on, or congregations could only afford these poorer sites. You will find that chapels are usually simple buildings, made from local materials and designed to blend in with the surrounding houses.

Revealing facts Look at the inscriptions: the foundation stone for Heptonstall Methodist Chapel at Hebden Bridge, Yorkshire, was laid by John Wesley, the founder of Methodism, in 1764. Gravestones will give you clues about the early worshippers.

Identifying marks An inscription over the entrance will provide the name and denomination of the chapel and the date of the building. Some, especially Welsh chapels, have names taken from the Bible, such as Bethesda, Bethel, Mount Zion or Pisgah.

- On entering you will find an interior focused on the pulpit, in a prominent position. There is little on the walls to distract the congregation's attention.
- The plainest meeting houses are likely to belong to the Quakers, founded as the Society of Friends by George Fox, who began preaching in 1647. Some, such as Briggflatts, near Sedbergh in Yorkshire, and Jordans, near Chalfont St Peter in Buckinghamshire, survive from the late 17th and early 18th centuries.

Date and denomination A plaque may tell you when the chapel was built and for whom. The Primitive Methodists split from the main body in 1810.

Nonconformist records Your local record office will hold surviving chapel records, such as membership lists, photographs of Whitsuntide Sunday School processions, and programmes of events.

The National Archives (see DIRECTORY) has a large collection of Nonconformist registers for births, marriages and burials, although in the 17th and 18th centuries Nonconformists generally used the Church of England for their baptism, marriage and burial services.

Scottish churches

If you live in Scotland, your town may have more than one large ecclesiastical building. This is because for a hundred years after the Reformation, Scottish Protestants dithered between Presbyterianism and Episcopalianism. Finally, in 1690, the official Church of Scotland chose Presbyterianism. Many existing churches, such as St Giles in Edinburgh, were converted from Catholic to Presbyterian places of worship. New churches built from 1700 to 1850 can be identified by galleries and a pulpit sited along a side wall facing a half-circle of pews.

- Subsequent schisms resulted in The Free Church of Scotland in 1843 and the United Presbyterian Church in 1847. Both have plain, sparsely furnished churches of local stone.
- You will find records, such as kirk (church) session minutes, in the National Archives of Scotland (see DIRECTORY).

Worship on a grand scale Old illustrations or photographs may reveal a place of worship which no longer exists, but which once had a significant role in your community. The Great Synagogue in Dukes Place, London EC3, was destroyed by bombing in 1941. In its heyday in the 19th century (above), it served the large Jewish community in the East End and was the seat of the Chief Rabbi.

Catholic churches

The earliest Catholic chapels date from 1790. You may find one in your town that was built after 1829, when the Catholic Emancipation Act finally removed most of the restrictions and penalties imposed on Roman Catholics in Britain.

- The Victorian Catholic churches and cathedrals in the large industrial towns, such as Manchester or Middlesbrough, were built in Gothic style.
- Strikingly modern churches were built in the expanding suburbs in the 1960s and 70s. The outstanding example is Liverpool's Metropolitan Cathedral of Christ the King, designed by Sir Frederick Gibberd in 1960.

About Catholic records The best way to find the records of individual churches is to consult *Catholic Missions and Registers, 1700-1880* (M. Gandy, 6 vols, 1993). Few congregations kept registers before the mid 18th century for fear of persecution.

Synagogues

William the Conqueror invited the first Jewish settlers to Britain in the 11th century. The earliest communities were Sephardic Jews, who came from Portugal and around the Mediterranean. Many were wealthy traders and money lenders. Poor Ashkenazic Jews from Russia, Poland and Lithuania arrived in Britain in their thousands in Victorian times to escape persecution. They settled mainly in the East End of London, Manchester and Leeds.

Jewish records Britain has about 400 synagogues. You will find them listed in the *Jewish Year Book*, published by the *Jewish Chronicle* (see DIRECTORY). Copies of the *Jewish Chronicle* (founded 1841) are available at British Library Newspapers (see DIRECTORY). Visit your local record office to see synagogue records, including registers, minute books and details of benefactors.

Mosques and temples

In the second half of the 20th century, Asian and African immigrants settled in Britain, forming large communities in areas such as Leicester and Bradford. There may be a mosque or temple where you live. Some are purpose-built, but others occupy converted chapels and former schools and factories. You will find them marked on large-scale modern maps at your library.

FIND OUT MORE

- **http://rylibweb.man.ac.uk/data1/dg/text/method.html** The Methodist Archives and Research Centre.
- **www.catholic-library.org.uk** The Catholic Central Library houses records dating back to 1694.
- **www.catholic-history.org.uk/crs** The Catholic Record Society lists published records.
- **www.catholic-heritage.net/sca** The Scottish Catholic Archive holds church manuscripts.
- **www.jewishgen.org** A comprehensive website of Jewish records.

Back to local schooldays

Schools lie at the heart of any community. You may have been a pupil at the local primary or secondary school, as perhaps your parents or grandparents were before you. A close look at the buildings will provide clues about the school's history, while the distant voices of those who have filled its classrooms come closer through the photographs and log books in your local library and record office.

Early primary schools

The Victorians were the first major builders of schools in Britain. From 1870 the State began providing primary schools and in 1880 attendance was made compulsory. In some towns these schools are among the finest surviving Victorian buildings.

Sign of a school Many old school buildings have other uses today, but you will be able to identify them from their separate entrances for boys and girls.

School clues You may find a primary school in your area that dates back to this period.

- Look for steeply sloping roofs, mullioned windows and a bell turret in the Gothic style favoured by the Victorians.
- The school name and the date of its opening will be carved on the front.
- Look for a date stone and inscription on a building near a church or chapel. It may denote a Sunday school, which most children attended before 1880 to learn the 3Rs – reading, writing and arithmetic – as well as religious education.
- Some primary schools today are much older foundations, where children of all ages were taught. An inscription at Burnsall School, in the Yorkshire Dales, reads that it was founded in 1602 by Sir William Craven, a native of the parish who became Lord Mayor of London.

CHARITY SCHOOLS

The Society for the Promotion of Christian Knowledge (SPCK), founded in 1698, established charity schools in many areas of Britain, including remote parts of Wales and Scotland. Look out for small buildings, often bearing an inscription. You may find a charity school in your community, set up in the 19th century either by the National Society (Church of England) or the British and Foreign Schools Society (Nonconformists). They were often attached to churches or chapels and some may still have inscriptions saying who built them and when.

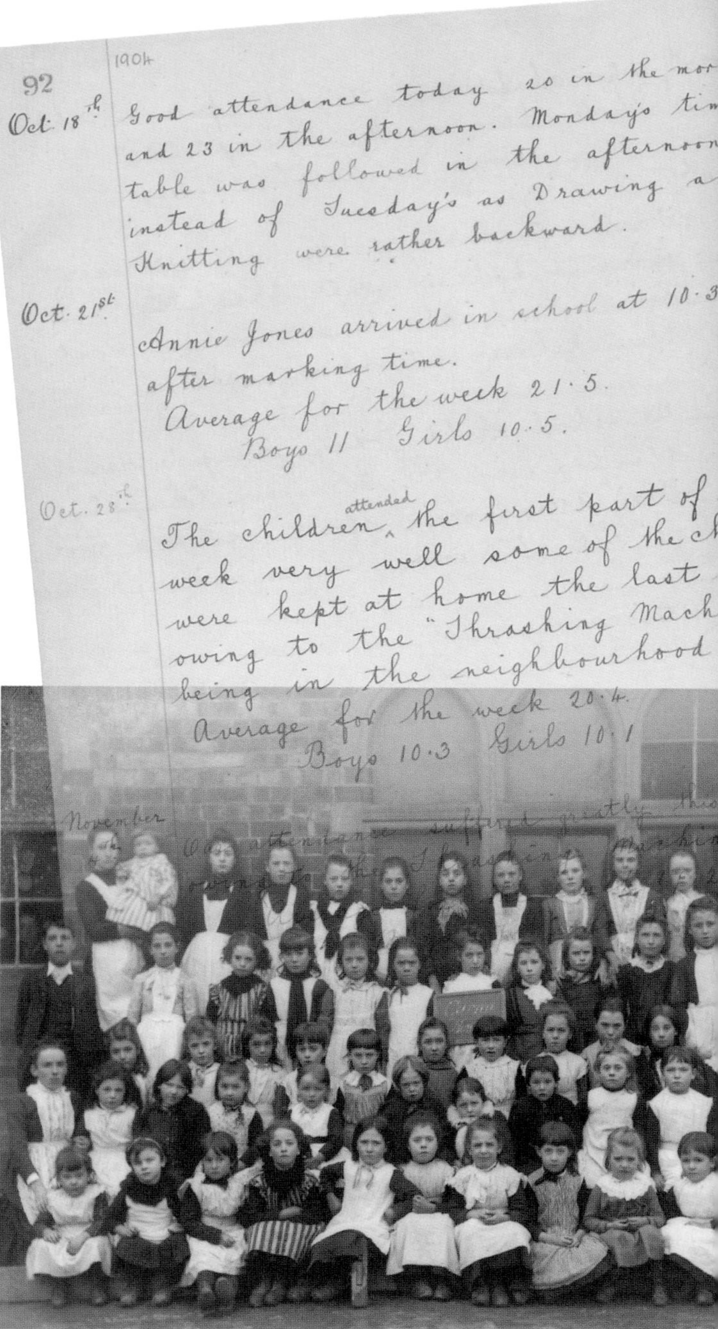

92 1904

Oct 18th Good attendance today 20 in the mor
and 23 in the afternoon. Monday's tim
table was followed in the afternoon
instead of Tuesday's as Drawing a
Knitting were rather backward.

Oct. 21st Annie Jones arrived in school at 10.3
after marking time.
Average for the week 21.5.
Boys 11 Girls 10.5.

Oct. 28th The children attended the first part of
week very well some of the c
were kept at home the last
owing to the "Thrashing Mach
being in the neighbourhood
Average for the week 20.4.
Boys 10.3 Girls 10.1

November

Skipping school School log books provide a fascinating picture of local life. In rural districts, assisting with farm work often took precedence over going to school, such as at Rhydygorlan 'Cwm' School in Merionethshire, when for the week ending October 28, 1904, the teacher noted that some children were not present because the 'thrashing machine' was in the district. Posing for the school photograph, such as at Carno School, Wales, in 1890, was an annual event. Look for captions listing the pupils' names, some of which may crop up elsewhere in your research.

Finding the paperwork
In your local record office you may find school log books (daily records kept by head teachers) dating from the 1840s and also admission registers, which had to be kept from 1870. Some log books are still held by schools.

- Look in your local library and record office for class photographs, magazines, reports, examination certificates and leaving certificates. Books of old photographs (see pages 70-71) often contain class groups.
- Parliamentary papers, such as the reports of the Charity Commission (1839-40, 1896-1907) and the Newcastle Commission (1857), provide information about elementary education, such as the types of school building, size of classes and what was taught. They can be seen at public reference libraries.
- For the 20th century, look in your local or county record office for the annual reports of the local education authority's education committee. They note class sizes and attendance, and the building of new schools.

Something old, something new Your local state secondary school may have a longer history than you think. Look for clues, such as old buildings on the present site. The Tudor red-brick range at the core of Boston Grammar School in Lincolnshire (above) was erected in 1567, using materials from a former Franciscan friary. It remained like this for 300 years before being extended. Today, Boston Grammar is a state secondary, and the Tudor building is the school library, surrounded by modern blocks (left).

Looking at secondary schools

You may find several different types of secondary schools in your area, including grammar and public schools. Although the oldest public schools, such as Eton and Winchester, have medieval or Tudor buildings at their core, most are Victorian Gothic in style and set in spacious grounds. These schools may have published an account of their history, which you can buy from the school, or you may find a copy at your local library.

History in the making Admissions registers, school magazines and class photographs may have been deposited at your local record office or kept at the school. Look out for printed histories that were produced to mark anniversaries or for the Millennium. Schools often provide an account of their history on their websites.

- Schoolmasters in the 17th and 18th centuries had to conform to the Established Church and their licences can be found among ecclesiastical court records at your county record office. Volumes of the *Victoria County History*, kept at your local public reference library, include information taken from documentary and printed sources on schools since the Middle Ages for some areas. The *Victoria County History* is an ongoing project to create a comprehensive history of each county of England. Visit **www.victoriacountyhistory.ac.uk** for details.
- Trade directories (see pages 74-75) will include the addresses of schools that have since been closed, but records are unlikely to have survived.
- In old copies of your local newspaper (see pages 74-75), you may find advertisements for the numerous 'dame-schools' that existed before 1870. They were run by older women in their homes.
- Before 1872, Scotland had burgh and parish schools. Records are held in the Burgh, Heritors' and Kirk Session records at the National Archives. Later records are also held there, in the Scottish Office Education Department archive.

FIND OUT MORE

- **www.scit.wlv.ac.uk/ukinfo** A website with links to universities and colleges of further education.
- **www.applebymagna.org.uk** Local history site covering education.
- **www.victoriantimes.org** Information on the Victorian education system and Victorian life.

Uncovering two hundred years of a seaside school

All villages, towns and cities have their primary schools – places where, often for more than a hundred years, the youngest community members have been nurtured in their earliest days of education. In central Brighton is a modern-looking primary school that disguises a rich history revealed in a search through local records.

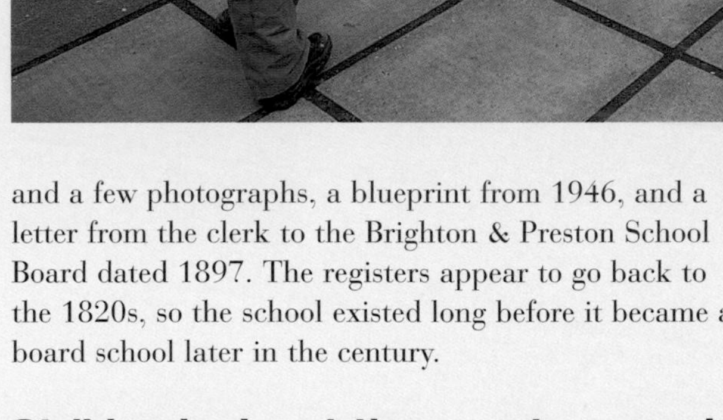

The old school A rare photograph shows Middle Street before it was demolished in the 1970s. The tall windows and imposing façade were typical of Victorian schools.

Starting out

Middle Street Primary School in Brighton is a boxy 1970s building, shoehorned into a corner plot in the heart of the medieval part of the town. How did it come to be in such an unlikely spot?

The first place to start looking into the school's past is the local history centre. At the Brighton centre a card index lists all the town's schools under 'Education'. Middle Street was one of many board schools formed after the Education Act of 1870, but the local archivist suggests that there will be more to be found at the county archive.

The catalogue of East Sussex County Archive is accessible on-line via the Access to Archives (A2A) website **www.a2a.org.uk** (see page 16). Initial results for Middle Street School look disappointing: a log book, some registers, title deeds and a few photographs, a blueprint from 1946, and a letter from the clerk to the Brighton & Preston School Board dated 1897. The registers appear to go back to the 1820s, so the school existed long before it became a board school later in the century.

Striking lucky at the county records

A visit to the county archive produces a fuller list of its holdings. A brief history states that Brighton Middle Street School began as the Union Charity School, founded and maintained by subscription and by payment of a penny a week from scholars. The school became a board school in 1875, and a new building was erected. The Boys' and Girls' Junior Schools were combined as a Junior Mixed school in July 1930; and in 1935 this was amalgamated with the Infants' school. It was rebuilt on the same site in 1974.

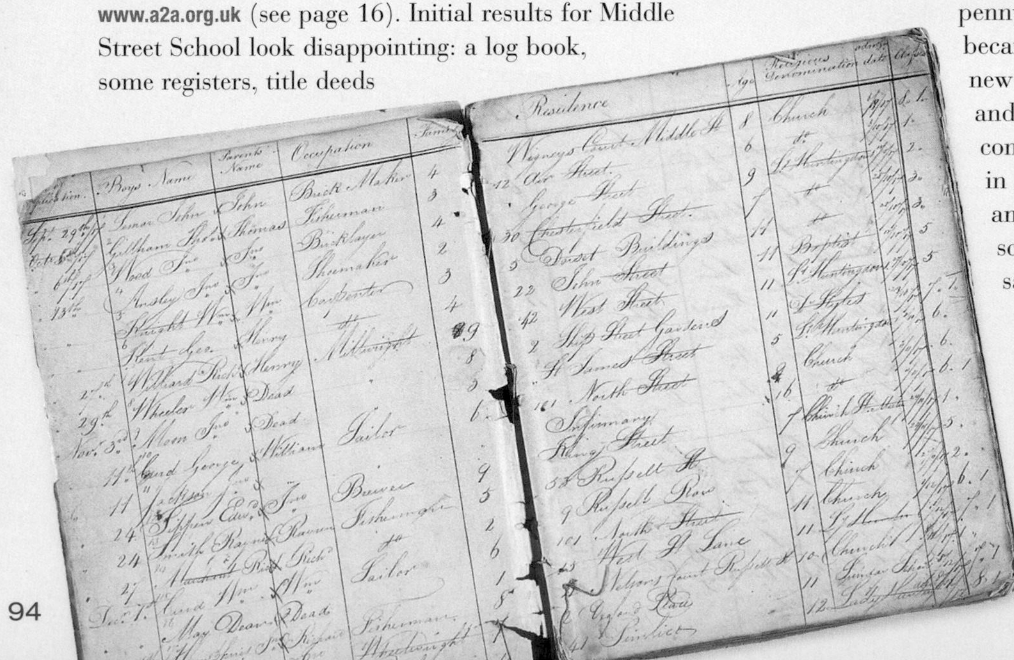

First day at school In an admissions register of 1817, the father of each new pupil is named and his occupation given, as well as the address and religious denomination of each child. The occupations include fisherman, millwright, shoemaker, tailor and brickmaker.

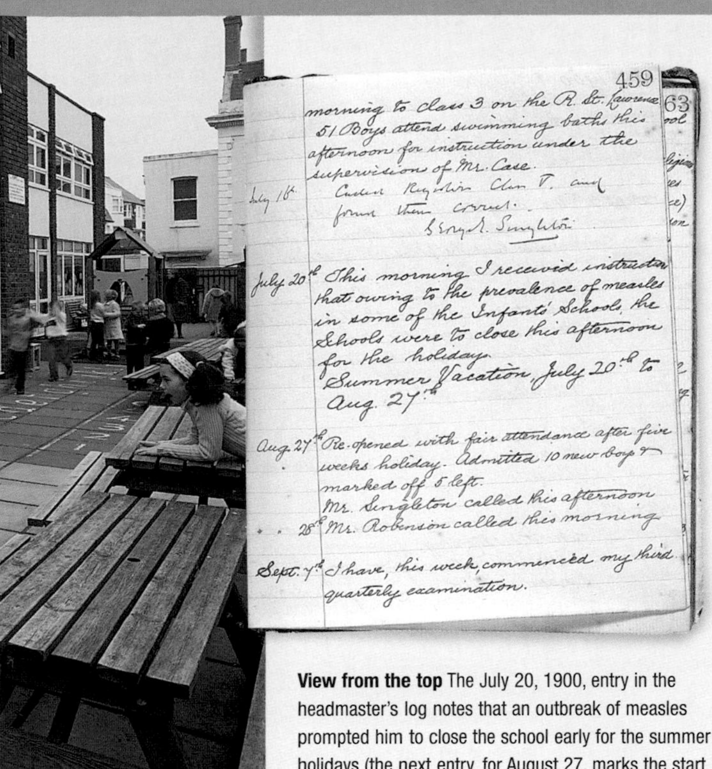

459

morning to class 3 on the R. St. Lawrence
51 Boys attend swimming baths this afternoon for instruction under the supervision of Mr. Case.

July 18th [illegible] Register Class V. and found them correct.
[illegible] Singleton

July 20th This morning I received instruction that owing to the prevalence of measles in some of the Infants' Schools, the Schools were to close this afternoon for the holidays.
Summer Vacation, July 20th to Aug. 27th

Aug. 27th Re-opened with fair attendance after five weeks holiday. Admitted 10 new boys & marked off 5 left.
Mr. Singleton called this afternoon

28th Mr. Robinson called this morning

Sept. 7th I have, this week, commenced my third quarterly examination.

View from the top The July 20, 1900, entry in the headmaster's log notes that an outbreak of measles prompted him to close the school early for the summer holidays (the next entry, for August 27, marks the start of the new term). The kindly nature of the man shines through the log, and many of the themes would be familiar to teachers at Middle Street School today (left).

The documents from the stacks put flesh onto these bare historical bones. There are admissions registers dating from 1817, and the single log book turns out to be fascinating. The heavy metal clasp is now broken, but it is still an imposing volume, an almost day-by-day account of the life of the school as seen from the top. What emerges are the broad themes and the seasonal rhythms of life in a Victorian board school. The head constantly laments that boys come to him from the infants' not knowing their letters, and visits from inspectors are noted.

The title deeds, sheets of vellum with wax seals and dense calligraphic writing, show that some of the land on which the school now stands was acquired by compulsory purchase in 1875, when the school was taken on by the board. Presumably, compulsory education meant more children so more space was needed: the Brighthelmstome Dispensary at No. 29 Middle Street had to make way.

Getting under the skin of the school

The plan of the school from 1946 gives an indication of what the Victorian building was like. The head's office looked down from the upper floor onto the playground and onto the street: the perfect headmasterly eyrie. And there are far more photographs than the on-line listings suggested: a snap of the Christmas pantomime from 1938, and of Empire Day celebrations; group portraits of sports teams and of evacuees in the school yard before they were sent away to the safety of rural Yorkshire.

The press cuttings are especially useful as they point to highlights in the school's history and draw on sources lost to present-day researchers. One cutting reports the school centenary dinner in 1905. Speeches are recorded verbatim, with men describing in detail the life and layout of the school they attended in their youth – before the Victorian rebuild. This cutting also states that in the first weeks of the school's existence, the pupils were marched to the sea front to see the passing cortege of the dead hero Nelson. This explains why the school badge, in the years when pupils wore uniform, depicted a warship in full sail.

Going back to school

A visit to the school, with the headmistress's permission, turns up more material still. A teacher and a parent who works in the Brighton history centre are preparing an exhibition for the school's bicentenary in 2005. They have most of the missing log books and registers, which the school had kept, and – at last – photographs of the Victorian building demolished in the 1970s. These show an engraved stone plaque set over the entrance to the old building that recorded the school's history from charity institution in 1805 to board school. It turns out that this one scrap was salvaged after the demolition, and is now set in a corner of the playground. Illegible in places, and slightly mossy, it is a testament to this little school's 200 years of history.

Forties memorablia The front cover of a wartime evacuee's diary dated 1941 (right) shows the Middle Street badge depicting Nelson's warship. A press cutting found in the country records shed light on the origin of the motif in 1805. After the war, it was back to school as usual – with daily rations of free milk for pupils (above, in 1948).

Learning about big industry

Your town or city might owe its existence to a large industry such as cotton and textiles, coal mining, iron and steel production or car-making. You can find out how it influenced your community by visiting some of Britain's outstanding industrial museums. Your local record office or public library can also help you to build up a picture of industrial life in your area.

From heyday to today

Although many industries, such as cotton manufacture and coal-mining, have disappeared or shrunk out of all recognition, local societies and museums take great interest in preserving signs in the landscape and investigating the past. Many mill towns, pit villages and manufacturing centres have been in existence for less than four generations, which makes it easy to track their history back to their origins. By visiting museums and record offices, you can trace the stories of working communities as they flourished, declined and then slowly transformed again into the places we know today.

Every picture tells a story Visual records, such as the photograph of workers leaving the Jaguar Foleshill car plant in Coventry (top) in the late 1940s, and the advertisement for the British Motor Show (above) from *Punch* magazine, 1958, give an idea of what goods were produced in your area and the people employed in these industries. Study the buildings; you may recognise some that have other uses today.

Picturing the industrial life

Old photographs (see pages 70-71) are a good starting point for learning about the industries that made your community. To see a new ship rising above a row of terraced houses at the end of a street in Sunderland, or on the banks of the Clyde, is to grasp how an entire community depended on the fluctuating fortunes of shipbuilding.

- Look for illustrations of factory buildings and workers' houses that have been demolished. You will find these places if you work back through Ordnance Survey (OS) maps (see pages 72-73) at your local record office.

- Note the distinctive dress of some workers, such as the shawls and clogs of the Lancashire cotton mill girls or the lamps, helmets and knee pads of the miners.
- Look for photographs of social events, such as galas, when trade unionists marched behind banners, led by a brass band. Churches, musical groups and sports teams also played a key role in the lives of workers.

Getting involved

Support local efforts to preserve the remains of the past by joining an industrial history or archaeological society.

- Ask at your library for details of any local society's activities, such as its programme of events and the membership secretary's contact details.
- Take part in projects to restore industrial premises. Local societies have restored many old mills and forges, such as the Chedleston flint mill in Staffordshire and Wortley Top Forge in Yorkshire.
- Join members of a society who are researching the documentary history of a local industry. Ask at your record office for information.

Talking to people

Recording the memories of former workers is an important way of preserving the past. Once an industry goes, the skills and dialects of the workforce gradually become forgotten.

- Ask former workers the purpose of tools that you have seen in a museum or photograph. How were they used?
- Ask about the words that were used in a craft or industry. What did a miner mean by a 'motty'? In the cutlery industry, what exactly is 'hollow ware'?

Powerful images Today, one of the few places where you can experience the sounds and smells of a working steam mill engine is in an industrial museum, such as the Museum of Science and Industry in Manchester. Steam power played a key role in the city's industrial development as a centre of the cotton trade. Other local industries, such as locomotive building (Beyer, Peacock & Co, 1854-1966) and early car manufacture (Rolls-Royce and Ford), are also represented here.

Tracking down company records

The companies involved in each industry will have kept records about their operations, workforces and buildings.

- Search the catalogues at your local record office for company records. Look for board minutes, accounts, annual reports, catalogues and correspondence, which detail the running of the business, the number of employees, what was made and who the customers were.
- Search the internet or ask at the local record office for the whereabouts of special collections, such as the archives of the British motor industry at the Heritage Motor Centre (see below).
- For information about local trade union activity, visit your record office or contact the Modern Records Centre at the University of Warwick (see DIRECTORY). For Scottish records, try the Department of Manuscripts at the National Library of Scotland (see DIRECTORY).
- The Guildhall Library, London (see DIRECTORY), has a collection of fire insurance records, starting with the Sun Fire Office in 1710. The registers include names of owners of industrial sites and descriptions of buildings.

FIND OUT MORE

The following museums, some housed on the sites of old mills, mines and docks, can tell you much about the industries and the communities that grew up around them.

- **Derwent Valley Mills World Heritage Site** Look round the water-powered cotton mills and factories that Sir Richard Arkwright built in the valley from 1771 onwards. You can explore the village of Cromford that Arkwright built for his workers and get a feel for the community that once lived here. www.derwentvalleymills.org; www.cromfordmill.co.uk
- **Beamish, The North of England Open Air Museum** Experience life in the north of England in the 19th and early 20th century. You can go down a coal mine, ride on a tram and visit a re-created colliery village at this museum outside Newcastle upon Tyne. www.beamish.org.uk
- **Museum of Science and Industry, Manchester** Find out about Britain's first industrial city. Based in an 1830s railway station complex, the museum has an impressive collection of working steam mill engines (see left). www.msim.org.uk
- **Museum in Docklands, London** Historic boats, a Georgian warehouse of artefacts, and recorded interviews with dock-workers recall a time when this was a bustling port. www.museumindocklands.org.uk
- **Heritage Motor Centre** All the records of the British motor industry, including a collection of cars and photographs, tell the story of the car-producing communities at this museum in Gaydon, Warwickshire. www.heritage-motor-centre.co.uk

Tasting the life of industrial Britain

Every one of Britain's traditional heavy industries, from coal mining and slate quarrying to iron and steel working, shipbuilding, heavy engineering and textile manufacture, declined in the late 20th century. Now, after decades of demolition and scrapping, their relics and remnants are being preserved and converted into hands-on museums, where you can gain a sense of what it was like to hew coal, quarry slate, operate a loom or shape white-hot metal.

King Coal

The heavy industry that, more than any other, epitomises Britain's days as an industrial powerhouse is coal mining. The combination of hard, heavy work in dangerous, difficult conditions, allied to the legendary close-knit character of mining communities, gives coal miners a special place in the hearts of people who would shudder at the thought of going underground.

Several mining museums trace the story of King Coal from its 19th-century peak to the present day. At preserved mines such as the Big Pit National Mining Museum of Wales (Blaenavon, south Wales) and the National Coal Mining Museum for England at Caphouse Colliery (Wakefield, west Yorkshire) you can take a tour through the underground workings. In the dark, dank, claustrophobic tunnels you can see the narrow seams where men dug coal lying on their sides in puddles of water. The guides, ex-miners themselves, know exactly how to set the scene with tales both grim and inspiring.

Places to visit

- National Coal Mining Museum for England, Caphouse Colliery. **www.ncm.org.uk**
- Scottish Mining Museum, Lady Victoria Colliery. **www.scottishminingmuseum.com**
- Big Pit National Coal Museum. **www.museumwales.ac.uk/en/bigpit**

Illuminating story Underground tours bring the history of coal mining to life. Here a guide from the National Coal Mining Museum demonstrates a Davy lamp. It was invented by Sir Humphry Davy in 1815 to give miners a safe form of lighting, and the basic design has not changed since.

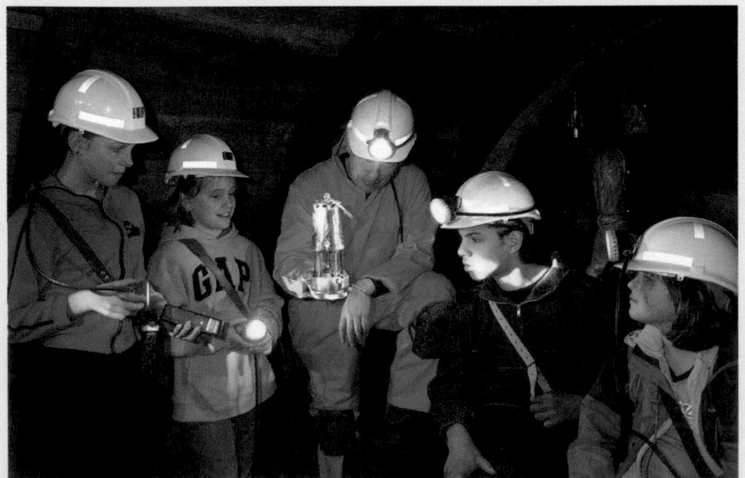

Digging for metal and rock

Coal miners were not the only men to work long hours under the earth. The extraction of iron, lead and tin ore demanded the same qualities of strength and endurance, and led to the establishment of the same kinds of exclusive industrial settlements – as did the quarrying of Welsh slate.

There are subterranean workings to explore, as well as the surface plant where the metal was separated from the rock, in museums dedicated to each of these industries: iron ore in the spooky Clearwell Caves in Gloucestershire's Forest of Dean; lead in the museums at Wanlockhead in the Lowther Hills south of Lanark and at Killhope in Upper Weardale, County Durham; and tin in Geevor mine at Pendeen in far west Cornwall. As for slate, there are several quarry workings open to the public in north Wales, notably the Welsh Slate Museum at Llanberis and the vast underground caverns at Llechwedd.

Close encounter A wander down the 1.25m (4ft) wide, 2.25m (7ft) high passages of Locknell Mine in Wanlockhead, Scotland, gives a sense of the cramped conditions in which miners worked.

Places to visit

- Clearwell Caves Ancient Iron Mines. **www.clearwellcaves.com**
- Scotland's Museum of Lead Mining, Wanlockhead. **www.leadminingmuseum.co.uk**
- North of England Lead Mining Museum, Killhope. **www.durham.gov.uk/killhope**
- Geevor Tin Mine. **www.geevor.com**
- Welsh Slate Museum, Llanberis. **www.museumwales.ac.uk/en/slate**
- Llechwedd Slate Caverns. **www.llechwedd-slate-caverns.co.uk**

A working mill At Quarry Bank Mill you can see the machinery in action, including the 500-spool mule (above). The Lancashire looms are still powered by waterwheel and weave cloth that is sold in the museum's shop. The steam room tells how steam power was added in 1810 as a power back-up in the event of water shortages.

Cotton and wool

Along with coal mining and metal-working, it was the textile trade that underpinned the Industrial Revolution. The mills with their gaunt silhouettes, towering chimneys and many rows of windows still stand in many towns and cities; some still work, but most are now redundant, killed off by competition. You can get an excellent idea of the noise, exhaustion and camaraderie of cotton mill work in Quarry Bank Mill at Styal in Cheshire with its steam engines, clattering looms and ex-millworker guides; while for wool mill history there is Coldharbour Mill at Uffculme in east Devon, where you can see carding and spinning operations as well as more fine steam engines.

Places to visit

- Quarry Bank Mill, Styal. **www.quarrybankmill.org.uk**
- Coldharbour Mill Working Wool Museum. **www.coldharbourmill.org.uk**

Working the metal

The processes of metal working with their fire, steam and clangorous tools and machinery are brought vividly to life at Ironbridge in Shropshire, cradle of the Industrial Revolution, with tours of the huge blast furnaces at Blists Hill set in a re-creation of a Victorian working town. At Abbeydale Industrial Hamlet in Sheffield you can see how craftsmen used great tilt hammers and grinding wheels to make steel scythe blades and other sharp-edged items. At Blaenavon in south Wales vast ironworks buildings from the late 18th century have been preserved, including furnaces, cast houses, kilns and workers' cottages.

Places to visit

- Ironbridge Gorge Museums. **www.ironbridge.org.uk**
- Abbeydale Industrial Hamlet. **www.tilthammer.com/hamlet/index.html**
- Blaenavon Ironworks Museum. **www.btinternet.com/~blaenavon.ironworks/Pages/ironworks.htm**

Moulding the clay

The pottery business dominated its landscape (chiefly the Midlands) with deep clay extraction holes, spoil heaps and the smoking chimneys of the conical kilns. At Gladstone Pottery Museum at Longton, Stoke-on-Trent, in the heart of the Potteries district of Staffordshire, you can experience pottery throwing, bone china flower making and pottery painting. The Etruscan Bone & Flint Mill at the nearby Etruria Industrial Museum gives an insight into what else besides clay went into pottery.

Places to visit

- Gladstone Pottery Museum. **www.stoke.gov.uk/ccm/navigation/leisure/museums**
- Etruria Industrial Museum. **www.stoke.gov.uk/ccm/navigation/leisure/museums**

Turning clay into gold To walk across the cobbled yard of the Gladstone Pottery Museum is like walking back in time. The old workshops and coal-fired bottle kilns go back to Victorian times, when the factory was manufacturing the world's finest bone china.

Town hives of small industry

Wherever you live, there will be signs to spot and records to follow of the numerous small industries, such as malting, brewing, milling, printing and textile spinning, that once supported the needs of the population and gave them employment. You will not have to go back far in history to find your town buzzing with a variety of activities that have since disappeared.

Looking for the signs of industry

A walk round your town may provide clues, such as water channels, lime kilns, the remnants of a furnace hearth or simply street names, which will help you to spot the signs of former thriving industries. Many buildings will survive, perhaps turned into a garage, shops or even a restaurant. Looking at old Ordnance Survey (OS) maps (see pages 72-73) first will give you leads on where to search.

- To identify a corn mill site, look for the banks of the former dam, the head leat (or goit in north England) that brings water along a channel from the river to the dam, the foundations of the water wheel, and the tail leat that takes the water back to the river.
- Maltings, dating from the late 18th and 19th centuries, produced the malted barley essential for brewing. Many have survived, to be turned into shops or housing. Look out for their distinctive conical chimneys, the vast floors where barley was dried and grain germinated, and for the tank used for steeping the barley. Close by will be the river or canal that supplied the water and the means of transporting the grain.
- The charcoal blast furnaces of the 17th and 18th centuries were water-powered. Look for the dam and the channel that brought the water to the bellows. The hearth, or its former position, will be close to the bellows site, where the molten iron was tapped.
- Lime kilns for making quicklime were worked in a similar fashion. They may have been built into a limestone or chalk hillside or close to a canal terminus for transporting goods and materials. You can judge the scale of the enterprise from the size of the kilns.
- Windmills were used not just for corn-milling, but for drainage. If you live near a windmill, look at the design. Post mills, such as the one at Mountnessing, Essex, have a central post and the sails can be turned to face the wind. The tower mill at Holbeach, Lincolnshire, has its sails fixed to a rotating cap on the top of the tower. Cranbrook in Kent has a smock mill, so-called because it resembles a man dressed in a smock. If a windmill has gone, look for the circular mound on which it stood.

Looking at the records

The local record office will hold a wide range of records to help you to build up a picture of industrial life in your locality.

Census returns Explore the census returns for your community from 1841 onwards (see pages 76-77) and note the occupations that are recorded for the population. Your search will give you a good idea of all the businesses and industries and who worked in them.

- Look at people's places of birth to see if they came from long-resident families or if they were newcomers.
- See whether they lived close together, perhaps in specially built rows of houses.
- The occupations column might tell you how many women and girls were employed in small factories or as outworkers in their own homes. Find out how old they were by looking at the age column.

Cracking a local riverside nut

Follow a waterway in any town and you will soon find clues to activities that kept its people in employment years ago. The ancient market town of Kingston upon Thames in Surrey is known today more for its shopping centre and university than for any industry. But if you track its little fast-flowing Thames tributary, the Hogsmill river, you soon find a waterside university hall of residence called Middle Mill and a narrow road, Mill Street, lined with workers' cottages – clear evidence of former milling activity. But what did the mill produce, and could the exotically named local pub, The Cocoanut, provide a clue?

Trade names Look out for street signs, such as Mill Street, pub signs, or the names of new buildings that may indicate a long-gone industry in your neighbourhood. You might find the enterprise marked on an old map.

Directories You can trace small businesses by looking at entries in trade directories from the 19th and early 20th centuries (see pages 74-75) and, more recently, telephone directories, which can be found at the British Telecom Archives (see DIRECTORY).

Newspapers Look at old newspapers (see pages 74-75) for business advertisements.

Old photographs Books of old photographs (see pages 70-71) or collections in local libraries will often show the premises of light industries in the background or groups of workers posed at their tasks.

Maps Spot the sites of small industries on OS, tithe award and town maps (see pages 72-73). They will show places such as brickworks, mills and brewhouses. Street names, such as Windmill Close, also give clues.

Delving further back in time

Parish and other records might help you to follow local industries beyond the 19th century.

Parish records At your local record office, look at parish registers of baptisms, marriages and burials – some of them give the men's trades or occupations (see page 85).

Probate inventories These documents, attached to wills and kept at county record offices, show a deceased's personal estate, which might include the tools of his trade.

Title deeds By looking at title deeds in your local record office, you might be able to pinpoint the origins of a business and the names of any partners. The deeds are often accompanied by small maps of the site.

Apprenticeship indentures The National Archives at Kew (see DIRECTORY) has registers of apprentices for 1710-1811, which record the name, place of residence and trade of the master, and the name of the apprentice. These may give you a further insight into local industries.

Company and guild records Records of an old industry may be held locally by a long-established company or trade guild. The Cutlers' Hall, Sheffield, founded in 1624, holds registers of apprentices and freemen.

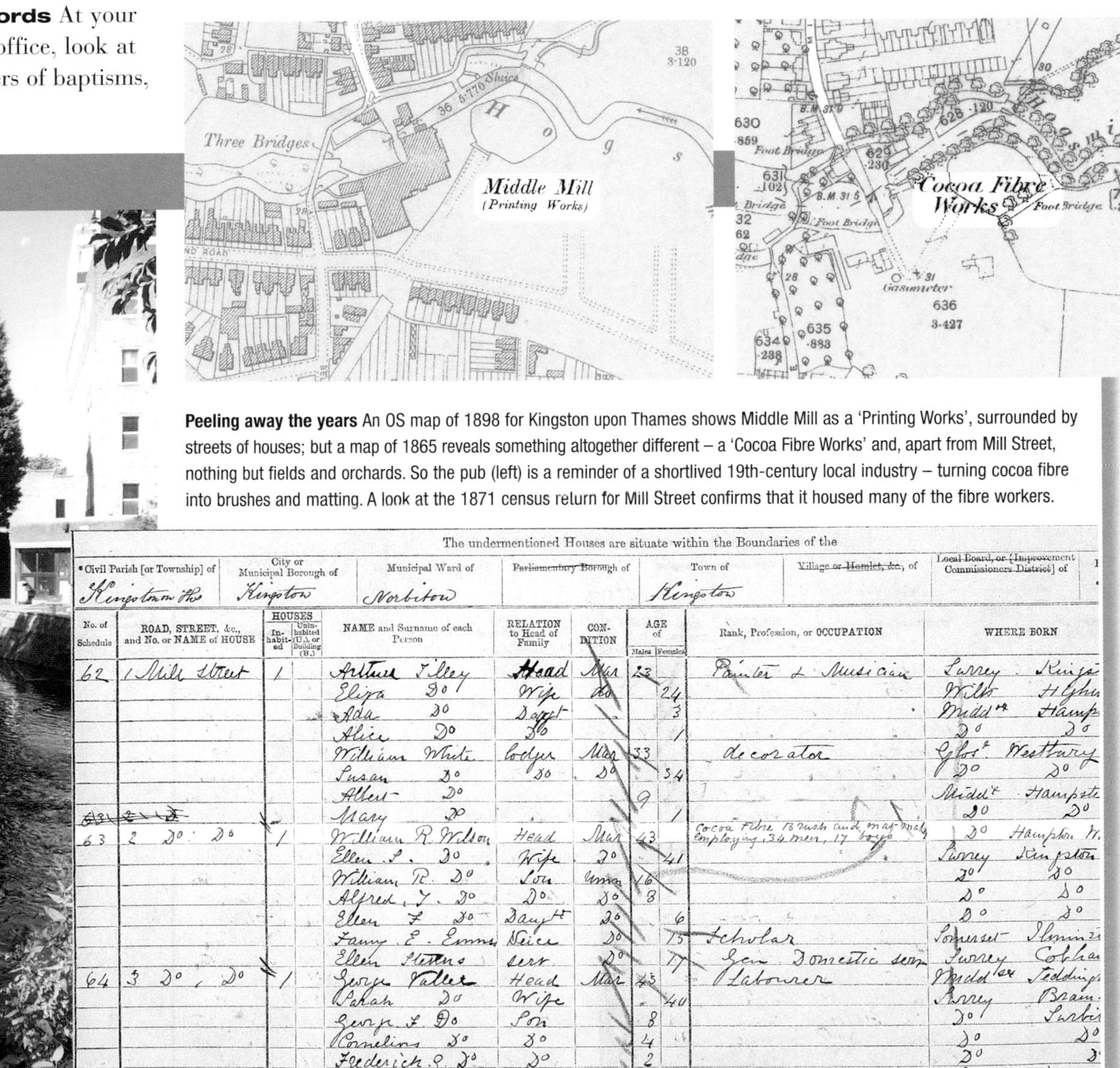

Peeling away the years An OS map of 1898 for Kingston upon Thames shows Middle Mill as a 'Printing Works', surrounded by streets of houses; but a map of 1865 reveals something altogether different – a 'Cocoa Fibre Works' and, apart from Mill Street, nothing but fields and orchards. So the pub (left) is a reminder of a shortlived 19th-century local industry – turning cocoa fibre into brushes and matting. A look at the 1871 census return for Mill Street confirms that it housed many of the fibre workers.

The undermentioned Houses are situate within the Boundaries of the

Civil Parish [or Township] of	City or Municipal Borough of	Municipal Ward of	Parliamentary Borough of	Town of	Village or Hamlet, &c., of	Local Board, or [Improvement Commissioners District] of
Kingston on Thames	Kingston	Norbiton		Kingston		

No. of Schedule	ROAD, STREET, &c., and No. or NAME of HOUSE	HOUSES In-habited	NAME and Surname of each Person	RELATION to Head of Family	CONDITION	AGE Males	AGE Females	Rank, Profession, or OCCUPATION	WHERE BORN
62	1 Mill Street	1	Arthur Tilley	Head	Mar	23		Painter & Musician	Surrey Kingston
			Eliza Do	Wife	Do		24		Wilts Highw…
			Ada Do	Daur			3		Midd^x Hamp…
			Alice Do	Do			1		Do Do
			William White	Lodger	Mar	33		decorator	Glos^r Westbury
			Susan Do	Do	Do		34		Do Do
			Albert Do			9			Midd^x Hampstead
			Mary Do				1		Do Do
63	2 Do Do	1	William R. Wilson	Head	Mar	43		Cocoa Fibre Brush and mat maker employing 34 men, 17 boys	Do Hampton W.
			Ellen S. Do	Wife	Do		41		Surrey Kingston
			William R. Do	Son	Unm	16			Do Do
			Alfred T. Do	Do	Do	8			Do Do
			Ellen F. Do	Daur	Do		6		Do Do
			Fanny E. Emms	Niece	Do		15	Scholar	Somerset Ilminster
			Ellen Stevens	Serv	Do		17	Gen Domestic serv	Surrey Cobham
64	3 Do Do	1	George Vallee	Head	Mar	43		Labourer	Midd^x Teddington
			Sarah Do	Wife			40		Surrey Bram…
			George F. Do	Son		8			Do Surbiton
			Cornelius Do	Do		4			Do Do
			Frederick G. Do	Do		2			Do Do

Cottage and village industry

Farming was not the only occupation in the countryside. The blacksmith, the carpenter and the village cobbler were familiar figures who served essential local needs and in some villages there were far more people working at a craft than working the land. Many rural communities were semi-industrial, often having a long-held association with a particular product or craft, such as hand-knitting or scythemaking.

Signs of village industry

Numerous small workshops were once dotted across rural Britain. Even in what are now sleepy villages, there is still ample evidence of these once bustling activities.

- Look for houses or pubs called 'The Old Forge', 'The Old Smithy' or any other name that suggests a craft formerly practised there.
- Keep an eye open for traces of faded advertisements for a trade above doorways or on gable ends of buildings.
- In wool-weaving areas, look for a row of large windows in the top storey of a house, allowing in extra light for a weaver to work by.
- Observe any outbuildings close to a house, especially those with chimneys. An old metalworker's workshop, for instance, might still have its hearth.

What the records reveal

You are unlikely to have to go far to uncover a mass of documentary evidence on rural industries in your area.

Old photographs and maps The practice of crafts, such as lacemaking or thatching, was a popular subject with Victorian photographers. But do check against other local records to make sure that such scenes were typical of when they were captured. You may also be able to site former local businesses by examining collections of old photographs (see page 70), perhaps with the help of an old OS map (see pages 72-73). You could discover that your local garage started life as a blacksmith's forge.

Directories Search through the old trade directories (see page 75) in your local reference library, being aware that a craftsman may have done much more varied work than his brief description suggests. Carpenters and joiners often acted as undertakers, while most blacksmiths were happy to forge anything in metal that a customer asked for.

Parish registers At your local record office look through the parish registers of baptisms, marriages and burials (see page 85) from the 16th to the 19th centuries. After 1813 a man's occupation was always recorded, and some earlier records include it too.

Census returns By searching the returns (see pages 76-77) for a village from 1841 to 1901, you can build up the story of its trade and industry during that time and follow family businesses through successive generations.

Militia returns Your local record office may have a militia return from the late 18th or early 19th century, when men aged between 18 and 45 were trained for military service in case Britain was invaded. These lists

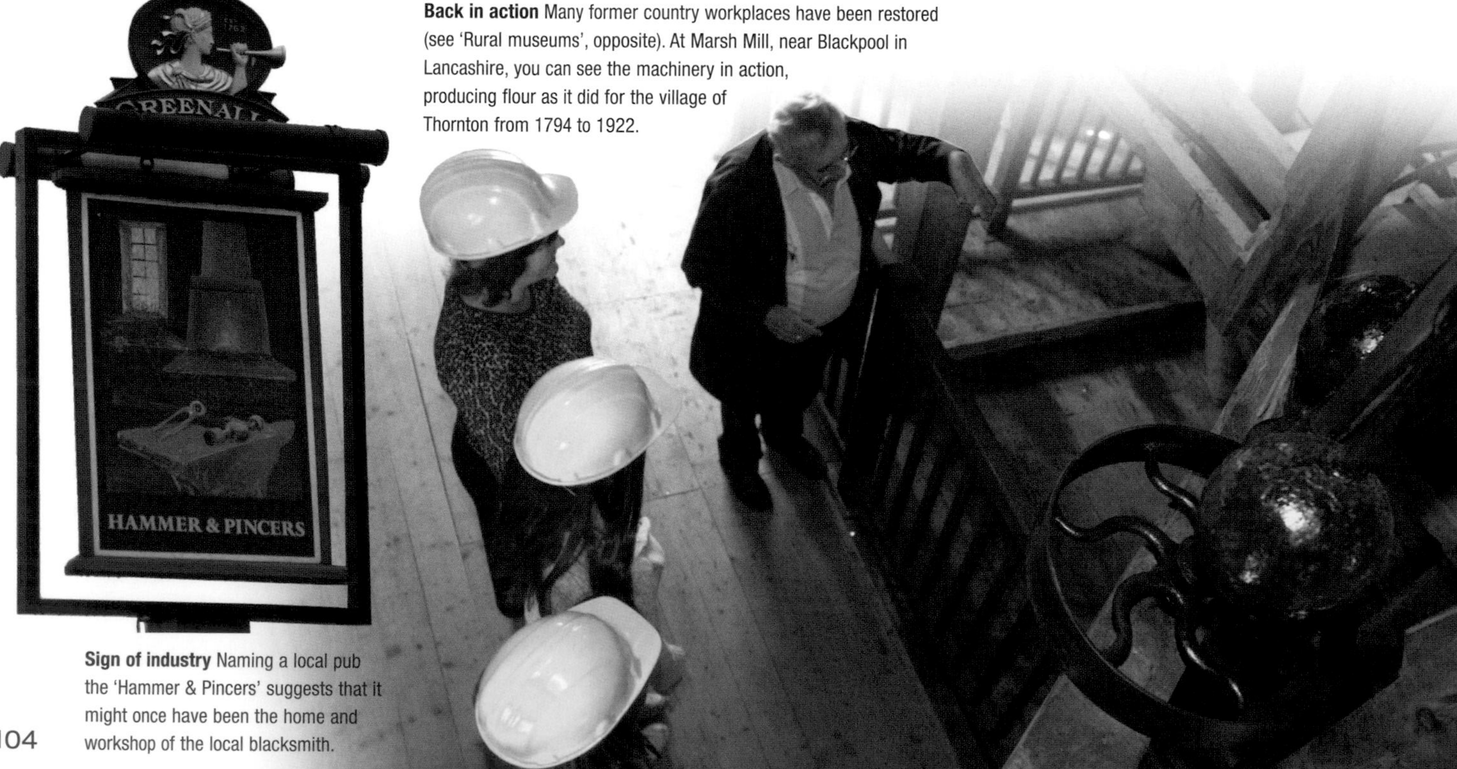

Back in action Many former country workplaces have been restored (see 'Rural museums', opposite). At Marsh Mill, near Blackpool in Lancashire, you can see the machinery in action, producing flour as it did for the village of Thornton from 1794 to 1922.

Sign of industry Naming a local pub the 'Hammer & Pincers' suggests that it might once have been the home and workshop of the local blacksmith.

The framework knitters of Leicestershire

The framework-knitting trade of the East Midlands grew quickly from the late 17th century, so that by 1800 knitters were found in at least 118 Leicestershire villages and hamlets. Socks, shirts, gloves, cravats and various fabrics were knitted on a frame in cottages, long after workshops using powered knitting machines were introduced during the mid 19th century. Much of the story of this small but essential industry can be followed through the records.

- Local parish registers often noted the occupation in the abbreviated form 'FWK'. Between January 1, 1813, and December 31, 1817, the register of Countesthorpe parish in Leicestershire recorded 51 framework-knitters, nearly 70 per cent of the workforce.
- Directories (see page 75) list the middlemen, known as 'bag hosiers', and the owners of workshops.
- Large volumes known as Parliamentary Papers, kept at local reference libraries, cover many enquiries into 19th-century trades and industries. Felkin's Enquiry of 1845 into the hosiery trade included interviews with framework knitters and employers.
- Wills and inventories (see pages 154-155) for the area show that the earliest knitters were usually part-time farmers as well.

Family affair A 1901 census return (right) for the village of Barton upon Soar, near Loughborough, shows that the framework-knitting cottage industry still persisted into the 20th century. At the top of the return is 58-year-old George Marlow, his occupation 'frame work knitter', while three of his eight children are either weavers or machinists.

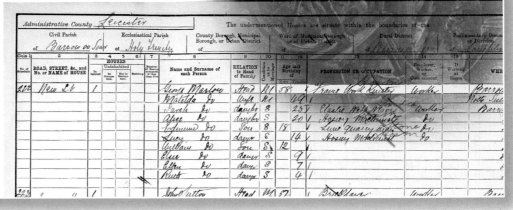

record each man's occupation. The Northamptonshire return for 1777 includes 94 men from the village of Raunds. Most were farmers, labourers or servants, but there were also several shoemakers, tailors, butchers, blacksmiths, carpenters, stonemasons, flax-dressers and lacemakers, plus a weaver, a miller and a baker.

Wills and inventories In the archives of your local record office, you will find the probate inventories that were attached to wills (see pages 154-155). These list the personal possessions of the deceased, including any tools or goods he might have manufactured.

The decline of rural crafts

By the late 19th century, cottage industries, faced with competition from factories and foreign imports, were no longer making a significant contribution to the household economy. In 1871, more than 20,000 Bedfordshire women plaited straw bonnets for a living – within 30 years their number had dropped to below 500. Meanwhile, the great agricultural depression cut the number of jobs for farm labourers, leading to a sharp fall in the rural population as people left to find work in the cities.

RURAL MUSEUMS

A number of museums give you a taste of what it was like to live and work as a cottage labourer (see DIRECTORY for addresses).

- Black Country Living Museum Reconstructions of former workshops and demonstrations of traditional local crafts, including glass-cutting, metalwork and sweet-making. www.bclm.co.uk
- Museum of English Rural Life Exhibition and demonstrations of old machinery and tools, and a large archive that includes books, old photographs, films and sound recordings. www.ruralhistory.org
- National Museum of Rural Life Displays of machinery and tools and a children's learning centre. www.nms.ac.uk/museumofrurallifehomepage.aspx
- St Fagans National History Museum Exhibitions and workshops with demonstrations of rural crafts. www.museumwales.ac.uk/en/stfagans
- Weald and Downland Open Air Museum A working smithy, watermill, windpump and brick-drying shed are among the 50 reconstructed village buildings, dating from the 13th century to Victorian times. www.wealddown.co.uk

Keeping things moving Trams proved an effective solution to Bristol's growing transport needs in the early 20th century. By the 1930s, they offered one of the cheapest and quickest ways of getting large numbers of people around the city.

From A to B by road, water and rail

Until fairly recently, the way most people got around was on foot or on horseback, and many public paths and bridleways in your area will be centuries old. But from the late 18th century onward, the growth of industry and urban expansion made swifter transport essential. Across Britain you can still spot traces of the rail, tram and canal systems that emerged during the later 18th and 19th centuries.

Following the highways and byways

The industrial boom of the 19th century led to many new rights of way, making it more convenient for people to get to work before buses, trams and trains were widespread.

- Compare the footpaths and bridleways in your village or town on a modern Ordnance Survey (OS) map with those on a first edition six-inch OS map drawn up in the 1850s or 60s (see pages 18-19). Were there more paths 150 years ago, and where did they lead to?
- At your local record office (see pages 10-11) look for enclosure awards and their maps (see page 73), setting out which lanes and highways in your local area were granted general public access.

Down your street

A stroll around your neighbourhood should help raise a host of questions about local streets that can then be answered by a visit to your city or county archives.

- The name of a street may contain clues to its age and to any former purpose or use. It is likely that a street named after a battle will date back to the time that it was fought. One named after an eminent person may suggest local links with that person (see pages 82-83). Look out also for the use of local names for alleyways or narrow passages, such as 'gennell', 'snicket' or 'wynd'.
- Note the names of roads leading to neighbouring towns, then check at the county record office to see if they were turnpike roads (see pages 60-61) in the 18th and 19th centuries. Glossop Road, Sheffield, was a new turnpike road in 1821 that soon attracted a middle-class suburb around it.
- A road that curves and bends in an irregular fashion may have grown up along old field or woodland boundaries. Find out by looking at old OS, tithe or enclosure maps (see pages 72-73).
- A straight road will have been planned. Look to see where such new roads were built to meet up with an old one as suburbs expanded in the late 19th century.
- Look for old photographs at your local record office of streets you know. Was the shape different a hundred years or so ago, and can you see what was there before the suburban houses or new shops were built?

Buses and trams

By the 1870s, the efficient new way to travel around many of Britain's towns and cities was by horse-drawn bus or tram. London had a network of 860 such vehicles in the 1890s. Electricity began to take over from horse-power around the turn of the 20th century, and motorised buses made their debut just before the First World War.

- Look at old photographs of your town (see pages 70-71) taken over the past 150 years, and see how much transport has changed during that time.
- Search through the records of bus and tram companies at your local record office or at the Guildhall Library in London (see DIRECTORY). Note which routes served your community, and who worked on them.

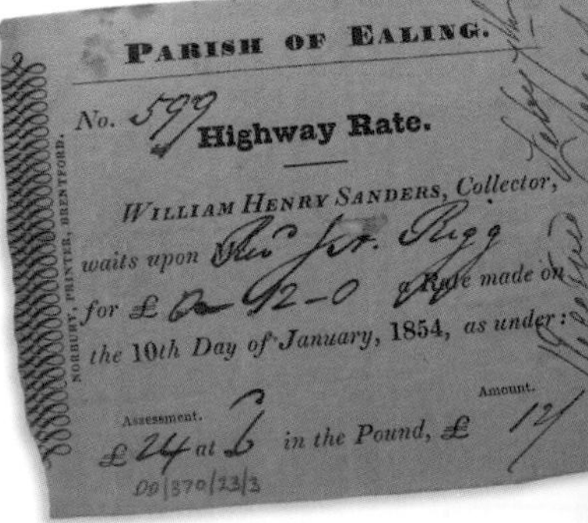
PARISH OF EALING.
No. 599 Highway Rate.
WILLIAM HENRY SANDERS, Collector,
waits upon
for £ of Rate made on the 10th Day of January, 1854, as under:
Assessment. Amount.
£24 at 6 in the Pound, £ 12/

Community tax Under an Act of 1555, the parish was responsible for the maintenance of local highways, and could levy a tax to pay for the work. Every able-bodied householder was also obliged to work on the roads for up to six days a year. Documents relating to this, including details of the frequent disputes that arose, can be seen along with other parish records at county record offices.

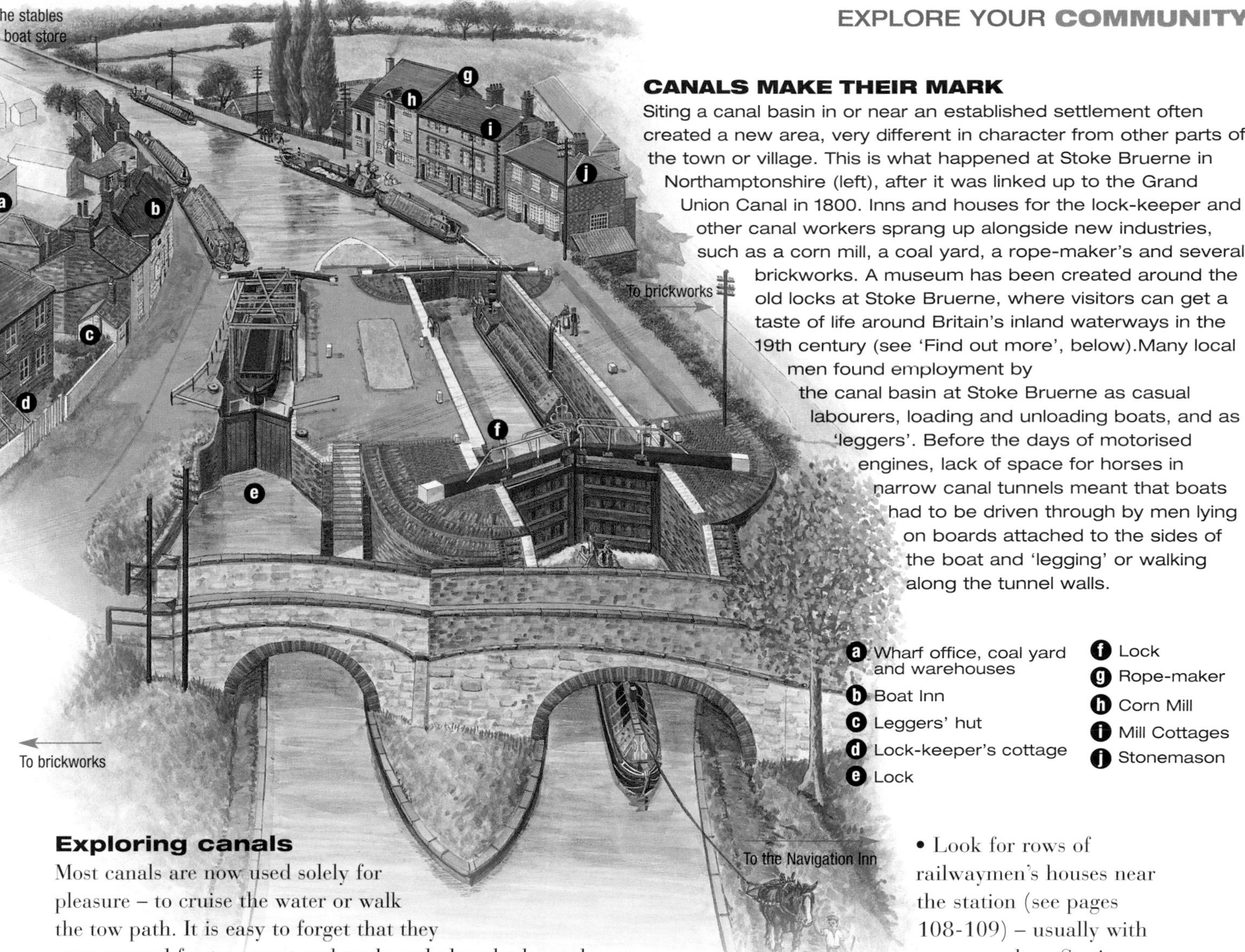

CANALS MAKE THEIR MARK

Siting a canal basin in or near an established settlement often created a new area, very different in character from other parts of the town or village. This is what happened at Stoke Bruerne in Northamptonshire (left), after it was linked up to the Grand Union Canal in 1800. Inns and houses for the lock-keeper and other canal workers sprang up alongside new industries, such as a corn mill, a coal yard, a rope-maker's and several brickworks. A museum has been created around the old locks at Stoke Bruerne, where visitors can get a taste of life around Britain's inland waterways in the 19th century (see 'Find out more', below).Many local men found employment by the canal basin at Stoke Bruerne as casual labourers, loading and unloading boats, and as 'leggers'. Before the days of motorised engines, lack of space for horses in narrow canal tunnels meant that boats had to be driven through by men lying on boards attached to the sides of the boat and 'legging' or walking along the tunnel walls.

Exploring canals

Most canals are now used solely for pleasure – to cruise the water or walk the tow path. It is easy to forget that they were created for transport and trade and played a key role in the economy of the communities they served. Canals were responsible for the rapid growth of ports such as Runcorn in Cheshire and for the character of the small settlements that formed around junctions, such as Shardlow in Derbyshire.

- At your local reference library you may find information on your local canal in the printed volumes of Parliamentary Papers, especially in the 12-volume *Report of the Royal Commission on Canals* (1906-11) and its accompanying maps. They are indexed by place name, so you can quickly find any local material.
- Search for records of canal companies at your local record office. Read through their accounts, minute books, correspondence, and engineers' reports on the everyday running and maintenance of the waterways.
- Look at local census returns (see pages 76-77) and try to identify boat people. They were often included as part of the community they were in on census day.

The railway comes to town

Railways that were constructed during the Victorian age have left their mark on most towns.

- Look for rows of railwaymen's houses near the station (see pages 108-109) – usually with names such as Station Road – and for pubs called the Railway Tavern.
- Search through your local census returns for people who worked on the railway – ticket collectors, firemen, porters and stokers.
- Records of many former railway companies survive, either in the National Archives at Kew, the National Archives of Scotland or the House of Lords Record Office (see DIRECTORY). Look for company reports, accounts, staff records, maps and plans, and even collections of old photographs. Staff records sometimes give complete service histories of the various workers.

FIND OUT MORE

- *The Railways of Britain: A Journey Through History* (Jack Simmons, Sheldrake Press, 1991)
- *Francis Frith's Trains and Buses* (Francis Frith, Frith Book Company, 2003)
- **www.nwm.org.uk** The National Waterways Museum's site includes details of canal history, along with numerous links to the websites of canal museums throughout Britain, including the one at Stoke Bruerne (see above).

Local station clues

The station that you pass through every day is worth a closer look, especially if it is one of the thousands built in the 19th century: the golden age of the train. See if you can spot the features that once made it the pride and joy of its community. Ornate wrought-iron footbridges, former coal yards and segregated waiting rooms are just some of the clues you may find that give a glimpse into your station's past.

The heyday of the railway station

In the hectic decades of the 19th century, railway companies joined in a competitive rush that sent lines first through every major town and then to far-flung corners of Britain, bringing travel within the reach of the poorest citizen. Stations sprang up everywhere. Many of these have today been stripped of their embellishments, and satellite buildings and yards sold off or put to other purposes. But some – like Settle in the main picture, which opened in 1876 – are remarkably well preserved.

As there were no railway stations before we started building them in Britain, the architects based the structures on familiar models such as estate cottages or suburban villas, each echoing the corporate style of the company that owned the line. Passengers had their comfort and convenience catered for with a refreshment room, waiting rooms, lavatories and a bridge connecting the platforms.

Station clock Take a look at the clock in your station – the Victorian original still takes pride of place in many stations, as at Great Malvern (left). Station clocks transformed the way people thought about time. Until the railways arrived, London and other cities kept different times – there was no need to do otherwise. But an efficient train service demanded a standard time – Greenwich Mean Time – and co-ordinated timetables. Every guard had a watch, and when a train pulled into a station, he would pass the correct time on to station staff, who would then sychronise the clock.

Waiting room Your station may still have a single waiting room, but once there were probably at least two, segregated into 'Ladies' and 'Gentlemen', with lavatories attached. A coal fire in winter, a solid table and horsehair-stuffed benches would have added home comforts.

Refreshment room Few trains in Victorian times carried their own stock of food and drink. Passengers changing trains would make for the station refreshment room to order something from a menu that might range from 'Breakfast with Cold Meat & Marmalade' for 2 shillings to sherry, port and champagne for 5 to 8 shillings a bottle.

Spotting the signs of your station's Victorian heritage

Take a look at the layout of your station and see if you can work out how this has changed since its heyday (see right). The Victorian station typically comprised a central block of platforms with waiting rooms and a ticket office, which have often survived unscathed.

Nearby lay the goods yard, coal yard and sidings. When the railways lost out to road haulage, many goods yards closed, as did coal yards once the steam train was phased out in the 1960s. Look around your station and you may find that the car park occupies the old coal yard, the house over the road was the stationmaster's, and the shabby hut down the line was the original signal box. Near the station you may also spot terraces of houses in a similar style, which were built for workers by the railway company.

Footbridge A gracefully curved footbridge, with lattice sides and decorative ironwork, is a feature of many Victorian stations. Look for initials in the ironwork that may give you the identity of the company that built the station, such as LCDR for London, Chatham & Dover Railway, one of more than 20 operating companies in the early 1900s.

Ticket office Often the only way to buy a ticket now is through an automated machine even though the old booking hall has survived in most stations. Step inside and see if the little hutch-like window of the Victorian ticket office still remains.

Platforms The two platforms (one for 'up' trains, the other for 'down') were raised as near as possible to the height of the carriage floors, so that passengers could step easily in and out. If your station has one, examine the canopy that shelters the platforms: Victorian canopies were often very elaborate, embellished with cast-iron columns and a valance or decorative board that hung down from the canopy edge.

Transports of delight

Britain, as a pioneer of trains, bicycles, passenger jets and many other forms of conveyance, has some of the best transport museums in the world. Visit them to see the story of travel in your community come alive.

Out for a ride You can catch a tram, such as the Southampton tram car of 1903 (above) – or drive one – at the National Tramway Museum in Crich, as well as journey back in time, passing the historic buildings of the Tramway Village. Vehicles of all kinds belong to the National Motoring Museum collection at Beaulieu, Hampshire, including the sporty 1956 Austin Healey 100M (left), a 1933 Morris Mobile Grocery Shop and mass-market saloons like the 1960s' Ford Cortina.

Freedom of the road

More than 100 years of British motoring is represented at the Heritage Motor Centre at Gaydon in Warwickshire. Here you can see the first cars to cause a flurry of excitement on Britain's streets, such as the 1896 Wolseley, and a walk along the museum's Time Road will give you an idea of how cars developed during the 20th century. The centre also holds the archives for Britain's car industry.

Motorbike fanatics get all the oil and leather smells, the buffed paintwork and engine intricacies they desire at the National Motorcycle Museum, Solihull. The collection includes more than 650 models.

The quieter, slower art of pushbiking is explored at the National Cycle Collection, Llandrindod Wells, Powys. Here you can see 250 machines, starting with an 1819 Hobby Horse and continuing with Boneshakers, Penny Farthings up to bicycles of today.

London's Transport Museum in Covent Garden tells the story of how people have got around the crowded capital. Exhibits include trams, horse-drawn buses, underground trains, trolleybuses and the celebrated London taxi. More vehicles can be seen at the Museum Depot in Acton Town, where uniforms, engineering drawings and poster artwork are on show. Tube and bus drivers can be heard reminiscing about the 'old days' as part of the museum's oral history project.

In Derbyshire, the National Tramway Museum at Crich has a collection of superbly maintained trams from around Britain, many of them offering rides (see above).

Places to visit

- Heritage Motor Centre, Gaydon. **www.heritage-motor-centre.co.uk**
- National Motorcycle Museum, Solihull. **www.nationalmotorcyclemuseum.co.uk**
- National Cycle Collection, Llandrindod Wells. **www.cyclemuseum.org.uk**
- London's Transport Museum, Covent Garden, London. **www.ltmuseum.co.uk**
- National Tramway Museum, Crich. **www.tramway.co.uk**
- National Motor Museum, Beaulieu. **www.beaulieu.co.uk**

On the water

As a seafaring nation Britain has many maritime museums – around 300 in all. Our coastal and sea trade, and defence, are explored in the displays and exhibits at the National Maritime Museum at Greenwich, and its sister at Falmouth, Cornwall, which holds the Small Boat Collection. All things maritime are covered, from slaving to passenger liners, naval warfare to international trade. Paintings, photographs and oral accounts show how seafaring communities were shaped.

Life and commerce on the canals (see page 107) and rivers is the topic at the National Waterways Museum in Gloucester Docks and the Boat Museum at Ellesmere Port in Cheshire, with their displays and collections of narrow-boats, barges and tugs. You can climb aboard some of the vessels to get a taste of the living conditions.

Places to visit

- National Maritime Museum, Greenwich. **www.nmm.ac.uk**
- National Maritime Museum, Falmouth. **www.nmmc.co.uk**
- National Waterways Museum, Gloucester. **www.nwm.org.uk**
- The Boat Museum, Ellesmere Port. **www.boatmuseum.org.uk**

On the rails

The National Railway Museum at York is a train-lover's dream – steam, diesel and electric locomotives, dining cars and Royal Saloons, snow ploughs and parcel vans. Other

Record breaker The *Mallard* (above), now at York's National Railway Museum, set a new world speed record for steam locomotives when it reached 126mph between Grantham and Peterborough in 1938.

attractions at the museum include railway story-telling, train rides, and thousands of items of train paraphernalia, including original posters. A fine collection of photographs and ephemera, signal boxes and equipment, as well as more than 20 steam locomotives, can be seen at the Didcot Railway Centre, while more gleaming locomotives take pride of place at STEAM, the museum of the Great Western Railway in Swindon's former railway works, established by Isambard Kingdom Brunel.

Places to visit

- National Railway Museum, York. www.nrm.org.uk
- Didcot Railway Centre. www.didcotrailwaycentre.org.uk
- STEAM, Museum of the Great Western Railway, Swindon. www.steam-museum.org.uk

In the air

Air travel has developed more dramatically during its short life than any other form of transport. The collections at the Royal Air Force Museums at Hendon in London and Cosford, Shropshire, range from the pioneer 'stringbag' planes of the early 20th-century to the modern Eurofighter. Civil aircraft include a BOAC Bristol Britannia 312, which operated on the London-New York route in the 1950s, and a 1960s' Vickers VC10. Among the Imperial War Museum's vast collection of military aircraft at Duxford, Cambridgeshire, you can see a de Havilland Comet 4, which in 1958 made history as the first jet to cross the Atlantic carrying fare-paying passengers. Twenty years later, Concorde was transporting people across the Atlantic at twice the speed of sound – a prototype is on display.

The Shuttleworth Collection at Biggleswade, Bedfordshire, features a notable collection of restored aeroplanes, including the scarlet de Havilland Comet which won the 1934 England-Australia race, and a 1941 Hawker Sea Hurricane designed for landing on aircraft carriers.

Places to visit

- Royal Air Force Museums, London and Cosford. www.rafmuseum.org.uk
- Imperial War Museum, Duxford. http://duxford.iwm.org.uk
- Shuttleworth Collection, Biggleswade. www.shuttleworth.org

OTHER MUSEUMS TO VISIT

- Scottish Vintage Bus Museum, Lathalmond, Dunfermline. www.busweb.co.uk/svbm
- National Museums and Galleries of Wales (Maritime and Transport), Cardiff. www.museumwales.ac.uk/en/200
- C.M. Booth Collection of Historic Vehicles, Rolvenden, Kent. www.motorsnippets.com/motormuseums/directory.asp?Letter=C
- Trolleybus Museum, Sandtoft. www.sandtoft.org.uk
- Benson Veteran Cycle Museum, Wallingford, Oxfordshire (open by appointment only, April-August, Tel. 01491 83841).
- The Canal Museum, Stoke Bruerne, Northamptonshire. www.canaljunction.com/museum/stoke_bruerne.htm
- Windermere Steamboats Museum, Cumbria. The website gives information on its current refurbishment. www.steamboat.co.uk
- Museum of Flight, East Lothian. www.nms.ac.uk/flight/index.asp

Up and away British Airways advertised its first flights to Europe from the new Gatwick Airport in 1936.

The public face of prosperity

If you stroll around your town and look at the street layout, the style of the public buildings and any parks and walks, you will uncover all kinds of clues about the character of the place. Was it shaped by the profits of medieval wool traders, fashionable Georgians or Victorian industrialists? What did people think of the new town hall design all those years ago? A visit to your local record office may uncover the answers.

Pride of the town

Take a close look at your local guildhall or town hall. It may reveal important clues to when and why it was built.

Prime location If you live in a town with a 16th or 17th-century centre, it may have a timber-framed hall raised on columns above an open arcade. The design provided shelter for traders at street level. The room or rooms above often served as a market hall and meeting place for the manorial court, as well as a school or cloth hall. Some public halls stood alone in the middle of the market place, at the heart of the town's commercial district. Today many, such as the 18th-century market hall at Dursley in Gloucestershire, are marooned by traffic.

Working under cover The local cutlers met upstairs in the 14th-century guildhall in Thaxted, Essex, while traders worked in the arcade at street level.

Perhaps your town has a guildhall that projects into the main street, like those of Plympton and South Molton in Devon. It would have been built this way because it required more space than the houses and shops around it.

Proud landmark If your town hall is in a striking classical design, with columns and a portico, it was probably built in the late 17th or 18th century to enhance the town's prestige.

The Victorians erected large town halls to accommodate splendid reception and dining rooms, chambers for meetings and offices for staff. Trading activities were moved out to new market halls and corn exchanges. The public buildings of the period share a grandeur imbued with civic pride. Manchester has a huge Gothic-style building, with arches, gables, spires and a tall clock tower; neighbouring Bolton favoured a classical style, with a flight of steps rising to six columns and a pediment, and a pair of lions framing the entrance.

Modern aspirations Even if your town hall was built in the 20th century, it could be an imposing classical-style structure, such as Barnsley (1932), or a part-Modernist, part-classical design, such as Waltham Forest (1938).

A sense of space

Walk around your town and look for the elegant parades and promenades, squares and crescents that were features of Georgian town planning. You may discover public walks, which were especially popular at this time in spa towns such as Bath and Epsom, and seaside resorts like Brighton and Scarborough. New promenades were built in many towns in the 18th century, such as Leicester's New Walk, originally called Queen's Walk, which was built

Status symbol Bradford's town hall, which opened in 1873, symbolised the city's new-found wealth as a manufacturing centre.

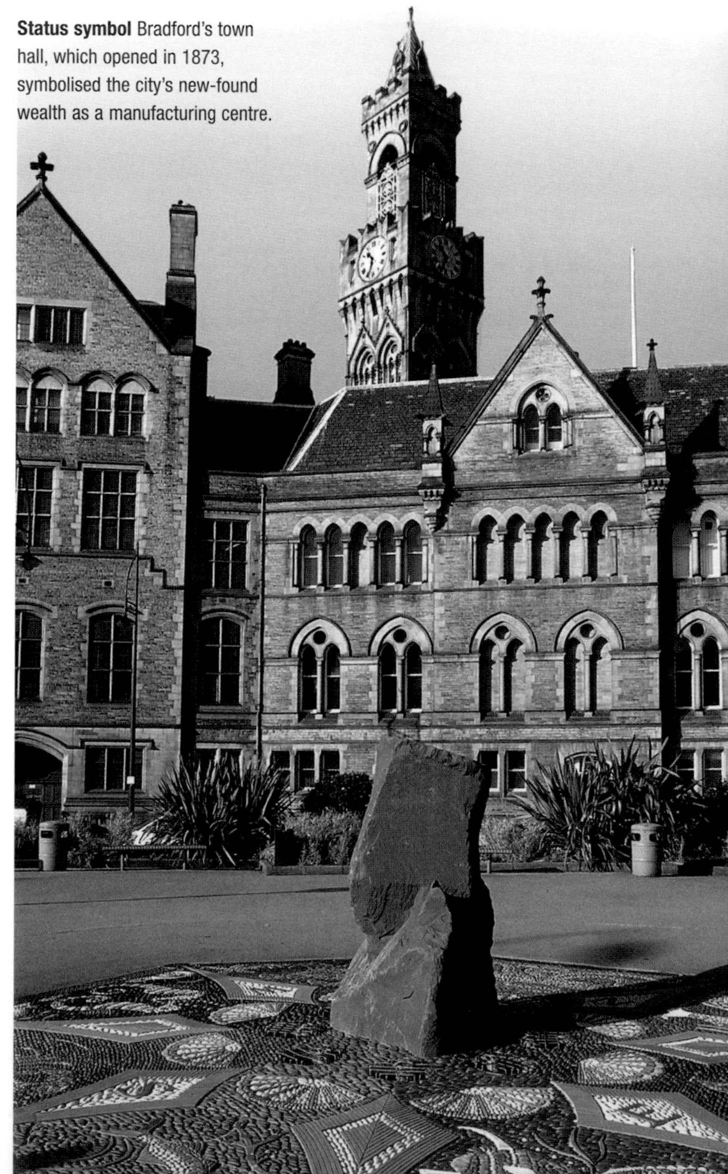

FOLLOW THE BANDSTANDS

The public parks that became a popular feature in the larger Victorian and Edwardian towns retain much of their original character. At the city or county record office, look for local authority plans and accounts, old maps and prints to find out when landmarks such as fountains or bandstands were built.

Spot the position Bandstands needed to be slightly elevated and have plenty of space around them to accommodate seated audiences for Sunday concerts.

• Look for an inscription on the bandstand – it might give you a clue about why it was built or who paid for it.

• Study an old town map (see pages 72-73) to see if a bandstand might once have stood in your park.

• Bandstands such as the one in Magdalen Green, Dundee (below), were designed to be decorative, often with elaborate ironwork, because they were focal points even when not in use.

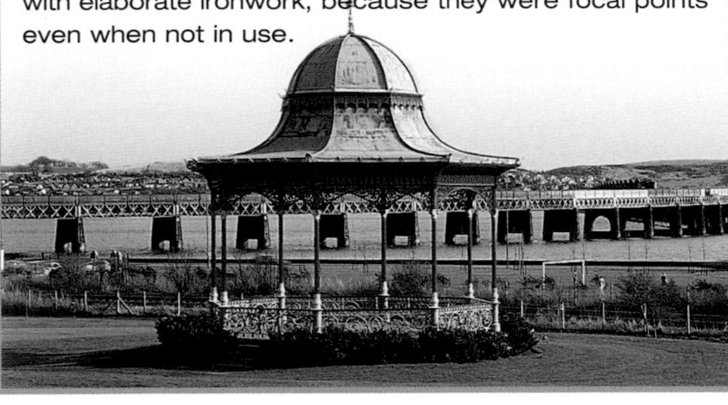

in 1785 as a pedestrian link between the town and the racecourse. Old town walls sometimes became walkways, as at York, and Dorchester's Roman fortifications were turned into public walks and planted with lime, sycamore and chestnut trees.

Your public park may be the setting for a museum or art gallery. Many were built during the reign of Queen Victoria and, like town halls, the styles could be either Gothic or classical.

Research tips

Find out how your town developed by looking at plans, prints and documents in your local library or record office.

- Look for old prints of your town, known as 'prospects'. Samuel and Nathaniel Buck drew many prospects for local authorities in the mid 18th century.
- 'Proposed new developments' may be marked on old maps, and often completed by the time of the next map.
- Trace the story of a civic building by looking for plans, contracts, accounts and correspondence.
- In the late 19th century, streets had to be widened for electric trams. You will find the revelant private Act of Parliament at your local record office.
- Georgian towns had to move the livestock markets from the centres to improve public health and ease traffic congestion. Look for street names, such as Beast Market, which reveal where the old markets were held.

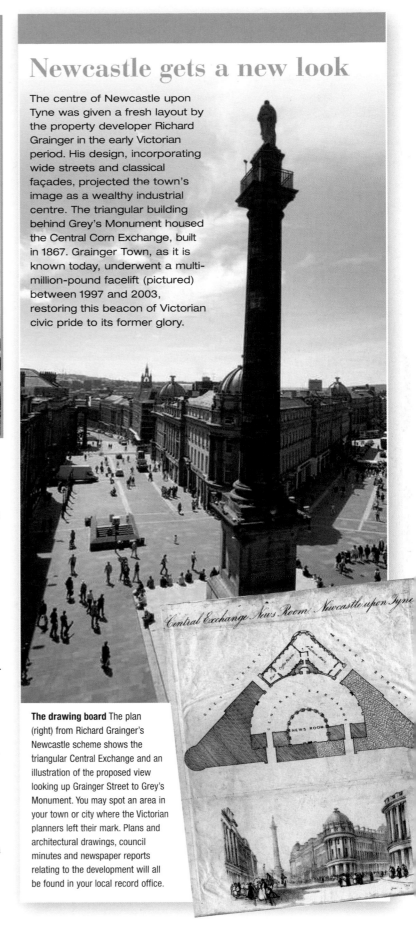

Newcastle gets a new look

The centre of Newcastle upon Tyne was given a fresh layout by the property developer Richard Grainger in the early Victorian period. His design, incorporating wide streets and classical façades, projected the town's image as a wealthy industrial centre. The triangular building behind Grey's Monument housed the Central Corn Exchange, built in 1867. Grainger Town, as it is known today, underwent a multi-million-pound facelift (pictured) between 1997 and 2003, restoring this beacon of Victorian civic pride to its former glory.

The drawing board The plan (right) from Richard Grainger's Newcastle scheme shows the triangular Central Exchange and an illustration of the proposed view looking up Grainger Street to Grey's Monument. You may spot an area in your town or city where the Victorian planners left their mark. Plans and architectural drawings, council minutes and newspaper reports relating to the development will all be found in your local record office.

Monuments and memorials

Every community remembers its dead, in cemeteries and on war memorials and other monuments. Take a look at the stones and statues, read the inscriptions, and you will discover another chapter in the story of where you live.

War memorials

When you walk around your neighbourhood, look for street names commemorating a British military or naval victory, such as the battles of Trafalgar (1805) or Waterloo (1815). The first public war memorials to list the names of the dead were erected in the 1850s after the Crimean War, but it was only after the First World War (1914-18) that monuments were put up by public subscription in a mass act of remembrance. There are now some 54,000 war memorials throughout Britain.

Where to look Memorials were placed in prominent positions at crossroads, beside churchyards, or in parks, market places and public gardens.

- Look for memorials on plaques and boards in churches, chapels and community halls.
- The names of those who died in the Second World War are normally inscribed on the same memorial as the fallen of the First World War.
- At your local record office, search for newspaper reports and photographs of annual parades to the memorials on the nearest Sunday to Armistice Day, November 11; or look for the original unveiling of a monument.

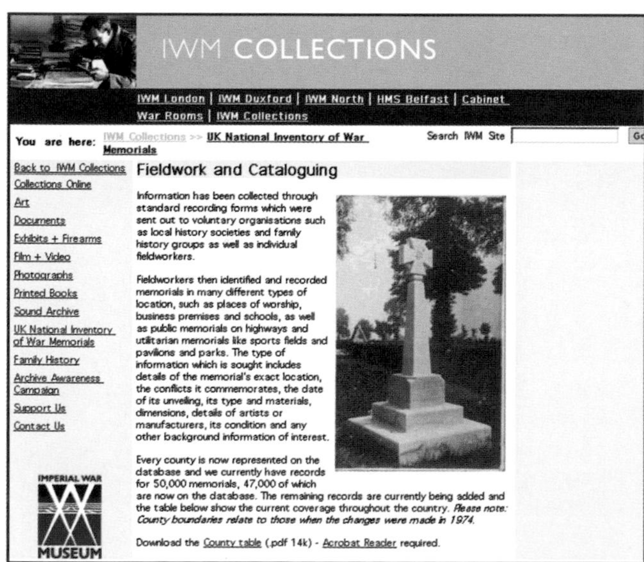

In lasting memory The Imperial War Museum estimates that there are 1.5 million names on Britain's war memorials. You will find them not just on public monuments, but on plaques in places of worship, memorial parks, sports fields, schools and hospitals. A remarkable initiative by the museum, involving 500 volunteers and local history and veterans' societies, has produced the UK National Inventory of War Memorials. To find out how you can access the database and obtain a copy of the *War Memorials Handbook*, go to the museum's website, **collections.iwm.org.uk**.

Public cemeteries

The overcrowding of churchyards in the mid 19th century, caused by a huge growth in population, forced local authorities to build public cemeteries in most towns. Nowadays, some of the largest of these have fallen into disrepair, but their grand memorials in Gothic designs vividly capture the Victorian age.

Reading monuments Study the memorials in your local cemetery to find out about former prominent members of your town. Inscriptions can reveal their standing in the local community and even their view of their own importance.

Out of town Cemeteries were usually sited in areas that were on the outskirts of town at the time, such as Highgate, founded on London's northern extremity in 1839.

- Look at how the grounds were landscaped and divided into sections so that graves would be easier to find.
- Check to see if a plan of the cemetery is on display. It will give an overview of the layout of the whole cemetery.
- You may see an imposing entrance and drive, leading to separate chapels for Anglicans, Nonconformists and Catholics. Some cemeteries have areas for Jewish burials.

Cemetery records If a cemetery is still open, its records may be kept at the office on the site. Otherwise, you may find them at your local record office. The records, arranged chronologically, usually provide the name, address, age and occupation of the deceased person and the date of death and burial. Each burial plot was given a number which will enable you to find the grave on the plan of the cemetery.

- The National Archives of Scotland (see DIRECTORY) has cemetery records for 1900-75, under the code DOD 7/6.
- Cremation was ruled legal in 1885. Memorials include books of remembrance at the crematorium, and sometimes plaques, benches and trees in the grounds.

Sculpture on the street

The Victorians injected their sense of occasion and love of decoration into all areas of day-to-day street life. If you look around your town centre, you may still find examples of their functional street 'furniture'.

- Among the most striking items are the ornamental fountains built at the junctions of main streets or in public parks. They were erected by the local authority or benefactors wishing to improve the town's facilities.
- Look for boundary posts that name the old townships before the Urban District Council was created in 1894. They will be marked on Ordnance Survey (OS) maps (see pages 72-73).

Drinks on the house The Victorians, concerned by the poor quality of the water supply, founded London's Metropolitan Drinking Fountain and Cattle Trough Association in 1859 to provide fresh water for all. Wealthy benefactors also paid for drinking fountains. Look out for their names in the inscriptions; one at Low Bradfield, Yorkshire, says: 'In memory of Mary Ann Smith: God's gift to man'.

Every statue tells a story

The Victorians, in particular, were fond of statues. Many still stand in public squares while others have been removed to a secluded spot in a park.

- Most towns have a statue of Queen Victoria. Some commemorate a royal visit, in which case photographs and a full report would have appeared in your local newspaper. You may find these at your record office.
- Look for statues of earlier monarchs, such as those of William III in Bristol and Hull, which celebrate the Glorious Revolution of 1688. Statues of Queen Anne, such as the one beside St Paul's Cathedral in London, are often mistaken for Victoria.
- Local aristocrats or Members of Parliament might have a statue, perhaps set on a column like that of Earl Grey in Newcastle upon Tyne (see page 113).
- Local worthies often merit statues: Lichfield in Staffordshire has one to the writer Dr Johnson (1709-84) and another to Commander Edward J. Smith, captain of the *Titanic*.
- Read the inscription on a statue. It may praise the person's achievements and enable you to see why he or she was held in such high esteem by contemporaries. It may also tell you who was responsible for putting up the statue. Armed with this information, you can find out more about the person's role in your community from your local library or record office.

Life history Take a close look at statues for clues about their origin. A memorial in Lister Park, Bradford (right), honours the inventor Samuel Lister (1815-1906), who gave the park to the city. Panels around the base of the statue (above) illustrate his innovations in the field of textile machinery.

FIND OUT MORE

- *The English Town* (Mark Girouard, Yale University Press, 1990). An excellent guide on what to look out for in urban areas.
- **www.bereavement-services.org** A directory of Britain's cemeteries, crematoria and burial sites, with maps, contact details and links to related websites.
- **www.tchevalier.com/fallingangels/bckgrnd/cemeteries/** A guide to Victorian cemeteries and funerary monuments.
- **www.vintageviews.org/vv-tl/pages/Cem_Symbolism.htm** A helpful glossary for interpreting Victorian cemetery symbolism.

Following the essential supplies

Find out where your water, gas and electricity come from, how and when your city, town or village was provided with these services, and when the postal and telephone services began. Each one of these improvements would have been momentous events in the story of your community.

Hidden assets Look for wells that were enhanced with stone structures or converted into cast-iron pumps in the 19th-century. Some are inscribed with their date of construction, which may indicate when improvements were made to the local water supply.

Drawing up the water

Look around your neighbourhood for clues to how your local water was supplied in the past.

- Street names can indicate the location of public wells. Barker's Pool in Sheffield was a major source of water for the city from the 15th to 18th centuries. Today, only its name marks the site.
- Wells are marked on early editions of large-scale Ordnance Survey (OS) maps (see pages 72-73).
- Search through manor court rolls (see page 152) in your county record office for references to wells in Tudor and Stuart times. In 1608 the manor court at Ecclesfield, Yorkshire, ordered that items of clothing must not be washed at drinking wells.

Dealing with waste

Three Public Health Acts in the 19th century gave local authorities the power to improve sanitation and generated many records.

- Search the archives of the local authority at your record office for council minutes, surveys and reports, maps and plans of public works.
- Government inspections were carried out between 1848 and 1857. Ask your library if they hold a copy of a local sanitation report and its accompanying plans.

Gas and electricity

It is hard to imagine life without gas or electricity. But it took the inventive skill of our 19th-century forebears to harness them. You can still see signs of their ingenuity.

- Look out for any surviving gasometers, or at least their frames. To find out when they first appeared study the large-scale 19th-century OS maps in your record office.

Water comes to Nottingham

You can follow the story of your local water supply by searching the archives of private waterworks companies from the 17th century onwards at your county record office. Look for maps and plans of reservoirs, conduits and pipelines to trace the route by which water reached your city, town or village. In the case of Nottingham, the records of the Derwent Valley Water Board reveal how water was supplied to the city and its neighbours, Derby, Leicester and Sheffield, in the early 20th century. The Derwent Valley Water Act of 1901 signalled the construction of three dams across the Derwent and Ashop valleys high in the Peak District. An old photograph reveals that the building of the Derwent Dam was marked with the laying of a record stone (right) on June 21, 1907. Old plans (above) show how water was transported from the Derwent and Howden reservoirs through an aqueduct to Ambergate Reservoir in the east. From here pipes branched off to Nottingham in the north and Leicester and Derby in the east. In Nottingham, the water flowed into a further reservoir pumped by the Papplewick station before it joined the city's system.

- See if you can spot an electric power station in your area on an early 20th-century OS map. Bradford was the first town to have one, in 1889, but electricity did not replace gas to light houses until the 1920s. You can find today's power stations by following the lines of pylons marked on modern OS maps.
- Electric street lamps were first used in the 1860s and 1870s. Look for any surviving Victorian cast-iron lamps. Old photographs (see pages 70-71) of dimly lit streets may give you clues for where to search.
- Look also for advertisements in old newspapers (see pages 74-75) from the 1860s, when gas burners were first used for heating and cooking.
- Before pipelines brought gas from the North Sea in the 1960s, gas was produced from coal. If you live near a former coalfield, look for the coke-ovens that created gas as a by-product of the coal distillation process.
- You may find the records of early 19th-century supply companies at your county record office. These include maps, plans, architects' drawings and accounts.

What's in a post box? Look at the post boxes in the streets where you live; they might offer you a clue about when the surrounding houses were built. You can identify the ages of your local boxes by their royal ciphers: clockwise, from top left, Edward VII (1901-10), George V (1910-36), Edward VIII (1936), George VI (1936-52) and Elizabeth II (reigned since 1952). The design of the box can also be revealing. A post box in Dudley, Worcestershire (left), was built in neighbouring Birmingham in 1866 in the distinctive design of J.W. Penfold, known as the Penfold Hexagonal. It carries the cipher VR, for Queen Victoria, the monarch from 1837 to 1901.

Postal services

A feature that links every town in the land is the red post box, another Victorian innovation. You may also find evidence of early mail services carried by coach and horse.

- At your local record office or library, look for paintings of mail coaches, which were used from 1784 until they were replaced by the railways. Old directories (see pages 74-75) carry details of these postal services.
- See if the Post Office Archives and Records Centre (see DIRECTORY) has records or photographs for your post office.
- Is your local post office the original one? Check its present appearance against old photographs.
- Members of the Postal History Society have written local histories of the postal service. Ask if there are any at your library.

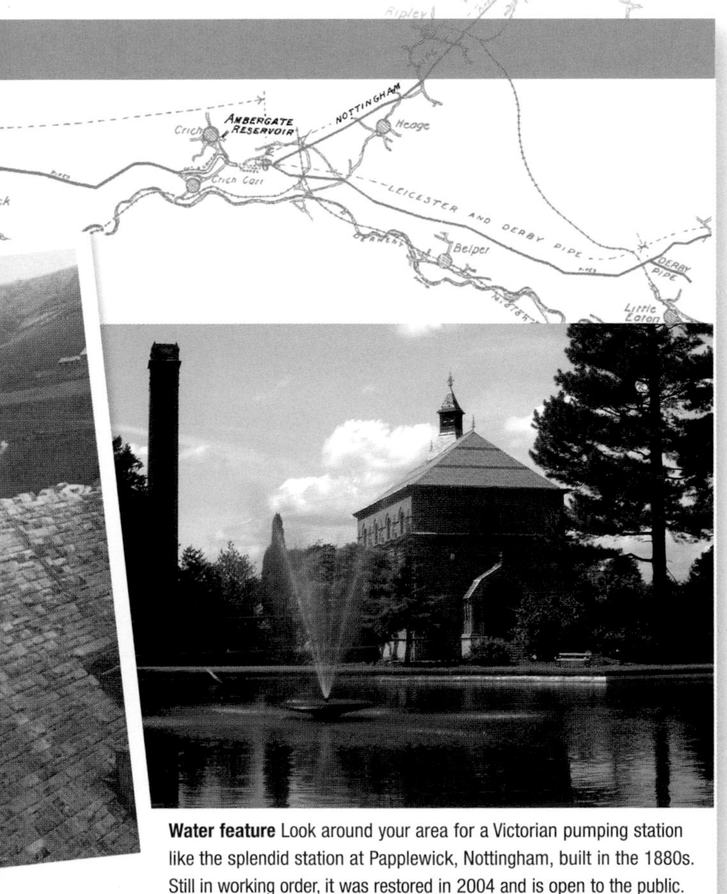

Water feature Look around your area for a Victorian pumping station like the splendid station at Papplewick, Nottingham, built in the 1880s. Still in working order, it was restored in 2004 and is open to the public.

Telephone services

The first telephone exchange opened in 1879 at 36 Coleman Street, London. Check to see if your town has one. Some are housed in elegant 1930s or 50s buildings.

- The first public telephone boxes date from 1921. You may still have one of the cast-iron dome-topped boxes in your neighbourhood designed by Sir Giles Gilbert Scott in 1924. They feature the monarch's crown over the door and are painted in the same red colour as post boxes.
- Old photographs show telephone wires criss-crossing urban streets. To find out when they disappeared underground, ask at your local record office or the British Telecom Archives (see DIRECTORY). Among its records are telephone directories dating from 1880.

In search of fun and games

By the mid 19th century, working people had more free time and began to look for entertainment. Impresarios and developers were quick to take advantage of new audiences and you may find that your town acquired a theatre and music hall at this time. Spectator sports were also popular, especially as even the professional football teams recruited their players from the local community, which helped to give a place a strong sense of identity.

Pantomime palace The lavishly appointed Alhambra Theatre in Bradford was built in 1914 by the impresario Francis Laidler to stage large-scale productions for the city's increasingly prosperous population. It was – and still is – renowned for its pantomimes.

Theatres of dreams

Many of Britain's towns have a long theatrical tradition. This may have begun with medieval mystery plays, and developed through the flowerings of Elizabethan and Restoration drama to the farces, musicals and 'angry young men' of the 20th century. Some Georgian and many Victorian and Edwardian auditoriums survive, but not always as theatres.

Most towns had a theatre or playhouse by the 18th century. You can spot any survivors by their plain, classical exteriors. They may be sited away from the central streets, such as the small Georgian theatres at Richmond in Yorkshire and Bury St Edmunds in Suffolk. Look in your library at the earliest town maps (see pages 72-73) and photographs (see pages 70-71) to see if there was a theatre in your town.

- Early Victorian theatres were much larger than their Georgian predecessors. They still used classical features, such as columns supporting a pediment over the entrance, as at the Theatre Royal, Newcastle, which opened in 1837.
- Look for the exuberant carvings decorating the late-Victorian or early 20th-century theatres: their auditoriums were embellished with cherubs, chandeliers and carved woodwork. They were often given exotic names, such as the Adelphi, Alhambra or Lyceum.

Music hall entertainment

Music halls and variety theatres started as extensions to pubs before they flourished in their own right in the second half of the 19th century, serving up a diet of song, dance and comedy to city working classes. The best-preserved is the City Varieties Music Hall, Leeds, which developed from the White Swan pub and in 1865 became the City Palace of Varieties.

By 1875 London had more than 375 music halls or variety theatres. Wilton's Music Hall (opened 1858) was one of the most successful in the East End of London. It has been restored to its original condition and use, and is lit by a gas-burning chandelier of 27,000 cut crystals.

- The theatre history website **www.peopleplayuk.org.uk** has a 'guided tour' of the story of the music hall.

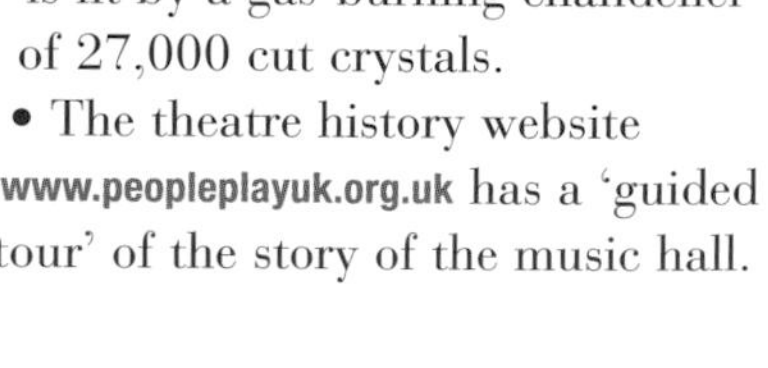

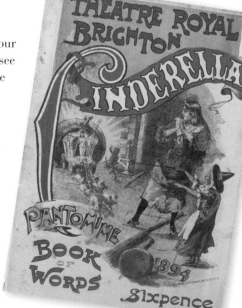

Show stopper Look out for ephemera, such as a theatre programme (left, 1894), to discover what was staged locally.

Come on, you Owls!

Sheffield Wednesday is one of the oldest football clubs in Britain. It was formed in 1867 and joined the Football League First Division in 1892 (defeating Notts County in its first game). You can follow its history, as you can with many clubs, through newspaper reports, census returns and other records, along with ephemera such as match programmes and old photographs.

- You might want to find out how your football team got its name. Sheffield Wednesday started as a cricket club that played mid-week from 1820. In 1867 it formed a football team to keep members together during the winter months. But by 1883 the football team had become so successful that it separated from the cricketers and formed its own club, turning professional in 1887.
- Clubs often moved once or twice before a permanent home was found at a new site in a working-class district or on the edge of town. You can spot these earlier sites on first-edition, large-scale Ordnance Survey (OS) maps (see pages 72-73).
- Wednesday's first permanent ground was at Olive Grove, on the southeast edge of the city. It is marked on first-edition OS maps. In 1899 the club moved across town to its present ground at Hillsborough, near Owlerton, hence the team's nickname The Owls.

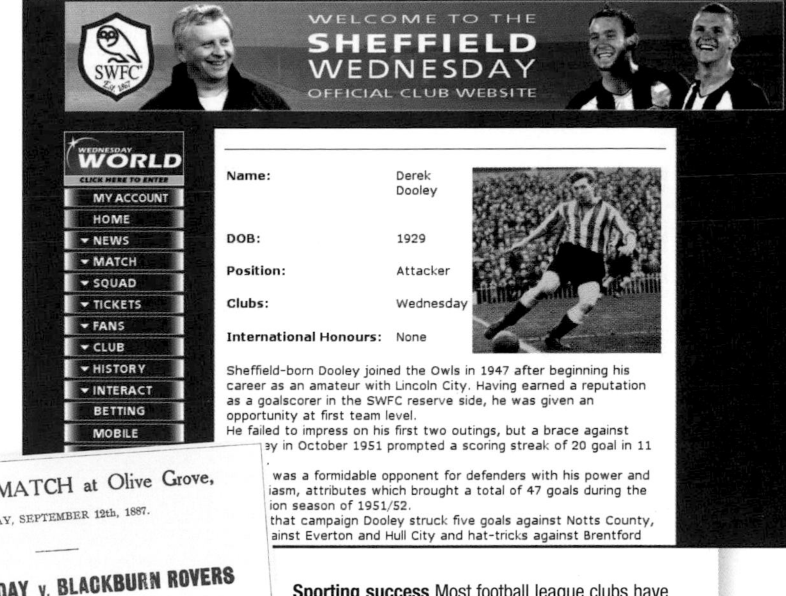

OPENING MATCH at Olive Grove,

MONDAY, SEPTEMBER 12th, 1887.

THE WEDNESDAY v. BLACKBURN ROVERS

BLACKBURN TEAM.

Right Wing. *Goal.* *Left Wing.*

H. Arthur.

Jos. Beverley. A. Chadwick.

Jos. Heyes. John Barton. Jas. H. Forrest.

S. Douglas. N. Walton. R. Rushton. L. H. Heyes. J. Berisford.

WEDNESDAY TEAM.

J. Smith.

F. Thompson. J. Hudson.

E. Brayshaw. W. Betts. A. Beckett.

H. Winterbottom. G. Waller. T. E. B. Wilson. T. Cawley. W. Mosforth.

Sporting success Most football league clubs have official and unofficial websites that often contain complete club histories. The official Sheffield Wednesday site is at **www.swfc.co.uk** It can tell you that the club won the Football League championship in 1902-3 and 1903-4, and again in 1928-9 and 1929-30, and added the FA Cup to this in 1896, 1907 and 1935.

Marking time Your local club may have a collection of memorabilia, such as Wednesday's team sheet (left) for its first match at its Olive Grove ground in 1887, just after the club had turned professional.

- Inside music halls or variety theatres, or at your local library or record office, look for posters, programmes, photographs and newspaper cuttings. These are likely to survive if the leading performers were star attractions.

Sport for all

Look at the ways in which the people of your community actively participated in sports and games. League and cup competitions for amateur football and cricket teams flourished from the mid-Victorian period onwards.

- Search past editions of your local newspapers (see pages 74-75) for reports of games played by local teams and photographs of competition winners.
- At your record office, look for the documents of local branches of the Football Association, including minutes of meetings, results and presentations to winners.

Football crazy Britain's national game is part of the fabric of most towns, from school and amateur teams' pitches to the stadiums that rise above city centres. Your local team might have published an official history. Also search the catalogues at your library or record office for match programmes, newspaper cuttings and photographs of former teams or star players. Many footballers would have lived in houses near a ground and you may find out more about them in census returns (see pages 76-77).

FIND OUT MORE

- **www.cinema-theatre.org.uk** The Cinema Theatre Association campaigns for the preservation of cinemas, theatres and music halls, publishes books about the buildings, and holds an archive for use by its members.
- **www.thefa.com** The Football Association's official website contains a directory of clubs and contact links. For details of Scottish teams, go to **www.scottishfa.co.uk**
- **www.rfu.com** The Rugby Football Union's official website contains a list of clubs and contact links as well as details of its Museum of Rugby at Twickenham.

Going down to your local pub

For centuries, places where people gathered to chat over a drink have served as the social heart of the community. Wherever you live, you will spot such establishments, from traditional inns to 1960s and 70s estate pubs, and a search through any records relating to them is likely to uncover a mine of information about the history of your neighbourhood.

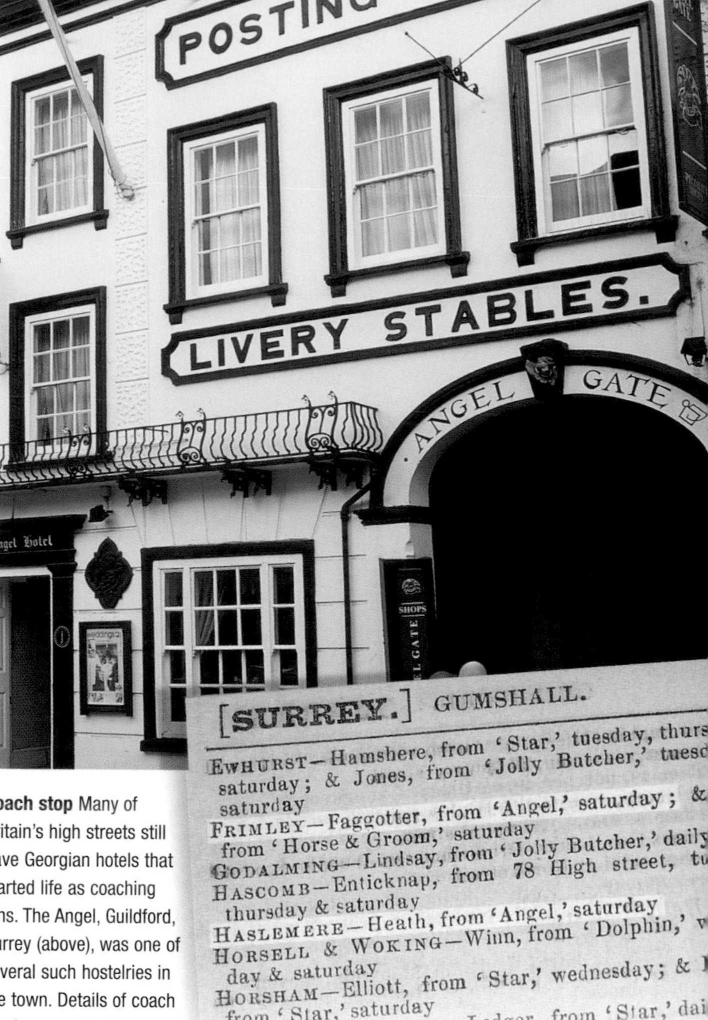

Coach stop Many of Britain's high streets still have Georgian hotels that started life as coaching inns. The Angel, Guildford, Surrey (above), was one of several such hostelries in the town. Details of coach services running from it are given in Kelly's 1855 directory for Surrey (right).

The earliest 'pubs'

The term 'public house' came into use only gradually during the 18th century. Before then, alcohol was served in licensed alehouses or inns. Many did not last long and some were merely a room in a private house, where ale was brewed and served to provide useful extra income.

Tracing alehouse records Some communities had an amazing number of premises licensed to serve alcohol. Derby had 120 alehouses to just 684 domestic dwellings in 1693, and the Scottish town of Dunbar in East Lothian supported 46 in the 1790s, compared with just ten today.

- Search through quarter-sessions records at your county record office for details of brewster sessions, when town and parish constables had to present a list of all the licensed inn and alehouse keepers in their areas.
- Probate inventories attached to wills, which are kept at local record offices and the National Archives (see DIRECTORY), often record brewhouses and stocks of ale stored in their cellars (see also pages 154-155).
- Burgh records held at the National Archives of Scotland (see DIRECTORY) sometimes include applications for alehouse licences.

One for the road

Growth in trade during the Middle Ages led to a marked increase in the traffic on the roads. Travellers needed somewhere to stop for refreshment and rest.

- Look for pub signs, such as the Travellers' Rest, the Packhorse, or the Coach and Horses along main roads, especially on those that were once packhorse or drovers' routes (see page 58) or one of the many essential coaching routes that criss-crossed Britain.
- Many former coaching inns have retained their Georgian appearance – look for sash or bow windows arranged symmetrically around a central doorway, perhaps framed by a pediment and pillars. A large, arched entrance at the side that allowed coaches and waggons to pass through into a courtyard will be a clue to a building's use as an inn.
- See if you can spot any old mounting blocks in front of an inn or in its courtyard. These were to help customers clamber back up on to their horses.

Documentary evidence As well as looking around you, a search at your local record office (see pages 10-11) should yield information about any local coaching inns.

- Inns that were boarding points for coaches may be listed in early trade directories (see page 75).
- Look at old newspapers (see page 74) for any mention of an inn as the venue for social events.
- Inns often feature in old photographs (see pages 70-71).

Service station The facilities on offer for horses at the Commercial Inn, Fressingfield, Suffolk, in the early 1900s were as important as those for the coach passengers.

Country pubs

In the countryside, the pub was often the only alternative social centre to the church or chapel.

- Many a country pub started as a farmhouse-cum-alehouse with just one room for drinking. You might recognise the original part of a pub that has been extended to serve food and to provide games rooms.
- Some pubs were attached to the workshop of a craftsman, such as a blacksmith or a wheelwright. Look for pub names in fading paint on the walls of village shops and houses.
- Many rural pubs bear the name of a local landowner. On the Duke of Rutland's estates in Derbyshire, there are several Rutland Arms as well as a few pubs called the Peacock, after the emblem on the duke's coat-of-arms.

Sign of the times The elaborate glass and tiled panels featured in numerous 19th and early 20th century pubs have often remained in place long after the buildings they adorned ceased to serve food, drink and a warm welcome. Some are more than just decorative: they carry information about ownership and the arrangement of rooms (right and below).

Country pub records Again, start by searching in local archives, such as your record office or reference library.

- Many pub names have changed over time. The old names can be traced by following a pub back through trade directories (see page 75).
- Look for innkeepers and publicans identified in census returns (see pages 76-77) and electoral registers.
- Ask individual breweries if you can see the title deeds to pubs they own. These give every change of ownership.

Town pubs

In England and Wales alone, there were more than 102,000 pubs in 1900, mostly in urban areas. They were generally comfortable places, full of colourful tiling and etched glass, reflecting the improved living standards of their largely working-class customers. Today there are only around 60,000, a good number of 'locals' having simply disappeared or been turned into something else.

- In the late 18th and 19th centuries, many towns had large 'common breweries' that served the local pubs. Try and find them on first-edition, six-inch Ordnance Survey (OS) maps (see pages 18-19), then go and see what survives today on the same site.
- Some pubs had an offsales counter. Look for evidence in words like 'Jug & Bottle', 'Family Department' or 'Outdoor', etched on glass panels above the bar.
- In the 1920s and 30s, the popularity of the car and buses encouraged the building of roadhouses, large pubs catering for day-trippers. They had plenty of parking space, rooms big enough for a busload of people, and overnight accommodation. Note any near your town, usually by roundabouts and A-road intersections.

FIND OUT MORE

- *Licensed to Sell: The History and Heritage of the Public House* (G. Brandwood, English Heritage Publications, 2004)
- **www.pubs.com/pub_history.cfm** A lively account of the evolution of the public house in Britain from the alehouse to the gin palace.
- **www.pubhistory.freeserve.co.uk** Website of the Pub History Society, giving details of special events, useful links and advice on carrying out research.
- **www.heritagepubs.org.uk** Campaign for Real Ale (CAMRA) has a dedicated website for historic pubs.
- **www.archives.gla.ac.uk/sba/** Scottish Brewing Archive, which collects and preserves the records of the Scottish brewing industry.

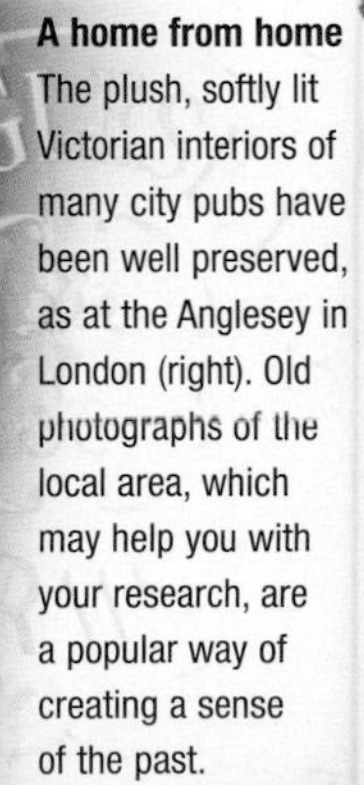

A home from home The plush, softly lit Victorian interiors of many city pubs have been well preserved, as at the Anglesey in London (right). Old photographs of the local area, which may help you with your research, are a popular way of creating a sense of the past.

The stories behind pub signs and names

Looking at the pub signs in your area and then trying to discover what lies behind the names and images on them can reveal a great deal about the history of where you live. Some of the names are popular in most parts of Britain and may relate to national and even international events, but many focus on local heroes and their deeds.

The Granby connection In the 18th-century the Marquis of Granby set up many of his retired army officers as innkeepers – who gratefully named their pubs after him.

Romans, the Church and royalty

It all began with the Romans, whose symbol to identify a public house to an illiterate population was a trail of vine leaves. The British took up the idea but, more appropriately for a colder climate, displayed a bush instead. In 1393, a law was passed making it compulsory for every pub and hostelry to show a symbol on a signboard, and the names of the symbols soon became associated with the establishments themselves.

At first many of these images and names were of a religious nature, such as the Cross Keys (of St Peter) and the Sun (a symbol of Christ). But after the Reformation in the late 16th century, many publicans thought it wiser to choose secular names, especially those with royal overtones – the Rose and Crown, or the King's or Queen's Head.

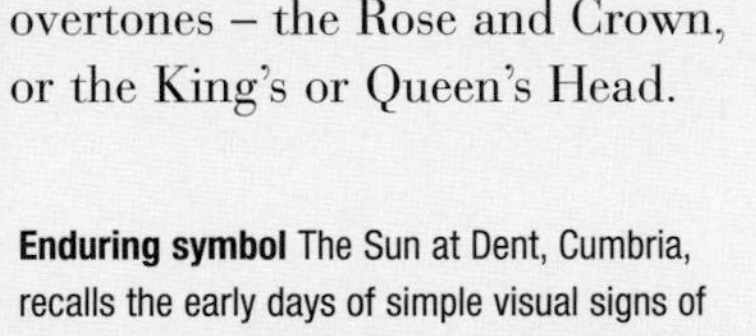

Enduring symbol The Sun at Dent, Cumbria, recalls the early days of simple visual signs of religious symbols, including the Cross and the Star.

Some refer to romantic royal adventures. The Royal Oak (left, at York) is the third most common pub name and commemorates where the future Charles II hid from his enemies after his defeat at the Battle of Worcester in 1651. Having a long reign seems to be the key to a king or queen having a pub named after them: the commonest royal pub names are the George (after George III, 1760-1820) and the Queen Victoria (1837-1901). The latter can be given a modern twist: the woman depicted on the sign outside Bristol's Queen Victoria pub is not the long-serving monarch but Victoria Beckham, Posh Spice.

WHEN IS A CAT NOT A CAT?

The Cat Head at Chiselborough in Somerset shows a cat on its signboard, but the 'cat head' referred to is the name for the beam in a sailing ship to which the anchor is secured. Maybe a past landlord had been a sailor and had found this snug berth after leaving the sea. And the 'cat' of the Cat and Bagpipes at Northallerton in Yorkshire is actually a short form of 'catphractes', a Roman term for troopers in body armour, and recalls the Scottish border raiders in their iron breastplates who terrified the northern English throughout the late Middle Ages and beyond.

The good, the bad and the plug-ugly

Drinkers have always enjoyed raising a glass to their heroes, and many publicans have immortalised the great, the good and the bad by naming their establishments after them. Pubs might be named after powerful local landowners as an act of flattery – the Waldegrave Arms in Chewton Mendip, Somerset, and the Raby Arms in Barnard Castle, County Durham. Widely commemorated wartime heroes include the dukes of Marlborough and Wellington, Admiral Nelson and Winston Churchill; also that much-honoured 18th-century general, the Marquis of Granby.

Very popular are sporting heroes such as boxing champions – the Bendigo in Nottingham (taking the professional name of local 19th-century champion, William Thompson), and the Tom Cribb (see right) and the Henry Cooper in London. In some cases, the signs might display likenesses of sportsmen, such as Ian Botham (at the Cricketers in Blackhall, County Durham) and Lester Piggott (at the Jockey in Baughton,

Worcestershire). Folk villains take their place, too, with romantic baddies such as the pirate Captain Kidd having a pub in Wapping named after him and the highwayman Dick Turpin being commemorated by one in York. Generally the named figure has some connection with the location of the establishment – Kidd was hanged in Wapping and Turpin in York.

Bloody memories The Bucket of Blood at Phillack, Cornwall, was so-called after a murder victim was found in the pub's well. The Lamb and Flag in London's Covent Garden once had the same gory name – in this case because of the bare-knuckle prize fights that took place there.

Birds and bees

Nature has been an inspiration to the namers of pubs. The Birch Tree, the Blackbird, the Honey Bee and the Spotted Dog were probably chosen for connotations that were particularly pleasant to their choosers. But there are plenty of clues to stories behind some pretty names. The Rose and Daffodil near Swansea in south Wales hints at harmony between two neighbouring and often antagonistic countries, as does the Rose and Thistle at Alwinton near the Scottish border in Northumberland; while the Pheasant, the Stag, the Fox and Hounds and the Leaping Salmon tell you about field sports that have traditionally been popular locally. Local insects (the Red Admiral or the Grasshopper) are commonly recalled, although the Ladybird is relatively rare.

Blazing Donkeys and Buckets of Blood

Best of all, perhaps, are the pub names that have you scratching your head for an explanation. The Blazing Donkey (Ramsgate, Kent) refers to a fire in the 1780s that gutted the stables. But what are we to make of Portsmouth's Sociable Plover, or the Bucket of Blood at Phillack in Cornwall (see above)? One of the strangest, the Shrew Beshrewed at Hersden, Kent, refers to the custom of punishing a scolding woman by tying her to a chair and ducking her in the river – the phrase 'Beshrew thee' meant 'Devil take thee'. The peversely named Nobody Inn at Doddiscomsleigh, near Exeter, Devon, came by its present name after a former owner took it into his head to refuse entry to customers.

Boxing champion Londoner Tom Cribb, commemorated in a Panton Street pub, fought and won the first international prize fight on 28 September, 1811, against American Tom Molyneux (inset). Cribb won £2600 and a cup valued at 80 guineas.

FIND OUT MORE

- **www.bjcurtis.force9.co.uk** The Inn Sign Society's informative website.
- **www.heritagepubs.org.uk** Campaign for Real Ale (CAMRA) has a dedicated website for historic pubs.

EXPLORE YOUR HOME

Have you ever wondered when your home was built, who used to live there and what events have taken place within its walls? You may even wish to find out what was there before it was built. By looking for clues, talking to neighbours and exploring records, local and national, you can start to work back and piece together the story of your home, inside and out.

Where to begin Before you start researching the story of your home, ask yourself what you want to achieve. There are three paths to follow – you can find out when a property was built, discover the people who lived there or uncover what was on the land before your home existed. You may find that you have to switch between the goals, depending on how the trail unfolds, and no two homes will follow the same path. The following tips should make the research process easier.

- Find out to which administrative district your home belongs. It will help to know the parliamentary ward, civil or church parish, census registration district, historic estate or manor. Your local record office (see pages 10-11) should have this information. Remember that the boundaries sometimes change (for example, many counties changed in 1974), so as your search takes you back in time, you will need to refer to contemporary maps and records.
- Work backwards in time, moving from clue to clue. Start with recent records such as electoral registers (see pages 156-157) or title deeds (see page 132) and use the information to look for other sources such as wills (see pages 154-155) and census returns (see pages 76-77, 158-159).
- Sometimes researching properties next to your home can yield useful information. If you obtain names of past neighbours, they may lead to documents (such as title deeds) that refer to your property.

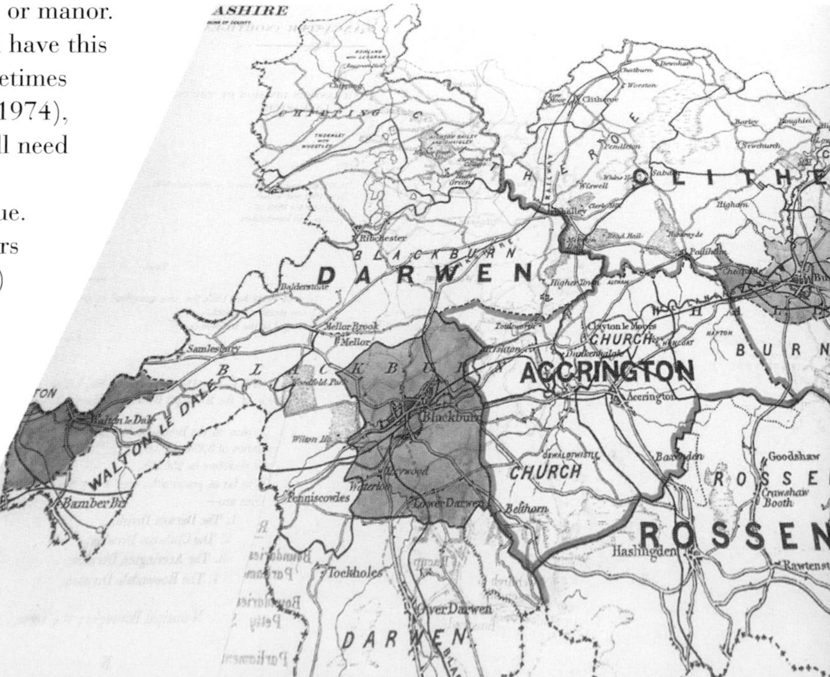

Know your boundaries A map dating from 1885 shows the parliamentary boundaries for North East Lancashire. It is important to have a clear idea of the administrative districts your home falls in so you can easily locate it on older maps or records grouped by district.

Key research sources

The following resources are all potentially helpful in your research, but the order in which you use them will depend on the information you discover as you progress.

- title deeds (see pages 132, 140, 148, 159)
- maps such as tithe and estate maps (see pages 18-19)
- sale catalogues (see pages 134-135)
- estate records (see pages 148-149, 152, 159)
- rate books (see page 157)
- census returns (see pages 76-77, 158-159)
- tax records (see pages 77, 140, 160-161)
- wills (see pages 154-155, 161)
- street directories (see pages 75, 135, 145, 157)
- photographs (see pages 70-71)
- newspapers (see page 74).

The hunt begins

The records you will need are stored in local study centres, record offices or specialist archives, and you will almost certainly need to visit more than one of these places. Start locally and then explore further afield: local sources may hold the information you need and so save you a longer trip. See 'Getting started', pages 10-13.

Local study centres These hold records, newspapers and photographs linked to the local area. If you live in a large town or city, you should also keep an eye open for city record offices. Most are listed in the 'Directory of sources' (see pages 162-169).

County record offices Look here for material relating to the administration of the county, plus privately deposited documents such as title deeds. All county record offices are listed in the 'Directory of sources' (see pages 162-169).

National archives Government surveys and records are held here. These include the National Archives, the National Archives of Scotland, the National Monuments Record Centre, the British Library, the National Library of Wales, the National Library of Scotland and the General Register Office for Scotland (see DIRECTORY).

FIND OUT MORE

- **www.nationalarchives.gov.uk/househistory** A National Archives guide to using records to research the history of your home.
- **www.nas.gov.uk/guides/buildings.asp** National Archives of Scotland factsheet giving a general introduction to useful records for researching the history of your house in Scotland.
- **www.bricksandbrass.co.uk/houseage/ageform.htm** A comprehensive questionnaire that helps you to work out the date that your house was built with lots of information and pictures showing period styles and furnishings.

Visiting the archives

If you have never used an archive before, the following tips should help (see 'Getting started', pages 10-11).

- Make contact in advance to ensure you are looking in the right place. Ask about opening times, the location of the archive and entry requirements - for example, most record offices require you to register as a user, which means you may have to bring some form of identification.
- Rules and regulations are fairly strict - you will not be allowed to bring certain items into the reading area, such as pens, erasers, pencil sharpeners, food or drink, as they could harm the documents.
- Always seek advice when you arrive. Most archives employ staff to help get you started, and can usually provide leaflets or guidebooks that explain in more detail how to undertake specific lines of research.

Time to search The information held in county or city record offices in your region may date back to the Middle Ages. To make the most of your visit you should check beforehand whether the office holds the documents you are looking for. Allow yourself plenty of time with the records – you may find they reveal some unexpected information that can broaden your search.

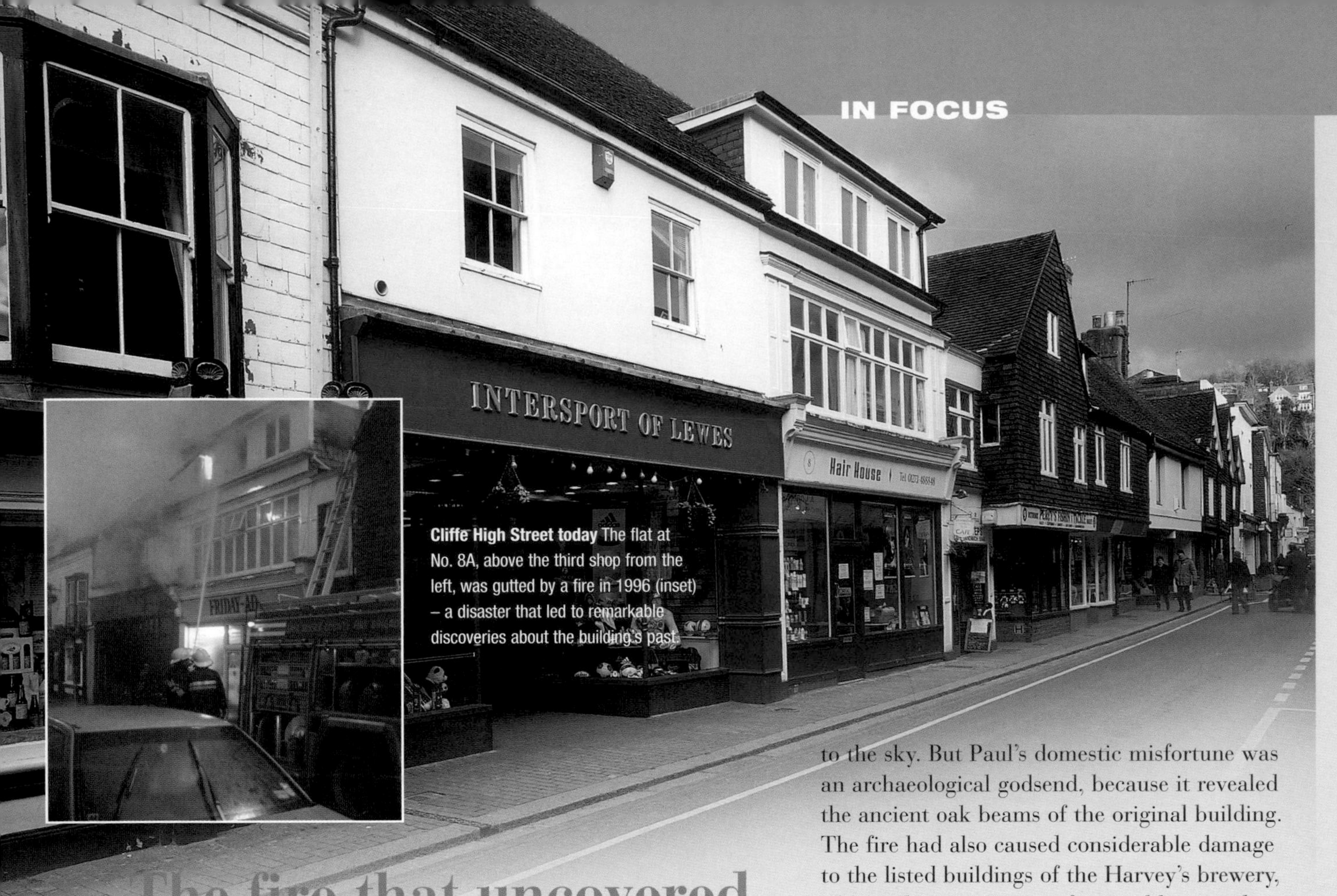

Cliffe High Street today The flat at No. 8A, above the third shop from the left, was gutted by a fire in 1996 (inset) – a disaster that led to remarkable discoveries about the building's past.

The fire that uncovered a flat's hidden secrets

Even the most ordinary-seeming homes may have a story that stretches further back than anyone would imagine. A flat above a shop in Lewes, East Sussex, surprised the owner when a seemingly disastrous fire revealed its history.

Appearances can deceive

No. 8A Cliffe High Street is at first glance an entirely unremarkable home. It is a flat above a row of shops at the end of the main shopping street in Lewes. There are four shops in the row, and the tiled façade of the shop at the far end looks old. But the frontage of the shop next door at No. 7 is fairly modern: 1930s at the latest. It is hard to say whether the building is genuinely old or not.

Paul Manners has lived above No. 8 for decades. His father bought the whole block, and in the 1950s ran a café called The Polar Bear in the shop below his son's present home. But it was not until 1996, when a fire gutted the building, that its true history was revealed.

The truth rises from the flames

The fire swept through the open roof cavity of the block and destroyed Paul Manners' home. It consumed furniture, plasterboard dividing walls, as well as some of the much older lath-and-plaster, and left the roof open to the sky. But Paul's domestic misfortune was an archaeological godsend, because it revealed the ancient oak beams of the original building. The fire had also caused considerable damage to the listed buildings of the Harvey's brewery, 100 yards away, so a professional historical surveyor was on the site soon after the flames were doused. The surveyor looked at the exposed and blackened oak beams in the flat at No. 8, which over the centuries had become as hard and impervious to flame as steel. His hunch, based on the configuration of the beams, was that Paul's building was around 350 years old.

The sophisticated construction led the surveyor to surmise that the building had been put up by London craftsmen and was a home of some importance. This fitted with the fact that Lewes was a fashionable place to live from the mid 17th century, as it became increasingly an administrative centre for Sussex. Paul, meanwhile, had noted other oddities. There was an original window frame close to the floor of his upper rooms, and the floor of the first storey ran through the centre of a very old door jamb. He guessed that the ceiling below must have been raised in the 19th century, after the building was converted into a row of shops. The remains of a Victorian awning, entombed behind a later street-side wall, made this theory seem more plausible.

Backed up by the records

While Paul set about the long task of rebuilding his home, the surveyor did some digging in the county archives. He found that the whole row was once known as the Great House, and that in 1685 the owner was a widow called

Ancient workmanship The fire uncovered an original window frame near the floor of the present-day flat, suggesting a change in floor height, and two vertical beams joined together by a beautifully crafted metal strap, pointed out by the owner (inset).

Judith Stevenson. She had inherited the house from her father, Samuel Towers of Cliffe (who also owned the Ann of Cleves house, still a tourist attraction in the town). The Great House and its attendant buildings are described in one 17th-century document as comprising 'messuage, barns, stables, warehouse, dyehouse and shoppes'. The need for more than one stable points to the main building having served as lodgings for several gentry families, and the jumble of other buildings suggests that they were all involved in commerce. In the early 1700s the building was divided into four homes. Each was then altered in its own higgledy-piggledy way: staircases, chimneys and outhouses were added in subsequent decades. The line of one chimney is still discernible in Paul's study, and a diagonal sawmark in one timber suggests it was made in connection with a now-forgotten banister.

The evidence uncovered by the surveyor sent Paul back to his own files. He has the deeds of the building, with maps, plans and indenture documents, all passed down from his father. These papers fill in other details in the house's history. They show that in Victorian times the owner of the shop below was Mr Tickner, who sold clothes, boots and shoes at No. 7 and china at No. 8. Tickner wanted a showroom for his china on the first floor (where Paul's sitting room is now). Perhaps it was the ambitious Mr Tickner who also raised the ceiling below, to make his ground-floor shop more commodious for his customers.

A lasting legacy

It took Paul almost a year to restore his home. It is now a bright modern flat, but in every room there is evidence of its long past. A great beam runs like a dark stripe across the white walls of his sitting room. It is blacker at the streetward end – a visible reminder of the 1996 fire. In the kitchen a supporting beam runs vertically from floor to high ceiling. It is in fact two huge pieces of wood, held together by a finely crafted metal strap at the height of the kitchen table. This strap has probably been in the same spot for centuries, despite the changes and traumas the building has endured – a pleasing thought for the homeowner each time he sits down next to that ancient, functional piece of workmanship.

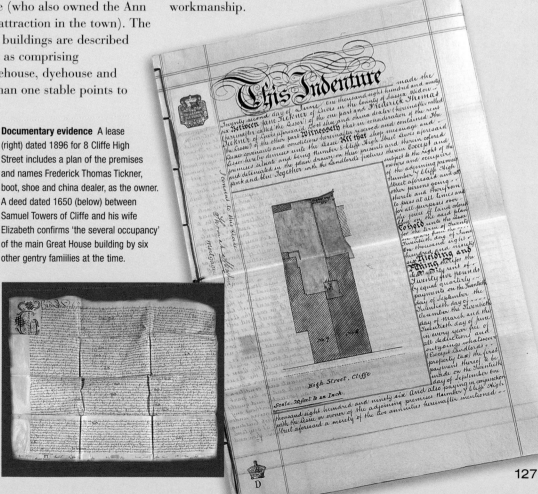

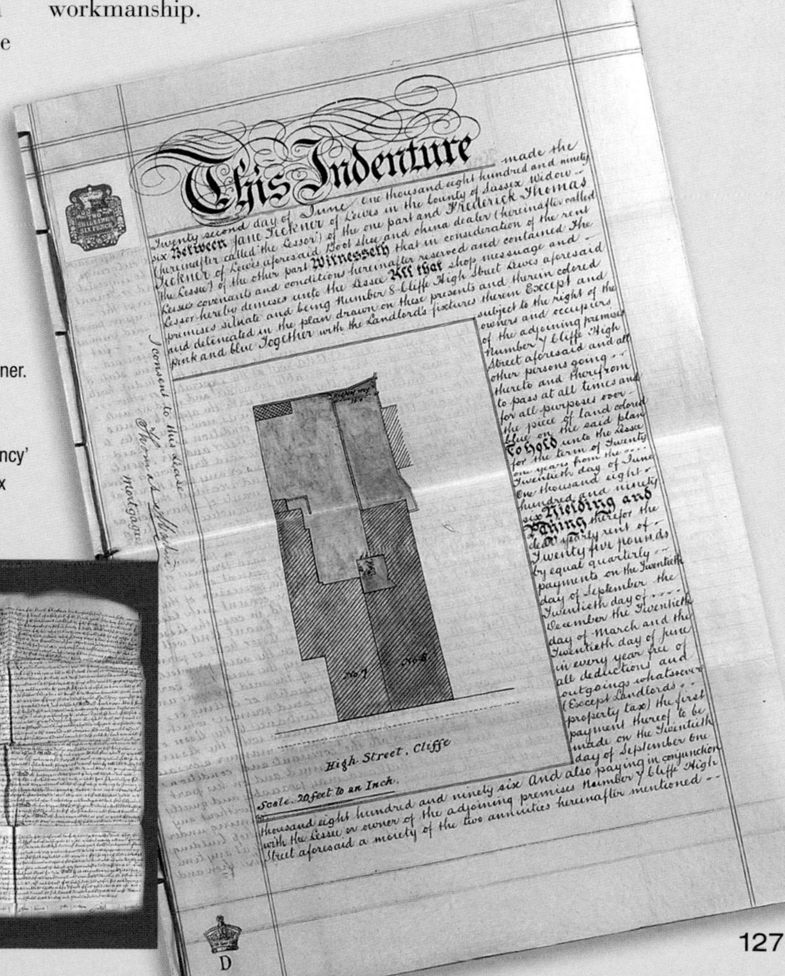

This Indenture made the Twenty second day of June One thousand eight hundred and ninety six Between Jane Tickner of Lewes in the County of Sussex Widow (hereinafter called the Lessor) of the one part and Frederick Thomas Tickner of Lewes aforesaid Boot shoe and china dealer (hereinafter called the Lessee) of the other part Witnesseth that in consideration of the rent Lessee covenants and conditions hereinafter reserved and contained The Lessor hereby demises unto the Lessee All that shop messuage and premises situate and being Number 8 Cliffe High Street Lewes aforesaid and delineated in the plan drawn on these presents and therein colored pink and blue Together with the Landlord's fixtures therein Except and subject to the right of the owners and occupiers of the adjoining premises Number 7 Cliffe High Street aforesaid and all other persons going thereto and therefrom to pass at all times and for all purposes over the piece of land colored blue on the said plan To hold unto the Lessee for the term of Twenty one years from the Twentieth day of June One thousand eight hundred and ninety six Yielding and Paying therefor the clear yearly rent of Twenty five pounds by equal quarterly payments on the Twentieth day of September the Twentieth day of December the Twentieth day of March and the Twentieth day of June in every year free of all deductions and outgoings whatsoever (Except Landlords property tax) the first payment thereof to be made on the Twentieth day of September One thousand eight hundred and ninety six And also paying in conjunction with the Lessee or owner of the adjoining premises Number 7 Cliffe High Street aforesaid a moiety of the two annuities hereinafter mentioned

High Street, Cliffe

Scale 20 feet to an Inch.

Documentary evidence A lease (right) dated 1896 for 8 Cliffe High Street includes a plan of the premises and names Frederick Thomas Tickner, boot, shoe and china dealer, as the owner. A deed dated 1650 (below) between Samuel Towers of Cliffe and his wife Elizabeth confirms 'the several occupancy' of the main Great House building by six other gentry famiilies at the time.

Looking out for visual clues

Before you even begin to explore the archives, look around closer to home. You can find clues to the age of your property from the local neighbourhood and even inside your own four walls. Architectural features might indicate a rough construction date, while house or street names can provide further clues. Even boxes of 'rubbish' in an attic may contain useful documents.

Building up a picture

An initial information-gathering process will help you to place your house in the context of your road or street, making it easier to establish when it was built.

A question of style Ask yourself whether the style of house that you live in is similar to those around it – which would suggest they were built at the same time, or designed by the same architect – or whether it is markedly different. Is your house more modern or more old-fashioned than the rest?

Clues in the location Where is your house situated? Houses nearer the centre of a town or village are likely to be older than those on the outskirts, which could have been added during the 19th-century population explosion or as part of the mass expansion of town and city suburbs in the 1920s and 30s. You can search for these patterns of development on old maps and plans held in local and national archives (see pages 18-19).

Ask the neighbours Talk to local residents, especially those who have lived in the area the longest. They should be able to tell you about former occupants of your house, how the street has changed, or if there are any interesting anecdotes that can be followed up during your research.

Period features

The architectural style of your home can offer key clues about when it was constructed. By taking account of building materials, the shape and style of the home and its roof, the size and position of windows, the number of chimney stacks and even door furniture, you can begin to assign a rough date to when your property was built.

Walls and windows Building materials and styles have changed over the years and can help you to date your home.

- Patterns of wooden beams and the wall materials used can indicate the age of the building. Irregularly sized bricks laid on a thick bed of mortar (see left) date from the 17th century. From the mid 19th century onwards, even-sized, manufactured bricks were used.
- Windows have changed perhaps more than any other feature. Different styles, such as casement, sash, metal-framed or stained glass, all provide pointers to the age of a home.

What's in a name? House names such as 'The Old Bakery' (above) and 'Miller's Cottage' can provide clues about the former use of a house. Many homes were once places of trade. A name may also help you to date your home. 'Railway Cottage' is likely to have been built for a family of railway workers and so can be dated to the mid 19th century onwards.

Local namesakes

A good line of research to pursue is the name of the house or street (see pages 82-83), which can give clues to its age and previous use. Many roads are named after famous people or battles, which can give you an idea of when they were built. But you should exercise caution, because a road name could have been based on a character or event from a more distant past. The names of people who exerted local influence or owned land were often used to describe property. The district of Brighton known as Kemptown was named after the principal architect who designed the building façades, Thomas Kemp. Sometimes road names can give you clues about local industries, such as Brick Pit Lane, or old landmarks that may no longer be standing, such as Gallows Corner.

> **WATCH OUT**
> 'Reading' the architectural fingerprints of a house can be misleading. In some areas regional styles continued to be employed long after the national trend had changed. Also, some styles can conceal an older core, as in the Georgian façades that were commonly erected on the front of medieval buildings, especially in marketplaces. There have also been fashions down the years that have rekindled and drawn upon past architectural styles, such as the Victorian use of Tudor-style chimneys.

A step back Taking a good look at your home from the front and back can reveal much about how the house has changed. The arched window (above) looks as though it may once have been a doorway. At the back of the house (below) the window frames look original (unlike the white, modern replacements at the front).

Surveying your land

You should also explore the extent of your property and the land surrounding it.

- Inspect any odd lumps and bumps in your garden; they may be remnants of former structures such as outhouses, sheds or stabling, all of which can be checked on maps and plans. You may even find the remains of an air-raid shelter, many of which were filled in and buried after the Second World War.
- Outbuildings or extensions may help to date your property. Coal sheds were introduced in late Victorian times while houses with attached garages are likely to date from the 20th century.
- If you have a garden, check to see how old the trees are; recent planting indicates a more modern development, whereas large, ancient trees suggest an older property or one that was built on woodland or an old orchard.
- The boundaries of your house can tell you about its age. Look at whether modern fencing or young hedging has been used. Flint walls and mature hedgerows indicate older boundaries.

What the interior can tell you

You are not restricted to the outside of the house. The design, layout, fixtures and fittings on the inside of your house will also yield clues about the age of the property (see pages 136-139, 146-147, 150-151, 153).

- Look out for period features, styles, designs or décor. Small stone mullioned windows may suggest that the house dates from a time when glass was an expensive luxury.
- Consider where the stairs are, and how they are constructed. By the Georgian period, grand or large staircases were often placed centrally in the entrance hall compared to earlier houses when staircases were placed at the side.
- The height, size and shape of a room are revealing as fashions changed over time, leading to different periods being associated with certain designs and layouts.
- Interior doors, door frames, window frames, picture rails, position of fireplaces and use of tiles can also indicate when the room was originally furnished.

Houses that were something else

All kinds of buildings that once served a functional purpose have been turned into homes. Converted mills, barns, oast houses and railway stations are fairly easy to spot, but less obvious are the former post offices, shops and public houses.

Rooms with a view A converted lighthouse makes the perfect living space for those who like curves, and its position almost guarantees peace and quiet. Fixtures and fittings are necessarily made to measure to cope with the circular layout. This lighthouse near lonely Guy's Head in Lincolnshire looks out over The Wash.

The past lives of buildings

Upheavals in agriculture and industry have often left buildings devoid of a purpose. The decline in traditional farming, particularly after the Second World War, made many farm buildings redundant. Some decayed, but others were sold and converted into houses. Similarly, in the cities, large warehouses stood empty for years before their potential as flats was spotted by developers in the 1970s. Almost anywhere you go, you will spot practical buildings of bygone eras now being used as homes.

Country converts

Perhaps the most common rural conversions are barns that have become surplus to a farmer's requirements. Their imposing exteriors and cavernous interiors with huge old beams open up many possibilities for those who like unrestricted space. Look for barn conversions close to farm buildings. But bear in mind that the barn could have been part of a farm that has long been demolished.

Drive around the southeastern counties of Essex, Suffolk, Norfolk and Lincolnshire and you will come across plenty of windmills. Their corn-grinding or pumping days now over, most have been converted into a particularly romantic kind of accommodation. A good example is the mill at Cley-next-the-Sea in north Norfolk, which is now a guesthouse with its former stables and boatshed turned into self-catering units.

Look out also for oast houses, especially in Kent. With their distinctive conical tops they are more likely to be homes these days than places to dry hops. But the ultimate in high living is the lighthouse (above), with rooms far above ground and walls up to 1m (3ft) thick.

HOMES THAT HIDE THEIR PAST

It is usually straightforward to work out if a building was once a windmill or a railway station. But what if your home was once a post office, bakery, vicarage or public house? Sometimes there are clues in the structure of the building itself. Look at the layout and how it differs from other houses in the same street. Does it have a large window at the front, where the others have smaller windows (it may once have been the display window of a shop)?

You should also consider a building's location, such as a vicarage sited close to a church or a forge at the heart of a village. The house in Stedham, Sussex (right), at first betrays little of its former use, but the stone name plaque and the covered entrance porch, now a window, are clues to what was once a pub. Other clues may be more subtle, such as a blocked up posting box indicating a former post office.

If you suspect that your home once had a commercial use, you will need to do some research in local archives. A good place to start is with local directories (see page 75).

Recycling the Industrial Revolution

In towns and cities the warehouses, textile mills and factories have been snapped up for development, mostly because of the grandeur imparted by their enormous proportions. The old run-down dock area of east London, re-christened Docklands as part of its late 20th-century clean-up, yielded hundreds of handsome large warehouses that had been empty for years. They have been quickly converted into flats, townhouses and lofts for artists, film-makers and workers in the City.

The Stroud Valley in south Gloucestershire is another area that has undergone rapid redevelopment. It was once lined with textile works, such as the late-Victorian Hill Paul clothing factory and the enormous early 19th-century Dunkirk Mill, that are now well-appointed apartments.

Following the railways

Hundreds of rural railway stations were closed in the 1960s under the notorious 'Beeching Axe'. Most have been demolished or lie ruined, but some have been converted into private houses. At Lynton in Devon even the goods shed has become a home, and at Dent on the Settle & Carlisle line, high in the moorlands of east Cumbria, a three-bedroomed house stands right on the platform, the decorative bargeboards of its twin gables revealing its railway company origin. At Great Moulton, between Diss and Norwich in Norfolk, the former level-crossing keeper's cottage has become a two-bedroomed house, while the old signal box at Shelley in west Yorkshire is now a house with three bedrooms.

FIND OUT MORE

- **www.diydoctor.org.uk/projects/barn_conversion.htm** Tips on converting a barn.
- **www.shipleywindmill.org.uk** Website for Shipley Windmill.
- **www.property.org.uk/unique/rail.html** Converted railway buildings.
- **www.martello-towers.co.uk** Martello tower conversions.
- **www.ecastles.co.uk/albert.html** Website for Fort Albert, Isle of Wight.
- **www.sealandgov.org** Website of the Principality of Sealand.

Towers and forts

Former military buildings seem to exert endless fascination. It is hard to make a home in a Napoleonic-era Martello Tower because of its inherent cold, damp and dark, not to mention the awkward elliptical shape. But that has not deterred the owners of towers at Folkestone, Sandwich and Dymchurch in Kent, and Pevensey in East Sussex. Likewise the immense and formidably grim-looking Fort Albert was built in 1856 to glower threateningly across The Solent at any potential invaders. It looks the least likely place to be turned into cosy apartments, but that is exactly what has happened to it.

Perhaps the most bizarre story of all belongs to Roughs Tower, a Second World War gun platform measuring just 137m x 43m (450ft x 140ft), situated in the North Sea, some 6 miles off the Essex coast. It has been converted not only into a comfortable home but also into a self-proclaimed sovereign state, the Principality of Sealand, complete with its own head of state, currency, flag and passports.

All change Brentor Station, near Tavistock, Devon, was built by the London and South Westen Railway Company in 1890. Made from local granite and carefully restored, it is now a charming and unusual setting for a guesthouse.

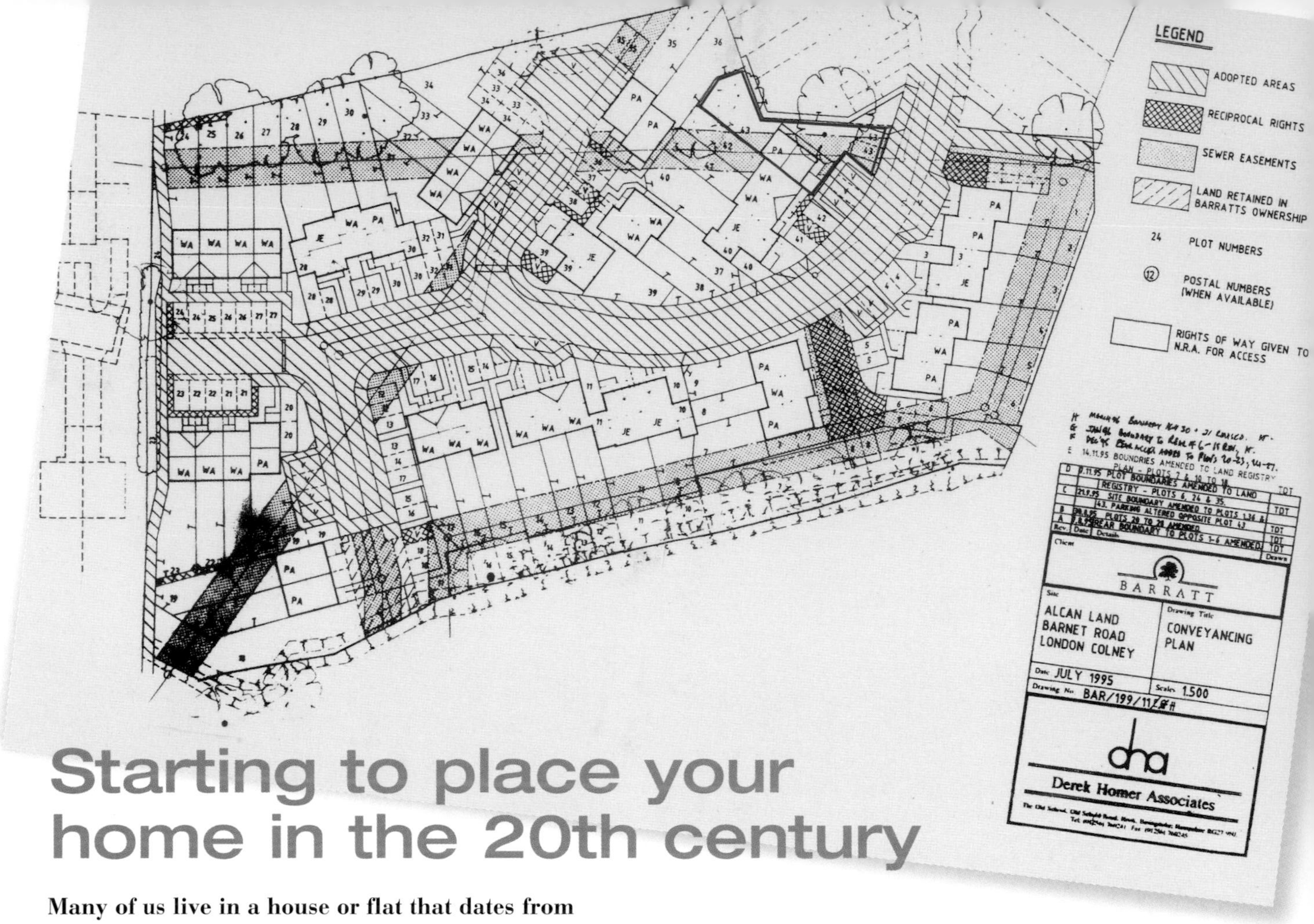

Starting to place your home in the 20th century

Many of us live in a house or flat that dates from the 20th century, probably from the 1920s onwards. To discover when the property was built, who built it and who lived in it you can take a clear series of fairly straightforward steps. If your home is older, you can follow the same path to see what was happening to it over the past 100 years.

Your first ports of call

There are two initial steps you can take to start to fill in the story of your home.

Title deeds First, try to track down your title deeds, which will give you information about the names of previous owners. If you have a mortgage, your lender will hold these documents, so you will need to make a formal approach to view them. Many companies charge a fee for access.

Land Registry records Next approach the Land Registry (see DIRECTORY) and request (for a small fee) the latest registered title (see right) along with the plan accompanying the registration. The plan will show the extent of the property – a useful document that you can use during your research to compare with older maps (see pages 18-19). The registered title may refer to former owners, although it will probably simply mention yourself since the Land Registry only holds details relating to the date of the last sale. The Land Registry was not set up to hold historic records, and you will need to search for earlier title deeds in local archives, or in the possession of former owners.

Property registration in Scotland Transfers of land in Scotland are carried out by a deed called an Instrument of Sasine (see pages 148-149). The Register of Sasines has printed summaries of transactions in the 20th century arranged by county and year. Indexes of places and names also help to speed up your search. The register is held at the National Archives of Scotland (see DIRECTORY).

Modern developments The Barratts estate plan (above) shows that the houses were built in 1995 on land belonging to Alcan (an aluminium producer). If your house was part of a housing development the estate plan may be held with the land registry documents (below).

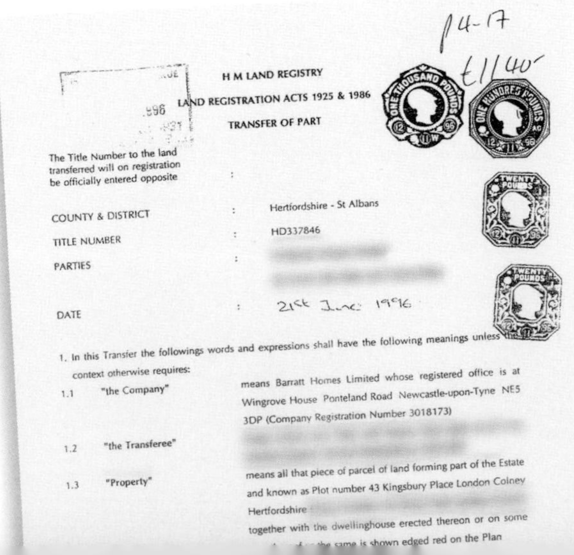

H M LAND REGISTRY

LAND REGISTRATION ACTS 1925 & 1986

TRANSFER OF PART

The Title Number to the land transferred will on registration be officially entered opposite :

COUNTY & DISTRICT : Hertfordshire - St Albans

TITLE NUMBER : HD337846

PARTIES

DATE : 21st June 1996

1. In this Transfer the followings words and expressions shall have the following meanings unless the context otherwise requires:

1.1 "the Company" means Barratt Homes Limited whose registered office is at Wingrove House Ponteland Road Newcastle-upon-Tyne NE5 3DP (Company Registration Number 3018173)

1.2 "the Transferee"

1.3 "Property" means all that piece of parcel of land forming part of the Estate and known as Plot number 43 Kingsbury Place London Colney Hertfordshire together with the dwellinghouse erected thereon or on some ... the same is shown edged red on the Plan

Slum clearance developments

In the 1920s successive legislation gave powers to local authorities to demolish unsanitary dwellings and create modern housing for the working classes in urban areas. The planning regulations are well documented in local records, including planning schemes, local authority orders and legal documents.

Where to find records Search in local records and the National Archives (see DIRECTORY), particularly among the records of the Ministry of Health (Housing Department).

Post-war redevelopment records

After the Second World War, plans were drawn up for large-scale reconstruction of the towns and cities damaged by bombing. Following the Town and Country Planning Act in 1947, developers had to seek planning permission from local authorities before any building work could go ahead. Similarly, all local authorities were required to prepare a development plan for their local area.

Where to find records Many of these records are held in county archives. Duplicate plans and paperwork were also passed on to the Ministry of Town and Country Planning whose records can be viewed at the National Archives (see DIRECTORY). Bomb census maps and papers (see below) are also stored at the National Archives.

The birth of new towns

As new housing developments sprang up they created a mass of documentation, held in local record offices.

Local government and planning records Your local council should hold records of planning applications (after 1947, following the Town and Country Planning Act). These consist of plans, maps and building specifications relating to advice on street layout, materials to be used, planting of trees and landscaping, the provision of public utilities and even street lighting. These records can also be found at the National Archives (see DIRECTORY). Some local authorities have databases that contain planning and building details of each property in the district.

Records of services Utility company records include maps and plans showing when houses were connected to gas mains, water supplies or the National Grid. Many refer by name to the occupiers or owners of the house. These are stored at your local record office.

Construction company brochures These brochures can be linked to a precise construction date. Also look out for advertisements in local newspapers (see pages 74-75).

FIND OUT MORE

- **www.landreg.gov.uk** On-line access to the Land Registry.

After the bombs Thousands of properties were rebuilt following the damage caused by the Blitz. Bomb census maps will show you how the war affected your area, while accompanying reports can add details such as how many bombs were dropped and when. The map below shows the destruction in part of Lambeth, London. Walcot Square (circled) was badly hit; today (inset) it is much restored, but the light-coloured bricks give a clue to where new properties were erected on top of bomb sites.

Filling in the 20th-century story of your home

If you live in a 20th-century house or flat you may think there is little history to uncover, but whatever the age or style of a property, there is much to learn. You can find details of a property when first built, or learn out about the site on which it was constructed – perhaps an earlier property stood there, or the land could have been part of a farm or estate.

What used to be there?

To find out what was once on the site your home now occupies, look at Ordnance Survey (OS) maps (see pages 18-19) dating from before the property was built. The 1910-15 Valuation Office Survey (see page 140) or earlier records such as tithe and enclosure maps (see pages 18-19) will also show you how an area has changed, and where your home fits in to the story.

Digging for Britain

If your home was built in the latter part of the 20th century on what was previously agricultural land, you should look up the area in the National Farm Survey records (see page 66). The survey was carried out in 1941-3 to assess the productivity of farms in order to help the war effort. Copies of OS maps were marked up to show the boundary of each farm, with a code assigned to every individual holding. Assessment forms include details of the size and extent of the property, the name and address of the owner, the name of the tenant farmer (if applicable), and information on the quality of the farm and how the land was being used.

Where to find the records The records are stored at the National Archives (see DIRECTORY) for England and Wales, with limited records for Scotland in the National Archives of Scotland (see DIRECTORY).

What did your house look like?

Perhaps your house has been modernised and you wish to see what it looked like when it was new. There are several types of record that will help you.

- Old sales catalogues belonging to local estate agents often contain photographs of exteriors and specify the internal period features of houses, so you may be able to see how your house looked when it was brand new.
- Local newspapers (see pages 74-75) often carry advertisements for property sales or rentals. You will need to have a rough idea of when a sale took place.
- Auctioneers' records are worth checking as they list sales and sometimes the contents of the property, which may have been sold at the same time.

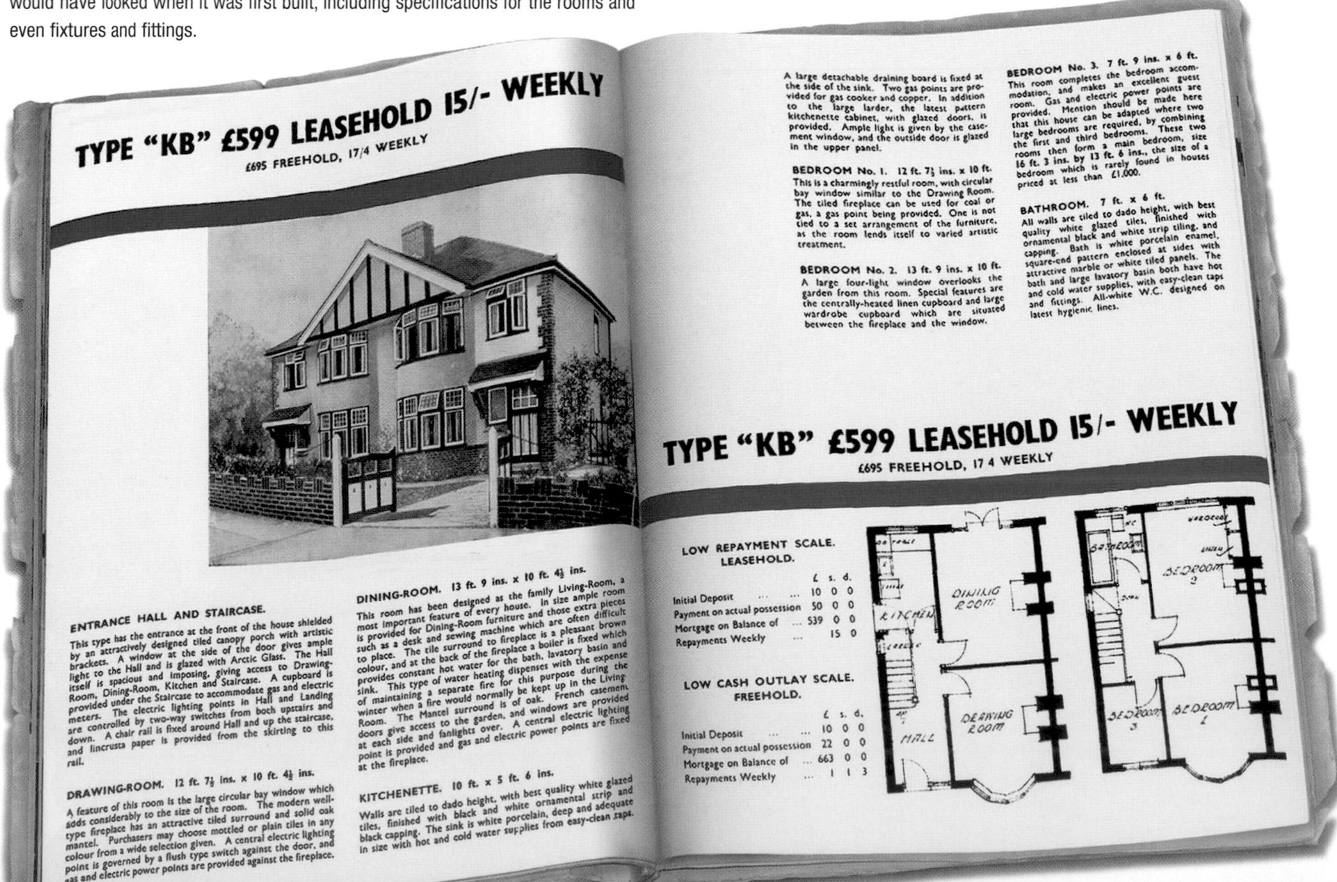

TYPE "KB" £599 LEASEHOLD 15/- WEEKLY

£695 FREEHOLD, 17/4 WEEKLY

ENTRANCE HALL AND STAIRCASE.

This type has the entrance at the front of the house shielded by an attractively designed tiled canopy porch with artistic brackets. A window at the side of the door gives ample light to the Hall and is glazed with Arctic Glass. The Hall itself is spacious and imposing, giving access to Drawing-Room, Dining-Room, Kitchen and Staircase. A cupboard is provided under the Staircase to accommodate gas and electric meters. The electric lighting points in Hall and Landing are controlled by two-way switches from both upstairs and down. A chair rail is fixed around Hall and up the staircase, and lincrusta paper is provided from the skirting to this rail.

DRAWING-ROOM. 12 ft. 7½ ins. x 10 ft. 4½ ins.

A feature of this room is the large circular bay window which adds considerably to the size of the room. The modern well-type fireplace has an attractive tiled surround and solid oak mantel. Purchasers may choose mottled or plain tiles in any colour from a wide selection given. A central electric lighting point is governed by a flush type switch against the door, and gas and electric power points are provided against the fireplace.

DINING-ROOM. 13 ft. 9 ins. x 10 ft. 4½ ins.

This room has been designed as the family Living-Room, a most important feature of every house. In size ample room is provided for Dining-Room furniture and those extra pieces such as a desk and sewing machine which are often difficult to place. The tile surround to fireplace is a pleasant brown colour, and at the back of the fireplace a boiler is fixed which provides constant hot water for the bath, lavatory basin and sink. This type of water heating dispenses with the expense of maintaining a separate fire for this purpose during the winter when a fire would normally be kept up in the Living-Room. The Mantel surround is of oak. French casement doors give access to the garden, and windows are provided at each side and fanlights over. A central electric lighting point is provided and gas and electric power points are fixed at the fireplace.

KITCHENETTE. 10 ft. x 5 ft. 6 ins.

Walls are tiled to dado height, with best quality white glazed tiles, finished with black and white ornamental strip and black capping. The sink is white porcelain, deep and adequate in size with hot and cold water supplies from easy-clean taps. A large detachable draining board is fixed at the side of the sink. Two gas points are provided for gas cooker and copper. In addition to the large larder, the latest pattern kitchenette cabinet, with glazed doors, is provided. Ample light is given by the casement window, and the outside door is glazed in the upper panel.

BEDROOM No. 1. 12 ft. 7½ ins. x 10 ft.

This is a charmingly restful room, with circular bay window similar to the Drawing Room. The tiled fireplace can be used for coal or gas, a gas point being provided. One is not tied to a set arrangement of the furniture, as the room lends itself to varied artistic treatment.

BEDROOM No. 2. 13 ft. 9 ins. x 10 ft.

A large four-light window overlooks the garden from this room. Special features are the centrally-heated linen cupboard and large wardrobe cupboard which are situated between the fireplace and the window.

BEDROOM No. 3. 7 ft. 9 ins. x 6 ft.

This room completes the bedroom accommodation, and makes an excellent guest room. Gas and electric power points are provided. Mention should be made here that this house can be adapted where two large bedrooms are required, by combining the first and third bedrooms. These two rooms then form a main bedroom, size 16 ft. 3 ins. by 13 ft. 6 ins., the size of a bedroom which is rarely found in houses priced at less than £1,000.

BATHROOM. 7 ft. x 6 ft.

All walls are tiled to dado height, with best quality white glazed tiles, finished with ornamental black and white strip tiling, and capping. Bath is white porcelain enamel, square-end pattern enclosed at sides with attractive marble or white tiled panels. The bath and large lavatory basin both have hot and cold water supplies, with easy-clean taps and fittings. All-white W.C. designed on latest hygienic lines.

TYPE "KB" £599 LEASEHOLD 15/- WEEKLY

£695 FREEHOLD, 17 4 WEEKLY

LOW REPAYMENT SCALE.
LEASEHOLD.

	£	s.	d.
Initial Deposit	10	0	0
Payment on actual possession	50	0	0
Mortgage on Balance of ...	539	0	0
Repayments Weekly ...		15	0

LOW CASH OUTLAY SCALE.
FREEHOLD.

	£	s.	d.
Initial Deposit	10	0	0
Payment on actual possession	22	0	0
Mortgage on Balance of ...	663	0	0
Repayments Weekly ...	1	1	3

Studying the property market A 1930 brochure for Huxley Road on the Grove Park Estate in Welling, Kent, gives detailed information on how a property on this estate would have looked when it was first built, including specifications for the rooms and even fixtures and fittings.

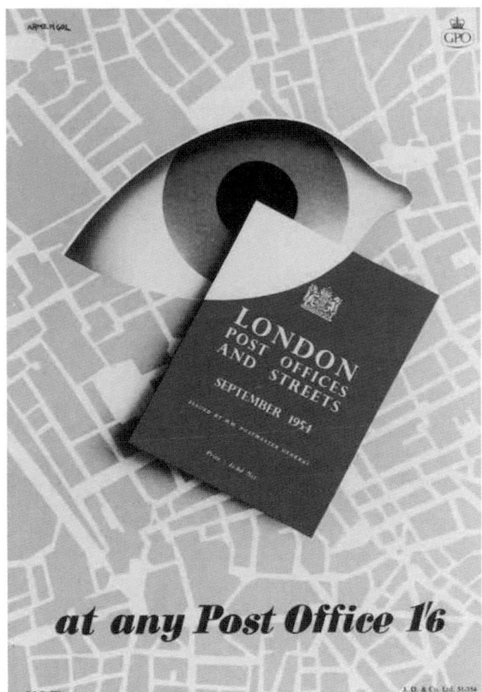

Logging the streets Old Post Office directories from the 20th century exist for most towns. If you follow the street names back from year to year, you could find when a street was built.

Where to find the records Estate agents' catalogues may have been deposited in your local studies library or at the county record office. Local newspapers are stored in local archives, with copies at British Library Newspapers (see DIRECTORY). Check for local auctioneers' records in local archives.

Architectural records

If your home is architecturally imposing or has an unusual design, it is worth checking at the Royal Institute of British Architects (see DIRECTORY) to see if any building accounts or architects' plans have been deposited. You could also check whether your home is mentioned in the Pevsner architectural guide for your area (held at your library). Each volume describes local notable buildings, and includes a gazetteer arranged alphabetically by place.

Where to find the records Look for architectural records in your county record office. In Scotland the Royal Commission on the Ancient and Historical Monuments (see DIRECTORY) has a wide collection of architects' papers.

Local directories

Many local trade, postal and telephone directories cover the 20th century. The volumes will usually include a street index, and often have a map. They can be found at local record offices and reference libraries.

Trade directories Properties that were associated with a trade or profession, such as shops or inns, can be traced in trade or commercial directories (see page 75). You can find out the names of the occupants and the business that was run from the property. Then it should be possible to cross-reference with trade licences, local newspaper advertisements, trade journals and photographs (all at local archives) to find when it was converted to a domestic property.

FIND OUT MORE

- **www.nationalarchives.gov.uk/catalogue/RdLeaflet.asp?sLeafletID=309** Advice on how to use the National Farm Survey.
- **www.pevsner.co.uk** Website giving information about architectural guides to Britain.
- **www.bl.uk/collections/newspapers.html** An on-line catalogue of national and local papers.
- **www.historicaldirectories.org** An on-line catalogue of national and local directories.

When research takes you back to bare land

As you look back to a period before your home was built, you will need to keep in mind the social history of your area. In the 1920s and 30s there was a rapid expansion of the suburbs, and land from large estates was often sold off and developed. Your street could be one of the many thousands built at this time on what was then the rural fringes of a town. In many cases the large estate house was converted to flats, or a non-domestic use such as a hotel or residential home. Sometimes it was demolished to make way for more housing. You can find demolition orders and slum clearance files at the National Archives (see DIRECTORY) or in local archives. You do not have to restrict your searches to 'wordy' documents. Most local study centres have extensive photographic archives. The photograph on the right shows the junction of Pinner Road and Headstone Lane in North Harrow, where Aish & Cartwright were building 'labour-saving' semis in 1924.

Interior clues in post-war homes

The home in the 1950s, 60s and 70s cast aside the austere look of the pre-war period. New properties were often smaller than their predecessors, so built-in furniture was used to make the most of the space. Modern living demanded flexible use of living areas and the convenience of easy-clean surfaces. Key features to look out for in the post-war home are room partitions, fitted kitchens with Formica worktops, linoleum floors and washable vinyl wallpaper.

Room partition

Open-tread staircase

1970s bathroom suite

Formica worktop

The open plan room

The concept of 'open planning' was widely adopted providing a feeling of increased space and light, with interior walls kept to a minimum, large picture windows and open-tread staircases. Room partitions or dividers acted as a wall substitute.

- **Room partitions or dividers** If you have an open-plan living, kitchen or dining area, you may still have in place the original 1950s or 60s open storage units which acted as 'room dividers'. These were usually finished in teak, or in a plastic veneer if adjoining the kitchen. Built-in sliding screens or 'foldaway' room partitions also became popular, allowing for a more flexible approach to space. Look out for those made from imitation leather, which covered collapsible partitions in a wide range of colours and patterns.
- **Windows** Large, single-pane floor-to-ceiling windows, known as 'picture windows', are a good indication that a property was built in the later 1950s or 60s. Pilkington made double-glazed units as large as 10ft by 6ft (3m by 1.8m). You may also find original sliding windows or patio doors, again double-glazed and often mahogany framed.
- **Staircases** Look at the location and style of your staircase. Stairs in 1950s homes generally rose directly from the open-plan living room and were a wooden open-tread ladder design to enhance the effect of light and space.

Built-in aesthetics

Modernist styling called for furniture and fittings that saved space. Look out for built-in cupboards in the hall, fitted wardrobes in the bedroom or fitted units in the kitchen or bathroom. You should examine the finishes and surfaces carefully, as they are the key to dating your interiors accurately.

- **Fitted kitchens** Worktops with plastic laminates from companies such as Formica and Warerite were popular in the 1950s and 60s. These materials were hard-wearing, easy to clean and readily manufactured in the latest decorative colours and patterns, including fashionable fake leather and wood finishes. A pressed steel or coloured enamel sink unit is also a clue to a 1950s or 60s kitchen.
- **Bathrooms** Look out for the panelled baths and built-in storage ('vanity') units found in many post-war bathrooms. Baths, toilets and wash basins were increasingly being made of Fibreglass or Perspex from the mid 1960s onwards, usually in colour co-ordinated pastel shades, particularly pink, blue and 'avocado'.
- **Fitted wardrobes** Veneers in teak, maple or mahogany were a strong element in designs of 1960s and early 70s, as were louvered doors. Wardrobes might also form part of a built-in bedroom suite, or act as a room partition.

HEATING

Increasingly sophisticated plumbing and heating systems provided the standard of comfort demanded by the modern consumer in the 1950s and 60s. As a result there was less reliance on the fireplace as a form of heating.

- **Fireplaces** With the increasing popularity of the television, a fire ceased to be the focal point of the living-room. Fireplaces became decorative rather than functional. If your home has one dating from the 1950s or 60s, it will probably be faced in stone or brick. Sometimes a built-in storage or shelving unit would be incorporated.
- **Central heating** Most new homes built from the 1960s onwards had central heating installed, giving a better standard of all-over draught-free warmth.

Exposed brickwork

Vinyl flooring

FIND OUT MORE

- Museum of Domestic Design and Architecture Collection includes 1950s wallpapers and textiles and trade catalogues. www.moda.mdx.ac.uk
- The Twentieth Century Society www.c20society.org.uk
- Geffrye Museum Has a 1950s-60s room set. www.geffrye-museum.org.uk
- *Fiftiestyle: Home Decorating and Furnishing from the 1950s* (Lesley Hoskins, Middlesex University Press, 2004)
- *Sixtiestyle: Home Decoration and Furnishings from the 1960s* (David Heathcote, Middlesex University Press, 2004)
- *Contemporary: Architecture and Interiors of the 1950s* A survey of trends in taste and interior design (Lesley Jackson, Phaidon Press, 1998)
- *Decorative Arts, 1970s* (Charlotte and Peter Fiell, Taschen, 2000)
- *Formica and Design* (S.G. Lewin, Rizzoli International Publications, 1991)

Poly-flor flexible vinyl floor tiles, 1960

Wallpaper 1958, by Shand Kydd

Textured 1960 wallpaper, by Lightbown Aspinall

'Spartacus', 1970s vinyl wallpaper, by Mayfair

Floors

If you have a 1950s, 60s or 70s home, man-made fibre tufted carpets may still exist in some areas. But a more likely survivor is the synthetic floor tile, in vinyl or linoleum. Look for these in hallways, landings, kitchens and bathrooms, and also for surviving pieces inside cupboards and fitted wardrobes or beneath fitted carpets.

- **Linoleum** Lino was commonly used as a floor covering in post-war homes, especially in the kitchen, and came in an array of mottled patterns designed not to show dirt.
- **Vinyl tiles** These tiles were hard-wearing and easy to install and keep clean. They were also very cheap, and in the 1950s and 60s gradually replaced lino as the material of choice for areas that were in constant use. Tiles with a faux marbling effect were available in a range of colours. Chequerboard vinyl floors in combinations of black and white, red and white, and yellow and white were popular during the 1950s.
- **Rubber or cork tiles, or hardwood block or strip** By the mid 1960s and in the 70s, these were considered a more stylish alternative to vinyl tiles for flooring, giving a room a more sophisticated, ultra-modern look.

Walls and wallpaper

Although there were fewer internal walls in homes of this era, walls still had an important role to play, giving a sense of space through surface texture, colour and pattern. Dados and picture rails disappeared and the decorative border or frieze became obsolete. The ceilings of the period were plain, with no mouldings to cover awkward edges.

- **Wall finishes** Look out for exposed brick and tongue-and-groove pine panelling, which were both popular in the 1960s and early 70s, as were textured wall finishes such as hessian and the more synthetic products such as textured paint and wallpapers, or vinyl wall tiles. Often a variety of textures – both natural and simulated – were used together.
- **Wallpaper** Washable vinyl-coated papers were commonly used in bathrooms and kitchens in the 1960s, but you are more likely to find textured 'woodchip' wallpaper which was widely used throughout the home in the 1960s and 70s and remains in many today. Remnants of screen-printed contemporary patterns may also survive. These were often bold and colourful, in abstract or geometric designs, inspired by graphic art.

Early 20th-century interior clues

The Edwardian home had many similarities to that of the Victorian era. But after the upheaval of the First World War ideas about living space took a new turn, bringing in the elegant, functional fashions of Art Deco. Change did not happen overnight. So when you try to date aspects of your home between 1900 and 1945, remember that the original features you see will owe as much to tradition as they do to the fashions of the day.

FIND OUT MORE

- *20s and 30s Style* (M. Horsham, Grange Books, 1989)
- *The 1930s Home* (G. Stephenson, Shire, 2000)
- **www.bbc.co.uk/homes/design/period_index.shtml** An introduction to period styles of the early 20th century.
- **www.bricksandbrass.co.uk** Information on how to identify the designs of elements such as wallpaper, stained glass and fireplaces in homes built in the 1920s and 30s.
- The Twentieth Century Society See DIRECTORY.
- The Bakelite Museum See DIRECTORY.

Art Nouveau

Art Deco

1930s stained glass

Bakelite switches

1930s bellboard

Fireplaces

If your home has original fireplaces, you can get close to establishing the decade in which it was built. The elaborate decoration of the late Victorian period was not repeated in 20th-century fireplaces. Instead of fussy little bouquets, representations of flowers were elongated, curved and stylised in the Art Nouveau fashion, which began in the 1890s and took off in the early 1900s. A fireplace installed in the decade before the First World War is more likely to be made of brightly burnished steel or copper than the black-leaded cast-iron of the late 19th century. In the 1920s and 30s, Art Deco style brought long straight lines and bold patterns. Not much then changed until the 1950s.

- **Art Nouveau** Like their Victorian predecessors, the Edwardians used tiles in fire surrounds, but the colours were bright and the floral imagery kept simple. Look for flowers that are more a brief freehand sketch in ceramic than an oil painting on clay. This style was popular until the 1920s.
- **Art Deco** The geometric, angular and functional lines of Art Deco are quite distinctive. If your fireplace has a chunky, stepped profile (see above), it is likely to be 1930s or possibly later. Typically the tiles are shades of pink, green or beige. Look out for Art Deco motifs such as shells, foliage, flowers and the more abstract designs such as the sunburst. An Art Deco fireplace in your home suggests that the house was built in the 1920s or 30s.
- **Tudorbethan fireplaces** An imposing inglenook fireplace featuring large expanses of tiling is likely to date from the 1920s and 30s, when there was a retrospective fashion for mock-Tudor detail in newly built large suburban houses.

Windows

The style of windows in your home can give a clue to its age. Painted steel-framed windows became popular in the 1920s and 30s, and were widely used into the 1960s, although by then the frames enclosed larger, single planes of glass. It was thought that the steel frames would be more durable than old-fashioned wood, but in fact they were prone to condensation and rust. Many have been replaced.

- **Stained glass** Art Nouveau or Art Deco motifs can be seen in many early 20th-century homes. Leaded stained glass door panels were popular, featuring colourful images of flora and fauna or stylised images such as the galleon ship or sunburst motif (see pages 288-289)

Fixtures

If your home has Bakelite doorknobs, escutcheons and light switches, it is a clear indication that the property dates from the early 20th century, particularly the 1920s and 30s. Bakelite, first introduced in the USA in 1909, was a popular material for electrics because it was totally non-conductive and practically indestructible. 'It will not burn; it will not melt,' declared *Time* magazine in 1924. Anyone who carries out wiring work in a pre-Second World War house may well find a jumble of brown Bakelite junction boxes beneath the floorboards.

Design for living Signs of a typical 1930s lounge might include large metal-framed windows, flush-fitting cupboards, tiled fireplace and unadorned Art Deco furnishings.

Floors

In the early 20th century, floorboards went out of fashion and linoleum and parquet floors were all the rage. Take a look under your carpet and see what is there. A design may be incorporated around the edge of the floor to frame a centrally placed rug.

- **Parquet floors** These were made in oak or walnut and laid in 9in by 2in blocks. A common pattern was 'herringbone' – a repeating series of v-shapes. Although they were fashionable in the 1920s and 30s, many parquet floors have not survived because they were ripped up in the 1940s and 50s by homeowners who needed to get beneath the floor to install central heating pipes.
- **Linoleum floors** The pattern will indicate the linoleum's age. Subtle colours belong to the Edwardian era and bold geometric designs to the 1930s.

Walls and ceilings

Does your home have oak panelling? This form of decoration was adopted after 1905, as it gave an appearance of comfort and luxury. It was a feature of the Tudorbethan style of the 1920s and 30s that aimed to recreate a medieval look.

- **False oak beams** Should your home have such beams it is likely that it was built in the 1920s or 30s when the Tudorbethan style was popular. The beams, in-filled with plaster, play no structural role and have a purely decorative purpose.

Wallpaper

When stripping wallpaper, it is common to find layers of old wallpaper underneath. You can literally peel back the years as you strip off the layers. Wallpaper designs can readily be linked to a certain period and go right back to Edwardian times, when wallpapered friezes were fashionable (as were stencils).

- **Muted colours and flat, curving patterns** The Art Nouveau style in the early 1900s favoured scenes from nature with stylised flowers, birds, plants and peacock feathers.
- **Moulded papers** Imitation exotic woods or simulated fabric finishes were popular in the Edwardian period. Designs were generally plain and patterns simple.
- **Bold motifs** Bright colours and geometric patterns are typical of Art Deco wallpapers from the 1920s and 30s. Their popularity persisted into the 1950s.

Art Nouveau wallpaper 1902, Silver Studio

Wallpaper c.1910, Silver Studio

Art Deco wallpaper c.1935

The home scene at the turn of the 20th century

Between 1910 and 1915 the surveyors of the Inland Revenue compiled the most comprehensive set of property records that had ever been made for the whole of Britain. If your home was built at or before this time you will be able to find out who was living there, how much the property was worth and much more besides.

The Valuation Office Survey

Between 1910 and 1915 the government carried out a national survey to assess the value of property for tax purposes. The records consist of valuation books, Ordnance Survey (OS) maps and field books.

The valuation books summarise the ownership and value of the property. OS maps record the extent of each property, and assign each one a 'hereditament number' marked in red. These numbers can be looked up in the field books, which describe each property, recording the number and uses of rooms and outbuildings. They also comment on the general condition, water supply and sanitation of each property (see also pages 66-67).

The records can show you where your property boundaries were, or indeed whether your house had even been built by this date. In some areas, proposed housing developments were drawn in pencil on the maps, which may help you to work out the construction date of a house. Most of the survey records survive although there are occasional gaps due to accidental loss.

Where to find the records The English and Welsh records are held at the National Archives (see DIRECTORY), in classes IR 58, 121 and 124-135. The Scottish records are stored at the National Archives in Edinburgh (see DIRECTORY) as field books (IRS 51-87), maps (IRS 101-133) and a few on-site notebooks for the Dundee area (IRS 88). A set of valuation books were also made for local record offices.

Lack of title deeds

Title deeds are usually a good way to find out who owned your home in the past. But in 1925 the Law of Property Act stated that deeds had to be held for only 30 years, so many were simply thrown away, which means that deeds dating from before the 20th century are scarce. Some were deposited at local record offices, while others may survive in private hands, with the former owners of the property.

Valuable survey If your property is part of a Victorian terrace, it may well be listed in the Valuation Office Survey. Find its hereditament number on the OS map and cross-reference it with the relevant field book. The field book entries (right) list the name and address of the owner, the occupier (if different) and whether the property is freehold, copyhold or leasehold.

The story of 14 Walcot Square

In the Victorian era huge numbers of properties were built to cater for the growing urban populations. Walcot Square in Lambeth, London, is one such development and a good example of how you can follow the history of a house through the 19th century and into the 20th.

No. 1 or 14? When researching the history of a property you should keep in mind that the street number may have changed. No. 14 Walcot Square was No. 1 when Charles Newnham took up the first lease (below). Old leases can also give you an idea of a tenant's social standing, since class was closely associated with a person's job at the turn of the 20th century. As a builder, Mr Newnham was middle class.

Early history

In 1667 Edmund Walcott bequeathed the land on which Walcot Square stands to a charity, in order to raise money for the poor of the area. This information can be found in probate records of the Prerogative Courts of Canterbury (see pages 154-155). By searching in the Walcot Charity estate papers, held at the Lambeth archives and a local reference library, we know that by 1837 the trustees of the charity had decided to develop the site. They wanted to build housing for people who sought accommodation within easy reach of the City of London.

A Victorian redevelopment

Plans stored with the charity's estate papers show that between 1837 and 1839 Walcot Square was designed and constructed by the architect John Woodward. The first lease for No. 1 Walcot Square in 1837 was granted to a local builder, Charles Newnham. This indicates that well-to-do, professional people were taking up residence in the square. The property remained in the Newnham family until the late 1890s, by which time it had been renumbered as No. 14. The occupations recorded for residents in the census returns from 1881 and 1891 indicate that the area in general was by then home to people from lower levels of society (see pages 76-77 for information on using census records).

Walcot Square in the 20th century

The 1901 census and tenancy papers show that predominantly working class tenants were living at the property until it was damaged during the Blitz in 1940 (see page 133). The building was renovated after the war and today has one owner-occupier.

FIND OUT MORE

- *Old Title Deeds* (N.W. Alcock, Phillimore, 2001)
- **www.nationalarchives.gov.uk/pathways/localhistory/gallery1/valuation.htm** Information on how to find and use the Valuation Office maps and field books.

Homes for the working class The 1901 census return shows that No. 14 had been converted to flats, with three separate households, 14 people in all, inhabiting the building (see below). The flats were let out to working-class tenants, including a labourer, messenger, porter and, more exotically, an Italian mosaic layer and a feather curler.

Victorian home comforts

Today it is hard to imagine life without central heating, electric lighting, flushing toilets and hot running water. Yet all these appliances were unavailable to our ancestors at the turn of the 19th century. It was the innovative, practical and optimistic Victorians who either invented them or persevered in making them work properly. The arrival of these 'mod cons' gradually changed the way people lived and had an impact on the way houses were constructed and furnished.

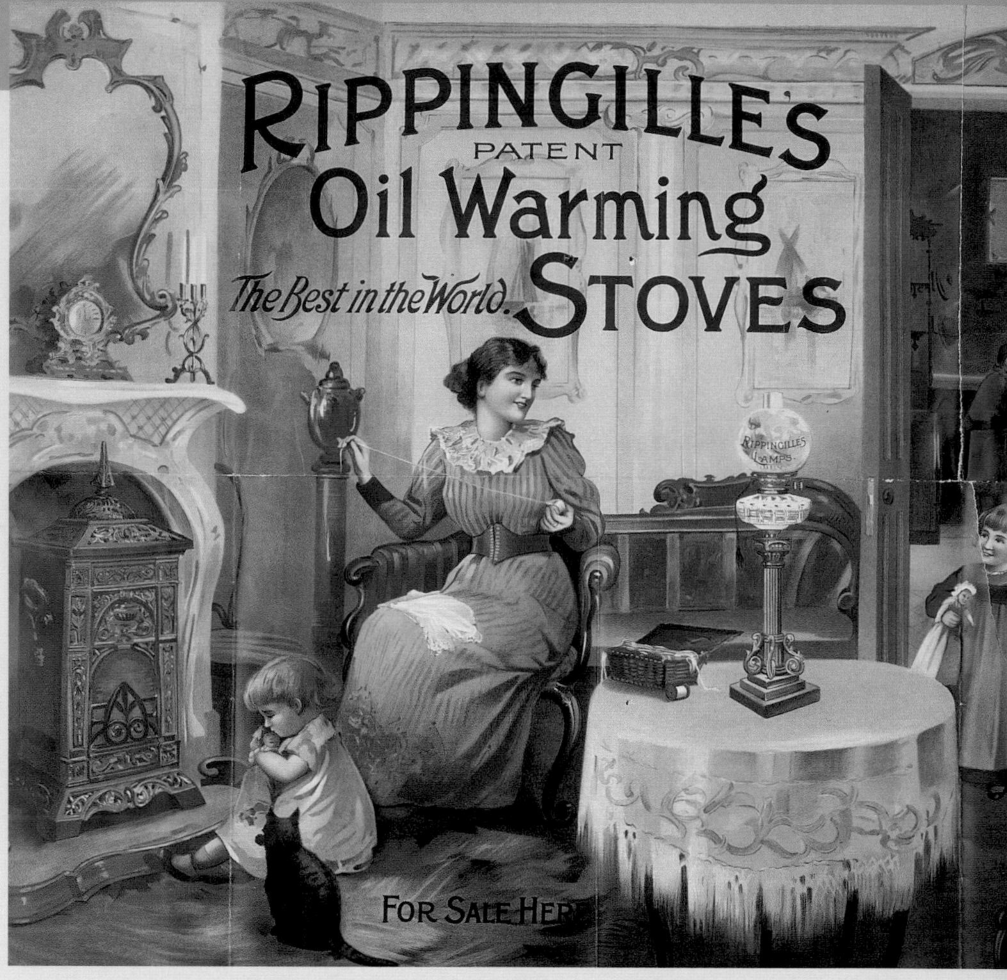

Domestic bliss The well-to-do Victorian was keen to make her home a haven with the latest gadgets. An 1894 advertisement (above) for oil-warming stoves seems to offer the way to a contented family, not just better heating. Gas lamps (right) also offered a happier home – they were brighter and safer than candles and cleaner than paraffin.

Turning up the heat

Gas was available from the early 19th century, but it was not introduced into many homes until the 1830s. A welcome invention for the better-off householder was the gas-fired water heater, in which a gas burner heated water flowing through a copper pipe. There were snags – it was hard to regulate the temperature and flow of the water, so that the contraption could become overheated to the point of explosion. Once the public water supply at a regulated pressure had been introduced, it became possible to develop the storage tank water heater, which was more reliable. Heating by means of steam pipes had been introduced into factories decades before Victorian pioneers began experimenting with domestic central heating. By the end of the 19th century cast iron radiators were being mass-produced, and most affluent householders had installed a heating system based on the circulation of hot water.

Estimates for Heating Apparatus, Ventilation,
Hot-Water Supply, Cooking Apparatus, &c.

RADIATORS,
HOT WATER,
STEAM, AND GAS.
ROSSER & RUSSELL,
OFFICES—
22, CHARING CROSS, LONDON.
WORKS—
Queen's Wharf, Hammersmith, W.
PATENTEES & MANUFACTURERS
Have in stock or progress in various sizes from 10 ft. to 200 ft. superficial heating surface each.
BOILERS, PIPES, STEAM-WATER HEATERS.
TRADE SUPPLIED. PRICE LISTS FREE.

Cast-iron monsters Rosser & Russell's advertisement for hot water, steam and gas radiators in an 1888 issue of *The Builder* was aimed at the wealthier Victorian. Central heating would not be widely available until the 1950s.

Let there be light

After the flickering light of candles, the introduction of gas lighting was a boon to the Victorians. Gas lighting was far brighter than candlelight, especially after the invention in the 1880s of the incandescent gas mantle, consisting of a skirt of silk or cotton soaked in soluble salts (thorium and cerium), and suspended over a fierce flame. The light shone upwards rather than downwards, but this disadvantage was

FLUSHED WITH PRIDE

Contrary to general belief and despite his name, the London plumber Thomas Crapper (1836-1910) did not give us the flush lavatory. In 1775 Alexander Cummings invented a flush mechanism, and three years later Joseph Bramah produced the first effective flush water closet, although the sewers at the time were unable to cope with the waste. The Victorians provided the necessary sewerage, and even applied their love of decoration to the lavatory itself (right, the Humber bowl of 1880).

overcome late in the 1890s with the introduction of the inverted mantle. Many homes used both gas lights and paraffin lamps, introduced in the 1860s. Paraffin gave a better light than candles, but it was smokier, smellier and more dangerous than gas.

By the turn of the 20th century, electric lighting was beginning to appear in the home. The carbon filament bulbs burned with a soft light but because they gave out negligible heat and no fumes, unlike gas and paraffin, they could be positioned anywhere within a room.

Brightening up the walls

In the early 19th century, interior wall coverings (see page 151) were often made of expensive fabrics such as silk, satin or cotton, and restricted to the better-off households. In the 1830s cheaper roller-printed wallpapers became available, and more houseowners could afford to cover their walls in bright, cheerful paper with printed designs (see page 147).

These wallpapers were shown off to best advantage in natural light, and technological advances in glass-making meant that larger pieces of plate glass, rather than many smaller panes, became the window glazing of choice. Windows themselves became more numerous after the heavy tax on glass was abolished in 1845, followed by the window tax in 1851 .

Damp and drains

Most early Victorian houses suffered from rising damp. Damp-proof courses – initially a layer of slates 15cm (6in) above ground level, and later a layer of bitumen – started to be incorporated into new buildings after the Public Health Act of 1875. The Act laid down statutory requirements for public health that included the provision of unpolluted water, rubbish collection, street cleaning and the hygienic disposal of sewage. It was the culmination of 27 years of legislation that began with an Act of 1848 that established a General Board of Health for London. Soon similar local Boards spread all across Britain, responding to a growing public concern about the disgusting state of many rivers, wells and streets, which had become the unregulated sewage and garbage dumps of overcrowded cities, causing regular outbreaks of cholera, typhoid and diarrhoea among the population.

The 1875 Act also decreed that every house should have either a flush lavatory, a privy or an ash pit. By the late 19th century every household that could afford it had an indoor lavatory with a high-level flush cistern and a dispenser full of lavatory paper (invented in America in 1857). The houses of the poorest still made do with an outside hut in which there was an earth or ash closet. The human waste, dirty water and other liquid sewage was carried away, and fresh water brought in, through cast-iron, lead or glazed ceramic piping.

Bright idea Although he did not invent the lightbulb, Thomas Edison made it considerably more efficient and long-lasting in the 1880s by using first a carbon and then a tungsten filament. By 1926 electricity networks were gradually linking up the country to power stations so that every home could enjoy the benefits of clean, safe lighting at the flick of a switch.

FIND OUT MORE

- The Gas Museum, Leicester Includes displays on the use of gas in the home. www.gasmuseum.co.uk
- Abbey Pumping Station Museum Covers the history of plumbing and sewage control. www.leicestermuseums.ac.uk
- www.periodproperty.co.uk/article018.htm Information about lighting in the Victorian home.

Charting your home through Victorian times

Throughout the 19th century there was a huge movement of people from the countryside into the towns and as a result thousands of houses were built to accommodate them. Whether you live in a detached 'villa', terraced house, 'two-up-two-down' worker's cottage or converted flat, there is an array of documents that can help you to find out when your house was built.

Mapping evidence

Victorian houses have distinctive architectural styles, but if you want to find out the precise year in which your home was built you will need to begin by searching through maps (see pages 18-19). By looking at the various types of map made in the 19th century you will be able to see when your home first appears. You will need to work back in time, in roughly the following order:

- town plans
- Ordnance Survey (OS) maps
- tithe maps
- enclosure maps.

Victorian town plans If you live in an urban area, look up some old town plans. These started to be produced during the Victorian period in great numbers by urban district councils, which used the maps when designing sewers and implementing improvements such as gas street lights and pedestrian paving. In many cases, maps are detailed enough to be able to identify individual properties.

Town plans are often held in local and city archives and county record offices. Between 1847 and 1895, the OS mapped 61 Scottish towns in great detail and the maps can be seen at the National Library of Scotland and on-line (see DIRECTORY).

Ordnance Survey maps You will be able to find OS maps at a scale of six inches to the mile going back decade by decade to the 1850s. (There are earlier OS sheets going back to 1801, but the scale of one inch to the mile means that they are unhelpful for locating individual properties.) Most county or local archives have a good selection. The British Library in London (see DIRECTORY) holds a copy of all OS maps, while the National Archives and the National Library of Scotland also hold OS material as part of their collections (see DIRECTORY).

Tithe awards If your home is still on an OS map of the 1850s, the next step is to see if it appears on a tithe map of the area (see pages 19, 73). Drawn up

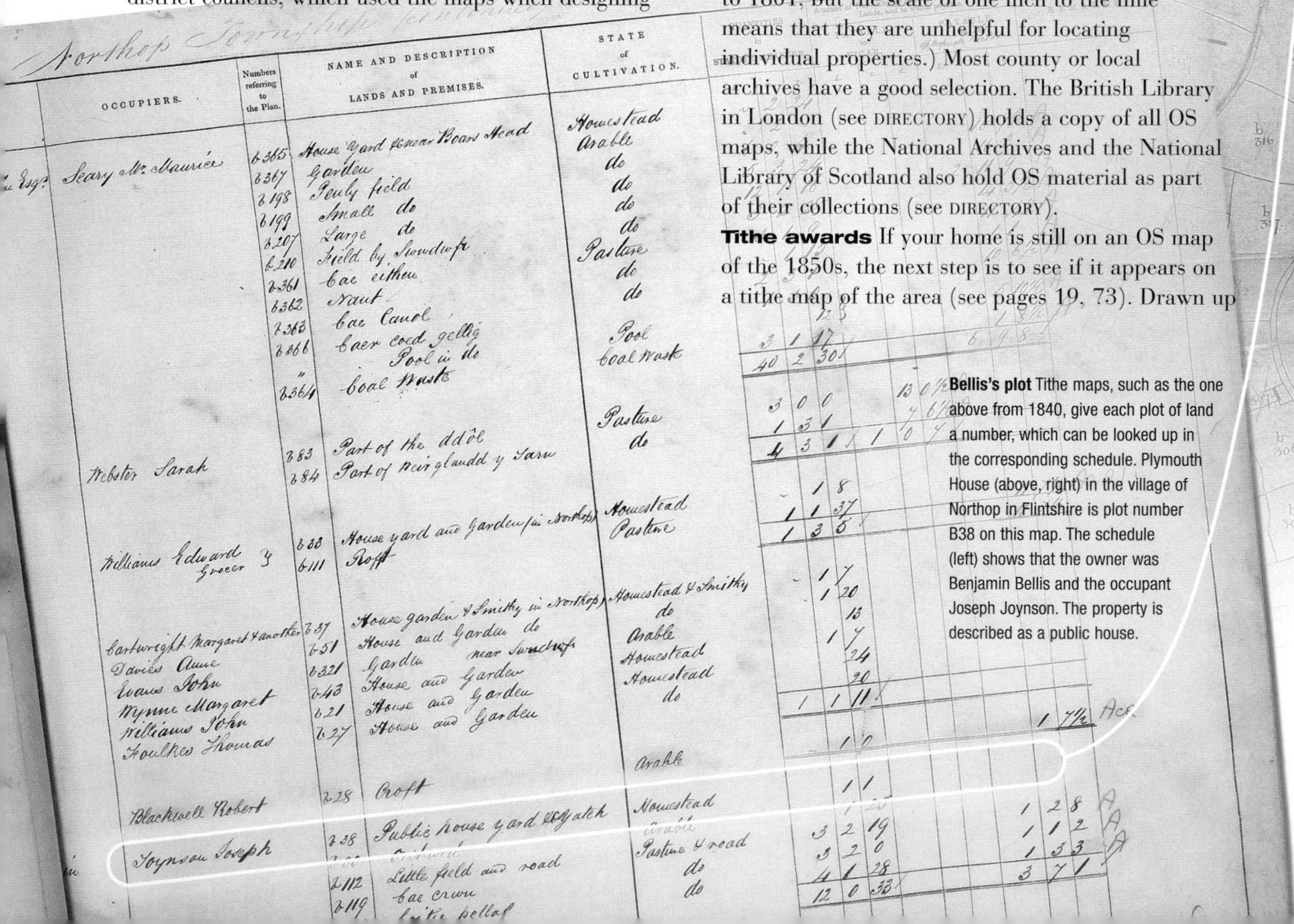

Bellis's plot Tithe maps, such as the one above from 1840, give each plot of land a number, which can be looked up in the corresponding schedule. Plymouth House (above, right) in the village of Northop in Flintshire is plot number B38 on this map. The schedule (left) shows that the owner was Benjamin Bellis and the occupant Joseph Joynson. The property is described as a public house.

Past life as a pub
Tithe records and trade directories from the 19th century reveal that Plymouth House in Northop, Flintshire, was a public house called the Yacht Inn, providing accommodation for travellers on the Chester to Holyrood coach route.

between 1836 and 1852. following the Tithe Commutation Act of 1836, tithe maps and schedules detail each parcel of land, house and outbuilding within more than 11,000 parishes in England and Wales. If your home was built after 1836, a tithe map can also show who owned the land and how it was worked previously.

Three sets of maps and schedules were made, with one set deposited at the National Archives (see DIRECTORY) and other copies usually sent to the relevant county record office. The National Library of Wales (see DIRECTORY) also has an extensive collection of tithe documents.

Enclosure maps These maps can take you back even further. From 1750 to around 1850, numerous Acts of Parliament authorised the enclosure of open-fields and common land into smaller rectangular fields. The enclosure awards (see pages 19, 73) incorporate a map and index book or schedule where you can identify who owned your property or the land on which it would later be built. These records are deposited at the National Archives (see DIRECTORY) or in local record offices.

Now for some lateral thinking

After tracing your home on the various maps, you may be left with a gap in its history due to incomplete records. For example, your home may appear on OS maps for the 1890s, but not on a map of 1870. Now you need to think of ways to narrow down your search.

FIND OUT MORE

- **www.historicaldirectories.org** An on-line library of local and trade directories for England and Wales (1750-1919).
- **www.nls.uk/maps/townplans** An on-line collection of Victorian Scottish town plans.
- **www.old-maps.co.uk** An on-line collection of late 19th-century OS maps, searchable by county, place name or grid reference.

Census records

The Victorians carried out a census every ten years (see pages 76-77), listing every household and its occupants. These records will narrow your search to within ten years. Using the example above, you would look up the 1871, 1881 and 1891 census records. If your home is not in the census for 1871 or 1881 but appears in the 1891 census, then you can deduce that it was built between 1881 and 1891.

OTHER USEFUL SOURCES OF INFORMATION

Estate papers If your house was part of an estate you may find these records of interest. They often contain maps and written surveys of properties, as well as correspondence, leases and rentals. See page 159.

Old photographs Use these to see what your house once looked like. See pages 70-71.

Directories As a final way of pinpointing the date your home was built you can use old local directories (see page 75). From the later 19th century most local directories list house numbers and street names. In the above example you would need to look at directories between 1881 and 1891. This should give you the year of construction.

Health and sanitation records

The work carried out to improve living standards in the Victorian era generated plenty of records in which your home may be listed. In London the Metropolitan Board of Works was set up in 1855 to build a network of sewers and install paving and lighting. It even assigned road names and numbers to individual properties. The records of the Metropolitan Board of Works are held at the London Metropolitan Archives (see DIRECTORY). You will find similar resources for other cities and towns in your local record office.

street, Newcastle-on-Tyne.

MARINE RESIDENCE, CULLERCOATS, NEAR TYNEMOUTH.

TO BE SOLD BY PRIVATE CONTRACT, the FREEHOLD MESSUAGE, named Cliff House, containing Entrance Hall, Dining Room, Library, Housekeeper's Room, Butler's Pantry, Mangling Room, and two Kitchens on the Ground Floor; Drawing Room, and seven Bedrooms on the First Floor. There are five Attics, spacious Wine, Beer, and Coal Cellars; two small Inner Yards, with a Larder, and three other small Outer Rooms. Under the Larder is a very large Cistern for Rain Water, and there is also an abundant supply of water from the adjoining Whitley Water Works, at a moderate cost.

The House is in excellent Repair, and is well drained. It is distant one mile and a half from

For sale notices Old local newspapers can reveal gems of information about a home. The advertisement above for Cliff House, in Cullercoats, Northumberland, appeared in the *Shields Daily News* in 1868. It gives an illuminating room-by-room description of the house, even down to its 'spacious wine, beer and coal cellars'. Newspaper clippings can be found at local archives (see pages 74-75).

Victorian interior clues

The Victorians liked to adorn their houses with ironmongery, ceramics and woodwork. These fittings, including tiles, dado rails, ceiling roses and doorknobs, were mass-produced and so affordable to all. They followed the fashion, so the smallest surviving feature in your home can help to pinpoint its age, and even give an insight into the tastes and aspirations of owners long ago.

Register grate

Tile surrounds

Brass finger-plate and door knob

Four-panelled door

Fireplaces

If your house is Victorian, it is likely to have cast-iron fireplaces. The drawing room – the place for entertaining – would have had the most impressive arrangement, with surrounds of black or grey slate, veined or painted marbles, or painted tiles. The bedrooms had smaller, simpler hearths. Fireplace technology evolved during the 19th century and you can tell whether a fireplace is early, mid or late Victorian from the style of the grate.

- **Cast-iron hob grate** Early Victorian fireplaces had square or rectangular openings and the decoration was restrained, with classical motifs.
- **Cast-iron register grate** This type of fireplace, with an arched top, was introduced in about 1850. The grate had a moveable iron plate to adjust the flue.
- **Straight-topped register grate** In the 1870s and 1880s fireplaces went back to having square openings and cast-iron surrounds. But they featured splayed sides, or 'cheeks', bearing tiles that would reflect heat into the room. The ceramic tiles were highly decorative, showing stylised flowers and animals.

Windows

Victorian houses were built with large-paned sash windows. You may also come across panels of stained glass in fanlights, front doors and landings. Typical motifs were floral, geometric or medieval, such as the fleurs-de-lys.

Interior shutters These were popular in the 19th century because the Victorians were concerned about the damaging effects on sunlight on their furniture.

Fixtures

The Victorians embellished their homes with brass fittings, leaded lights and mouldings. The amount of decoration reflected the importance of the room, with more elaborate designs in rooms used for entertaining.

- **Doors** In the 1960s internal doors were often covered over to create a more modern look. Look beneath the plywood to see if an original four-panelled Victorian door survives.
- **Fingerplates** These were brass, and screwed to doors above the knob to stop the paintwork getting dirty. Early Victorian fingerplates were plain, but as the century progressed they became more ornate. After the 1850s there were Japanese-style and mock-rococo fingerplates.
- **Door knobs** These have often been replaced many times, but you may still find Victorian doorknobs made of brass, bronze or porcelain.

Floors

The Victorians continued the Georgian practice of showcasing the parts of the house where visitors would be received (see pages 150-151). A tiled hallway is a strong indication that your home dates from the Victorian era.

Tiled floors From the 1850s through to the end of the Edwardian era, there was a vogue for encaustic tiles – coloured tiles in geometric shapes which were laid in intricate mosaic patterns. These tiles often survive because they are so hardy and practical. Common colours were reds, browns and buffs, with the occasional green, blue or white tile thrown in for relief. Tiles were only ever laid in the front hallway, so if you see a mosaic kitchen floor in a late Victorian house it can only be a modern attempt to introduce period flavour into the kitchen.

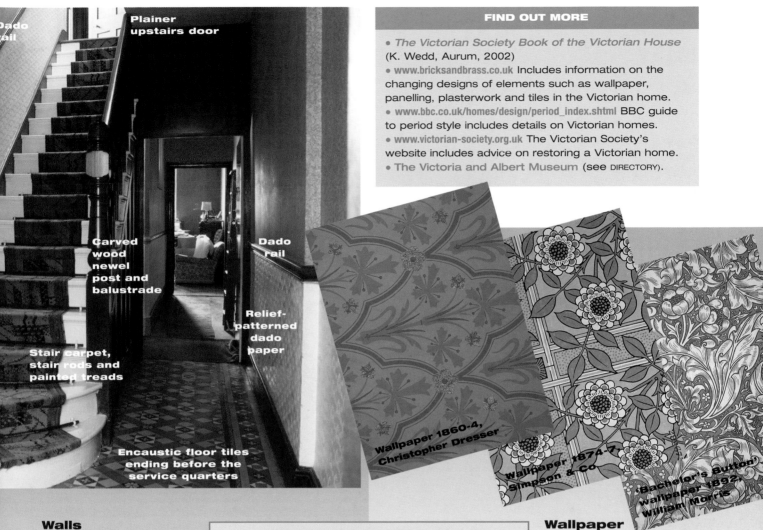

Dado rail

Plainer upstairs door

Carved wood newel post and balustrade

Dado rail

Relief-patterned dado paper

Stair carpet, stair rods and painted treads

Encaustic floor tiles ending before the service quarters

FIND OUT MORE

- *The Victorian Society Book of the Victorian House* (K. Wedd, Aurum, 2002)
- www.bricksandbrass.co.uk Includes information on the changing designs of elements such as wallpaper, panelling, plasterwork and tiles in the Victorian home.
- www.bbc.co.uk/homes/design/period_index.shtml BBC guide to period style includes details on Victorian homes.
- www.victorian-society.org.uk The Victorian Society's website includes advice on restoring a Victorian home.
- The Victoria and Albert Museum (see DIRECTORY).

Wallpaper 1860-4, Christopher Dresser

Wallpaper 1874-7, Simpson & Co

'Bachelor's Button' wallpaper 1892, William Morris

Walls

A wooden rail fixed to the wall at about waist height (a dado rail) was a universal feature. Below the rail the wall was panelled or, in halls and passageways, tiled so that it could be easily washed. A cheap alternative was a relief-patterned paper such as Lincrusta (from 1877) or Anaglypta (from 1887) – mixtures of wood pulp, linseed oil, gums, resin and wax. They were so hard wearing that many survive. The space above the dado – the field – was then free to be decorated with wallpaper. Dado rails (and picture rails) became less common in dining and drawing rooms from the 1890s and were often removed in the 20th century. But when you strip a wall in a Victorian house you can usually see the old scars in the plaster where the rails used to be.

DECORATIVE PLASTERWORK

Ready-made decorative plasterwork for walls and ceilings proliferated in the Victorian period, such as the ceiling rose, a circular feature from which a chandelier or a crystal lantern would hang. Handmade plaster or timber ceiling roses (see a selection of designs below from the 1830s) were typical of the early Victorian period. They used naturalistic designs and were more delicate and flatter than later counterparts.

Intricately detailed garlands of oakleaves began to appear on ceilings and cornices in the 1850s. Sculpted ceilings, painted salmon pink and pale green, were common in the 1860s. The mouldings became increasingly bulky and more ornate and stretched across the whole ceiling with plaster ribs or vaulting in Gothic revival styles.

Factory-made cardboard ceiling roses date from the 1880s. These were much simpler in style with little floral embellishment. Such roses survive in many late Victorian houses, where, despite bright electric light, they can still easily be mistaken for plaster versions.

Wallpaper

Check inside cupboards and behind plasterwork and you may find some original Victorian wallpaper. From the 1830s patterned fabrics became widely available, and cheap mass-produced papers were used in every room in every home by the 1870s. Wallpaper borders and friezes were also common.

- **Moiré wallpaper** A wall covering popular in early Victorian times that imitated textiles or panelling and featured sprig and trellis designs. It was a style hangover from the Georgian period.
- **Strong geometric patterns** Inspired by the Gothic Revival of the mid-Victorian period, wallpaper was produced in rich colours such as dark greens and burgundy. The patterns were elaborate, often flock or velvet-textured. Christopher Dresser was one of the most popular designers.
- **Detailed naturalistic plant-inspired designs** Willow and acanthus leaves were popular in the late Victorian period. William Morris-style flowers or large dahlias and hydrangeas were typical.
- **Embossed wallpapers** At the end of the Victorian era, wallpapers began to imitate moulded plaster, wainscot, carved wood and stamped leather.

Taking the story back to the 18th century

The 18th century was a time of increasing commercial prosperity, as trade links developed across the world. The newly rich poured their wealth into impressive homes. Towns such as Bath, Bristol and Newcastle underwent large-scale redevelopment during the Georgian period, and many of the houses are still standing. Outside the towns, grand houses were built in country estates, some of which have since been converted into flats. If you live in a town house, flat or more modest Georgian building, there is much you can discover about its history.

Georgian property deeds

In the early years of the 18th century several local deed registries were established by Acts of Parliament. They were the forerunners of the national Land Registry established in 1862. The local registries enabled people to record property transactions, although the records created were not deeds as such, merely the memorial of when and how a property changed hands. The registries are an important resource, as they allow you to trace the history of houses for which original title deeds no longer survive (see page 140). The parts of England covered by these local registries are London and Middlesex, the 'Bedford level' (including Bedfordshire and extending across neighbouring counties), as well as the North, East and West Ridings of Yorkshire.

Further deed registration took place in many of the central English courts, often by way of a fictitious lawsuit. The buyer – in full knowledge of the landowner – would come up with some reason why the landowner should be removed from his land and then take him to court. The dispute would inevitably be 'settled out of court', but it would leave an official record of a property transaction. The documents can tell you the names of owners and the dates the property changed hands.

Where to find the records The National Archives (see DIRECTORY) holds a variety of property records, including title deeds. You will also find title deeds and court records (quarter sessions) in local or county record offices.

Property registration in Scotland Scotland operated a different system of property registration. Transfers and mortgages of property were carried out by a deed called an Instrument of Sasine. After 1617 copies of the records have been kept in a central Register of Sasines. From 1783, detailed summaries of the documents, known as abridgements, were created. They are arranged by county and year. These, and name indexes, will speed up your search and can be viewed at the National Archives of Scotland (see DIRECTORY).

Estate records

Many town or country estates were built during the Georgian and Regency periods. Some of the estates were so large that they included whole villages (see

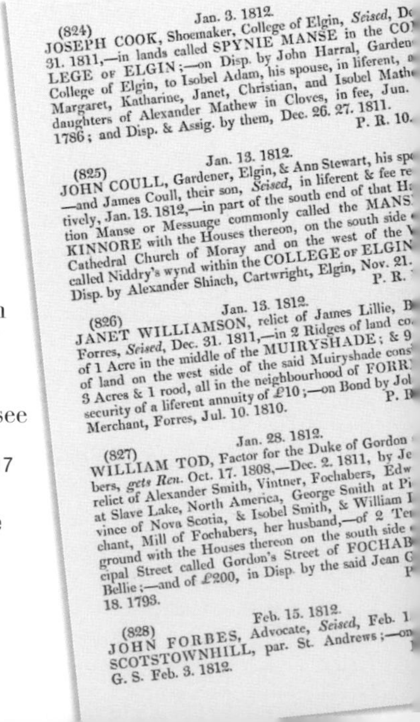

Jan. 3. 1812.
(824)
JOSEPH COOK, Shoemaker, College of Elgin, *Seised*, De
31. 1811,—in lands called SPYNIE MANSE in the CO
LEGE OF ELGIN;—on Disp. by John Harral, Garden
College of Elgin, to Isobel Adam, his spouse, in liferent, a
Margaret, Katharine, Janet, Christian, and Isobel Math
daughters of Alexander Mathew in Cloves, in fee, Jun.
1786; and Disp. & Assig. by them, Dec. 26. 27. 1811.
P. R. 10.

Jan. 13. 1812.
(825)
JOHN COULL, Gardener, Elgin, & Ann Stewart, his sp
—and James Coull, their son, *Seised*, in liferent & fee re
tively, Jan. 13. 1812,—in part of the south end of that H
tion Manse or Messuage commonly called the MANS
KINNORE with the Houses thereon, on the south side
Cathedral Church of Moray and on the west of the
called Niddry's wynd within the COLLEGE OF ELGIN
Disp. by Alexander Shinch, Cartwright, Elgin, Nov. 21.
P. R.

Jan. 13. 1812.
(826)
JANET WILLIAMSON, relict of James Lillie, B
Forres, *Seised*, Dec. 31. 1811,—in 2 Ridges of land co
of 1 Acre in the middle of the MUIRYSHADE; & 9
of land on the west side of the said Muiryshade cons
3 Acres & 1 rood, all in the neighbourhood of FORR
security of a liferent annuity of £10;—on Bond by Jo
Merchant, Forres, Jul. 10. 1810.
P. R

Jan. 28. 1812.
(827)
WILLIAM TOD, Factor for the Duke of Gordon
bers, *gets Ren.* Oct. 17. 1808,—Dec. 2. 1811, by Je
relict of Alexander Smith, Vintner, Fochabers, Edw
at Slave Lake, North America, George Smith at Pi
vince of Nova Scotia, & Isobel Smith, & William
chant, Mill of Fochabers, her husband,—of 2 Te
ground with the Houses thereon on the south side
cipal Street called Gordon's Street of FOCHAB
Bellie;—and of £200, in Disp. by the said Jean G
18. 1793.
P

Feb. 15. 1812.
(828)
JOHN FORBES, Advocate, *Seised*, Feb. 1
SCOTSTOWNHILL, par. St. Andrews;—on
G. S. Feb. 3. 1812.

Scottish sasine Property transfers after 1617 in Scotland were recorded in the Register of Sasines. Summaries of these documents are fully indexed by place and partly by name.

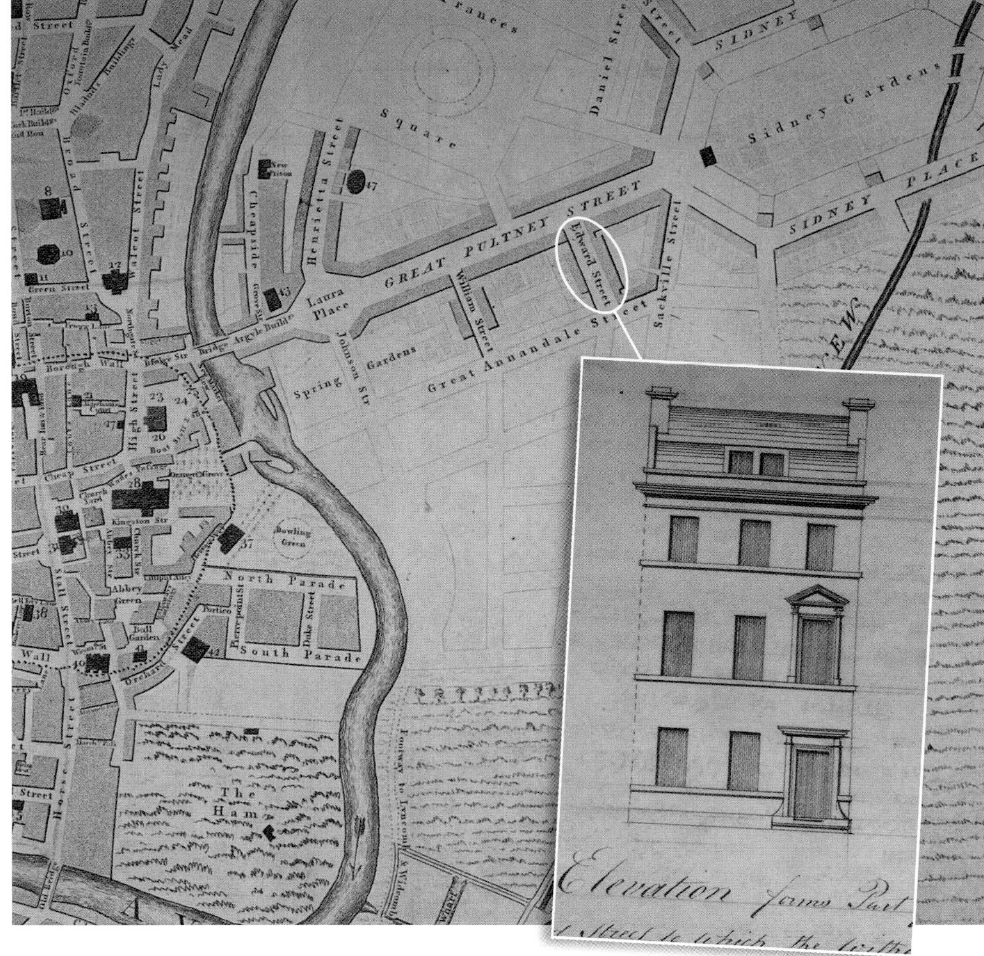

Bath estate records Landowners' estate papers can tell you much about urban properties built during the speculative housing boom in the Georgian period. The detailed 1799 estate plan (left) shows the position of Edward Street, where the terraced house (inset) was built during the development of Bath to the east of the River Avon.

pages 48-49). If your house was part of such an estate you will need to locate the estate papers. The following records may turn up in estate papers (see page 49) and can help you to build up a picture of how and when your house was designed and who commissioned the work.

Estate records will also give you the names of the first owners or tenants, and how much it cost to build the property or rent it from the owners. Records include:

- architects' plans and drawings
- building leases and contracts
- tenancy agreements
- schedules of rent and payments
- stewards' accounts
- penalties for non-maintenance of property
- accounts for repairs and improvements
- estate maps.

Where to find the records Since estate papers and accounts are private property you are only likely to see them if they have been deposited in a local archive or county record office.

See you in court

One underused but rich source for 18th-century property history is equity court records (see page 161). Many people contested property inheritance, and brought civil actions to court. Sometimes the cases dragged on for years, and generated piles of documents that reveal details about house occupancy, ownership and even construction. Sometimes the papers include details of furniture and other possessions.

The two main equity courts active during the 18th century were those of Chancery and Exchequer. Equity court records include:

- bills of complaint filed by the plaintiff
- answers from the defendants
- decrees and orders made by the judges
- depositions supplied by witnesses
- evidence supporting rival cases.

Supporting documents were also archived, so you may find title deeds, property plans, marriage settlements and building contracts among the records.

Where to find the records Equity court records are stored at the National Archives (see DIRECTORY).

FIND OUT MORE

- *Old Deeds* (N.W. Alcock, Phillimore, 2001)
- 'The deeds registries of Middlesex and Yorkshire' (F. Sheppard and V. Belcher, *Journal of the Society of Archivists*, vol.6, pages 274-286).
- **www.nationalarchives.gov.uk/catalogue/RdLeaflet.asp?sLeafletID=160** On-line guide to the records of the Court of Exchequer held at the National Archives.
- **www.ros.gov.uk** The website for the Registers of Scotland.
- **www.nas.gov.uk/guides/sasines.asp** National Archives of Scotland fact sheet on how to use the Register of Sasines.
- **www.nas.gov.uk/guides/estateRecords.asp** National Archives of Scotland fact sheet providing information on estate records in Scotland.

OTHER USEFUL SOURCES OF INFORMATION

Historic buildings and those of special architectural merit are often awarded listed building status. They can be investigated further through organisations such as English Heritage (see DIRECTORY) or the National Trust (see DIRECTORY).

Georgian interior clues

The guiding principles of interior design in the Georgian period were symmetry and proportion, combined with a desire to display wealth and status. Money and attention were lavished on the rooms used by guests, most on the ground floor. You are likely to find the fireplaces, the plaster cornices, even the architrave around the doors to be more elaborate in these rooms than in the upper rooms or basement – the domain of children and servants.

Mid-Georgian fireplace

Simple Georgian upper room fireplace

Fireplaces

The Georgian period extends over more than 100 years, but by looking at the fireplaces you can date a home to within a few decades. The grandest houses had white marble surrounds with inlays of coloured marble. The less well off made do with 'scagliola' – plaster mixed with marble chips and polished to resemble the real thing. These faux-marble fittings were light and easy to install.

Over the years many Georgian fireplaces, particularly the grandest marble examples, will have been ripped out and sold, often replaced with a more modern imitation. The fireplaces that are more likely to have survived are the simple, functional surrounds on an upper floor that was not used for entertaining.

- **Early Georgian** Palladian-style fireplaces were popular from around 1714 to 1760. These featured columns, swags, scrolls and shells. The mantelpieces were narrow and supported by brackets or pairs of carved figures. The grates began as free-standing wrought-iron baskets. But these were soon eclipsed by cast-iron 'hob grates'. The flat-topped hobs, on which pots and kettles were kept warm, were introduced in the 1720s and widespread by 1780.
- **Mid Georgian** The Neo-Classical period (from 1750) favoured more delicate designs, using figures from Greek mythology and other Classical motifs. Delftware imitation fireplace tiles were popular by 1750.
- **Regency** Late Georgian fireplaces were simpler than their predecessors, with few adornments and decoration.

Floors

The type of flooring indicated the homeowner's affluence. If you have a floor made of wide planks of English oak – more than 30cm (12in) wide and fitted tightly with tongue-and-groove joints – you can assume the Georgian homeowner was fairly wealthy. Many people saved money by using pine or fir wood, imported in vast quantities from Scandinavia and around the Baltic. These floors were nailed down in narrower planks (oak trees are thicker than pine) and scrubbed with lime and sand until they shone. Boards became increasingly narrow over time, down to 20cm (10in), and more uniform in width as machines for planing timber were introduced. Floorboards were made to be seen, with rugs placed in the centre of rooms. Wilton carpets date from 1655, but it was not until the mid to late 18th century that fitted carpets came into fashion.

Ceilings

The Georgians applied decorative mouldings to their ceilings in abundance. The mouldings were originally made from wood – by 1720 plaster was also used.

- **Early Georgian** Early 18th-century designs followed Classical styles and were large and chunky, such as the egg-and-dart moulding – alternating egg and dart-shaped figures – often seen on cornices.
- **Mid Georgian** Mouldings became progressively more subtle with a lower profile and the details were Classically inspired.
- **Regency** By the end of the 18th century mouldings were light and simple. Bead moulding was popular, and known as 'reeding', where several beads were linked together to mimic the ornamentation on Classical columns. Look for reeding on cornices, fireplaces, door surrounds, dados and skirting.

FIND OUT MORE

- The Georgian Group
Charity dedicated to preserving Georgian buildings and gardens.
www.georgiangroup.org.uk
- *The Georgian Group Book of the Georgian House* (S. Parissien, Aurum, 1995)
- *Georgian House Style* (I. Cranfield, David & Charles, 2001)

Classical wallpaper 1769

Georgian dining room interior

Chinoiserie wallpaper 1740

Walls

Wood panelling to the full height of the room was fashionable until the 1740s. After that point, panelling stopped at the dado rail and the walls above would be papered or painted. Common colour schemes were sage green, blue grey or oxblood red. The wooden panels were usually made from cheap pine rather than pricey oak. There was no point in using expensive wood because panelling was never left bare. Pine panels were painted in colours to mimic more prestigious woods such as mahogany or cedar. Panelling was often removed in later years, and usually leaves little trace.

Doors

The ground and first floor rooms of early 18th-century town houses often had mahogany double panelled doors. They gave an impression of space and light, and lent the rooms an air of grandeur. The number of panels in doors varied. Six was the norm on early Georgian doors; by the end of the period two or three-panel doors were common.

- **Doorframes** Compare the mouldings on the doorframes of rooms upstairs to those in the main reception rooms and you may find that they are different. The entrance to an upper room might be as plain and rectilinear as a matchbox, while the lower doorway is framed in an elaborate moulding made up of ovolos (convex shapes), fillets (flat surfaces) and beads (cylindrical shapes). In the grandest houses the doorframes to the best rooms resemble the porticos of Greek temples with Classical pediments and architrave mouldings displaying Classical motifs such as ancathus leaves, shells and scrolling foliage.
- **Glazing** Internal doors were sometimes glazed – usually with four or six panes in the upper half of the door.
- **Door furniture** Rooms reserved for entertaining might have brass or bronze fittings, with glass, ebony and white china also used for door handles. Elsewhere handles and hinges were usually made of cast iron painted black.

Wallpaper

It is possible to find a scrap of Georgian wallpaper in the back of a fitted cupboard, underneath newer layers of plaster, or behind a patch of skirting board. Wallpaper was a luxury item until the production process was mechanised in the Victorian era, and Georgian patterns were as flamboyant as a peacock's tail. The common themes included Grecian pillars and arches (above, top), Classical motifs featuring urns, swags and niches, and Chinese birds and fishes (reflecting the fashion for chinoiserie – above, bottom). Flock wallpaper was also the height of fashion.

TIPS ON DATING WALLPAPER

- Blue wallpapers date from the first half of the 18th century as an embargo to protect the indigo-dying trade prevented the use of any other colours.
- The quality of Georgian handblocked wallpaper is a clue to its age. The paper is thick and is watermarked. It may even have a tax stamp on the back.

Following the story of a home back to its earliest days

Most simple early medieval homes have disappeared because the organic materials used to build them have perished, but many later timber-framed houses have survived. You may find that an apparently Georgian or Victorian building hides an older core or that your home was once part of a larger structure now demolished. Even if your home is modern, it can be intriguing to find out what was once on the site it now occupies.

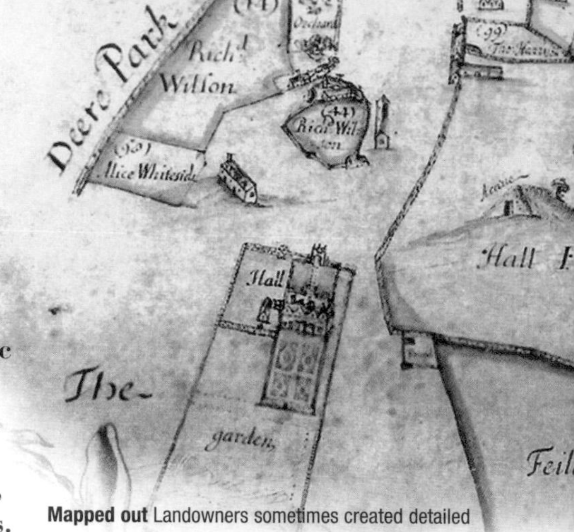

Mapped out Landowners sometimes created detailed maps of their estates to keep track of tenants. The 1665 estate map of Bidston, Cheshire (above), includes the church, a useful marker for surrounding buildings.

Manorial records

Whether you live in a medieval structure or just want to know what the landscape around your home looked like in medieval times, your first port of call should be manorial records. These go back to the introduction of the feudal system to England and Wales in the 11th century. Under this system the basic unit of land was called a manor. The lord of the manor would lease property to individuals in return for a service or money. The transaction was recorded in the manor court roll and copies of the entry were handed to each new tenant, or 'copyholder'. Copyholders had to seek the approval of the lord before they sold, inherited or mortgaged their property and this, too, was recorded in court rolls. Bear in mind that up to around 1733 the documents were written in Latin (see pages 14-15). Most archives have Latin dictionaries and guides to help you with interpretation.

The Manorial Register at the National Archives (see DIRECTORY) lists the manors of a particular parish. It will tell you what manorial records survive for your area.

What the court rolls tell you Surviving court rolls, dating from the 1230s, describe the property in some detail and name previous occupants. By the 17th century place name indexes start to appear more frequently and can help you to track property occupancy quickly. If you find the name or a description of your home in the court rolls, you can work backwards and forwards among surviving rolls to compile a list of tenants.

Estate maps and surveys Often the lord of the manor made maps of his estate, cross-referenced to survey books, to keep track of who rented which property. Owners also made lists of tenants and freeholders in their manor. The maps (see page 19) can show you the position of your home (or its absence) within the manor and whether the house was part of a larger property that has since been demolished.

Where to find manorial records The National Archives (see DIRECTORY) has a wide collection of court rolls, estate maps and surveys, although most are stored in county record offices. Some manorial records are available from the internet (see 'Find out more' box).

Dividing up the manor

When the lord of the manor died an 'inquisition post mortem' would take place to identify what lands were held and who should succeed to them. Local residents were asked to provide information on property held by the deceased, including houses, tenements or cottages. Inquisitions post mortem can also provide information (called an assignment of dower) about what part of an estate had been set aside for the lord's widow. In many cases specific rooms are mentioned and listed. These documents can be found at the National Archives (see DIRECTORY) as well as at local record offices.

Old timers Black-and-white, half-timbered houses are typical of Montgomeryshire. The style indicates that they were built between the 15th and 17th century.

Medieval interior clues

Most medieval houses will have undergone considerable structural and cosmetic changes over the years, but you can sometimes find clues to their original structure and design, especially in attics and cellars.

Changes in floor level Check if part of the house is lower at one end: this may indicate that it was originally a medieval longhouse, where animals were kept in a byre. The byre was on a lower level to prevent animal slurry from seeping into the living quarters.

Examine the rafters The heavier the timbers, the older the house is likely to be. Also note the type of wood: oak was the most common material until the late 17th century. If there is a complex skeleton of rafters they may have been the original structure of a medieval timber-framed house. Look out for blackened timbers: these indicate the house was an old medieval hall with a central, open hearth.

Check for old beams Many early beams were hidden during the 18th and 19th centuries behind false lowered ceilings, or were cased in plaster cornices. If you can get access to beams, look for chamfering on the outer corners (left) which was pronounced in the 16th century and before but became more subtle over time.

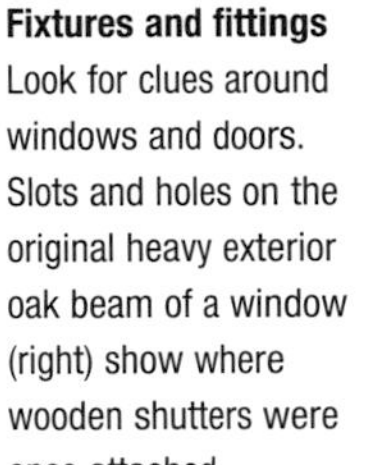

Medieval signs The fine mullioned window on the right is medieval. It has original bars but no shutters. Also look out for chamfered beams (below left) where a large amount of the edge has been cut away. These were a common embellishment in medieval houses.

Filled-in doors and windows Examine any recesses in walls and cracks in the plaster that may indicate former windows and doors (right). Check the windows for signs of medieval wooden shutters (below). Also check the door frames of internal doors: while many old doors were replaced in the 18th century, the original heavy oak frames often remain. Also check the outside of the house for signs of blocked-in windows or extra windows that could indicate a hidden room.

Fixtures and fittings Look for clues around windows and doors. Slots and holes on the original heavy exterior oak beam of a window (right) show where wooden shutters were once attached.

A licence to trade

Medieval housing in urban areas tended to combine a place of trade or shop with a dwelling area above. You might find information in title deeds, leases, records of boroughs and corporations, or even in the records of local courts if shopholders breached the numerous regulations about what they could sell. Most buildings required licences before they could be used for trade, so look for applications in local sources such as quarter session records, which are held at county records offices. The owners of alehouses or taverns had to apply to the local magistrates for bonds guaranteeing good behaviour.

FIND OUT MORE

- *Manorial Records* (D. Stuart, Phillimore, 1992)
- **www.nationalarchives.gov.uk/mdr** Manorial records for the Isle of Wight, Hampshire, Norfolk, Middlesex, Yorkshire, Cumberland, Westmorland, Cumbria, Surrey and Wales.
- **www.nationalarchives.gov.uk/catalogue/Rdleaflet.asp?sLeafletID= 226** Guide to pre-1689 taxation records held at the National Archives.

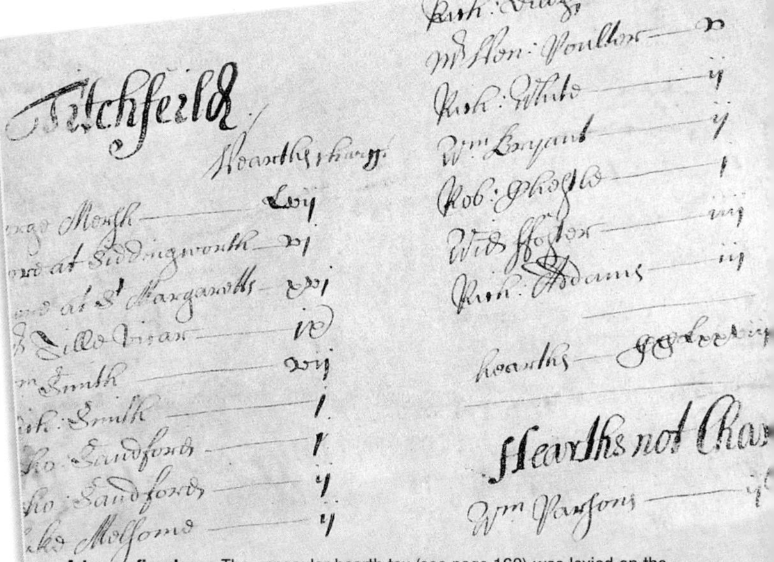

Titchfeild

Hearths not Chargeable

A tax on fireplaces The unpopular hearth tax (see page 160) was levied on the number of hearths in a property. The tax returns list the liable houses in each parish and the name of the owner. The one above of around 1665 is for Titchfield, Hampshire. Comparing hearth tax returns with manorial records can help you to establish the rough size of a property and its owner's means. Wealthier people could afford more hearths.

Through the keyhole: looking at previous owners' possessions

If your house is more than a century old, you might have trouble envisaging how it was furnished. Wills and probate inventories can help tremendously here. They list previous owners' possessions and can help you to picture how the rooms once looked based on objects that were actually there.

Where there's a will...

In 1540 the Statute of Wills allowed property to be given to a person of a man's choosing (and not automatically to his heir). But wills tell you more than simply who owned or inherited your home. They often contain specific instructions about the disposal of household possessions, clothing and heirlooms.

Worldly goods A will may be accompanied by a probate inventory itemising all the deceased's possessions complete with valuations. These lists were made to assist the executors of a will in carrying out final bequests, and to protect them against claims of fraud. From 1530 to 1750 many probate courts required inventories, but later they were not mandatory. So you are less likely to find a probate inventory for someone who died in the 19th or 20th centuries, although inventories were sometimes made to avoid disputes among relatives. If you are lucky enough to find a probate inventory for a previous owner of your home, you may be able to deduce how the house was furnished since many inventories list goods room by room.

Finding names of previous owners Before you start looking for a particular property in a will, you need the names of previous owners. You can find these out using census records (see pages 76-77), title deeds (see pages 132, 140, 148, 159) or rate books (see page 157). You can then start to look for the death of the owner in parish records or in civil records held at the Family Records Centre (see DIRECTORY), and check to see if a will was left.

Where to find wills

A will may be held in local archives or personal papers, but should also be registered with the court that had responsibility for 'proving' its authenticity.

Before 1858

- Wills were registered with the church courts (the main ones being the Prerogative Courts of Canterbury and the Prerogative Courts of York).

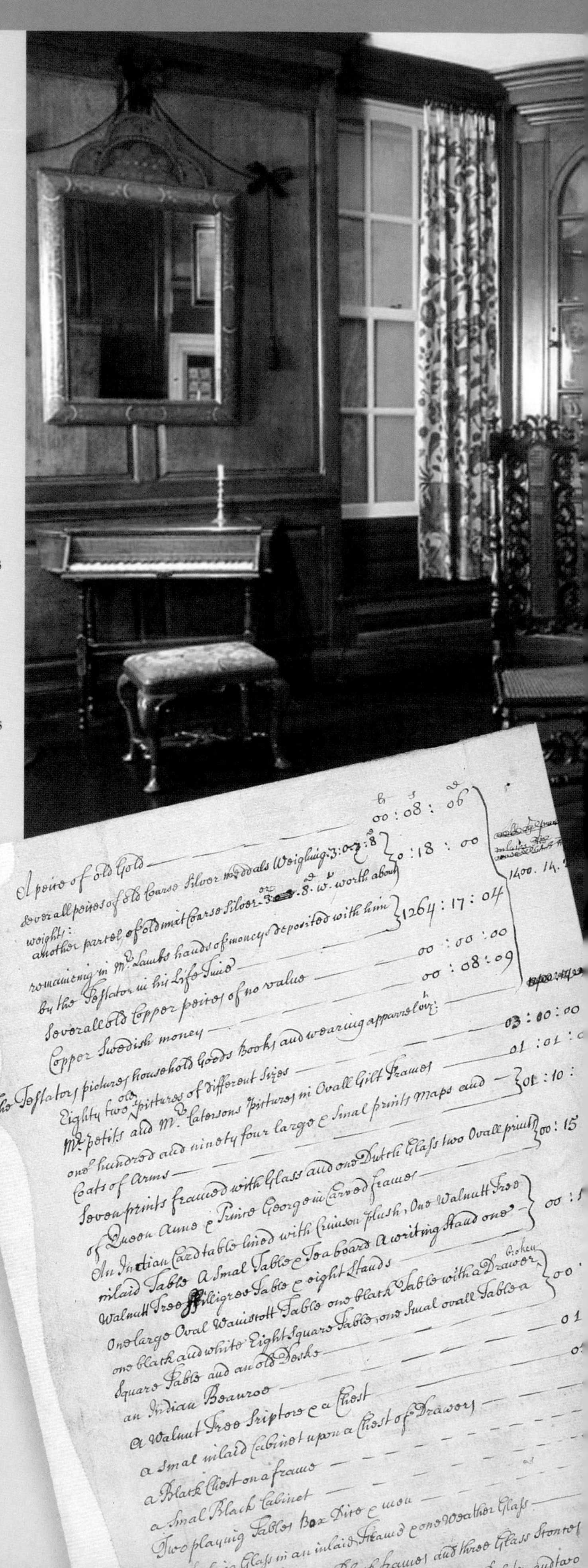

A paire of old Gold — 00 : 08 : 06
Severall peices of old Coarse Silver Meddals Weighing 3:oz:8 weight: another parcel of old mixt Coarse Silver 3 oz 8 d w't worth about — 0 : 18 : 00
remaining in Mr Lambs hands of money deposited with him by the Testator in his Life time — 1264 : 17 : 04
Severall old Copper peices of no value — 00 : 00 : 00
Copper Swedish money — 00 : 08 : 09
The Testators pictures household Goods Books and wearing apparell viz:
Eighty two old pictures of different sizes — 03 : 00 : 00
Mr Petits and Mr Catersons pictures in Ovall Gilt frames — 01 : 01
one hundred and ninety four large & smal prints maps and Coats of Arms — 01 : 10
Seven prints framed with Glass and one Dutch Glass two Ovall prints of Queen Anne & Prince George in Carved frames — 00 : 15
An Indian Card table lined with Crimson plush, One Walnutt Tree inlaid Table A Smal Table & Tea board A writing Stand one Walnutt Tree filligree Table & eight Stands
One large Oval Wainscott Table one black Table with a Drawer one black and white Eight Square Table one Smal ovall Table a Square Table and an old Desk
an Indian Bearoe
A Walnut Tree Scriptore & a Chest
a Smal inlaid Cabinet upon a Chest of Drawers
a Black Chest on a frame
a Smal Black Cabinet
Two playing Tables Box Dice & men

Designs of the day The National Archives (see DIRECTORY) holds collections of registered designs for a huge array of domestic items, ranging from wallpaper samples to drawings and photographs of furniture, lamps and household appliances. They will help you to picture any items listed in an inventory. So if you wanted to find out about fixtures from 1868, for example, you would need to look through the registered designs for that year.

- Records of the Prerogative Courts of Canterbury (for southern England and Wales) are held at the National Archives (see DIRECTORY).
- Records of the Prerogative Courts of York (for northern England) are held at the Borthwick Institute, York (see DIRECTORY).
- Local record offices and probate registries also hold probate information.

After 1858

- English and Welsh wills were registered at the Court of Probate, later the Principal Registry, London (see DIRECTORY). You can order copies of wills from the registry or arrange a visit in person.
- A detailed index to wills – the National Probate Calendar – is available at the National Archives, Family Records Centre and the Guildhall Library (see DIRECTORY).

Scotland

Until 1868 land and buildings were inherited by the eldest son alone. Personal property could be left in a 'testamentary dispensation'. The National Archives of Scotland (see DIRECTORY) is the best place to start researching bequests.

Living in style The probate inventory of Silvester Petyt (left) reveals the personal possessions of a London lawyer in the early 18th century. The assessors produced a full account of Petyt's clothes, furnishings and treasured belongings. His rooms were furnished with the latest goods from around the world, including carpets and chairs from Turkey, a card table from India, tea tables, several clocks, cutlery, maps, prints and a fine array of miniature portraits of friends, family, nobility and royalty. Petyt's house may have looked something like the one above – a reconstruction of an early 18th-century house, decorated in the Queen Anne style, on display at the Geffrye Museum in London.

In case of fire

Fire insurance records can provide a list of household items that would have been insured against loss. They survive from the 17th century onwards, although only in large numbers from the 18th and 19th centuries. The records are not easy to use without a policy number, but if you have a fire mark on the outside of your home – placed there to alert the insurance company's fire brigade that the householder was insured – the policy number should be inscribed on it.

Where to find fire insurance records The records are usually held in local archives. The City of Westminster Archives (see DIRECTORY, under 'London boroughs') has a particularly fine collection for London companies.

FIND OUT MORE

- Geffrye Museum The museum, sited within a set of 18th-century almshouses in Shoreditch, London, shows the changing style of English domestic interiors from 1600 to the present day. Reconstructed period rooms contain collections of furniture, textiles, paintings and decorative arts. www.geffrye-museum.org.uk

- *Probate jurisdictions: where to look for wills* (ed. J. Gibson and B. Langston, 5th ed., FFHS, 1995)
- *Prerogative Court of Canterbury wills and other probate records* (M. Scott, National Archives, 1997)
- *Index to the Probate Accounts of England and Wales* (ed. P. Spufford, London, British Record Society, 1999)
- www.nationalarchives.gov.uk/househistory/guide/probate.htm National Archives leaflet on where to find probate records.
- www.nationalarchives.gov.uk/documentsonline/wills.asp Information about using the records of the Prerogative Courts of Canterbury.
- www.scottishdocuments.com Advanced search option allows you to search for Scottish wills by name, court and place.

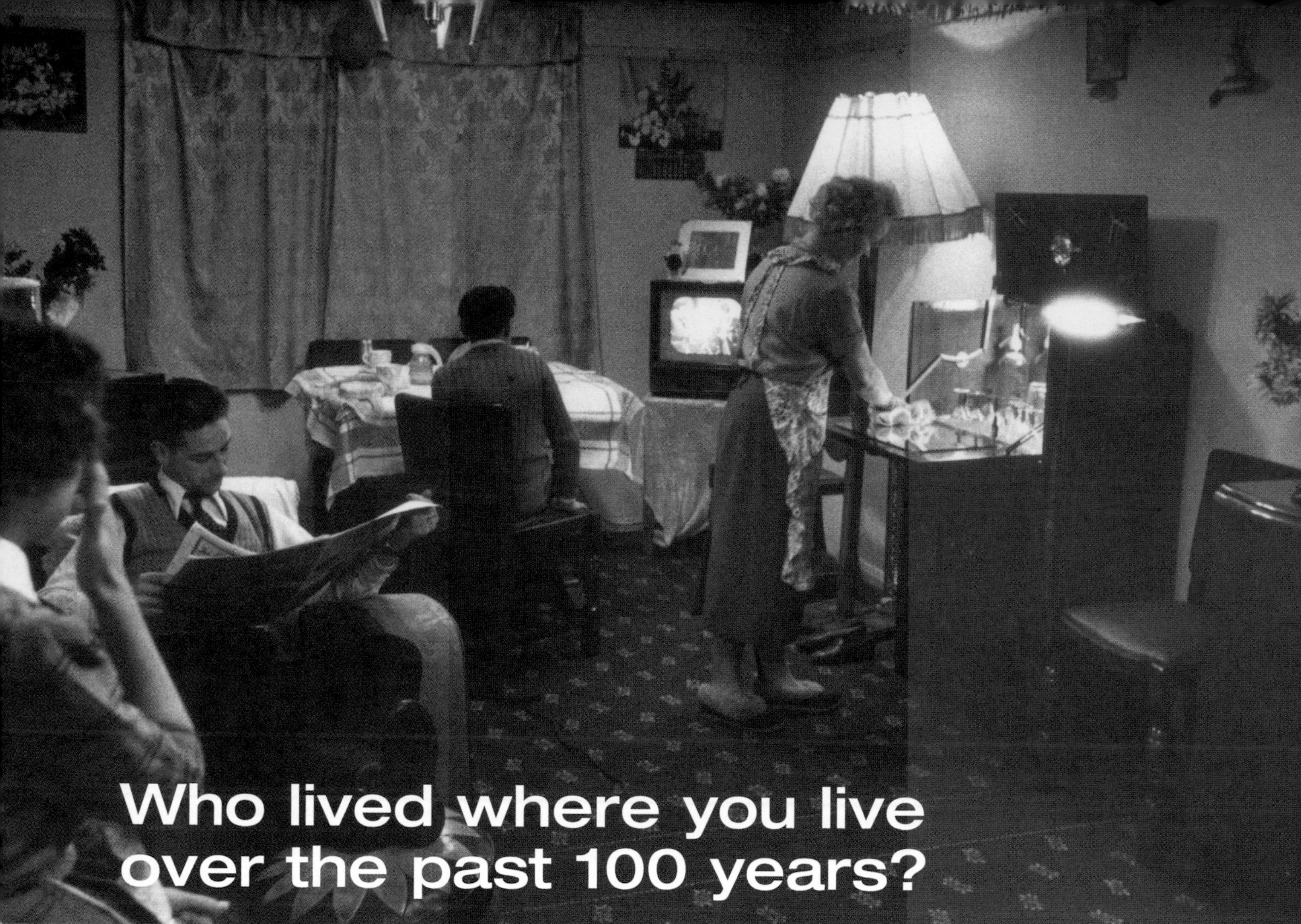

Who lived where you live over the past 100 years?

There is more to tracing the history of your home than simply finding out how old the property is – you can put its history into context by digging up some information about the people who used to live there before you did. Find out about the lives they led and where they came from and you can begin to see how they turned the bricks and mortar of a house into a home.

Ask the neighbours

Your first step is to undertake some local detective work. Ask your neighbours about your house, especially if they have been in the area for a number of years. If the property was built within living memory, they may even remember when it was first erected and who the first occupant was. At the least you should be able to obtain a list of names of former owners or occupants that can help you with your research.

Questions to ask Try to adopt a diplomatic approach when making enquiries. People may be suspicious of your motives at first and your questions may seem intrusive. Explain what you are trying to achieve and they will be more likely to open up. The following questions should start you off:

- What sort of people lived in the house?
- How many people lived there?
- What jobs did they do?
- What were their backgrounds?
- When did they move there?
- Where did they move to when they left?
- Are there any interesting stories and legends about the house or the people who lived there?

Local societies Try asking local history groups (see page 9) about the people who lived in your house. Many groups have collated gravestone information from local cemeteries and graveyards, which may be of use to you.

Registered to vote

Electoral lists (see pages 80-81) record the names of all residents who were eligible to vote and a description of the property. They should help you to compile a list of previous inhabitants of your home. It is best to start with the most recent records and work backwards in time, because modern lists tend to include street indexes, house numbers or names and reflect modern parliamentary boundaries, making them easier to use.

Property values The local authority rate book for Upper North Street, Poplar, London, in 1925, gives a description of the properties and the level of rate due, information that can reveal the wealth and status of the inhabitants of the houses.

Gaps in the story

Electoral records may not always yield the information you hoped for. Bear the following points in mind.

- There may be people missing from the list because they were ineligible to vote. The vote was extended to women over 30 only in 1918 and to women over 21 in 1928.
- Some people may have been registered elsewhere and so your house may not always appear in the lists. This may well be an indication that your home was once used as a commercial site or had a non-domestic use, which may require further research in other records (see pages 132-135).

Where to find the records Most main reference libraries hold current electoral lists, although you may need to go to a county record office or local studies library to track down older lists. The British Library in London (see DIRECTORY) holds an extensive collection for the 20th century. Some 19th-century Scottish electoral registers are held at the National Archives of Scotland (see DIRECTORY). The National Library of Scotland (see DIRECTORY) has 20th-century material, dating from the 1940s.

Checking title deeds

If you can obtain the title deeds of your property – usually held by your mortgage provider (see page 132) – you should be able to see the names of former owners. Remember that since 1970 title deeds need only extend back 15 years (between 1925 and 1970, they had to go back 30 years). If you know where the previous owners moved to, you might be able to track them down through phone books or other local directories. Ask them if they have any interesting stories about your house, or whether they recall the name of the people from whom they purchased the property.

Rate books

Over the last century rates were allocated based on the size of property and location. Rate books (Valuation Rolls from 1854 in Scotland) recorded the level of tax to be paid to each local authority. They often give the name of both the owner and occupier of the property, as well as the contemporary value of the house. Look for rate books in county or city archives. In 1989 (Scotland) and 1990 (England and Wales), the poll tax (later community charge) briefly replaced property rates as a way of generating revenue for local authorities. It was superseded in 1993 by the Council Tax.

Using directories

Trade directories were introduced to help people find local businesses (see pages 74-75). Publishers such as Kelly's and the Post Office added street and name indexes to their volumes as well as lists of trades, making them excellent sources for finding out who lived in your house, and what occupations they had.

Where to find the records
Look for directories in local reference libraries or local and county record offices.

Names and numbers Working through a series of Post Office directories, such as this one for London dating from 1968, can help you track down who was living in your house and when they moved out.

FIND OUT MORE

- *Electoral Registers Since 1832 and Burgess Rolls* (J. Gibson and C. Rogers, FFHS, 1990)
- **www.genealogysupplies.com** Provides a list of county directories available on CD.

Who lived where you live in the Victorian period?

Thanks to census records you can discover more about Victorian inhabitants than those at any other time. The first census took place in 1801 and from then on was carried out every ten years. The earliest censuses were intended merely as population counts but from 1841 the returns include names, addresses, ages and occupations, and from 1851, relationships and places of birth, too.

Life downstairs If your home is a large Victorian house a variety of servants may have lived there, cooking, cleaning amd minding children for the family upstairs.

Census returns

If you want to find out about the people who lived in your home from the mid to late 19th century, the first place to look is the census returns that were taken every ten years throughout the 19th century (see pages 76-77 for more details).

- The 1841 census is the first where you can discover who were the occupants of homes. It also includes an indication (within five years) of their ages, as well as providing information on occupations, and house and street names.
- From 1851 census records are more useful as they include greater detail on each inhabitant, such as a full name, marital status, exact age, relationship to the head of the household and place of birth.
- The 1901 census (see page 76) is available on-line, with a facility to search by property.

Note that because of the personal nature of the content, census returns for England, Wales and Scotland are closed to the public for 100 years. The 1901 census is the most recent record available. When using census returns it is best to start with the most recent records and then work backwards in time.

> **TIP FOR USING THE 1901 CENSUS**
> In the 1901 returns your house may have had a different street number, or it may have had a name instead of a number. If so, you might be able to locate the property by comparing the occupants in the street or neighbourhood with other records, such as rate books (see page 157), the 1910 Valuation Office Survey (see page 140) or old directories (see pages 75, 145). This will help you to fill in the gaps.

How did previous occupants earn their living?

Census returns from 1841 onwards list occupations, and so you can start to build a picture of the type of people who lived in your home during the 19th century, and how the use of the house and status of the area changed over time. If you found that the people living in your property were associated with a particular trade, you could then start to search for employment documents (often in local archives) such as factory staff ledgers, trade union membership, pay books and disciplinary committees (see pages 98-99). Remember that as most businesses were privately owned, there is no guarantee that records will survive. Another source worth checking is a museum dedicated to the particular trade or industry.

Crowded homes You may be surprised at the number of people living in your house at the same time. In the 19th century many properties were the homes of extended families, with in-laws and grandparents all

The Vicar's household The number of live-in servants shown on a census return can be a clue to the wealth of the owners, as the 1901 return for The Vicarage in Great Yarmouth illustrates. There are five servants – a lady's maid, cook, parlour maid, house maid and kitchen maid – to administer to the small family of Francis Godolphin Pelham, his wife and daughter.

sharing the same roof as their children and grandchildren. Tenements and multi-storied properties often contained several families living together in shared accommodation. Higher up the class system, you might also find domestic servants, such as housemaids, cooks or, in more prosperous establishments, butlers, coachmen and governesses. These clues all provide rich detail about the former uses of your home and the status of the people who lived there.

Victorian title deeds

When the Law of Property Act was introduced in 1925, the requirement to prove ownership as far back as possible was reduced to only 30 years. Consequently, large numbers of title deeds were destroyed. But if you are lucky enough to find any at your local county record office, you will see that they often tell you more than just the names of previous owners. The status and sometimes profession of the buyer and seller are normally recorded, along with their usual address if they were not actually living in the house in question. Note the date of the sale and price paid as well as any sub-leases or loans raised against the property. Constant re-mortgaging would suggest that the owner was in need of money.

Estate papers

If your property was once part of a larger estate, you may be able to find some useful information in estate papers – usually deposited in local archives (see pages 49, 148-149). Documents may include account books, schedules, ledgers or pay books for rented houses. From such material you can learn more about the type of person who owned or lived in your property. Records relating to the management of an estate often reveal what mix of people were employed to keep things running smoothly. Although many people listed in estate rentals and surveys will simply be tenant farmers, who rented property and land as smallholders, other specialist occupations such as estate bailiff or steward might be recorded as well. Many properties for agricultural workers or tenant farmers were built on rural estates, and improvements to the houses are often reflected in increased rents or expenditure in the accounts of the estate steward.

REGULATIONS

The stairs to be swept every morning, and washed at least twice a week by the Tenants—week about—Tenants upstairs sweeping and washing the stairs below the flat in which they reside; and the Tenants on the ground floor sweeping and washing the close, the paint work of lower walls of stairs to be washed down regularly, also lower walls of closes. The staircase windows to be cleaned regularly by the Tenants in turn.

No clothes will be allowed to be hung out at the windows to dry.

Tenants must be careful not to allow their Children to break the staircase windows, or otherwise injure the property; and to keep clean and well-aired houses; and not to give offence or annoyance to their neighbours in any way; as none but cleanly and respectable persons will be allowed to remain Tenants.

Rugs and Mats only to be beaten between the hours of 8 a.m. and 12 noon, at back of property.

Any person casting filth over the window or laying it in any other place than the ashpit will be removed from the Property at the first terms of removal.

No Dogs allowed.

Following the rules Regulation cards issued to tenants can give an insight into their lives. An early 20th-century card (above) sets out a rigorous timetable of cleaning required, and even specifies when and where rugs may be beaten.

FIND OUT MORE

- **www.bricksandbrass.co.uk/people/people.htm**
A description of the daily lives of a late Victorian family living in a suburban home, describing clothes, room furnishings and daily routines.
- **www.1901census.nationalarchives.gov.uk**
On-line 1901 census for England and Wales (pay per view).
- **www.scotlandspeople.gov.uk**
On-line Scottish registers (pay per view).

Who lived where you live in Georgian days and beyond?

If your home was built in the Georgian period, or even earlier, many generations of people will have lived there before you. You can trace their names through tax records, and if they entered into a property dispute you may be able to find out much more about their personalities and the way they lived.

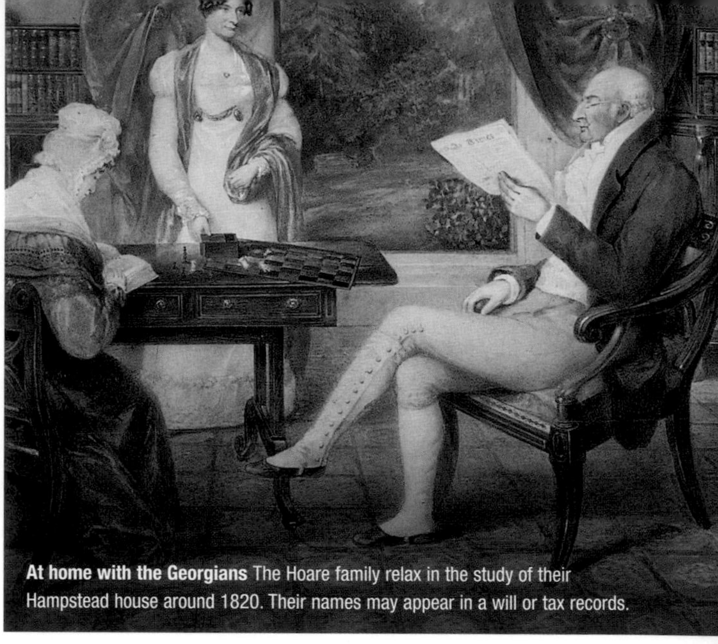

At home with the Georgians The Hoare family relax in the study of their Hampstead house around 1820. Their names may appear in a will or tax records.

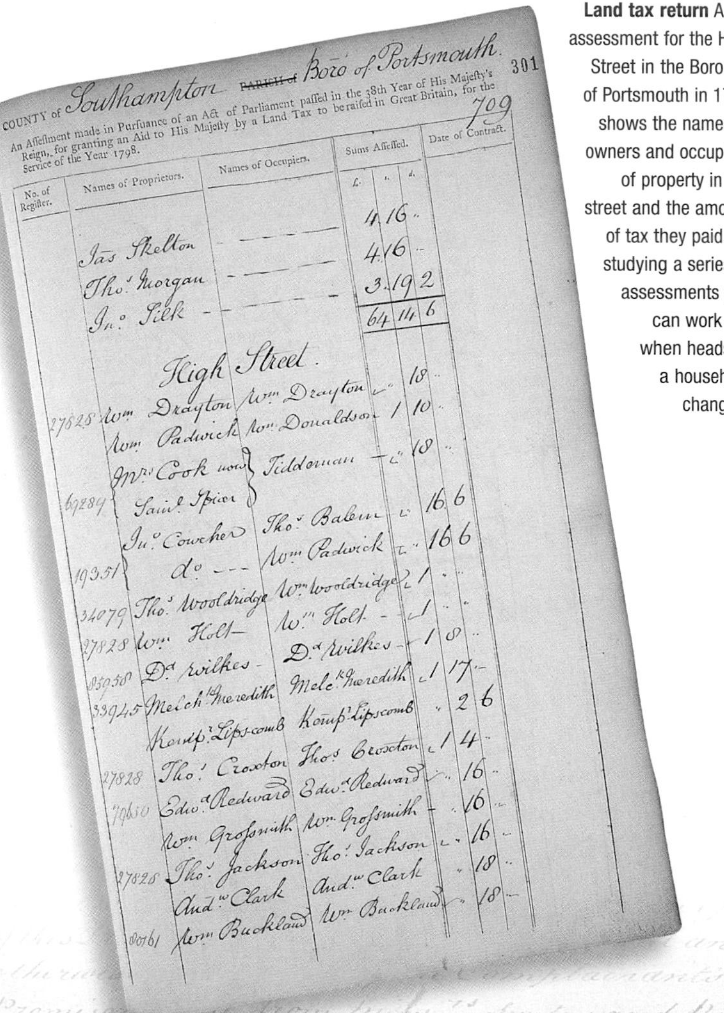

COUNTY of Southampton ~~PARISH of~~ Borō of Portsmouth. 301

An Assessment made in Pursuance of an Act of Parliament passed in the 38th Year of His Majesty's Reign, for granting an Aid to His Majesty by a Land Tax to be raised in Great Britain, for the Service of the Year 1798.

709

No. of Register.	Names of Proprietors.	Names of Occupiers.	Sums Assessed. £. s. d.	Date of Contract.
	Jas Shelton	—	4.16	
	Thos Morgan	—	4.16	
	Jno Silk	—	3.19.2	
			64.14.6	
	High Street.			
27828	Wm Drayton	Wm Drayton	18	
	Wm Padwick	Wm Donaldson	1.10	
	Mrs Cook now	Tilderman	18	
69289	Saml Spicer			
	Jno Courcher	Thos Balem	16.6	
19351	do	Wm Padwick	16.6	
34079	Thos Wooldridge	Wm Wooldridge	1	
27828	Wm Holt	Wm Holt	1	
23958	Dr Wilkes	Dr Wilkes	1.8	
33945	Melch Meredith	Melck Meredith	1.17	
	Kemp Lipscomb	Kemp Lipscomb	2.6	
	Thos Croxton	Thos Croxton	1.4	
27828	Edwd Redward	Edwd Redward	16	
70610	Wm Grossmith	Wm Grossmith	16	
27828	Thos Jackson	Thos Jackson	16	
	Andw Clark	Andw Clark	18	
20061	Wm Buckland	Wm Buckland	18	

Land tax return A tax assessment for the High Street in the Borough of Portsmouth in 1798 shows the names of owners and occupiers of property in the street and the amount of tax they paid. By studying a series of assessments you can work out when heads of a household changed.

Death and taxes

The two unavoidable aspects of life are good starting points when searching for names of previous owners of your home. A will can tell you what a person left behind, while tax records show how they lived.

The land tax This was a tax on the value of land in England and Wales, levied between 1692 and 1963. The annual assessments usually list both owners and occupiers, and many records survive, particularly between 1780 and 1832, when they were used to prove the entitlement to vote. From 1798 the returns often include a brief description of the property. Land tax returns are usually held at county record offices among quarter session records, and a complete set for 1798 is available at the National Archives (see DIRECTORY).

Hearth tax This tax – levied from 1662 to 1688 in England and Wales, and from 1691 to 1695 in Scotland – was based on the number of hearths in a property (see pages 77, 153). As well as the name of the owner or occupier, the records will give you an indication of the person's affluence and the size of the property.

Window tax Levied from 1696 to 1851, the window tax was always unpopular since it seemed to be a tax on fresh air, light and health. Blocked-in windows indicate where a previous owner reduced his tax bill. Records are held mostly at the National Archives (see DIRECTORY).

Local rates These were essentially taxes on property and they vary depending on where you live. Early church rates were levied on householders to help the poor in a particular parish, while in towns corporations taxed their citizens to raise money for improving local facilities. Look for rate returns in local record offices.

Last will and testament

If you are searching for an owner who lived 200 years ago or more, you may well unearth a probate inventory associated with the person's will (see pages 154-155). If one exists it will give you valuable information about a previous owner or occupier's work and belongings. From these scraps you can start to build up a picture of the person's social standing and circle of friends. Registered wills for southern England and Wales can be accessed on the National Archives website, while material for northern England is stored at the Borthwick Institute, York. Scottish testaments are housed at the National Archives of Scotland (see DIRECTORY).

Legal wrangles

Equity court records generated by property disputes can provide a colourful insight into the character of people who once lived in your home. The equity law courts were established as a system of justice based on conscience rather than the strict rules of law. All used the 'pleading' system, whereby an original bill of complaint was brought into the court by the plaintiff and was answered by the defendant. The Court of Chancery records go back to 1386, while the Court of Exchequer did not become an equity court until the mid 16th century. Other courts provided access to justice for lower ranks of society, such as the Court of Requests and the Court of Star Chamber.

Evidence often describes a property in detail, or at least names the owner or occupier. In many cases the contents of a property are itemised, showing you how the house was originally furnished or used.

Where to find records All surviving court records are held at the National Archives (see DIRECTORY).

FIND OUT MORE

- *Land and window tax assessments* (J. Gibson, M. Medleycott and D. Mills, 2nd ed., FFHS, 1998)
- *The Hearth Tax, other Later Stuart Tax Lists and the Association Oath Rolls* (J. Gibson, FFHS, 1985)
- **www.nationalarchives.gov.uk/e179**
An on-line catalogue of taxation records, some of which refer to property.
- **www.scotlandspeople.gov.uk**
An on-line index to Scottish wills from 1515 to 1901.
- **www.nas.gov.uk/guides/taxation.asp**
A National Archives of Scotland information sheet on taxation records.

An 18th-century property dispute

From the 17th century onwards people seemed to delight in bringing lawsuits against each other to settle grievances over an inheritance. A good example concerns Thomas Armstrong, a customs officer who built Cliff House in Cullercoats, Northumberland, during the 1750s. Armstrong's father-in-law, William Allison, died at sea in mysterious circumstances, and as executor Armstrong moved quickly to carry out what he claimed to be the terms of Allison's will. Allison's property in Cullercoats (left) was seized and placed under Armstrong's control, while Allison's widow Jane was forcibly ejected from the family home. We know of these events because Jane Allison brought a lawsuit against Armstrong in the Court of Chancery.

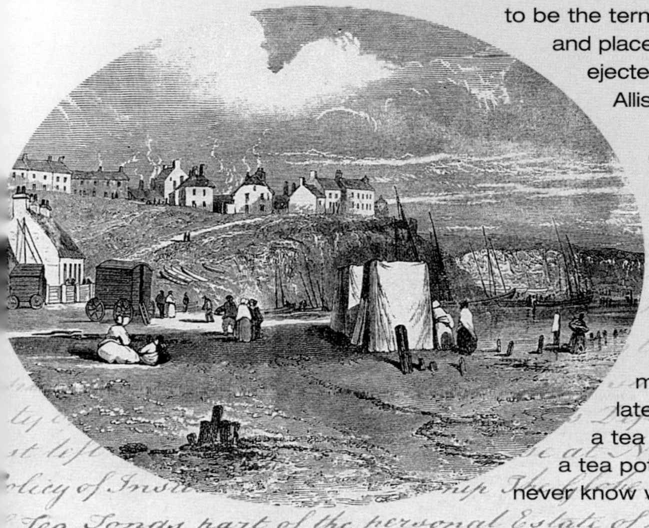

The story sheds light on the lengths that feuding families would go to in the search for material wealth. While Jane Allison travelled to London to make her complaint in the Court of Chancery, the devious customs officer took advantage of her absence and filed a complaint against her in the local courts. She was arrested on her return to Cullercoats and thrown into Northumberland gaol. The last we hear of Jane Allison is in a further petition to Chancery, where she claims one of Armstrong's men had stolen the paperwork she needed to prove her innocence. The document mentions some of the personal possessions she 'rescued' from her late husband's house, including 'six chairs, two tables, a looking glass, a tea box, a pair of bellows, a tea kettle, six china cups and saucers ... a tea pot and two silver spoons'. Although this level of detail is rare, you never know what you may uncover in your searches.

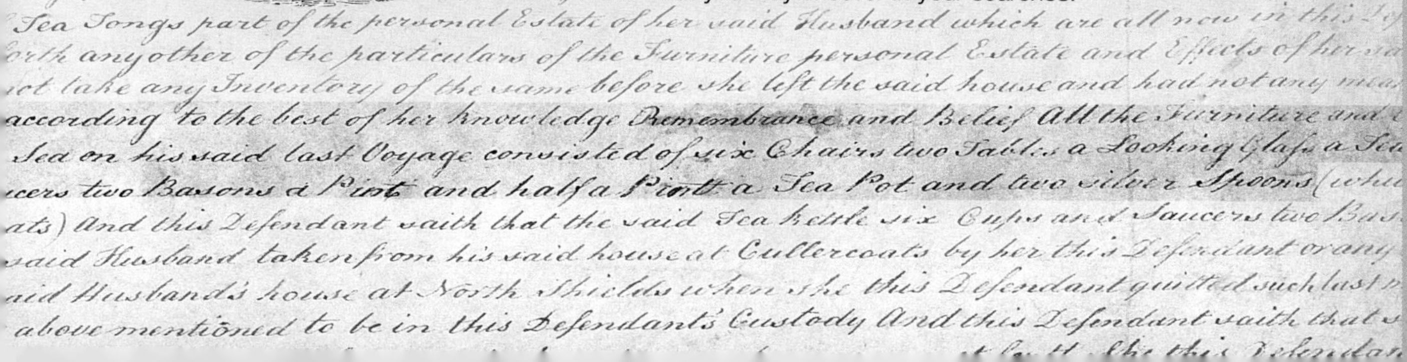
Tea Tongs part of the personal Estate of her said Husband which are all now in this
forth any other of the particulars of the Furniture personal Estate and Effects of her sa
not take any Inventory of the same before she left the said house and had not any mea
according to the best of her knowledge Remembrance and Belief All the Furniture and
Sea on his said last Voyage consisted of six Chairs two Tables a Looking Glass a Tea
cers two Basons a Pint and half a Pint a Tea Pot and two silver Spoons (whic
ats) And this Defendant saith that the said Tea kettle six Cups and Saucers two Bas
said Husband taken from his said house at Cullercoats by her this Defendant or any
aid Husband's house at North Shields when she this Defendant quitted such last
above mentioned to be in this Defendant's Custody And this Defendant saith that

Directory of sources

The directory lists sources of information mentioned in the book and other useful addresses. They are arranged alphabetically, including county and city record offices, except for London boroughs, which appear under 'L'.

Aberdeen City Archives
Town House, Broad Street
Aberdeen AB10 1AQ
Tel. 01224 522513
and
Old Aberdeen House Branch
Dunbar Street
Aberdeen AB24 3UJ
Tel. 01224 481775
www.aberdeencity.gov.uk/archives

Anglesey County Record Office
Shire Hall, Glanhwfa Road
Llangefni LL77 7TW
Tel. 01248 752080
www.anglesey.gov.uk

Angus Archives
Hunter Library
Restenneth Priory
By Forfar DD8 2SZ
Tel. 01307 468644
www.angus.gov.uk/history

Argyll and Bute Council Archives
Manse Brae
Lochgilphead PA31 8QU
Tel. 01546 604774
www.argyll-bute.gov.uk

Ayrshire Archives
Ayrshire Archives Centre
Craigie Estate
Ayr KA8 0SS
Tel. 01292 287584
www.south-ayrshire.gov.uk

North Ayrshire Libraries
Local History Library
39-41 Princes Street
Ardrossan KA22 8BT
Tel. 01294 469137
www.learning-north-ayrshire.com

The Bakelite Museum
Orchard Mill
Williton
Somerset TA4 4NS
Tel. 01984 632133
www.bakelitemuseum.co.uk

Bath and North East Somerset Record Office
Guildhall, High Street
Bath BA1 5AW
Tel. 01225 477421
www.batharchives.co.uk

Bath Central Library
19 The Podium
Northgate Street
Bath BA1 5AN
Tel. 01225 394041
www.librarieswest.org.uk

Bedfordshire and Luton Archives and Record Service
Riverside Building, County Hall
Bedford MK42 9AP
Tel. 01234 228833
www.bedfordshire.gov.uk/archive

Berkshire Record Office
9 Coley Avenue
Reading RG1 6AF
Tel. 0118 901 5132
www.berkshirerecordoffice.org.uk

Birmingham City Archives
Floor 7, Central Library
Chamberlain Square
Birmingham B3 3HQ
Tel. 0121 303 4217
www.birmingham.gov.uk/archives

Blackburn with Darwen *see*
LANCASHIRE RECORD OFFICE

Black Country Living Museum
Tipton Road, Dudley
West Midlands DY1 4SQ
Tel. 0121 557 9643
www.bclm.co.uk

Bodleian Library
Broad Street
Oxford OX1 3BG
Tel. 01865 277180
www.bodley.ox.ac.uk

Bolton Archives and Local Studies
Central Library, Civic Centre
Le Mans Crescent
Bolton BL1 1SE
Tel. 01204 332185
www.bolton.gov.uk

Borthwick Institute for Archives
University of York
Heslington
York YO10 5DD
Tel. 01904 321166
www.york.ac.uk/inst/bihr

Bournemouth Heritage Zone
Bournemouth Library
22 The Triangle
Bournemouth BH2 5RQ
Tel. 01202 454848
www.bournemouth.gov.uk/residents/libraries

Bracknell Record Office *see*
BERKSHIRE RECORD OFFICE

Bristol Record Office
'B' Bond Warehouse
Smeaton Road
Bristol BS1 6XN
Tel. 0117 922 4224
www.bristol-city.gov.uk

British Association for Local History
BALH PO Box 6549
Somersal Herbert
Ashbourne DE6 5WH
Tel. 01283 585947
www.balh.co.uk

British Library
96 Euston Road
London NW1 2DB
Tel. 020 7412 7000/
020 7412 7702 (map library)
www.bl.uk

British Library Newspapers
Colindale Avenue
London NW9 5HE
Tel. 020 7412 7353
www.bl.uk/catalogues/newspapers.html

British Telecom Archives
Holborn Telephone Exchange
268-270 High Holborn
London WC1V 7EE
Tel. 020 7440 4220

British Trust for Conservation Volunteers
Sedum House, Mallard Way
Potteric Carr
Doncaster DN4 8DB
Tel. 01302 388888
www.btcv.org

Centre for Buckinghamshire Studies
County Hall, Walton Street
Aylesbury HP20 1UU
Tel. 01296 382587
www.buckscc.gov.uk/archives

Bury Archive Service
Moss Street
Bury BL9 0DG
Tel. 0161 253 6782
www.bury.gov.uk/archives

Business Archives of Scotland
Archive Service
University of Glasgow
13 Thuro Street
Glasgow G11 6PE
Tel. 0141 330 5515
www.archives.gla.ac.uk

Cadw
Welsh Assembly Government
Plas Carew, Unit 5-7 Cefn Coed
Parc Nantgarw
Cardiff CF15 7QQ
Tel. 01443 336000
www.cadw.wales.gov.uk

Caerphilly Archives
Bargoed Library, The Square
Bargoed CF81 8QQ
Tel. 01443 875548
www.caerphilly.gov.uk/learning/libraries

Cambridgeshire County Record Office
Shire Hall, Castle Hill
Cambridge CB3 0AP
Tel. 01223 717281
www.cambridgeshire.gov.uk

Campaign to Protect Rural England
CPRE National Office
128 Southwark Street
London SE1 0SW
Tel. 020 7981 2800
www.cpre.org.uk

Carmarthenshire Archives Service
Parc Myrddin
Richmond Terrace
Carmarthen SA31 1DS
Tel. 01267 228232
www.carmarthenshire.gov.uk

Catholic Central Library
St Michael's Abbey
Farnborough Road
Farnborough GU14 7NQ
Tel. 01252 543818
www.catholic-library.org.uk

Catholic Record Society
12 Melbourne Place
Wolsingham
Co Durham DL13 3EH
Tel. 01388 527747
www.catholic-history.org.uk/crs

Ceredigion Archives
County Offices, Marine Terrace
Aberystwyth SY23 2DE
Tel. 01970 633697/8
www.archifdy-ceredigion.org.uk

Cheshire and Chester Archives and Local Studies Service
Duke Street
Chester CH1 1RL
Tel. 01244 602574
www.cheshire.gov.uk/recoff

Clackmannan Local Studies
Alloa Library
26-28 Drysdale Street
Alloa FK10 1JL
Tel. 01259 722262
www.clacksweb.org.uk/culture/localhistoryandlocalstudies/

Conwy Record Office
The Old Board School
Lloyd Street
Llandudno LL30 2YG
Tel. 01492 860882
www.conwy.gov.uk

Cornwall Record Office
Old County Hall
Truro TR1 3AY
Tel. 01872 323127
www.cornwall.gov.uk

Corporation of London Records Office
PO Box 270, Guildhall
London EC2P 2EJ
Tel. 020 7606 3030
www.corpoflondon.gov.uk

Cumbria Record Office (Carlisle)
The Castle
Carlisle CA3 8UR
Tel. 01228 607284/5
www.cumbria.gov.uk/archives/recordoffices

Cumbria Record Office (Kendal)
County Offices
Kendal LA9 4RQ
Tel. 01539 773540
www.cumbria.gov.uk/archives/recordoffices

COMPANY REGISTRIES

Companies House
(Main office for England and Wales)
Crown Way
Cardiff CF14 3UZ
Tel. 0870 3333636
www.companieshouse.gov.uk

Companies House
21 Bloomsbury Street
London WC1B 3XD
Tel. 0870 3333636
www.companieshouse.gov.uk

Companies House
37 Castle Terrace
Edinburgh EH1 2EB
Tel. 0870 3333636
www.companieshouse.gov.uk

d

Denbighshire Record Office
46 Clwyd Street
Ruthin LL15 1HP
Tel. 01824 708250
www.denbighshire.gov.uk

Derby Local Studies Library
25B Irongate
Derby DE1 3GL
Tel. 01332 255393
www.derby.gov.uk

Derbyshire Record Office
County Hall
Matlock DE4 3AG
Tel. 01629 580000/
01629 585347 (search room)
www.derbyshire.gov.uk

Devon Record Office
Great Moor House
Bittern Road, Sowton
Exeter EX2 7NL
Tel. 01392 384253
www.devon.gov.uk/record_office.htm

North Devon Library and Record Office
Tuly Street
Barnstaple EX31 1EL
Tel. 01271 388607/8
www.devon.gov.uk/north_record_office

Dorset History Centre
Bridport Road
Dorchester DT1 1RP
Tel. 01305 250550
www.dorsetcc.gov.uk/records.htm

Dry Stone Walling Association
Westmorland County Showground
Lane Farm, Crooklands
Milnthorpe
Cumbria LA7 7NH
Tel. 01539 567953
www.dswa.org.uk

Dudley Archives
Mount Pleasant Street
Roseville, Coseley
West Midlands WV14 9JR
Tel. 01384 812770
www.dudley.gov.uk

Dumfries and Galloway Archives
Archive Centre
33 Burns Street
Dumfries DG1 2PS
Tel. 01387 269254
www.dumgal.gov.uk

Durham County Record Office
County Hall
Durham DH1 5UL
Tel. 0191 383 3253
www.durham.gov.uk/recordoffice

e

East Dunbartonshire Archives
William Patrick Library
2-4 West High Street
Kirkintilloch G66 1AD
Tel. 0141 776 8090
or
Brookwood Library
166 Drymen Road
Bearsden G61 3RJ
Tel. 0141 942 6811
www.eastdunbarton.gov.uk

East Lothian Local History Centre
Haddington Library
Newton Port
Haddington EH41 3NA
Tel. 01620 823307
www.eastlothian.gov.uk

East Renfrewshire Heritage Centre
Giffnock Library
Station Road, Giffnock
East Renfewshire G46 6JF
Tel. 0141 577 4976
www.eastrenfrewshire.gov.uk

East Sussex Record Office
The Maltings, Castle Precincts
Lewes BN7 1YT
Tel. 01273 482349
www.eastsussexcc.gov.uk/useourarchives

Edinburgh City Archives
Dept of Corporate Services
City Chambers, High Street
Edinburgh EH1 1YJ
Tel. 0131 529 4616
www.edinburgh.gov.uk

English Heritage
PO Box 569
Swindon SN2 2YP
Tel. 0870 333 1181
www.english-heritage.org.uk

Essex Record Office
Wharf Road
Chelmsford CM2 6YT
Tel. 01245 244 644
www.essexcc.gov.uk/ero

f

Falkirk History Research Centre
Falkirk Council Archive
Callendar House
Callendar Park
Falkirk FK1 1YR
Tel. 01324 503779
www.falkirk.gov.uk

Family Records Centre
1 Myddelton Street
London EC1R 1UW
Tel. 020 8392 5300/
0845 603 7788 (certificates)
www.familyrecords.gov.uk/frc

Federation of Family History Societies (FFHS)
Administrator
PO Box 2425
Coventry CV5 6YX
www.ffhs.org.uk

FFHS (Publications) Ltd
Units 15 and 16
Chesham Industrial Centre
Oram Street
Bury BL9 6EN
Tel. 0161 797 3843
www.genfair.com

The Federation of Synagogues
65 Watford Way
London NW4 3AQ
Tel. 020 8202 2263
www.federationofsynagogues.com

Fife Archives
Carleton House
The Haig Business Park
Balgonie Road
Markinch KY7 6AQ
Tel. 01592 583352
www.fife.gov.uk

Flintshire Record Office
The Old Rectory, Hawarden
Flintshire CH5 3NR
Tel. 01244 532364
www.flintshire.gov.uk

General Register Office for Scotland
New Register House
3 West Register Street
Edinburgh EH1 3YT
Tel. 0131 334 0380
www.gro-scotland.gov.uk

Glamorgan Record Office
Glamorgan Building
King Edward VII Avenue
Cathays Park
Cardiff CF10 3NE
Tel. 029 2078 0282
www.glamro.gov.uk

Glasgow City Archives
The Mitchell Library
North Street
Glasgow G3 7DN
Tel. 0141 287 2876/2988
www.glasgow.gov.uk

Gloucestershire Record Office
Clarence Row, Alvin Street
Gloucester GL1 3DW
Tel. 01452 425295
www.gloucestershire.gov.uk/archives

Guildhall Library
Aldermanbury
London EC2P 7HH
Tel. 020 7332 1868/1870
www.cityoflondon.gov.uk/guildhalllibrary

Gwent Record Office
County Hall
Cwmbran NP44 2XH
Tel. 01633 644886/8
www.llgc.org.uk/cac/cac0004.htm

Gwynedd Archives and Museums Service
Caernarfon Record Office
County Offices,
Swyddfa'r Cyngor,
Caernarfon LL55 1SH
Tel. 01286 679095
www.gwynedd.gov.uk/Archives

h

Halton Local History Service
Halton Lea Library
Halton Lea, Runcorn
Cheshire WA7 2PF
Tel. 01928 715351
www2.halton.gov.uk

Hampshire Record Office
Sussex Street
Winchester SO23 8TH
Tel. 01962 846154
www.hants.gov.uk/record-office/index.html

Herefordshire Record Office
Harold Street
Hereford HR1 2QX
Tel. 01432 260750
www.herefordshire.gov.uk

Heritage Motor Centre
Banbury Road
Gaydon
Warwickshire CV35 0BJ
Tel. 01926 641188
www.heritage-motor-centre.co.uk

Hertfordshire Archives and Local Studies
County Hall, Pegs Lane
Hertford SG13 8EJ
Tel. 01438 737333
www.hertsdirect.org

North Highland Archive
Wick Library
Sinclair Terrace
Wick KW1 5AB
Tel. 01955 606432
www.highland.gov.uk/leisure/archives/northhighlandarchives

Highland Council Archive
Inverness Library
Farraline Park
Inverness IV1 1NH
Tel. 01463 220330
www.highland.gov.uk/leisure/archives/highlandcouncilarchives

Historic Scotland
Longmore House
Salisbury Place
Edinburgh EH9 1SH
Tel. 0131 668 8600
www.historic-scotland.gov.uk

House of Lords Record Office
House of Lords, Westminster
London SW1A 0PW
Tel. 020 7219 3074
www.parliament.uk

Huguenot Society of Great Britain and Ireland
Huguenot Library
University College
Gower Street
London WC1E 6BT
Tel. 020 7679 5199
www.huguenotsociety.org.uk

Huntingdonshire County Record Office
Grammar School Walk
Huntingdon
Cambridgeshire PE29 3LF
Tel. 01480 375842
www.cambridgeshire.gov.uk

i

Imperial War Museum
Lambeth Road
London SE1 6HZ
Tel. 020 7416 5320
www.iwm.org.uk

Imperial War Museum Duxford
Duxford
Cambridgeshire CB2 4QR
Tel. 01223 835000
www.iwm.org.uk

Institute for Name Studies
School of English Studies
University of Nottingham
Nottingham NG7 2RD
Tel. 0115 951 5919
www.nottingham.ac.uk/english/ins/index.html

Inverclyde Local History Library
The Watt Library
9 Union Street
Greenock PA16 8JH
Tel: 01475 715628
www.inverclyde.gov.uk/Libraries

Isle of Man Public Record Office
Unit 40A
Spring Valley Industrial Estate
Douglas, Isle of Man IM2 2QR
Tel. 01624 693569
www.gov.im/registries/publicrecords

Isle of Wight Record Office
26 Hillside, Newport
Isle of Wight PO30 2EB
Tel. 01983 823820/1
www.iwight.com/library/record_office

j, k, l

Jewish Chronicle
25 Furnival Street
London EC4A 1JT
Tel. 020 7415 1500
www.thejc.co.uk

Jewish Historical Society of England
33 Seymour Place
London W1H 5AP
Tel. 020 7723 5852
www.jhse.org

Jewish Museum
80 East End Road
London N3 2SY
Tel. 020 8349 1143
www.jewishmuseum.org.uk

Centre for Kentish Studies
Sessions House, County Hall
Maidstone ME14 1XQ
Tel. 01622 694363
www.kent.gov.uk/archives

Knowsley Local Studies
Huyton Library
Civic Way, Huyton
Knowsley L36 9GD
Tel. 0151 443 3738
http://www.knowsley.gov.uk/leisure/libraries/archives.html

Lambeth Palace Library
Lambeth Palace Road
London SE1 7JU
Tel. 020 7898 1400
www.lambethpalacelibrary.org

Lancashire Record Office
Bow Lane
Preston PR1 2RE
Tel. 01772 533039
http://www.lancashire.gov.uk/education/record_office/

Land registers (for Scotland)
see REGISTERS OF SCOTLAND EXECUTIVE AGENCY

Land Registry
Lincoln's Inn Fields
London WC2A 3PH
Tel. 020 7917 8888
www.landreg.gov.uk

Record Office for Leicestershire, Leicester and Rutland
Long Street, Wigston Magna
Leicester LE18 2AH
Tel. 0116 257 1080
www.leics.gov.uk

LONDON BOROUGHS

Barking and Dagenham
Valence House Museum
Becontree Avenue
Dagenham
Essex RM8 3HT
Tel. 020 8227 5296
www.barking-dagenham.gov.uk

Barnet
Local Studies and
Archives Centre
80 Daws Lane, Mill Hill
London NW7 4SL
Tel. 020 8359 3960
www.barnet.gov.uk/archives

Bexley Local Studies and Archive Centre
Townley Road
Bexleyheath
Kent DA6 7HJ
Tel. 020 8303 7777 Ext. 3470
www.bexley.gov.uk/localstudies

Brent
Brent Community History
Library and Archive
Cricklewood Library
152 Olive Road
London NW2 6UY
Tel. 020 8937 3541
www.brent.gov.uk/archive

Bromley
Local Studies and Archives
Central Library, High Street
Bromley
Kent BR1 1EX
Tel. 020 8461 7170
www.bromley.gov.uk

Camden
Camden Local Studies and
Archives Centre
Holborn Library
32-38 Theobald's Road
London WC1X 8PA
Tel. 020 7974 6342
www.camden.gov.uk/localstudies

Croydon
Local Studies Library
Central Library
Croydon Clocktower
Katharine Street
Croydon CR9 1ET
Tel. 020 8760 5400 Ext. 61112
www.croydon.gov.uk

Ealing
Ealing Local History Centre
Central Library
103 Ealing Broadway Centre
London W5 5JY
Tel. 020 8825 8194
www.ealing.gov.uk

Enfield
Archives and Local
History Unit
Southgate Town Hall
Green Lanes
London N13 4XD
Tel. 020 8379 2724
www.enfield.gov.uk

Greenwich
Greenwich Heritage Centre
Artillery Square
Royal Arsenal
Woolwich
London SE18 4DX
Tel. 020 8854 2452
www.greenwich.gov.uk

Hackney
Hackney Archives
43 De Beauvoir Road
London N1 5SQ
Tel. 020 7241 2886
www.hackney.gov.uk/ca-archives

Hammersmith and Fulham
Archives and Local
History Centre
The Lilla Huset
191 Talgarth Road
London W6 8BJ
Tel. 020 8741 5159
www.lbhf.gov.uk

Haringey
Haringey Archive Service
Bruce Castle Museum
Lordship Lane
London N17 8NU
Tel. 020 8808 8772
www.haringey.gov.uk/archives

Harrow
Harrow Reference Library
Civic Centre
Station Road
Harrow HA1 2UU
Tel. 020 8424 1055/6
www.harrow.gov.uk

Havering
Local Studies Library
St Edwards Way
Romford
Essex RM1 3AR
Tel. 01708 432 394/3
www.havering.gov.uk

Hillingdon
Hillingdon Local Studies
Central Library
14-15 High Street
Uxbridge
Middlesex UB8 1HD
Tel. 01895 250702
www.hillingdon.gov.uk

Hounslow
Chiswick Local Studies
Department
Dukes Avenue
Chiswick
London W4 2AB
Tel. 020 8994 1008
and
Hounslow Library
Local Studies Department
24 Treaty Centre
High Street
Hounslow
Middlesex TW3 1ES
Tel. 0845 456 2800
www.hounslow.info

Islington
Local History Centre
245 St John Street
London EC1V 4NB
Tel. 020 7527 7988
www.islington.gov.uk

Royal Borough of Kensington and Chelsea
Local Studies Section
Kensington Central Library
Phillimore Walk
London W8 7RX
Tel. 020 7361 3010
www.rbkc.gov.uk

Royal Borough of Kingston upon Thames
Kingston Local History Room
North Kingston Centre
Richmond Road
Kingston KT2 5PE
Tel. 020 8547 6738
www.kingston.gov.uk

Lambeth
Lambeth Archives
Minet Library
52 Knatchbull Road
London SE5 9QY
Tel. 020 7926 6076
www.lambeth.gov.uk

Lewisham
Lewisham Local History
and Archives Centre
Lewisham Library
199-201 Lewisham
High Street
London SE13 6LG
Tel. 020 8297 0682
www.lewisham.gov.uk

Merton
Local Studies Centre
Merton Civic Centre
London Road, Morden
Surrey SM4 5DX
Tel. 020 8545 3239
www.merton.gov.uk

Newham
Archives and Local
Studies Library
Stratford Library
3 The Grove
Stratford
London E15 1EL
Tel. 020 8430 6881
www.newham.gov.uk

Redbridge
Archives Service
Central Library
Clements Road
Ilford
Essex IG1 1EA
Tel. 020 8708 2414
www.redbridge.gov.uk

Richmond upon Thames
Local Studies Collection
Albert Barkas Room
Old Town Hall
Whittaker Avenue
Richmond TW9 1TP
Tel. 020 8332 6820
www.richmond.gov.uk

Southwark
Local History Library
211 Borough High Street
London SE1 1JA
Tel. 020 7525 2000
www.southwark.gov.uk

continued overleaf

continued from overleaf

LONDON BOROUGHS

Sutton
Archives and Local Studies
Sutton Central Library
St Nicholas Way
Sutton SM1 1EA
Tel. 020 8770 4747
www.sutton.gov.uk

Tower Hamlets
Local History and
Archives Library
277 Bancroft Road
London E1 4DQ
Tel. 020 7364 1289/90
www.towerhamlets.gov.uk

Waltham Forest
Local History Library
Vestry House Museum
Vestry Road, Walthamstow
London E17 9NH
Tel. 020 8509 1917
www.lbwf.gov.uk

Wandsworth
Local History Service
Battersea Library
265 Lavender Hill
London SW11 1JB
Tel. 020 8871 7753
www.wandsworth.gov.uk

Westminster
Westminster Archives
Centre, 10 St Ann's Street
London SW1P 2DE
Tel. 020 7641 5180
www.westminster.gov.uk/archives

Lincolnshire Archives
St Rumbold Street
Lincoln LN2 5AB
Tel. 01522 526204
www.lincolnshire.gov.uk/archives

North East Lincolnshire Archives
Town Hall, Town Hall Square
Grimsby DN31 1HX
Tel. 01472 323585
www.nelincs.gov.uk/Leisure/Archives

Liverpool Record Office and Local Studies Service
Central Library
William Brown Street
Liverpool L3 8EW
Tel. 0151 233 5817
http://archive.liverpool.gov.uk

London Library
14 St James's Square
London SW1Y 4LG
Tel. 020 7930 7705
www.londonlibrary.co.uk

London Metropolitan Archives
Corporation of London
40 Northampton Road
London EC1R 0HB
Tel. 020 7332 3820
www.cityoflondon.gov.uk/archives

m

Manchester City Archives
Archives and Local Studies
Central Library
St Peter's Square
Manchester M2 5PD
Tel. 0161 234 1979
www.manchester.gov.uk/libraries/arls

Greater Manchester County Record Office
56 Marshall Street, New Cross
Manchester M4 5FU
Tel. 0161 832 5284
www.gmcro.co.uk

Medway Archives and Local Studies Centre
Civic Centre
Strood, Rochester
Kent ME2 4AU
Tel. 01634 332714
www.medway.gov.uk/index/leisure/archives.htm

Merseyside
see LIVERPOOL RECORD OFFICE

Merthyr Tydfil Archives
Central Library
High Street
Merthyr Tydfil CF47 8AF
Tel. 01685 723057
www.merthyr.gov.uk

Metropolitan Police Archives
see NATIONAL ARCHIVES

Middlesex *for records of the former county see* LONDON BOROUGH OF WESTMINSTER *and* LONDON METROPOLITAN ARCHIVES

Midlothian Council Archives
Library Headquarters
2 Clerk Street
Loanhead EH20 9DR
Tel. 0131 271 3976
www.midlothian.gov.uk

MAGAZINES

Ancestors
PO BOX 38
Richmond
TW9 4AJ
Tel. 020 8392 5370
www.ancestorsmagazine.co.uk

The Local Historian (journal of BALH)
and
Local History News
see BRITISH ASSOCIATION FOR LOCAL HISTORY

Local History Magazine
Local History Press Ltd
3 Devonshire Promenade
Lenton
Nottingham NG7 2DS
Tel. 0115 970 6473
www.local-history.co.uk

Scottish Local History Journal
Department of
Scottish History
University of Edinburgh
17 Buccleuch Place
Edinburgh EH8 9LN
Tel. 0131 650 4030
www.slhf.gcal.ac.uk

Modern Records Centre
University Library
University of Warwick
Coventry CV4 7AL
Tel. 02476 524219
http://modernrecords.warwick.ac.uk

Moray Archives
East End School
Institution Road
Elgin
Moray IV30 1RP
Tel: 01343 569011

www.moray.gov.uk

Museum of English Rural Life
see RURAL HISTORY CENTRE

n

National Archives
Ruskin Avenue
Kew
Surrey TW9 4DU
Tel. 020 8876 3444
www.nationalarchives.gov.uk

National Archives of Scotland
HM General Register House
2 Princes Street
Edinburgh EH1 3YY
Tel. 0131 535 1314
and
West Search Room
West Register House
Charlotte Square
Edinburgh EH2 4DJ
Tel. 0131 535 1413
www.nas.gov.uk

National Army Museum
Department of Archives,
Photographs, Film and Sound
Royal Hospital Road
London SW3 4HT
Tel. 020 7730 0717
Ext. 2214/2
www.national-army-museum.ac.uk

National Hedgelaying Society
88 Manor Road
Tottington
Bedfordshire LU5 6AJ
www.hedgelaying.org.uk

National Library of Scotland
Department of Manuscripts
George IV Bridge
Edinburgh EH1 1EW
Tel. 0131 632 3700
www.nls.uk

National Library of Wales
Department of Manuscripts
and Records
Penglais, Aberystwyth
Ceredigion SY23 3BU
Tel. 01970 632 800
www.llgc.org.uk

National Maritime Museum
Park Row, Greenwich
London SE10 9NF
Tel. 020 8858 4422
www.nmm.ac.uk

National Monuments Record Centre
Kemble Drive
Swindon SN2 2GZ
Tel. 01793 414600
www.english-heritage.org.uk

National Monuments Record of Scotland *see* ROYAL COMMISSION ON THE ANCIENT AND HISTORICAL MONUMENTS OF SCOTLAND

National Museum of Rural Life
Kittochside
Philipshill Road
East Kilbride G76 9HR
Tel. 0131 247 4377
www.nms.ac.uk/museumofrurallife-homepage.aspx

National Museums of Scotland
Chambers Street
Edinburgh EH1 1JF
Tel. 0131 247 4422
www.nms.ac.uk

National Trust
PO Box 39
Warrington WA5 7WD
Tel. 0870 458 4000
www.nationaltrust.org.uk

National Trust for Scotland
Wemyss House
28 Charlotte Square
Edinburgh EH2 4ET
Tel. 0131 243 9300
www.nts.org.uk

Natural England
Northminster House
Peterborough PE1 1UA
Tel. 0845 600 3078
www.naturalengland.org.uk

Neath-Port Talbot Archives
Neath Library, Victoria Gardens
Neath SA11 3BA
Tel. 01639 644604
www.neath-porttalbot.gov.uk

Norfolk Record Office
The Archive Centre
Martineau Lane
Norwich NR1 2DQ
Tel. 01603 222599
www.archives.norfolk.gov.uk

Northamptonshire Record Office
Wootton Hall Park
Northampton NN4 8BQ
Tel. 01604 762129
www.northamptonshire.gov.uk

North Lanarkshire Archives
10 Kelvin Road
Lenziemill Road
Cumbernauld
Glasgow G67 2BA
Tel. 01236 638980
www.northlan.gov.uk

Nottinghamshire Archives
County House
Castle Meadow Road
Nottingham NG2 1AG
Tel. 0115 958 1634/950 4524
www.nottinghamshire.gov.uk/archives

O

Office for National Statistics
Customer Contact Centre
Room 1.015
Cardiff Road
Newport NP10 8XG
Tel. 0845 601 3034
www.statistics.gov.uk

Oldham Local Studies and Archives
84 Union Street
Oldham OL1 1DN
Tel. 0161 770 4654
www.oldham.gov.uk/community/local_studies

Orkney Library and Archives
44 Junction Road
Kirkwall
Orkney KW15 1AG
Tel. 01856 873166
www.orkneylibrary.org.uk

Oxfordshire Record Office
St Luke's Church
Temple Road
Cowley
Oxford OX4 2HT
Tel. 01865 398200
www.oxfordshire.gov.uk/oro

p,q

Pembrokeshire Record Office
The Castle
Haverfordwest SA61 2EF
Tel. 01437 763707
www.pembrokeshire.gov.uk

Perth and Kinross Council Archive
AK Bell Library
York Place, Perth PH2 8EP
Tel. 01738 477012
www.pkc.gov.uk

Plymouth and West Devon Record Office
Unit 3, Clare Place
Plymouth PL4 0JW
Tel. 01752 305940
www.plymouth.gov.uk/archives

Poole Local History Centre
Waterfront Museum
4 High Street
Poole BH15 1BW
Tel. 01202 262600
www.poole.gov.uk

Portsmouth City Museum and Records Office
Museum Road
Portsmouth PO1 2LJ
Tel. 023 9282 7261
www.portsmouth.gov.uk

PROBATE OFFICES

Birmingham
The Priory Courts
33 Bull Street
Birmingham B4 6DU
Tel. 0121 681 3400

Brighton
William Street
Brighton BN2 2LG
Tel. 01273 573510

Bristol
The Crescent Centre
Temple Back
Bristol BS1 6EP
Tel. 0117 927 3915/
0117 926 4619

Cardiff
PO Box 474
2 Park Street
Cardiff CF10 1TB
Tel. 029 2037 6479

Ipswich
Ground Floor
8 Arcade Street
Ipswich IP1 1EJ
Tel. 01473 284260

Isle of Man
General Registry
Isle of Man Courts of Justice
Deemsters Walk
Bucks Road
Douglas IM1 3AR
Tel. 01624 685 242

Leeds
3rd Floor, Coronet House
Queen Street
Leeds LS1 2BA
Tel. 0113 386 3540

Liverpool
Queen Elizabeth II
Law Courts
Derby Square
Liverpool L2 1XA
Tel. 0151 236 8264

London
Principal Registry of the Family Division
First Avenue House
42-49 High Holborn
London WC1V 6NP
Tel. 020 7947 6939/6043

Manchester
9th Floor, Astley House
23 Quay Street
Manchester M3 4AT
Tel. 0161 837 6070

Newcastle upon Tyne
Number One
Waterloo Square
Newcastle NE1 4AL
Tel. 0191 211 2170

Oxford
St Aldates
Oxford OX1 1LY
Tel. 01865 793055

Winchester
4th Floor, Cromwell House
Andover Road
Winchester SO23 7EW
Tel. 01962 897029

Scotland:

General Register Office
(probate up to 1985)
General Register House
2 Princes Street
Edinburgh EH1 3YY
Tel. 0131 535 1352

HM Commissary Office
(probate after 1985)
Sheriff Court House
27 Chambers Street
Edinburgh EH1 1LB
Tel. 0131 247 2850

PUBLISHERS

Countryside Books
Highfield House
2 Highfield Avenue
Newbury RG14 5DS
Tel. 01635 43816
www.countrysidebooks.co.uk

Sutton Publishing Ltd
Phoenix Mill
Thrupp, Stroud
Gloucestershire GL5 2BU
Tel. 01453 883300
www.suttonpublishing.co.uk

Tempus Publishing Ltd
The Mill, Brimscombe Port
Stroud GL5 2QG
Tel. 01453 883300
www.tempus-publishing.com

Powys County Archives
County Hall
Llandrindod Wells LD1 5LG
Tel. 01597 826088
www.powys.gov.uk/archives

Principal Registry, London
see PROBATE OFFICES *box*

Quakers
see RELIGIOUS SOCIETY OF FRIENDS LIBRARY

r

Reading *see* BERKSHIRE RECORD OFFICE

Registers of Scotland Executive Agency
Erskine House
68 Queen Street
Edinburgh EH2 4NF
Tel. 0845 607 0161
www.ros.gov.uk

Religious Society of Friends Library
Friends House
173-177 Euston Road
London NW1 2BJ
Tel. 020 7663 1135
www.quaker.org.uk/library

Renfrewshire Archives
Paisley Central Lending Library
High Street
Paisley PA1 2BB
Tel. 0141 887 3672
and
Reference and Local Studies Library
Central Library
68 High Street
Paisley PA1 2BB
Tel. 0141 889 2360
www.renfrewshire.gov.uk

Rhondda-Cynon-Taf Archives
Aberdare Library, Green Street
Aberdare CF44 7AG
Tel. 01685 880050
www.rhondda-cynon-taf.gov.uk

Rochdale Local Studies Library
Touchstones Rochdale
The Esplanade
Rochdale OL16 1AQ
Tel. 01706 924915
www.rochdale.gov.uk

Roehampton Hearth Tax Centre
Heart Tax Research Project
School of Arts
Digby Stuart College
Roehampton University
Roehampton Lane
London SW15 5PU
Tel. 020 8392 3731
www.roehampton.ac.uk/hearthtax

Royal Air Force Museum
Department of Research and Information Services
Grahame Park Way
Hendon
London NW9 5LL
Tel. 020 8205 2266
www.rafmuseum.org.uk

Royal Commission on Historical Manuscripts *see* NATIONAL ARCHIVES

Royal Commission on the Ancient and Historical Monuments of Scotland/National Monuments Record of Scotland
John Sinclair House
16 Bernard Terrace
Edinburgh EH8 9NX
Tel. 0131 662 1456
www.rcahms.gov.uk

Royal Institute of British Architects (RIBA)
66 Portland Place
London W1B 1AD
Tel. 020 7580 5533
www.riba.org

The Royal Mail Archive
Freeling House, Phoenix Place
London WC1X 0DL
Tel. 020 7239 2570
www.postalheritage.org.uk

Royal Naval Museum
HM Naval Base (PP66)
Portsmouth PO1 3NH
Tel. 023 9272 7562
www.royalnavalmuseum.org

Rural History Centre
The Museum of English Rural Life
The University of Reading
Redlands Road
Reading RG1 5EX
Tel. 0118 378 8660
www.ruralhistory.org

Rutland
see LEICESTERSHIRE, LEICESTER AND RUTLAND, THE RECORD OFFICE FOR

St Fagans Natural History Museum
St Fagan's Castle
Cardiff CF5 6XB
Tel. 029 2057 3500
www.museumwales.ac.uk/en/stfagans/

St Helen's Archives
Central Library
Gamble Institute
Victoria Square
St Helens WA10 1DY
Tel. 01744 456954
www.sthelens.gov.uk

Salford Local History Library
Peel Park
The Crescent
Salford M5 4WU
Tel. 0161 736 2649
www.salford.gov.uk/lhlibrary

Sandwell Community History & Archive Service
High Street
Smethwick B66 1AB
Tel. 0121 558 2561
www.lea.sandwell.gov.uk/libraries/chas.htm

Scottish Borders Archive and Local History Centre
Library HQ, St Mary's Mill
Selkirk TD7 5EW
Tel. 01750 20842
www.scotborders.gov.uk

Scottish Catholic Archive
Columba House
16 Drummond Place
Edinburgh EH3 6PL
Tel. 0131 556 3661
www.catholic-heritage.net/sca

Scottish Jewish Archives Centre
129 Hill Street
Garnethill
Glasgow G3 6UB
Tel. 0141 332 4911
www.sjac.org.uk

Scottish Record Society *see* NATIONAL ARCHIVES OF SCOTLAND

Sheffield Archives
52 Shoreham Street
Sheffield S1 4SP
Tel. 0114 203 9395
www.sheffield.gov.uk

Shetland Museum and Archives
Hay's Dock
Lerwick, Shetland ZE1 0WP
Tel. 01595 695057
www.shetland.gov.uk

Shropshire Archives
Castle Gates
Shrewsbury SY1 2AQ
Tel. 01743 255350
www.shropshirearchives.co.uk

Slough
see BERKSHIRE RECORD OFFICE

Society of Genealogists
14 Charterhouse Buildings
Goswell Road
London EC1M 7BA
Tel. 020 7251 8799
www.sog.org.uk

Solihull Heritage and Local Studies
Central Library, Homer Road
Solihull B91 3RG
Tel. 0121 704 6934
www.solihull.gov.uk

Somerset Archive and Record Service
Somerset Record Office
Obridge Road
Taunton TA2 7PU
Tel. 01823 278805/337600
www.somerset.gov.uk/archives

Southend-on-Sea
see ESSEX RECORD OFFICE

Southampton Archives Service
South Block, Civic Centre
Southampton SO14 7LY
Tel. 023 8083 2251
www.southampton.gov.uk

South Lanarkshire Council Records Centre
30 Hawbank Road
College Milton
East Kilbride G74 5EX
Tel. 01355 239193
www.southlanarkshire.gov.uk

Staffordshire and Stoke-on-Trent Archive Service
County Buildings
Eastgate Street
Stafford ST16 2LZ
Tel. 01785 278379
www.staffordshire.gov.uk/archives

Stirling Council Archives Services
5 Borrowmeadow Road
Stirling FK7 7UW
Tel. 01786 450745
www.stirling.gov.uk

Stockport
see CHESHIRE, DERBYSHIRE OR LANCASHIRE ARCHIVES

Suffolk
County archives are in three locations and share a website:
www.suffolkcc.gov.uk/libraries

Suffolk Record Office
77 Raingate Street
Bury St Edmunds IP33 2AR
Tel. 01284 352352

Suffolk Record Office
Gatacre Road
Ipswich IP1 2LQ
Tel. 01473 584541

Suffolk Record Office
Central Library
Clapham Road
Lowestoft NR32 1DR
Tel. 01502 405357

Surrey History Centre
130 Goldsworth Road
Woking GU21 1ND
Tel. 01483 518737
www.surreycc.gov.uk/surreyhistoryservice

Sussex
see EAST SUSSEX *and* WEST SUSSEX RECORD OFFICES

Swansea
see WEST GLAMORGAN ARCHIVE SERVICE

Tameside Local Studies and Archives Centre
Tameside Central Library
Old Street
Ashton-under-Lyne
Tameside OL6 7SG
Tel. 0161 342 4242
www.tameside.gov.uk/archives

Teesside Archives
Holds archives for Stockton-on-Tees and Middlesbrough
Exchange House
6 Marton Road
Middlesbrough TS1 1DB
Tel. 01642 248321
www.middlesbrough.gov.uk

Thurrock Archives
Grays Library
Orsett Road, Grays
Essex RM17 5DX
Tel. 01375 383611
www.thurrock.gov.uk/libraries

Torfaen Local Studies Centre
Abersychan Library
Brynteg, Abersychan
Pontypool NP4 7BG
Tel. 01495 772261
www.torfaen.gov.uk

Trafford Local Studies Centre
Sale Library, Sale Waterside
Sale M33 7ZF
Tel. 0161 912 3013
www.trafford.gov.uk

Twentieth Century Society
70 Cowcross Street
London EC1M 6EJ
Tel. 020 7250 3857
www.c20society.org.uk

Tyne & Wear Archive Service
Blandford House
Blandford Square
Newcastle upon Tyne NE1 4JA
Tel. 0191 277 2248
www.tyneandweararchives.org.uk

Victoria and Albert Museum
Cromwell Road
London SW7 2RL
Tel. 020 7942 2000
www.vam.ac.uk

Walsall Local History Centre
Essex Street, Walsall WS2 7AS
Tel. 01922 721305
www.walsall.gov.uk

Warrington Archives
Central Library, Museum Street
Warrington WA1 1JB
Tel. 01925 442889/90
www.warrington.gov.uk

Warwickshire County Record Office
Priory Park, Cape Road
Warwick CV34 4JS
Tel. 01926 738959
www.warwickshire.gov.uk/general/rcindex.htm

Weald and Downland Open Air Museum
Singleton Park, Chichester
West Sussex PO18 0EU
Tel. 01243 811 363
www.wealddown.co.uk

Wesley Historical Society Library
Wesley Centre
Oxford Brookes University
Harcourt Hill
Oxford OX2 9AT
Tel. 01865 488319
www.wesleyhistoricalsociety.org.uk/library.htm

West Country Studies Library
Castle Street, Exeter EX4 3PQ
Tel. 01392 384216
www.devon.gov.uk

West Dunbartonshire Archives
Strathleven Place
Dunbarton G82 1BD
Tel. 01389 733273
www.wdcweb.info/library

West Glamorgan Archive Service
County Hall
Oystermouth Road
Swansea SA1 3SN
Tel. 01792 636589
www.swansea.gov.uk/westglamorganarchives

West Lothian Council Archives
Local History Library
Library HQ, Hopefield Road
Blackburn
West Lothian EH47 7HZ
Tel. 01506 776331
www.westlothian.gov.uk/libraries

Westmorland *see* CUMBRIA RECORD OFFICE

West Sussex Record Office
3 Orchard Street
Chichester PO19 1DD
Tel. 01243 753600
www.westsussex.gov.uk

Wigan Archive Service
Town Hall, Leigh
Lancashire WN7 2DY
Tel. 01942 404430
www.wlct.org/Culture/Heritage/archives.htm

Wiltshire and Swindon Record Office
Bythesea Road
Trowbridge BA14 8BS
Tel. 01225 713138
www.wiltshire.gov.uk/archives

Windsor and Maidenhead Archives
Maidenhead Library
St Ives Road,
Maidenhead SL6 1QU
Tel. 01628 796 969
www.rbwm.gov.uk

Wokingham
see BERKSHIRE RECORD OFFICE

Wolverhampton Archive and Local Studies
42-50 Snow Hill
Wolverhampton WV2 4AG
Tel. 01902 552480
www.wolverhampton.gov.uk

Women's Library
London Metropolitan University
25 Old Castle Street
London E1 7NT
Tel. 020 7320 2222
www.londonmet.ac.uk/thewomenslibrary

Worcestershire Record Office
Headquarters Branch
County Hall, Spetchley Road
Worcester WR5 2NP
Tel. 01905 766351
www.worcestershire.gov.uk/records

Workers' Educational Association (WEA)
3rd Floor
70 Clifton Street
London EC2A 4HB
Tel. 020 7426 3450
www.wea.org.uk

York City Archives
Art Gallery Building
Exhibition Square
York YO1 7EW
Tel. 01904 551878
www.york.gov.uk

East Riding of Yorkshire Archives
County Hall, Beverley
East Riding of Yorkshire
HU17 9BA
Tel. 01482 392790
www.eastriding.gov.uk/libraries/archives/archives.html

North Yorkshire County Record Office
Malpas Road
Northallerton
North Yorkshire DL7 8TB
Tel. 01609 777585
www.northyorks.gov.uk

West Yorkshire Archive Service
Wakefield Headquarters
Registry of Deeds
Newstead Road
Wakefield WF1 2DE
Tel. 01924 305980
www.archives.wyjs.org.uk

Index

Page numbers in *italic* refer to illustrations and captions.

a

b

c

d

j&k

l

m

n

t

u

v

w

y

Acknowledgments

Illustrations in *Reader's Digest Local History Detective* were supplied by the following.
Some short forms of suppliers have been used: BAL – The Bridgeman Art Library, London; LRL – © Last Refuge Limited, Dae Sasitorn & Adrian Warren; MEPL – Mary Evans Picture Library; SSPL – Science and Society Picture Library; TSP – The Skyscan Photolibrary. The following abbreviations are also used: T top; C centre; B bottom; L left; R right. © RD indicates images that are copyright of The Reader's Digest Association Limited.

Cover TL MEPL/Roger Mayne Collection TR Alamy Images/David Robertson BL Popperfoto BR Popperfoto Background London Topographical Society **Endpapers** © RD/London Topographical Society **2-3** Hulton Getty Images **4** CL © RD/Jason Smalley B Popperfoto **4-5** T © RD/Jason Smalley **5** TR Aerofilms BL Topham Picture Library BR Edifice **6** (both) © RD/Jason Smalley **7** See pgs 261-2, 68-9 and 192 **8** (both)© RD/Jason Smalley **9** TL & TR © RD/Jason Smalley B © RD **10** C Powys County Archives Office B www.cornwall.gov.uk **10-11** © RD/Jason Smalley **11** TR © RD/Jason Smalley BR © RD **12** © RD/Jon Bouchier **13** © RD **14-15** The National Archives **15** L The National Archives R www.balh.co.uk **15-16** The National Archives **16** www.balh.co.uk **17** TR www.scotlandspeople.gov.uk B www.old-maps.co.uk **18** (all) Ordnance Survey/ © Crown Copyright **19** T The National Archives B © RD **20** T LRL B © RD/David Tarn **21** (all) © RD **22** © RD **23** L © RD TR John Cleare/Mountain Camera **24** © RD **25** T © RD BL Collections/Chris Blyth BR © RD **26** BL English Heritage/Bob Skingle BR © RD **27** TR The Travelsite/Jarrold Publishing CR BAL/Philip Mould, Historical Portraits, London UK BL TSP **28** T Carnegie Publishing Ltd/Sheffield Central Library, Local Studies Department BL Collections/Ian Walker **29** T © RD/Jason Smalley **30** Reproduced with the permission of the County Archivist, Lancashire Record Office/County Archivist, Lancashire Record Office (P29) **31** (map) Trustees of The National Library of Scotland/Trustees of the National Library of Scotland (photograph) Air Photo Library, University of Cambridge/Tillhill & Stirling Council CR © RD **32** L Carnegie Publishing Ltd/Sheffield Central Library, Local Studies Department R Carnegie Publishing Ltd/Sheffield Central Library, Local Studies Department **32-33** BAL/Sheffield Galleries and Museums Trust **33** TL Sheffield Central Library,/Local Studies Department TR Sheffield Industrial Museums Trust **34** T LRL **35** TC Ordnance Survey/ © Crown Copyright TR Neil Holmes B © RD/Jason Smalley **36** T Ordnance Survey/ © Crown Copyright B TSP/Kevin Allen **37** TL © RD/Jason Smalley CR Ecclesiastical & Eccentricities Picture Library/Dorothy Burrows B John Cleare/Mountain Camera **38** T Cath Marsh B Roger G Howard/Photographers Direct **39** TL The National Trust/Nick Meers R © RD **40** Collections/Robin Weaver **41** T © RD/Jason Smalley B West Glamorgan Archive Service **42** L Colin Molyneux R © RD/Eric Meacher **43** L David Hey/George Redmonds R Ordnance Survey/ © Crown Copyright **44** NHPA/David Woodfall **44-45** Ardea, London/Adrian Warren **45** T NHPA/Guy Edwards CR © RD/ Jason Smalley **46** B © RD **47** B St.Andrews University Library **48** BR Collections/Robin Weaver **48-49** © RD/Roger Hutchins **49** T By permission of the Trustees of the Chatsworth Settlement CL Garden Picture Library/Clive Boursnell R Topham Picture Library **50** T Institute of Agricultural History and Museum of English Rural Life, Reading C & B Hulton Getty Images **51** T Institute of Agricultural History and Museum of English Rural Life, Reading/Topical Press Agency Ltd B Hulton Getty Images **52** L Woodfall Wild Images R Woodfall Wild Images/Bob Gibbons **52-53** © RD/Jason Smalley **53** T Ordnance Survey/ © Crown Copyright L Natural Visions R Ardea, London/David Dixon **118** T David Hey C Edifice/Philippa Lewis B Topham Picture Library **55** T © RD/Jason Smalley B Nottinghamshire County Council: Culture and Community **56** (maps) © Crown copyright. Reproduced with permission of the Forestry Commission BL Woodfall Wild Images/Mark Hamblin **57** T Woodfall Wild Images TL Ardea, London B Forestry Commission/Neil Campbell **58** L Ordnance Survey/ © Crown Copyright TL Collections/David McGill BL © RD **58-59** John Cleare/Mountain Camera **123** TR Ecclesiastical & Eccentricities Picture Library/Dorothy Burrows C Collections CR © RD **60** C Ecclesiastical & Eccentricities Picture Library/Dorothy Burrows CR Ecclesiastical & Eccentricities Picture Library/Dorothy Burrows BL Neil Holmes BR © RD/Richard Turpin **60-61** Neil Holmes **61** C Alvey & Towers Picture Library BR © RD/Jason Smalley **62** R © RD **63** T © RD/Jason Smalley **64** TL Friends of Three Sisters/Wigan Leisure & Culture Trust CL Phil Jones Photography/photographersdirect.com **64-65** LRL **65** TL Cotswold Water Park Society TR Photograph © English Nature/Peter Wakely **66** (both) The National Archives **66-67** John Cleare/Mountain Camera **67** BC © RD BR The Illustrated London News Picture Library **68** T The John Frost Historical Newspaper Service BL © RD/Jason Smalley **69** Wandsworth Museum **70** B © RD **70-71** Historystore **71** C A Photograph from work by Frank Meadow Sutcliffe,Hon.F.R.P.S. (1853-1941) Copyright The Sutcliffe Gallery,Whitby, YO21 3BA/by agreement with Whitby Literary and Philosophical Society B © RD/Jason Smalley **72** T © RD/Jason Smalley BL Ordnance Survey/ © Crown Copyright **73** T Berkshire Record Office C Berkshire Record Office BL David Hey **74** B The John Frost Historical Newspaper Service **74-75** The National Archives **75** B © 2001 Archive CD Books. All rights reserved **76** C The National Archives B © RD/Jason Smalley Jason Smalley B The National Archives **76-77** The National Archives **77** B The National Archives **78** T Rex Features Ltd/GMC C www.scan.org.uk B Jonathan Smith/photographersdirect.com **79** T © National Library of Scotland B © RD **80** C Birmingham Central Library **80-81** T Alan Godfrey Maps/Sandwell Local History Library C © RD B Birmingham Central Library **82** T Collections/Michael Nicholson CR Alamy Images BL © RD/Jason Smalley BR Salisbury District Council **83** T Stan Kujawa Images/photographersdirect.com CL The Art Archive, London CR Hulton Getty Images BR Sithean Photo/photographersdirect.com **84** TL Liz King Media/photographersdirect.com C Stanley Pritchard/photographersdirect.com CR & BR www.oldbaileyonline.org **85** L © RD 228 L © RD/Jason Smalley BR www.churchplansonline.org.uk **86-87** Collections/Robert Hallmann **87** (all) © RD **88** L © RD/Jon Wyand **88-89** © RD/Roger Hutchins **89** T © RD/Jason Smalley B MEPL **90** T Neil Holmes B Neil Holmes **91** BAL **92** L The Photolibrary Wales TR Meirion Record Office BR National Library of Wales **93** (both) Nigel Roberson/photographersdirect.com **94** CL 'Royal Pavilion, Libraries and Museums, Brighton & Hove'/Royal Pavilion, Libraries and Museums, Brighton & Hove B © RD/Angelo Hornak/East Sussex Record Office ESC 24/2/1 **94-95** T © RD/Angelo Hornak **95** T © RD/Angelo Hornak/Middle Street Primary School/East Sussex Record Office (ESC 24/1/1) C © RD/Angelo Hornak/Middle Street Primary School/East Sussex Record Office ESC (24/7/73-73) B © RD/Angelo Hornak/Middle Street Primary School/East Sussex Record Office (ESC 82/A) **96** T Andrew Lawson C John Heseltine B Greenwich Heritage Centre **97** L © RD TR Beamish North of England Open Air Museum **98** T Jaguar Daimler Heritage Trust B The Advertising Archives **99** © RD/Jason Smalley **100** L National Coal Mining Museum for England R The Museum of Lead Mining-Wanlockhead **101** T The National Trust/Keith Hewitt L The National Trust/Dennis Gilbert R Bryan & Cherry Alexander **102** T © RD/John Andrews B © RD/John Andrews **102-103** © RD/John Andrews **103** TL © RD TR © RD B The National Archives **104** L Adrian Japp Photography, photographersdirect.com **105** T BAL B The National Archives **106** TL Hulton Getty Images BR Hammersmith & Fulham archives & local history centre **107** © RD/Roger Hutchins/Stoke Bruerne Canal Museum **108** L Milepost Ninety-Two and a Half **108-109** Rail Images **109** T © RD CR Milepost Ninety-Two and a Half **110** TR Collections/Liz Stares C The National Motor Museum, Beaulieu **111** T SSPL B MEPL **112** L The Travelsite/Jarrold Publishing R Pictures courtesy of Bradford Council **113** TL Collections/Archie Young TR City of Newcastle Upon Tyne BR Newcastle Libraries and Information Service **114** T © RD/Jason Smalley B Imperial War Museum **115** TR Popperfoto BR (both) Collections/Dorothy Burrows **116** TL © RD/Julie Bennett **116-117** © RD/from Walls across the valley by Brian Robinson © RD/from Walls across the valley by Brian Robinson **117** (post boxes) © RD TL Collections/Barbara West B © Michael Melbourne/Papplewick Pumping Station Trust **118** ArenaPAL T Collections/Dorothy Burrows **119** T Sheffield Wednesday FC B Sheffield Wednesday FC **120** T Collections/Andria Massey CR © RD/Guildhall Library, Corporation of London/Geremy Butler B Edifice/Philippa Lewis **121** TC Edifice/Philippa Lewis TR Edifice/Philippa Lewis B Collections/Kim Naylor **122** TR Neil Holmes C & BL Ecclesiastical & Eccentricities Picture Library/John Turner **123** T Ecclesiastical & Eccentricities Picture Library/H. Harrison L Edifice/Tom Thistlethwaite BR MEPL **124** T The Advertising Archives **124-125** B Reproduced with the permission of the County Archivist, Lancashire Record Office **125** © RD/Jason Smalley **126** T © RD/Angelo Hornak CL Phil Flowers **127** TL & TC © RD/Angelo Hornak BC © RD/Angelo Hornak/East Sussex Record Office, SAU/669 BR © RD/Paul Manners **128** TR Edifice C © RD BL © RD/Julie Bennett **129** L © RD/Jason Smalley R © RD/Jason Smalley **130** T Elizabeth Whiting & Associates B Edifice/Philippa Lewis **131** Travel Ink **132** T © RD B © RD **133** L London Metropolitan Archives B © RD **134** Harrow Local Studies **135** T Postal Heritage Trust B Harrow Local Studies **136** C The Advertising Archives **136-137** Elizabeth Whiting & Associates **137** C © RD CR & R Museum on Domestic Design and Architecture, Middlesex University/Angelo Hornak BR © RD/Angelo Hornak **138** CL The National Trust/Keith Paisley CR & BR The National Trust/Dennis Gilbert **139** T Martin Black (rest), Museum on Domestic Design and Architecture, Middlesex University **140** L Edifice R The National Archives **141** T Minet Library C Minet Library B The National Archives **142** T The National Archives BL © RD BR SSPL **143** T SSPL B SSPL **144** (both) The National Archives **144-145** The Photolibrary Wales **145** BR © RD **146** L Interior Archive Limited/Edina van der Wyck CR © RD CR Copyright Sylvia Cordaiy Photo Library Ltd **146-147** Elizabeth Whiting & Associates **147** C The National Archives CR The National Archives R The National Trust B © RD **148** T Edifice B The Scottish Record Office **149** Inset Bath Record Office TL Bath Record Office **150** CL Elizabeth Whiting & Associates C Elizabeth Whiting & Associates CR www.arcaid.co.uk/Benedict Luxmoore **151** TR Courtesy of the Trustees of the Victoria and Albert Museum, London CL Elizabeth Whiting & Associates CR Courtesy of the Trustees of the Victoria and Albert Museum, London **152** T Cheshire Record Office B © RD **153** TR, CL & CR Amy Browne BR The National Archives **154** B The National Archives **154-155** Geffrye Museum, London **155** T The National Archives **156** Hulton Getty Images **157** T Tower Hamlets Local History Library & Archives B BT Archives **158** Popperfoto **158-159** The National Archives **159** © Glasgow City Council (Museums) **160** T The Art Archive, London L The National Archives **160-161** The National Archives **161** The National Archives

Reader's Digest Local History Detective is based on material in *The Story of Where You Live* published by The Reader's Digest Association Limited, London.

First edition copyright © 2007
The Reader's Digest Association Limited,
11 Westferry Circus, Canary Wharf,
London E14 4HE

We are committed to both the quality of our products and the service we provide to our customers. We value your comments, so please feel free to contact us on **08705 113366** or via our website at: **www.readersdigest.co.uk**
If you have any comments or suggestions about the content of our books, email us at gbeditorial@readersdigest.co.uk

Book code 400-350 UP0000-1
ISBN (13) 978 0 276 44259 9
Oracle code 250011351S.00.24

READER'S DIGEST PROJECT TEAM

Editor
John Andrews

Art Editor
Julie Bennett

Senior Designer
Austin Taylor

Assistant Editors
Caroline Boucher
Liz Clasen
Celia Coyne
Jane Hutchings
Cécile Landau

Editorial Assistant
Gail Paten

Picture Research
Elizabeth Loving
Rosie Taylor

Proofreader
Ron Pankhurst

Indexer
Hilary Bird

READER'S DIGEST GENERAL BOOKS

Editorial Director
Julian Browne
Art Director
Anne-Marie Bulat
Managing Editor
Alastair Holmes
Head of Book Development
Sarah Bloxham
Picture Resource Manager
Sarah Stewart Richardson
Pre-press Account Manager
Penny Grose
Senior Production Controller
Deborah Trott
Product Production Manager
Claudette Bramble
Origination
Colour Systems Limited, London

Printed and bound in China

CONTRIBUTORS

Chief Consultant
David Hey
Emeritus Professor of Local and Family History, The University of Sheffield

Consultants
Sonia Baker
Peter Christian

Writers
Sonia Baker
Nick Barratt
Jonathan Bastable
Peter Christian
David Hey
Roger Hunt
Alice McEwan
Christopher Somerville

Photography
Angelo Hornak
Jason Smalley

Maps
Cartographica Limited

Illustration
Roger Hutchins

Digital Imaging
Ian Atkinson

Reader's Digest would like to thank the following for their help in the preparation of this book:

Andrew Bennett, East Sussex County Archives; Martin Bennett; Chorley Borough Council; Jane McKenna; Paul Manners and Marietta Van Dyck; The Museum of Science & Industry in Manchester; Diane Naylor, Andrew Petit and Stewart Mann, Chatsworth House, Derbyshire; Alison Smith, The Canal Museum, Stoke Bruerne; Donna Steele and David Dyer, Middle Street School, Brighton; Kingston Local History Room, Kingston upon Thames